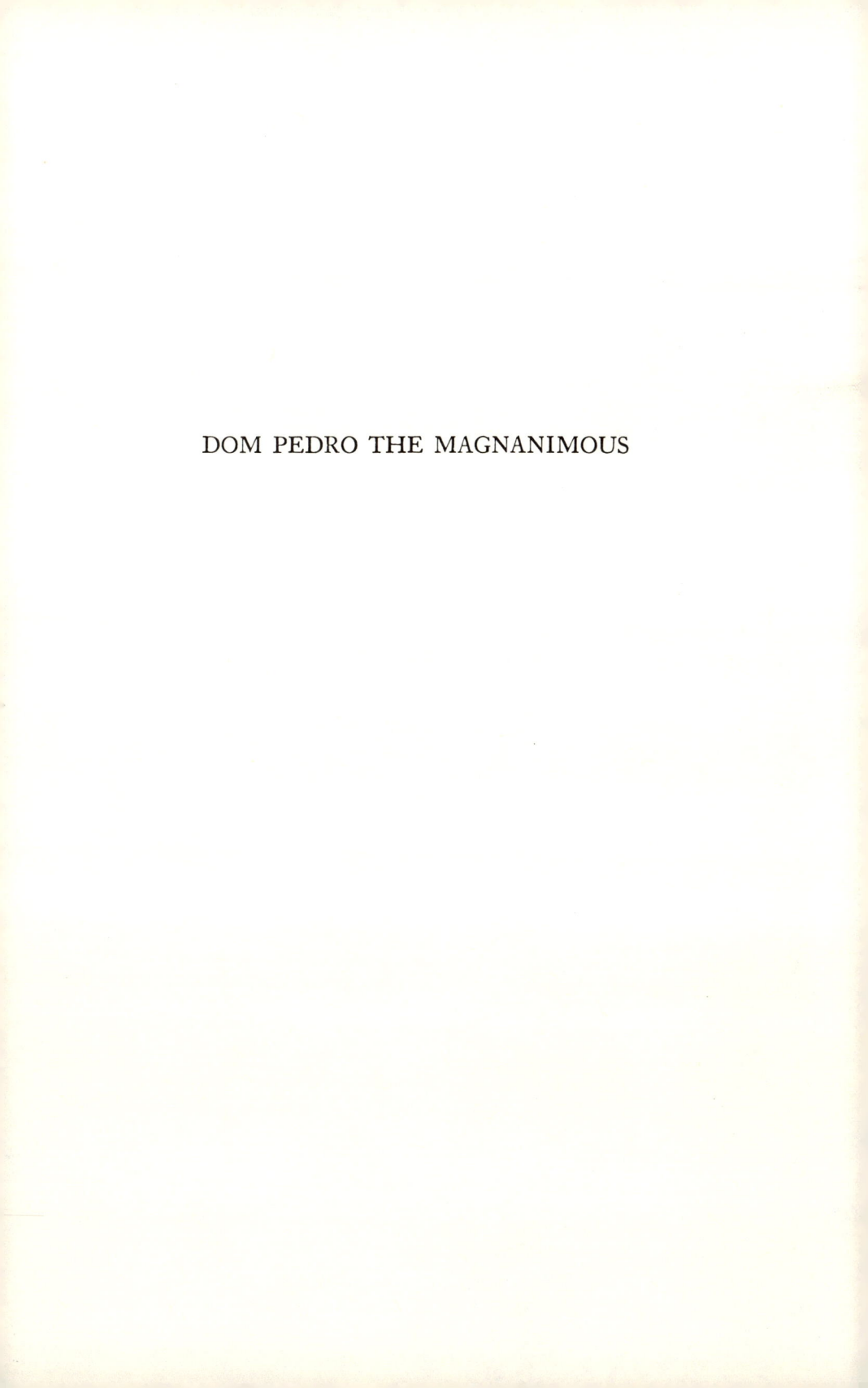

DOM PEDRO THE MAGNANIMOUS

From a painting by Monvoisin at the Château d'Eu
DOM PEDRO II IN 1847

DOM PEDRO THE MAGNANIMOUS

Second Emperor of Brazil

By

Mary Wilhelmine Williams

1966
OCTAGON BOOKS, INC.
New York

Copyright 1937 by The University of North Carolina Press

Reprinted 1966
by special arrangement with The University of North Carolina Press

OCTAGON BOOKS, INC.
175 FIFTH AVENUE
NEW YORK, N.Y. 10010

LIBRARY OF CONGRESS CATALOG CARD NUMBER: 66-18031

Printed in U.S.A. by
NOBLE OFFSET PRINTERS, INC.
NEW YORK 3, N. Y.

To the Friendly
CO-OPERATIVE BRAZILIANS
in Grateful Appreciation

PREFACE

UP TO NOW, there has been no biography in English of Dom Pedro II of Brazil, who should be ranked among the ablest rulers of his century and among the finest historical characters of modern times. The present volume was written with the aim of supplying this lack. In this connection I tried to find and weigh all important available data relating to the Emperor.

Many people have aided me in my work. To the staffs of the following-named libraries I am indebted:—Goucher College, Enoch Pratt, and the Library of the Peabody Institute in Baltimore, the Columbus Memorial Library of the Pan American Union, the Library of Congress, the Lima Library of the Catholic University of America, the *Bibliotheca Nacional* of Portugal, the *Bibliotheca Nacional* of Brazil, the *Archivo Nacional* of Brazil, and the Library of the *Instituto Historico e Geographico Brasileiro*. Miss Eleanor Falley, librarian at Goucher College, was tireless in her efforts to secure for me inter-library loans. Dona Maria Luiza de Maia Monteiro cheerfully kept me supplied with archival materials at the Château d'Eu.

For aid in gaining access to important sources I am indebted to Mrs. Manoel de Oliveira Lima of Washington, Dr. Bertha Lutz, Madame Jeronyma Mesquita, Dr. Max Fleiuss, and the Conde de Affonso Celso, all of Rio de Janeiro, the Honorable Walter C. Thurston, formerly chargé d'affaires in Brazil, Professor J. Fred Rippy of the University of Chicago, Professor Percy Alvin Martin of Stanford University, and, especially, to Professor Clarence H. Haring of Harvard University and to the late Edwin Vernon Morgan, for many years American ambassador to Brazil.

The Social Science Research Council made it financially possible for me to examine in 1933 important records in Europe and in Brazil relating to the Emperor.

In solving problems connected with my researches I received aid from Miss Clarissa Rolfs of Gainesville, Florida, Sra. Lucia Furquim Lahmeyer, librarian of the *Instituto Historico e Geographico Brasileiro*, Dr. Alcides Bezerra, director of the Brazilian *Archivo Nacional*, and Dr. Manoel A. Velho da Motta Maia, the son of Dom Pedro II's last physician.

I was helped by the following-named persons in securing certain illustrations for my book: Dr. E. Roquette Pinto, of the Brazilian *Museu Nacional*, Dr. Manoel A. Velho da Motta Maia, Mr. Paul A. McNeil, librarian of the Lima Library, Mr. Charles E. Babcock, librarian of the Columbus Memorial Library, and Miss Elsie Brown, editor of the *Bulletin* of the Pan American Union.

President Ada Comstock of Radcliffe College granted me permission to use a long quotation from Lucy Ellen Paton's *Elizabeth Cary Agassiz*, the copyright of which belongs to the trustees of the College.

Most of all, I am under obligations to His Highness Dom Pedro de Alcantara d'Orléans Bragança, grandson of Dom Pedro II, who not only gave me access to the Bragança archives at the Château d'Eu and permitted me to have copies made of many portraits at the Château, but also helped clear up obscurities by answering my numerous questions, and otherwise showed constant and sympathetic interest in my efforts to produce in English a worthy biography of the Emperor.

Dr. Raul d'Eça of Washington checked for me a number of translations from Portuguese, and my colleague Professor Eugene Newton Curtis of Goucher read and helpfully criticized the entire manuscript.

For all of this aid I am very grateful.

Finally, I wish to express appreciation of the courteous coöperation of my publishers.

M. W. W.

Baltimore, Maryland
September 24, 1937.

CONTENTS

	PAGE
Preface	vii

CHAPTER

I.	Founding of the Brazilian Empire	3
II.	Bending the Twig	20
III.	The Regency and the Boy Emperor	44
IV.	Dom Pedro's Brazil in the 1840's	66
V.	The Emperor's Family Life and General Routine	84
VI.	Twenty-five Years of Foreign Troubles	101
VII.	Dom Pedro's Struggles with a Premature Political System	128
VIII.	A Visit to the Old World	149
IX.	The Emperor's Religious Views and Church Policy	166
X.	Touring the United States of America	186
XI.	Dom Pedro as Teacher of the Brazilian Nation	214
XII.	Promotion of Internal Progress	228
XIII.	Among the Intellectuals	244
XIV.	Slavery and Abolition	264
XV.	Increasing Discontent toward the Monarchy	288
XVI.	The Menace of Militarism	310
XVII.	The Revolution	327
XVIII.	Banishment of the Imperial Family	344
XIX.	Dom Pedro in Exile	360
	Appendices	
	I. Pronunciation of Portuguese	383
	II. Prime Ministers of Brazil, 1847-1889	384
	Bibliography	386
	Index	405

ILLUSTRATIONS

Dom Pedro II in 1847	*Frontispiece*
Dom Pedro I	10
Empress Leopoldina	10
Dom Pedro II at About One Year	40
Dom Pedro II in Boyhood	40
Dom Pedro II and His Sisters at Their Lessons in São Christovão Palace	40
Coronation of Dom Pedro II	58
Map of the Brazilian Empire under Dom Pedro II	76
Dom Pedro II in Middle Age	116
Dona Thereza in Middle Age	116
Princess Isabel	116
Prince Gaston d'Orléans, Comte d'Eu	116
Dom Pedro at the Opening of the War Against Paraguay	120
The Imperial Party at Niagara Falls in 1876	202
Dom Pedro as Represented by a Contemporary Cartoon	202
The Imperial Family Shortly Before the Revolution	324
Empress Thereza in Old Age	364
Dom Pedro II and Dr. Motta Maia at the Hotel Beauséjour, Cannes, 1890	364

DOM PEDRO THE MAGNANIMOUS

I

FOUNDING OF THE BRAZILIAN EMPIRE

ONE AFTERNOON in April, 1831, Rio de Janeiro was festively decked and was stirred by unusual excitement. From windows and balconies hung gay damask draperies; flags and pennants of green and gold waved in the breeze. Crowds of people—black, brown, and white—were making for the large *praça* in front of the imperial City Palace on the margin of the Bay. Some of them carried green branches of the "national" croton shrub in yellow bloom. The military guard drawn up in front of the palace had decorated their caps and the barrels of their muskets with glossy sprigs from coffee trees spangled with starry blossoms and green and red berries. Also in the square were the municipal officers, on horseback and wearing ancient ceremonial uniform. Presently, from vessels in the harbor and fortresses on the hills came the boom of cannon. The crowds shouted joyfully, "Long live Dom Pedro II, Emperor of Brazil!"

On a second-floor balcony of the palace was their sovereign, surrounded by his sisters and his ministers of state, who were likewise splendid in the imperial green and gold. The tiny Emperor, little more than five years old, was standing on a chair, that the people might more easily see him. He was a delicate-looking child, with light golden hair, fair skin, and German blue eyes, and with a slightly projecting lower lip which betokened his Habsburg ancestry. In almost baby wonder he gazed upon his cheering subjects and responded to their *vivas* by waving a handkerchief. On an English war vessel in the harbor was his father, Dom Pedro I, who had abdicated the Brazilian throne two days before and was soon to leave for his native Portugal, to face even worse troubles than those left behind.[1]

The Bragança family and the two countries over which it ruled had long known perplexing problems; but difficulties had thickened about a generation ago, when Brazil was still a mere colony. Napoleon Bonaparte was at the time trying to make himself dictator of Europe and of lands beyond. England, the chief hindrance to his success, had been an ally of Portugal for more than four centuries. Repeatedly she had used her superior strength to impose upon and exploit the little Iberian kingdom, but Portugal, forced to choose between the devil of Napoleon's unscrupulousness and the deep, blue sea of British greed, inclined to the latter; for, after all, England was her best friend. Napoleon was bent upon starving England into submission, through strict enforcement of the continental blockade; but Portugal, bolstered by British agents, refused to coöperate. Since French invasion and conquest seemed imminent, it was decided that the Portuguese royal family and court should take refuge in the colony of Brazil. Accordingly, on November 29, 1807, a fleet of thirty-six vessels bearing the Bragança family and many thousands of nobles and hangers-on sailed out the mouth of the Tagus, under convoy of a British squadron, and set off across the Atlantic. Shortly afterwards Napoleon's army occupied Lisbon.

The leading members of the fugitive royal family were much inferior to some that the Bragança line had produced. The nominal ruler was Queen Maria, great-grandmother of the little Dom Pedro II who was joyfully acclaimed Emperor of Brazil on the April day in 1831; but she had long been hopelessly insane, and her son João was Regent. Dom João was mediocre mentally and poorly educated, slow, timid, and inde-

[1] João Alcides Bezerra Cavalcanti, ed., *Infancia e adolescencia de D. Pedro II: Documentos interessantes* . . . , pp. 32-33; J. B. Debret, *Voyage pittoresque et historique au Brésil*, III, 230-31, *Atlas*, pl. 51; "Traços biographicos de D. Pedro II extrahidos das collecções do *Jornal do Commercio*," *Rev. do Inst. Hist. e Geog. Bras.*, vol. 152, pp. 609-11.

cisive, but kindly and, on the whole, well-meaning.[2] His wife, Princess Carlota Joaquina, daughter of Carlos IV of Spain, was vulgar, bad-tempered, unscrupulous, and malicious, and given to political intrigue, even against her husband, whom she despised and from whom she was estranged.[3] The oldest child of this jarring couple was nine-year-old Prince Pedro. The boy was active and impulsive, and his liveliness helped cheer the Portuguese court during the long voyage to the New World.

Brazil had experienced economic repression and discrimination under Portugal, and also most of the other ills that were the lot of colonies at the time. Many of the Brazilian leaders, influenced by French revolutionary philosophy, had become restive. They had little fondness for the mother country, and less for Portuguese nationals as a whole. Yet they joyfully welcomed the royal fugitives, since the presence of the sovereigns would enhance Brazilian prestige and since it offered bright hopes of a better status for the colony. This was not vain optimism: a change for the better soon began. The Regent opened several ports to the direct commerce of friendly nations, removed various galling restrictions from industry, introduced the printing press, and made other changes which placed the big colony upon the road to economic and cultural progress. All of this was gratifying, but perhaps the Brazilians were most pleased when, in December, 1815, their land was made a coördinate part of the Kingdom of Portugal, Algarve, and Brazil. The change in status was largely aimed to pacify and consolidate the vast, straggling colony, to foster its loyalty, and to offer better protection to it from the suspected designs of England.[4] In 1816, Queen Maria died and the Prince Regent became King João VI.

By now, the Brazilians had learned that the presence of their sovereign was not an unmixed blessing. To keep satisfied

---

[2] Manoel de Oliveira Lima, *Dom João VI no Brasil*, II, 941-42; Pedro Calmon, *O rei do Brasil: a vida de D. João VI*, pp. 33-122, *passim*.
[3] Oliveira Lima, *op. cit.*, I, 261-82; Calmon, *op. cit.*, pp. 33-122, *passim*.
[4] Oliveira Lima, *op. cit.*, I, 529-39.

the horde of his subjects who had followed him into exile, King João distributed offices and titles with lavish hand, a procedure which added much to the original unpopularity of the Portuguese aristocrats. Moreover, the Brazilians found their taxes increasingly heavy, for the royal establishment and its hungry satellites were costly, as were also the wars in which King João engaged, especially that against the United Provinces of the Plata (Argentina) over the *Banda Oriental del Uruguay*, then hardly free from Spain. This conflict resulted partly from the ambitions of the energetic Carlota Joaquina, who had declared herself the heir of her brother Fernando VII of Spain when he was a prisoner of Napoleon Bonaparte. After six years of war, King João annexed the Banda Oriental to Brazil as the Cisplatine Province.

Though this territorial expansion pleased national vanity, the Brazilians were by now much dissatisfied with their refugee sovereigns. They heartily disliked Dona Carlota Joaquina, who frankly expressed her contempt for them and her preference for Portugal. Resentment towards the King had also grown, for he refused to grant a liberal constitution and he often acted tyrannically. As a result, there were uprisings in various parts of Brazil. Though these were crushed, the demand for a constitution was not silenced. The Crown Prince, Pedro, sympathized with the liberals, and Dom João, finding compromise necessary, planned to send Brazilian delegates to a meeting of the Cortes in Portugal. He also called a convention to discuss pending problems, but soon quarreled with it and dissolved it with troops. In the struggle a number of members were killed.[5]

Meanwhile, things had been going badly in Portugal, where, nominally, a council of regency had ruled since the French had been driven out. João's return was demanded and, though he

[5] John Armitage, *The History of Brazil*, I, 22-33; R. Walsh, *Notices of Brazil in 1828 and 1829*, I, 187-99; Calmon, *op. cit.*, pp. 265-68.

preferred to live in Brazil, he finally prepared to go back. He made his son Pedro Regent over the Brazilian hornet's nest, and suggested that he assume the crown of Brazil if it became free from Portugal, to prevent another from getting control. In April, 1821, João set sail for Lisbon, taking with him a large fraction of the Portuguese nobles—a good riddance in the eyes of the Brazilians.[6]

Recent events had caused nationalism to grow rapidly in Brazil, and the leaders watched fearfully for the results of João's return to Portugal. Their suspense was brief, for soon the government at Lisbon restored various discriminations against the former colony, and followed this by ordering the Prince Regent to return to Europe. Apparently the colonial status was to be restored.

Brazilian alarm spread, and action quickly followed. Under the leadership of José Bonifacio de Andrada e Silva, Dom Pedro's minister of the interior and of foreign affairs, a bold stand was made for independence. The Prince Regent's wife, the Archduchess Maria Leopoldina of Austria, aided and abetted the revolutionary movement. There was considerable republican sentiment among the leaders, but separation from the mother country seemed better assured if Dom Pedro was asked to remain as constitutional ruler. This was done and, after considerable hesitation, the Prince consented. On September 7, 1822, he took the final step, when he and his suite were riding near the city of São Paulo in the south. Besides the little stream called Ypiranga he drew rein on his horse, tore from his uniform the Portuguese colors, flourished his sword, and shouted a formal proclamation of freedom: "It is time! . . . Independence or death! We are separated from Portugal!" This is known as *O Grito do Ypiranga* (The Cry of Ypiranga), Brazil's declaration of independence. On October 12, he was officially pro-

[6] Oliveira Lima, *op. cit.*, II, 1125-26; Manoel de Oliveira Lima, *O movimiento da independencia, 1821-1822*, pp. 7-11; Calmon, *op. cit.*, pp. 246-47, 251, 277-78.

claimed Emperor of Brazil, and on December 1, 1822, was crowned.[7]

Dom Pedro I was twenty-four years old when he became sovereign of Brazil, which, under Portugal, had experienced three centuries of neglect and misrule. In appearance he was pleasing, for there was a courtly elegance about his short, sturdy figure, and his open countenance was dominated by large, expressive, dark eyes. He had an alert but poorly trained mind, and was fond of mechanics and the fine arts. For music he had decided talent and had composed a number of pieces. His disposition and character were now more pronounced and complicated than they were when, as an interesting little boy, he fled with his parents from the armies of Bonaparte. He was impulsive, but stubborn; energetic, but at times indecisive; democratic, generous, and friendly; but occasionally he resorted to wild fits of anger and to deeds of brutality. He was likewise romantic and sentimental, given to self-dramatization, and ambitious for glory. In morals as well as in character he was undisciplined, for as a child he had been permitted to run the streets freely and to associate with almost whomsoever he would. While still in his teens he had affairs with a number of women. In politics he inclined, theoretically, towards French revolutionary philosophy and liked to think of himself as a liberal. He took seriously his duties as a ruler and certainly he meant to do well by his subjects.[8]

His wife was an asset. Dona Maria Leopoldina—commonly known as Leopoldina—was the daughter of Emperor Francis I of Austria and great-granddaughter of the famous Maria Theresa, archduchess of Austria and queen of Hungary.

---

[7] Oliveira Lima, *O movimiento da independencia*; Manoel de Oliveira Lima, *Formation historique de la nationalité brésilienne*, pp. 154-67; Armitage, *op. cit.*, I, 80-98; Walsh, *op. cit.*, I, 206-17; Pedro Calmon, *O rei cavalleiro, a vida de D. Pedro I*, pp. 120-24.

[8] Max Fleiuss, *Paginas de historia*, pp. 80-82; Calmon, *O rei do Brasil*, pp. 36-45; Oliveira Lima, *Formation historique de la nationalité brésilienne*, pp. 149, 167; Alan K. Manchester, "The Paradoxical Pedro, First Emperor of Brazil," *Hisp. Amer. Hist. Rev.*, XII (May, 1932), 176-79.

Her mother—also named Maria Theresa—was a daughter of King Ferdinand IV of Naples, and her elder sister, Maria Louisa, was the second wife of Napoleon Bonaparte. Dona Leopoldina was of German appearance, with sturdy figure, curly flaxen hair, fair skin, and blue eyes. The lower part of her face showed the strong jaw and prominent under lip of the Habsburgs. Her marriage to Dom Pedro took place in 1817, without the young people's seeing each other in advance. But she had exchanged many a letter with the young Prince, who was nearly two years her junior, had received his portrait, and was much attracted to him. Furthermore, she was somewhat romantic, and the idea of life in the American tropics appealed to her strongly.[9]

Dona Leopoldina, who possessed a superior mind and great intellectual interest, had received an excellent education, was interested in the whole field of knowledge, and read much and widely. The library accumulated by her in the residential palace at Boa Vista was the best in Brazil at the time, and she constantly added to it by orders from Europe. One, probably typical, list that she sent asked for the best recent books in the fields of "history, geography, natural history, politics, philosophy, belles-lettres, botany, travels, and journals."[10] Specific items that she requested ranged from a French treatise on the flora of Benin in Africa to Solvyn's four-volume work on the Hindus, and Thomas Malthus's *Principles of Political Economy*.[11] She introduced into Rio de Janeiro various plants and trees from Europe, and had them set out in the park at Boa Vista. With the strange and luxuriant vegetation of her adopted land she was delighted and fascinated, and she sent specimens of it, and also of Brazilian minerals, back to Austria.[12]

The coming of Dona Leopoldina raised the intellectual and cultural tone of the Brazilian court, and gave it a needed touch

[9] Max Fleiuss, in *Contribuições para a Biographia de D. Pedro II*, Pt. I, p. 15.
[10] João Alcides Bezerra Cavalcanti, ed., *A Imperatriz Maria Leopoldina: Documentos interessantes . . .* , p. 120.   [11] *Ibid.*, pp. 105-10, 181-210.
[12] Fleiuss, *Paginas de historia*, pp. 205-47.

of refinement. She soon became a familiar figure to her new subjects, for she appeared often in public, usually on horseback, in company with Dom Pedro. Clad in blue dragoon uniform and boots with heavy silver spurs, she rode by his side when the troops were reviewed, and in parades and maneuvers. The people quickly became attached to her because of her friendly greetings and her kindliness, which caused her to dispense money with generous hand for the relief of the poor. And their hearts were completely won through her definite support of their cause when the struggle came for separation from Portugal.[13]

Her romantic attachment for Dom Pedro, formed in the days of betrothal, became a strong, deep affection. But it was not returned by her husband, for Dona Leopoldina lacked the charm needed to attract and hold his roaming heart. Both of them, however, delighted in their children, particularly the Empress, whose maternal instincts were unusually strong. The eldest child, Maria da Gloria, princess of Grão Pará, was born on April 4, 1819, while João was still ruler of Brazil, as was also the second child, Miguel, born April 26, 1820, and the third, João, born March 6, 1821. Miguel lived but a few weeks and in February, 1822, João died as a result of exposure suffered when the royal family fled into the country because of a military revolt in Rio de Janeiro during the struggle for independence. Another daughter, Januaria Maria, arrived on March 11, 1822, a little over a month after Prince João's death; Paula Marianna was born on February 17 of the next year; Francisca Carolina, on August 2, 1824; and on December 2, 1825, the parents were rejoiced by the birth of another boy, the subject of this book, who was named Pedro de Alcantara.[14]

---

[13] *Ibid.*, pp. 242-43, 291; Fleiuss, in *Contribuições para a Biographia de D. Pedro II*, Pt. I, p. 16, note; Bezerra Cavalcanti, ed., *A Imperatriz Maria Leopoldina: Documentos interessantes*, pp. 145-80.

[14] Bezerra Cavalcanti, ed., *A Imperatriz Maria Leopoldina: Documentos interessantes*, pp. 76-103; *passim*; Max Fleiuss, "D. Pedro II—seu nascimento—seus irmãos," *Rev. do Inst. Hist. e Geog. Bras.*, vol. 152, pp. 21-22.

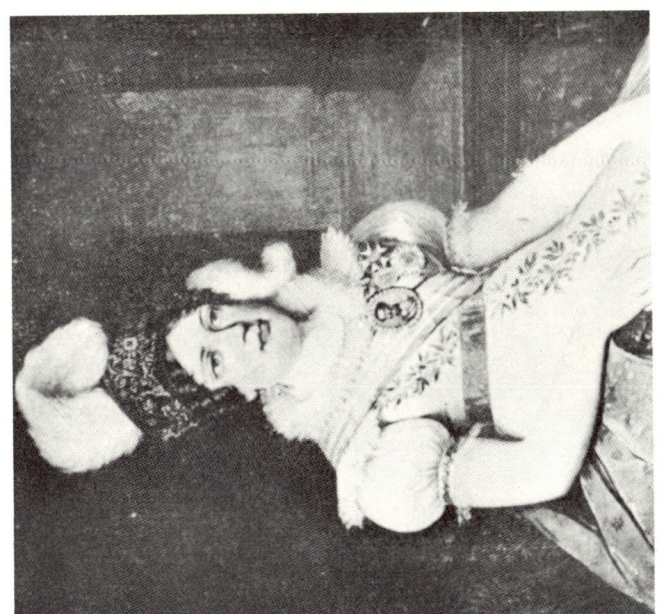

From a painting at the Château d'Eu

EMPRESS LEOPOLDINA

From a photograph in the Lima Library, Catholic University of America, of a miniature by Simplicio de Sá

DOM PEDRO I

Before the birth of Pedro, however, troubles had begun to harass both his parents. Dom Pedro I's problems were largely political, which was to be expected, for Brazil would have been a difficult country for any one to govern; and the young Emperor was poorly fitted for the task and was hopelessly handicapped by his Portuguese birth. Early in 1823 a convention met at his call to draw up the promised constitution. Here, Brazilian jealousy and resentment toward the Portuguese in the country caused serious discord and, finally, an open quarrel between the Emperor and many of the delegates. José Bonifacio de Andrada and his two brothers, three of the most enlightened liberals in the country, who had at first supported Dom Pedro, became estranged and began vigorously to oppose him. Dom Pedro, influenced by the Portuguese reactionaries, dissolved the convention in November, 1823, by use of troops, and exiled the three Andrada brothers.[15] This was his first serious mistake. Promptly afterwards he appointed a commission of ten which drew up a frame of government under his direction.

Even the declaration of independence and the coronation of Dom Pedro had not ended the unrest and dissatisfaction which was rife in Brazil when King João left for Portugal. When, therefore, the Emperor's high-handed treatment of the constituent assembly became known in the north it was used as justification for a republican revolt. Frightened by this, Dom Pedro swore to the new constitution on March 21, 1824, and it was proclaimed. The document provided for a two-house Parliament elected indirectly by limited suffrage, but it left much authority to the Emperor, through granting him *poder moderador*—moderating power.[16] On the whole, the constitution was as liberal as national progress justified.

It did not, however, satisfy the revolutionary provinces; and, led by Pernambuco, these organized and proclaimed the "Confederation of the Equator," using the United States of

[15] Calmon, *O rei cavalleiro*, pp. 132-46.
[16] Herman G. James, *The Constitutional System of Brazil*, pp. 237-52.

America as model. Only after considerable fighting were the refractory provinces subdued.[17]

But no sooner was this accomplished, than more serious trouble came in the south. The Cisplatine Province revolted and declared independence of Brazil. Political leaders of Buenos Aires came to the province's support, and soon Dom Pedro had a war on his hands with his transplatine neighbors. After a long and costly conflict the province, through British influence, was in 1828 given independence and became the Republic of Uruguay. The loss of it hurt the Emperor's prestige, for the expansionist spirit was strong in Brazil. In addition, many of the people resented the increased taxes caused by the futile war.

There was also dissatisfaction with the treaty of 1825, whereby Portugal recognized Brazil's independence, since the price the Empire had to pay for the boon was assumption of a considerable share of Portugal's debt.[18] This agreement increased hostility towards the mother country and made the Brazilians more suspicious of Dom Pedro's tendency to favor the Portuguese within the Empire.

The death of King João VI in March, 1826, heightened ill feeling, for the regency which João had appointed in Lisbon quickly proclaimed the young Brazilian Emperor as King Pedro IV of Portugal. The Brazilians were fearful that Dom Pedro would return to his native land and reduce Brazil to a subordinate position. Dom Pedro doubtless would have preferred to rule from Lisbon, but he knew that to attempt it would result in the loss of his New World empire. Therefore, after decreeing a constitution for Portugal, which the Liberals were demanding, he, on May 2, 1826, abdicated its throne in favor of

---

[17] Oliveira Lima, *Formation historique de la nationalité brésilienne*, p. 182; José Francisco de Rocha Pombo, *Historia do Brasil*, VIII, 33-39.

[18] Alan K. Manchester, *British Preëminence in Brazil*, pp. 186-219; Manoel de Oliveira Lima, *Historia diplomatica do Brazil; o reconhecimento do Imperio*, pp. 243-45.

his daughter Maria da Gloria, then seven years old.[19] His abdication was, however, conditioned upon Maria da Gloria's marrying his brother Miguel, and upon Dom Miguel's swearing to Portugal's new constitution. There was precedent in the Bragança dynasty for marriage of such close kin, since the law required that a sovereign queen of Portugal should marry a Portuguese.[20] The betrothal contract was signed at Vienna, in the presence of Emperor Francis I, the little Princess's grandfather; and Dom Miguel swore to the constitution that his brother had granted to Portugal. But before the marriage could take place that country was reduced almost to anarchy through strife between liberals and reactionaries. Therefore, on July 3, 1827, Dom Pedro made Miguel Regent. Opponents of constitutional rule and of Maria da Gloria as sovereign, who were numerous, urged Dom Miguel to set aside the constitution and to reign as absolute monarch. He yielded, and in July, 1828, took the oath as King.

One result of this was civil war in Portugal between the two brothers, during which conflict Dom Pedro spent Brazilian money in trying to uphold the claims of his daughter. His subjects resented this, and also the fact that Dom Pedro continued to call himself King Pedro IV of Portugal, until March, 1828, when he unconditionally abdicated.[21]

Even before the war of succession began in Portugal, the Emperor's private life had become a subject for serious criticism in Brazil, for he continued after his marriage the promiscuous habits of his early youth. It was his mistress Senhora Domitila de Castro Canto e Mello who caused the worst scandal at the

---

[19] Marquis de Rezende, *Éclaircissements historiques*, pp. 180-81; Manoel de Oliveira Lima, *Dom Pedro e Dom Miguel, a querela da successão*, pp. 52-59; Oliveira Lima, *Historia diplomatica do Brazil*, p. 254.

[20] Walsh, *op. cit.*, I, 310-12; Armitage, *op. cit.*, I, 232-34; João Pandiá Calogeras, *A politica exterior do Imperio*, III, 324.

[21] Tudor to Van Buren, no. 136, Aug. 23, 1829, Dept. of State, Despatches, Brazil; Fleiuss, "D. Pedro II—seu nascimento—seus irmãos," *Rev. do Inst. Hist. e Geog. Bras.*, vol. 152, p. 29; Armitage, *op. cit.*, I, 296; Walsh, *op. cit.*, I, 315-16; Rezende, *op. cit.*, pp. 181-82, 183-85, 188, 218, 239-40.

Brazilian court. In May, 1824, she bore him a daughter, but apparently the Empress did not learn of this gross infidelity until a year later. At about this time Dom Pedro made Domitila the Empress's first lady of the bedchamber, and later Marchioness of Santos. In public, the Empress maintained calm dignity in the face of these insults, but she suffered intensely from them, and finally, on October 23, 1826, she told the Austrian minister at Rio de Janeiro of her unhappiness and asked him to notify her father.[22] Subsequently, she had a violent quarrel with Dom Pedro over Domitila. But they seem to have become reconciled, and immediately afterwards, on November 24, the Emperor left for the south where frontier uprisings prompted by the war over the Cisplatine Province were in progress. Dona Leopoldina had been made Regent for the period of his absence, but she soon became ill, and grew rapidly worse. Miscarriage of a child followed, and puerperal infection developed. On December 11, 1826, she died in delirious horror over the presence of Domitila. At once there spread a rumor—which was probably false, but was generally accepted as fact by the Brazilians—that the Emperor had struck the beloved Dona Leopoldina during their last quarrel and that the injuries had caused her death. This added to the unpopularity of Dom Pedro, especially in the capital.[23]

After the death of the unhappy Empress, Dom Pedro's infatuation for Domitila increased. He gave her a voice in government councils, and even tried to secure for her full recognition at court. But to the nation as a whole, whose indignation grew with the scandalous situation, she was the "Madame Pompadour of Brazil."[24]

To help restore a semblance of respectability to the court,

---

[22] Alberto Rangel, *D. Pedro I e a Marquesa de Santos*, p. 154.

[23] *Ibid., passim*; Bezerra Cavalcanti, *A Imperatriz Maria Leopoldina: Documentos interessantes*, pp. 46-74, 143-44; Alcides Bezerra, *A vida domestica da Imperatriz Leopoldina (1797-1826)*; Fleiuss, *Paginas de historia*, pp. 249-50, 257-58; Walsh, *op. cit.*, I, 255-59, 266-67.

[24] Rangel, *op. cit.*, pp. 181 ff.

the ministry urged Dom Pedro to marry again. Finally, a match was arranged between him and Princess Amelia de Leuchtenberg, a daughter of Princess Augusta Amelia of Bavaria and Eugene de Beauharnais, the stepson of Napoleon Bonaparte. Before the bride arrived, Domitila was sent back to São Paulo, probably through the influence of José Bonifacio, who, with his brothers, had returned to Brazil the year before and had been restored to royal favor. Dom Pedro's second marriage took place in Rio de Janeiro, in October, 1829. Princess Amelia, who was but seventeen years old at the time, was beautiful, charming, and kind. The Brazilians were delighted with her, as was the Emperor, and she, like Dona Leopoldina, became deeply attached to her husband.[25]

It was the Portuguese question that caused the most hostility towards Pedro I and that was the basic reason for his downfall. This cropped out chiefly in his relations with Parliament, which he had delayed calling until May, 1826, when the demand for funds for the war in the Plata basin made it necessary. After that, regular sessions took place. But trouble between him and the lower house began almost immediately. The deputies demanded a cabinet system modeled on the British, with the ministers responsible to them. The constitution included no such democratic provision, and Dom Pedro was unwilling to grant it. Hence, much friction resulted over the personnel of the cabinet, for the Emperor tended to give preference to ministers from the Portuguese party, since he could rely more upon loyalty and support from them than from the Brazilians. The deputies, who did not trust these foreign sympathizers, retaliated by refusing to vote the budget and by ignoring imperial recommendations for the national good. Thus, deadlocks were frequent, little was accomplished by Parliament, and the country drifted. The opposition press, which Dom Pedro dared not muzzle, emphasized his faults and played up the French Revolution of

[25] *Ibid.*, pp. 203-56; Maria Junqueira Schmidt, *A segunda imperatriz do Brasil*; Tudor to Van Buren, no. 145, Oct. 26, 1829, Dept. of State, Despatches, Brazil.

1830 to his disadvantage. In this way, feeling against him was stimulated and crystallized.[26] Threatened uprisings in some of the provinces resulted in declaration of martial law.

The Emperor and his family spent the early part of 1831 in visiting Minas Geraes, where he hoped to revive some of the great popularity he had enjoyed there during the struggle for independence. It was in vain; even while he was present one of his ministerial supporters failed in the parliamentary election. Stimulated by his political friends, the Portuguese—some of whom were recently arrived fugitives from Dom Miguel—and other sympathizers celebrated his return to the capital, on March 11, by illuminations and bonfires. The opposition element refused to coöperate in the festivities. Insults were exchanged between the two factions, and a number of Brazilians were hurt in the street frays which followed during the nights of March 12 to 14.[27]

This produced a crisis. Parliament was not in session, but many members who opposed the Emperor were in Rio, and these met to plan for action. Evaristo da Veiga, editor of the *Aurora Fluminense*, the best paper in the Empire, was chosen to draw up a representation to the Emperor regarding the situation. This, after being signed by more than twenty deputies, was presented to Dom Pedro. It called special attention to the recent conduct of the Portuguese party and asked the Emperor to rid himself at once of the "traitors" with whom he was surrounded. Public confidence, it declared, was largely lost, and public order menaced; the tranquillity of the state, and even the throne itself, would be in danger if these representations did not receive attention.[28]

---

[26] Manoel de Oliveira Lima, *O Imperio brazileiro*, pp. 18-19; Walsh, *op. cit.*, II, 422-23; Alan K. Manchester, "Rise of the Brazilian Aristocracy," *Hisp. Amer. Hist. Rev.*, XI (May, 1931), 163-67.

[27] Rocha Pombo, *op. cit.*, VIII, 239-44; Armitage, *op. cit.*, II, 112-15; W. S. W. Ruschenberger, *Three Years in the Pacific, Containing Notices of Brazil*, I, 38.

[28] Rocha Pombo, *op. cit.*, VIII, 244-46; Armitage, *op. cit.*, II, 117-22.

Dom Pedro promptly replied that the steps necessary to preserve peace and quiet had been taken, but this did not calm the nation, and in some provinces there were frank outbursts of rebellion.[29] On March 25, the anniversary of the imperial oath to the constitution, when Dom Pedro was entering church to attend a *Te Deum*, some one cried, "Long live Dom Pedro II!" This was the first implied wish that the Emperor might be displaced by his son. Other bystanders shouted, "Long live the Emperor!" But voices from the crowd added—"in so far as he is constitutional." With characteristic impetuosity, Dom Pedro turned and called out, "I am, and always have been, a constitutional monarch!"[30] He probably had been since he put the constitution into effect, but the constitution was of his own dictation and did not satisfy the Brazilian liberals.

Realizing that matters were serious, he became conciliatory. On March 19, he made changes in his ministry, putting in Brazilian senators of mediocre ability. But he found it difficult to work with them, and on April 6 he abruptly dismissed this cabinet and appointed one from reactionaries among his unpopular titled aristocracy. When this action became known, an excited crowd gathered in the Campo de Acclamação near the residential palace. With them were the deputies who had signed the communication of March 17 to the Emperor. The gathering demanded reinstatement of the former cabinet. Dom Pedro issued a proclamation assuring his indignant subjects that the government was constitutional, and promising to maintain it so, but the paper was torn from the hands of the officer who tried to read it to those who waited in the Campo. In the afternoon a deputation from the opposition called upon the Emperor at São Christovão and asked that the dismissed members be reinstated. Knowing that his constitutional prerogatives

---

[29] Rocha Pombo, *op. cit.*, VIII, 246-48; Armitage, *op. cit.*, II, 122-24.
[30] Anfriso Fialho, *Dom Pedro II, empereur du Brésil*, pp. 13-14; Armitage, *op. cit.*, II, 125; Calogeras, *op. cit.*, II, 554-55.

were at stake, Dom Pedro refused to comply. He is reported to have told the deputation, "I will do everything for the people, but nothing by the people."³¹

Some of the troops joined the mob in the square; the Emperor's battalion followed; and then his guard of honor. After some hours of deadlock, Dom Pedro, though unwilling to reinstate the former cabinet, finally decided to appoint one to suit the popular wish. He therefore sent for Senator Vergueiro, who belonged to the reform element, intending to ask him to head the new ministry; but the messenger failed to find the senator and was delayed. Farías, an officer of the rebellious troops, who had come to report the situation, urged prompt action, lest the crowd in the Campo get out of control.³²

By now it was early morning of April 7, and Dom Pedro was weary, disgusted, and discouraged. To continue seemed futile. With characteristic impulsiveness, and without consulting his ministers, he took paper and wrote out an abdication in favor of his "much beloved and esteemed son, the Senhor Dom Pedro de Alcantara."³³ But he wept as he did so, and in his excitement he forgot to mention that it was the Brazilian throne he was giving up.³⁴ Handing the paper to Farías, he said, "Here is my abdication. May you be happy. I shall retire to Europe and leave the country which I have loved so much, and still love."³⁵ He next wrote out a statement naming as the tutor of his four youngest children José Bonifacio de Andrada, whom he called his "true friend." Farías galloped to the Campo with the abdication, which was received with joyful demonstrations. Soon afterwards the deputies and senators in the capital met and appointed a provisional regency.³⁶

---

[31] Armitage, *op. cit.*, II, 127-29.
[32] *Ibid.*, pp. 131-32; Calmon, *O rei cavalleiro*, p. 235.
[33] *Diario do Rio de Janeiro*, April 8, 1831; Calmon, *O rei cavalleiro*, pp. 235-36.
[34] Oliveira Lima, *O Imperio brazileiro*, pp. 20-21; Fleiuss, in *Contribuições para a Biographia de D. Pedro II*, Pt. I, pp. 49-50.
[35] Calmon, *O rei cavalleiro*, p. 236; Armitage, *op. cit.*, II, 132-33.
[36] Armitage, *op. cit.*, II, 134.

Meanwhile, Dom Pedro, Dona Amelia, and Princess Maria da Gloria[37] went aboard the British vessel "Warspite" which happened to be in the harbor. From there Dom Pedro heard the enthusiastic demonstrations in favor of his son when he was acclaimed in the praça before the City Palace. But he probably had no regrets, for, says Oliveira Lima, "His romantic soul was exalted by the idea of sacrifice."[38] Part of his time while awaiting departure was spent in fishing in the Bay. He also wrote for publication in the press a letter ending, "Farewell, Patria, farewell, friends, farewell forever!"[39] After some days on the "Warspite," he and Dona Amelia were transferred to the British frigate "Volage," which left for Europe on April 14.[40] Maria da Gloria sailed at about the same time aboard a French vessel.[41] Dom Pedro's remaining years were spent in warfare against his brother Miguel in behalf of his daughter's claims to the Portuguese throne. He was successful a short time before his death, on September 23, 1834.[42]

[37] Maria da Gloria, after futile attempts in Europe to get support for her claims to the Portuguese throne, had been recalled by her father late in 1829 and had since then remained in Brazil.—*Ibid.*, pp. 64-65.
[38] *O Imperio brazileiro*, p. 22.
[39] *Diario do Rio de Janeiro*, April 14, 1831; Ruschenberger, *op. cit.*, I, 43, note.
[40] Calmon, *O rei cavalleiro*, pp. 240-41; *Diario Mercantil*, April 15, 1831.
[41] Armitage, *op. cit.*, II, 133-34.
[42] Oliveira Lima, *Dom Pedro e Dom Miguel*.

II

BENDING THE TWIG

LITTLE Dom Pedro de Alcantara who became emperor of the vast land of Brazil in 1831 represented some of the bluest blood of the world. Ancestors of his, bad and good, had swayed European scepters for more than a thousand years. Among them were Charlemagne, Alfred the Great, William the Conqueror, Hugh Capet and Louis XIV of France, Ferdinand and Isabella, and the Emperor Charles the Fifth. More closely connected with his imperial crown were Count Henry of Burgundy, who founded Portugal; Emanuel, who, besides his Iberian heritage, ruled a far-flung empire in Asia; and also the eighth Duke of Bragança, who, in 1640, was crowned João IV of Portugal. The Bragança dynasty, from which the infant Emperor of Brazil was descended, had occupied the throne in Lisbon ever since.

Dom Pedro II was born December 2, 1825, at São Christovão, the imperial residential palace, which was then about three miles from Rio de Janeiro, on the estate of Boa Vista. Immediately after his arrival, the baby was formally presented to the court, assembled at the palace for the occasion. Following this, his father and his four little sisters gave thanks to God in two different chapels for the birth of the much-desired prince. The joy of the nation was expressed by cannon salutes fired at intervals for three days, and by a week of celebration, with *festas,* illuminations, and fireworks. In accordance with Bragança custom, the baby was baptized at the age of a week. Water from the River Jordan was used for the ceremony, in the Cathedral of Rio de Janeiro, with the principal royal chaplain in charge. The proud and happy Dom Pedro I carried the infant in the baptismal procession, and the baby's eldest sister, Maria da Gloria, then six years of age, was his godmother. Saint Pedro de Alcantara, Dom Pedro I's celestial protector, was made special guardian of the little Prince. In accordance with royal tradition, the child was given many names—Pedro de Alcantara João Carlos Leopoldo Salvador Bibiano Francisco Xavier de Paula Leocadio Miguel Gabriel Rafael Gonzaga. After the ceremony a *Te Deum* was sung, with music composed by Dom Pedro I.[1]

On January 2, when the baby was a month old, the Emperor brought him to the place of worship which had been his own father's favorite and was also his—the Chapel of Our Lady of Glory, for whom the Emperor's eldest daughter had been named. The shrine was situated on one of the hills overlooking the lovely Bay of Rio de Janeiro. Leaving his carriage on the street below, the Emperor, with the baby in his arms, climbed the steep slope—as King João had done in his day—and consecrated his son to the Madonna of the chapel by placing him on her altar.[2] In the following August, 1826, the Brazilian Parliament passed an act formally recognizing the infant as Prince Imperial and heir apparent to the throne.[3]

For the first two years of his life Dom Pedro II was nourished by a wet nurse, Senhora Maria Catharina Equey, a member of the Swiss colony of southern Brazil.[4]

His chief nurse, or governess, was Dona Marianna Carlota Verna de Magalhães Coutinho, a Portuguese aristocrat. Dona Marianna and her husband, Joaquin José Magalhães Coutinho, had come to Brazil in 1808, with the court of King João.

---

[1] Fleiuss, "D. Pedro II—seu nascimento—seus irmãos," *Rev. do Inst. Hist. e Geog. Bras.*, vol. 152, pp. 20-26; Bezerra Cavalcanti, *Infancia e adolescencia de D. Pedro II: Documentos interessantes*, pp. 11-23.

[2] Fleiuss, in *Contribuições para a Biographia de D. Pedro II*, Pt. I, pp. 38-39.

[3] Bezerra Cavalcanti, *Infancia e adolescencia de D. Pedro II: Documentos interessantes*, pp. 25-27.

[4] Fleiuss, in *Contribuições para a Biographia de D. Pedro II*, Pt. I, p. 19.

Joaquim José, who had been secretary of finance and keeper of the royal robes for Dom Pedro I, had died in 1823.

When the royal baby was barely a year old tragedy first came to him, in the death of his mother. Her body, clad in imperial robes reclined on cushions of green and gold silk ready for the solemn Portuguese ceremony of *beija mão mortuario*, which took place five days after she died. Little Prince Pedro, in charge of his chamberlain, was the first to kiss Dona Leopoldina's cold hand. His sisters came next, but only seven-year-old Maria da Gloria, who sobbed inconsolably, realized that it was a last farewell.[5]

Though not of robust health, for the Bragança line was weakly, the Prince made fair progress in physical growth as well as in mental development. A pleasing glimpse of him on his third birthday is given by Robert Walsh, rector of the Church of England parish in Rio de Janeiro, at the reception to the diplomatic corps in honor of the occasion. The little boy stood beside his father on the steps of the throne and was dressed in a "plain jacket and trousers such as he would play marbles in, and looked so simple and pretty that he interested every body. When I was presented," wrote the clergyman, "he put his hands in his breeches pockets, and looked very knowing at my dress, which was not exactly that of clergy he was accustomed to."[6]

The following year Prince Pedro acquired his stepmother, Empress Amelia. He became warmly attached to her and later called her his "second mother"; but she was young and inexperienced, and during her brief stay in Brazil of less than a year and a half she probably exercised very little real influence upon her husband's children.

Between father and son there was a strong, deep affection, and an incipient congeniality and understanding, despite the fact that the boy largely drew his mental as well as his physical char-

---

[5] Fleiuss, "D. Pedro II—seu nascimento—seus irmãos," *Rev. do Inst. Hist. e Geog. Bras.*, vol. 152, p. 27; Fleiuss, in *Contribuições para a Biographia de D. Pedro II*, Pt. I, pp. 43-44. [6] *Op. cit.*, I, 525.

acteristics from his mother. In the evening before the Emperor's abdication, as he paced in the palace grounds pondering the political crisis, he held the hand of his little son, who walked by his side. The boy did not see his father after that night, for Dom Pedro I avoided awakening his children when he kissed them goodbye in the early hours of the following day.[7]

At the seven o'clock mass that morning in the royal chapel at São Christovão the members of the court were sad and the chaplain wept openly as he officiated at the services, but the royal children were not then permitted to know the cause for these signs of distress. Perhaps not until two days later—when the infant Emperor was acclaimed—did they realize, in a childish way, what had happened.

It was on the afternoon of the 9th of April that the four children were brought into the city in charge of Dona Marianna, for various ceremonies and to satisfy the desire of the people to see their new sovereign. During the drive the little boy sat on his governess's lap and, following her instructions, smiled and bowed to right and left in acknowledgment of the enthusiastic applause of the crowds. At one point, the populace, in a delirium of joy, wished to unhitch the horses from the royal coach and to draw it themselves, but this was prevented by Dona Marianna. The infant Emperor was taken to the royal chapel, beside the City Palace, where a *Te Deum* was sung, then to the palace itself where he received the diplomatic corps. At the reception for his subjects in the balcony, which has been described, his tutor, José Bonifacio,[8] supported him in the arm chair in which he stood, and his sisters, Januaria, Paula, and Francisca, were at his side. The exciting events of the day ended with a reviewing of the troops.[9]

[7] Fleiuss, "D. Pedro II—seu nascimento—seus irmãos," *Rev. do Inst. Hist. e Geog. Bras.*, vol. 152, pp. 28-29.

[8] He was commonly referred to thus. In Brazil, all people—like royalty elsewhere—are often called by their first names, or by other parts of their full names, with or without titles.

[9] Debret, *op. cit.*, III, 230-31; Debret's *Atlas*, plate 51; "Traços biographicos de D. Pedro II," *Rev. do Inst. Hist. e Geog. Bras.*, vol. 152, pp. 608-11; D. P. Kidder

In a farewell letter from the "Warspite," Dona Amelia had asked Brazilian mothers to adopt the "crowned orphan," Dom Pedro II, and to give him a place in their hearts. After their father's abdication, the royal children were, indeed, broadly speaking, the wards of the whole nation. The ex-Emperor, nevertheless, kept in close touch with them by correspondence, especially with his son, and also with those who were responsible for the children's care and training. And to all he gave wise and zealous counsel. The letters between the two Pedros began before the father left Rio de Janeiro Bay, with a loving note from the boy, probably written with Dona Marianna guiding his hand. His father was deeply moved by it and, in a reply beginning, "My beloved son and my Emperor," he urged the child to follow the advice of those who had his education in charge and to love his country and strive to be worthy of it.[10] The little Prince wrote his father in 1833 that he was cherishing with particular care the letters received from him, "as true guides for my present and future life."[11]

By keeping in close touch with the children he had left in Brazil, the ex-Emperor preserved for himself their deep affection. When his death was made known to them late in 1834 their grief was overwhelming. Dressed in deep mourning, the sad little group attended in the imperial chapel solemn mass for the repose of their father's soul. At the time Dom Pedro II was just nine years of age. Affectionate, gentle, sensitive, and old for his years, he was much shaken over his loss. He

---

and J. C. Fletcher, *Brazil and the Brazilians*, p. 214; information supplied through the courtesy of the director of the National Archives of Brazil, Dr. Alcides Bezerra, in December, 1936.

There is lack of agreement in the contemporary accounts as to the day on which this first holding of court by Dom Pedro II took place. Debret gives the 7th as the date, but this is unquestionably an error. As the official records show, the acclamation occurred on April 9th. Debret is also mistaken in saying that the Emperor was brought into the city in charge of the Condessa de Rio Seco.

[10] Fleiuss, in *Contribuições para a Biographia de D. Pedro II*, Pt. I, pp. 25, 52-53, 71-72, 78.   [11] *Ibid.*, p. 72.

was reported to have been much changed by it, becoming more serious, almost somber, and his words and actions showed a new thoughtfulness.[12] In a letter of consolation to him, José Bonifacio wrote, "They err; Dom Pedro did not die. Common men die, but not heroes."[13]

Dom Pedro I's public record during his ten years' rule really contrasted pleasingly with the achievements of most contemporary European sovereigns. He granted independence and a reasonably liberal constitution to Brazil, under which the country progressed in some ways. He also gave Portugal a charter providing for representative government, and he spent the last years of his life as leader of the Portuguese liberal element in the effort, finally successful, to put the charter into effect. These aims and achievements, as well as his affectionate disposition and attractive personality, caused his son to have a lasting admiration and attachment for him.

During the first decade of the boy's life the person influencing him most was perhaps Dona Marianna, who was promoted in 1831 to the position of first lady of the Prince Imperial. She was forty-six years old when the baby was born and had at first objected, on the grounds of her age, to assuming the responsibility which his father asked her to take. But she was a good choice, for she was well-educated and cultured, and had high ideals and fine character, and was absolutely true to her trust. Towards her little charge she was tender and kindly, but sensible, firm, and strict. During his early, formative years she watched his health with loving care and directed his mental and spiritual development. The child, who called her "Dadama" (apparently a baby mispronunciation of "dama," the Portuguese for "lady"), came to love her like a son. His father, shortly before his death, declared that Dona Marianna had shown herself worthy to educate an em-

[12] *Ibid.*, p. 81; Fialho, *op. cit.*, p. 21.
[13] Pedro d'Orléans Bragança Archives, A, 4874, Dec. 4, 1834; Fleiuss, in *Contribuições para a Biographia de D. Pedro II*, Pt. I, p. 81, note 25.

peror. Doubtless she had an important share in making Dom Pedro II what he became.[14]

In the cooler months of the year the governess and her charges spent most of the time at the São Christovão Palace, but occasionally she took them for a change of air to the imperial *fazenda* (rural estate) of Santa Cruz, about forty miles to the south of the capital. During the summer, to escape the tropical heat, they usually stayed at a fazenda in the Organ Mountains, near the present Petropolis. Here, the nights were cool and comfortable, even from December to March, when the climate was oppressive in Rio de Janeiro.

Dom Pedro's earliest playmates were his sisters; but Princess Paula died in January, 1833, following a long illness. Dona Januaria and Dona Francisca, the two who remained in Brazil, were healthy, natural little girls who early satisfied domestic instincts by learning and practicing some of the mysteries of cookery. Whether Dom Pedro had a finger in these culinary activities is not apparent, but when he discovered what his sisters were doing he insisted upon sharing the dishes they prepared. Princess Francisca, her brother's favorite, who was unusually beautiful and lovable, had much initiative and a bubbling sense of humor. When the children played church, as they were fond of doing, she was usually the priest, dressed for the part, while Dom Pedro and Dona Januaria were acolytes.[15] All three of them had garden plots in the park at São Christovão, where they occupied themselves with planting and tending flowers. This perhaps helped foster the Emperor's later interest in agriculture.

Dona Marianna realized that the little Prince needed boy associates, and these she supplied by having several sons of Brazilian aristocrats come to the palace to be his companions. With

---

[14] Heitor Moniz, *A côrte de D. Pedro II*, pp. 129-37; Calogeras, *op. cit.*, III, 387.
[15] Mozart Monteiro, "A familia imperial," *Rev. do Inst. Hist. e Geog. Bras.*, vol. 152, p. 82; Fleiuss, in *Contribuições para a Biographia de D. Pedro II*, Pt. I, pp. 97, 109.

these he played soldiers and other boyish games. One of the boys, Luiz Pedreira do Couto Ferraz, later Visconde do Bom Retiro, proved congenial to Dom Pedro mentally as well as temperamentally and they became lifelong friends.[16]

Another companion of Dom Pedro's childhood was Rafael, a Negro soldier to whom his father had become attached on his visit to the southern province of Rio Grande. Rafael was the special servant, devoted friend, and military hero of the Prince, who during his early childhood loved to ride about the palace grounds on the Negro's broad shoulders. When the boy was a little older he delighted in visiting Rafael in his quarters on the southern slope of the palace grounds and in listening to his hair-raising tales of war and other adventures in the south of the Empire.[17]

It was Dona Marianna who gave Prince Pedro his first lessons in reading and writing when he was scarcely out of babyhood, and from her also he received his earliest training in religion and ethics. Before he was five she prepared for him a little book which was published in 1830 under the title *Introduction to the Small Historical Catechism offered to His Imperial Highness D. Pedro de Alcantara*. Her letter of dedication at the beginning of the volume shows some ideas she tried to plant in the child's mind. The Christian faith, she wrote, always makes for the happiness of society; and though mankind has invoked the name of religion while committing crimes, nothing can alter the purity and perfection of the faith. A truly Christian sovereign must not fail to work for the happiness of the people who are his subjects. Piety, justice, and charity are virtues of special importance in a ruler.[18] Dona Marianna's influence upon the young Emperor continued even after he reached manhood.

Soon after Dom Pedro I's abdication, however, the respon-

---
[16] Moniz, *op. cit.*, pp. 147-54.
[17] Mucio Teixeira, *O Imperador visto de perto*, p. 25.
[18] Fleiuss, in *Contribuições para a Biographia de D. Pedro II*, Pt. I, p. 48.

sibility for the intellectual training and general welfare of his four youngest children passed to José Bonifacio de Andrada. Owing to opposition from the chamber of deputies, there was some delay before he was permitted to assume his duties.[19] Meanwhile the Marquez de Itanhaén was provisional tutor.[20] The "Father of Independence," as José Bonifacio was called by some, was finally given charge of the royal children on August 24, 1831. He was then sixty-eight years old but was still alert and vigorous. He was the most distinguished scholar in Brazil, was remarkably versatile, possessed high ideals, was devoted to his country, and was fond of his young charges.[21]

Wise and kind in his attitude towards them, he had shown his sympathetic understanding promptly after their father's abdication by hurrying out to São Christovão early the next day and asking for them. With deep emotion he gathered the tiny Dom Pedro II into his arms, exclaiming, "My emperor and my son!" Dona Amelia had arranged that the children be given a certain portion of their toys each day, but José Bonifacio, bent upon helping them to forget their troubles, ordered that for the time they be permitted to play with them all.[22]

Though José Bonifacio had once been an ultra-liberal, by the time of Dom Pedro I's abdication he had developed a "furi-

[19] The chamber held that the appointment of a tutor rested with it, not with Dom Pedro I. José Bonifacio, at the time a deputy from Bahia, replied by publishing a *Protest to the Brazilian Nation and to the Entire World* against this attitude. Soon aferwards a permanent regency was appointed and it decreed that the tutor for the royal children should be named by, responsible to, and removable by the General Assembly. It also stipulated that the tutor should take no part in politics in the name of his pupils. On June 30, 1831, the two chambers met jointly as a General Assembly and—apparently in response to popular opinion—elected as tutor José Bonifacio.—Fleiuss, in *Contribuições para a Biographia de D. Pedro II*, Pt. I, pp. 63-65; Bezerra Cavalcanti, *Infancia e adolescencia de D. Pedro II*; *Documentos interessantes*, pp. 31-37.

[20] Fleiuss, in *Contribuições para a Biographia de D. Pedro II*, Pt. I, p. 63.

[21] José Maria Latino Coelho, *Elogio historico de José Bonifacio de Andrada e Silva*, pp. 1-31; Oliveira Lima, *Formation historique de la nationalité brésilienne*, p. 155.

[22] Affonso de Escragnolle Taunay, "A formação intellectual de Pedro II," *Rev. do Inst. Hist. e Geog. Bras.*, vol. 152, pp. 888-89; Fleiuss, in *Contribuições para a Biographia de D. Pedro II*, Pt. I, p. 92.

ous horror" of anti-monarchist principles. Influenced by the political turbulence in neighboring states, he was convinced that theoretical democracy, at least in Latin America, meant military despotism. Hence, his influence in the country tended to strengthen the throne. But he believed in progressive monarchy, and favored civilization of the Indians and abolition of the slave traffic; and he pointed out that Brazil was the only nation of European origin that still traded in African bondmen.[23] To what extent he influenced his imperial pupil along these lines is not apparent, for the records of his tutorship are meagre and his tenure was brief. At the time Brazil suffered from great unrest and from repeated political crises. This caused many to wish Dom Pedro I back, at least to serve as Regent until his son was old enough to rule. José Bonifacio was charged with being associated with the faction which worked for the former Emperor's return, and the accusation was perhaps just. He was, accordingly, dismissed from office on December 15, 1833.[24]

The Marquez de Itanhaén,[25] who had the general responsibility for Dom Pedro during the remainder of his minority, was very different from José Bonifacio. When he took up his new duties he was slightly past fifty years old, was tall, thin, and austere in appearance, but possessed of a dry sense of humor. While not bigoted, he was deeply religious, and during his afternoon walks at São Christovão Palace he carried his rosary in his hand and softly recited his prayers. His career had been agricultural rather than governmental, and he scrupulously avoided all political questions. The Marquez was not intellectually brilliant, and his education was in no way unusual,

---
[23] Oliveira Lima, *Formation historique de la nationalité brésilienne*, pp. 111-12, 154-56.

[24] Moniz, *op. cit.*, pp. 102-7. José Bonifacio took a defiant attitude saying that he would yield only to force, and was promptly arrested and imprisoned. Early in 1834 he was tried and acquitted, but he retired in disgust from politics. He died April 6, 1838.—Fleiuss, in *Contribuições para a Biographia de D. Pedro II*, Pt. I, p. 73.

[25] Manoel Ignacio de Andrade Souto Maior Pinto Coelho, Marquez de Itanhaén.

but he was modest and honorable and had a strong sense of duty. He came to love the boy Emperor deeply and worked constantly to make him a good man and a good king. For Dom Pedro II he had, indeed, an ideal of perfection.[26] He and Dona Marianna, in their aims for the boy, were much alike, but he was more exacting than she.

The Marquez established a very strict regimen, and during the six and a half years of his tutorship almost every minute of Dom Pedro II's time was accounted for. At seven o'clock—later, at six—the boy rose, dressed, and attended mass in the royal chapel; at eight, he breakfasted in the presence of the palace physician, who passed upon all of his food; after that, he rested until nine. From then until eleven-thirty he was at his lessons. During the next two hours he was free to play or walk in the palace grounds. At one-thirty he went to dress for dinner, which was served promptly at two, with the physician again present, and also his chamberlain and Dona Marianna. Conversation during the meal was expected to concern scientific or other useful subjects, with persons there who could foster the boy's education by answering any questions he might ask. After dinner came another period of rest. At four-thirty or five, according to the season, if the weather was good he went for a walk in the palace grounds, or for a horseback ride, which usually lasted until dusk; but care was taken that he not exercise to the point of fatigue. Returning to the palace, he spent some time in reading aloud, or in listening while another read to him. At first the matter selected was tales and stories, and during this period he probably read Scott's novels and Froissart's *Chronicles,* which he later remembered with delight; but as he grew older and stronger he was introduced to more informational works. Thus, the Marquez inspired in him a love for

---

[26] Moniz, *op. cit.*, p. 14; Mozart Monteiro, "A infancia do Imperador," *Rev. do Inst. Hist. e Geog. Bras.*, vol. 152, pp. 34-36; Fleiuss, in *Contribuições para a Biographia de D. Pedro II*, Pt. I, p. 79.

reading. At eight o'clock came evening prayers; at nine, supper; and at nine-thirty or ten he was put to bed.[27]

In May, 1835, as a result of the recommendations of a commission appointed by the General Assembly to study the question of the royal children's education, it was decided to appoint a headmaster. The position was filled by Pedro de Santa Marianna, a Carmelite friar of broad culture who for many years had taught mathematics in the Royal Marine Academy at Rio de Janeiro. Friar Pedro, who is a rather obscure figure, seems to have been well-educated and of high moral character, able and patient as a teacher, but somewhat exacting. To him was given the immediate supervision of the three children's training, and the responsibility for unifying the work of their various teachers, and for "preserving them from false ideas of things."[28]

It was later found that the general authority given Friar Pedro was not adequate for the training of the future ruler of Brazil, since the various teachers were still prone to follow their own ideas. Consequently, on December 2, 1838, the Emperor's thirteenth birthday, the Marquez de Itanhaén issued a definite code of *Instructions to be Observed by the Teachers of the Senhor Dom Pedro II, Constitutional Emperor and Perpetual Defender of Brazil*. This rambling but illuminating document is as much a political treatise as an educational one. It reveals the aims of the General Assembly for the training of the future ruler of Brazil, and shows what kind of ruler the nation, as represented by the Assembly, desired. Likewise it describes the ideals of manhood which the Marquez aspired to realize in his youthful charge.

In the introduction to the *Instructions* the tutor stated that Socrates's injunction, "Know thyself," was to be the basis for the education of the Emperor, in order that he might tell the

---

[27] Fleiuss, in *Contribuições para a Biographia de D. Pedro II*, Pt. I, pp. 83, 107-8.
[28] E. Vilhena de Moraes, "Frei Pedro de Santa Marianna, o preceptor de Pedro II," *Rev. do Inst. Hist. e Geog. Bras.*, vol. 152, pp. 45-55; Fleiuss, in *Contribuições para a Biographia de D. Pedro II*, Pt. I, p. 86.

true from the false, understand the dignity of humankind, and realize that the monarch is a man without any natural difference from other people. He must study the earth, on which mankind is born, lives, and dies, and also the relations between human beings and nature in general, so that he would come to see, whether he wished to or not, the absolute necessity for being a good, wise, and just ruler, prepared to be the loyal friend of the representatives of the nation, and of all influences and individuals making for the good of the country. He must be taught that tyranny, violence with the sword, and shedding of blood never brought good to any one. The masters must strive likewise to reveal clearly that religion and politics are in harmony, and that both are in accord with all science. This, the Marquez believed, would help the pupil to realize the importance of tolerance and mutual forgiveness of injuries, defects, and errors, which attitude was "the perfection of Christianity," and the test of fine souls in their relations with other peoples, regardless of their religion or their form of government. Without this quality of mutual forgiveness, declared the tutor, it was impossible to exist in a complex world.

The teachers must give the Emperor real and exact knowledge of things, and avoid verbose, worthless, and prejudicial displays of learning. Hence, they must all adopt the methods of instruction of the headmaster, Friar Pedro de Santa Marianna. Furthermore, time must not be wasted on useless theses, nor the child's memory burdened with abstract ideas. The teachers must at once get down to the classification of things and ideas, so that the Emperor could fully know that "bread is bread and cheese is cheese." For instance, the teacher of ethics must show the pupil all of the results of pride and arrogance, and, in contrast, all of the consequences of humility. Not only must the child be taught that people should never be arrogant, but he must also be shown the danger of a ruler's committing acts prompted by a haughty spirit, under the impression that such conduct is worthy of praise. The instructor of physical sciences must so present his subject that Dom Pedro would understand that, though the monarch is a representative of Divinity on earth, he was also a man, subject to the natural and spiritual laws made by God.

It is the love of humanity that is the end and aim of all learning, and learning should be directed towards promoting the happiness of mankind. Therefore, wrote the Marquez,

I desire that my August Pupil become a profound and thorough scholar, versed in all of the arts and sciences, and likewise in mechanical matters, so that he may learn to love labor as the foundation of the virtues, and to honor equally the men who toil and those who serve the state through political office. But I certainly do not want him to become a superstitious *literato,* wasting his time in religious discussions like the Emperor Justinian; nor that he become a political fanatic, squandering the money and blood of Brazilians in wars and conquests and in erecting luxurious buildings, like Louis XIV in France, completely absorbed by ideas of greatness; for the Senhor Dom Pedro II can well become a great monarch through being just, wise, honorable, and virtuous, a lover of the happiness of his subjects—without any need of vexing the people by tyranny and the violent extortion of money and blood.

Finally, the teachers must not fail to tell the Emperor every day that a monarch who does not regard seriously his duties as a ruler will always become the victim of the errors, caprices, and iniquities of his ministers, which are always the cause of revolutions and civil wars. . . . Therefore it is of great importance that the Monarch read carefully all of the newspapers and periodicals of the capital and the provinces, and, furthermore, that he receive with attention all representations and complaints made by any one against the Ministers of State, since only through knowing the public and private lives of each one of his ministers and agents can he decide whether he should retain them or should dismiss them immediately and appoint others who will perform better their duties and will work for the happiness of the nation.[29]

In conclusion, wrote the Marquez de Itanhaén, "I rely much upon the wisdom and prudence of the very respectable

---

[29] Bezerra Cavalcanti, *Infancia e adolescencia de D. Pedro II: Documentos interessantes,* pp. 63-70.

Senhor Master Friar Pedro de Santa Marianna, who, being obliged to preside always at all of the sessions of instruction of the Emperor as his chief preceptor, is entrusted with putting these instructions into practice, thus unifying the educational system of the Senhor D. Pedro II."[30]

The great responsibility that the Friar was to have for the child Emperor was shown by a special set of instructions from Itanhaén. These gave the headmaster full charge of the apartments of Dom Pedro, with all employes responsible to him. No servant might execute orders from the Emperor without permission of the headmaster. Friar Pedro must be present at formal functions to watch the Emperor's manners, and must supervise the instruction of the various teachers, and send to the Marquez each day reports on the progress of the pupils.[31]

How successful Friar Pedro was in developing the mind and character of the future ruler of Brazil to realize the ideals of the General Assembly and the Marquez de Itanhaén will appear later.

While changes were being made towards greater unity and efficiency in his training, the boy Emperor was making good progress in his studies. Since it had been the wish of Dom Pedro I that all of his children be well-educated, from the first the best teachers had been secured for them. As far as their progress permitted, they had, for many years, almost the same ones. When José Bonifacio took charge of their education, Dona Januaria was nine years old, Dona Francisca was seven, and Dom Pedro was five years and nine months. For a time, Luiz Alexio Boulanger, appointed in the latter part of 1831, was the boy's chief instructor, and gave him lessons in writing, reading in Portuguese, geography, and drawing. Dom Pedro soon learned to write a clear and attractive hand, for Boulanger was especially expert as a teacher of penmanship. He required the children to write to their father every fortnight, and oc-

---

[30] *Ibid.*, p. 70.
[31] Fleiuss, in *Contribuições para a Biographia de D. Pedro II*, Pt. I, 107-8.

casionally to their stepmother. Shortly after Dom Pedro's sixth birthday they began to correspond with their Austrian grandfather.[32]

The boy was fond of drawing and showed some talent for it. In 1833, he was having lessons in art from the Portuguese painter, Simplicio Rodrigues de Sá, who had made a crayon portrait of him when he was a year old.[33] Apparently at about this time Friar Pedro de Santa Marianna was his instructor in mathematics and also in religion. In the same period he was studying French and English under native teachers. From Dr. Roque Schuch, the Austrian who had been librarian for his mother, he was learning Latin; and he had begun natural science with Alexander Antonio Vandelli, son-in-law of José Bonifacio. He was also studying piano, dancing, and horsemanship.[34]

All concerned were much pleased with the royal pupil's attitude, for Dom Pedro was naturally inclined to do what was right and desirable: he was attentive, responsive, and studious. His mental qualities likewise were promising. In May, 1835, Itanhaén informed the General Assembly that his charge was a "most precocious child, full of docility and submission."[35] The next year he reported that the Emperor was highly gifted with vivacity, penetration, and memory.[36] This was in line with the views of his individual instructors. In fact, the chief concern that Dom Pedro gave his teachers seems to have been his extreme devotion to learning, for under the Marquez's strict regimen he became such a bookworm that it was difficult to induce him to take sufficient rest. At times after he had been put to bed for the night he lit his lamp and proceeded to read or study, thus incurring rebuke from Friar Pedro.[37]

Occasionally, however, the little boy revolted, fled from his

[32] *Ibid.*, p. 69.   [33] See p. 40 of this book.
[34] Escragnolle Taunay, "A formação intellectual de Pedro II," *Rev. do Inst. Hist. e Geog. Bras.*, vol. 152, pp. 888-90.
[35] *Ibid.;* Fleiuss, in *Contribuições para a Biographia de D. Pedro II*, Pt. I, p. 80.
[36] *Ibid.*, p. 92.   [37] Fialho, *op. cit.*, p. 23.

lessons, and took refuge in the quarters of his good friend black Rafael on the palace grounds at Boa Vista.[38] This was partly a mere childish reaction to the exacting system under which he was trained, but Friar Pedro's methods seem to have brought out in the boy a slightly wilful strain, inconsistent with his original docility, though akin to his great natural persistence. This headstrong tendency at times showed itself in the Emperor's mature years.[39]

As time passed Dom Pedro's training expanded, with some changes in the teaching personnel. Simplicio, because of ill health, was replaced by Felix Emilio Taunay, director of the National Academy of Fine Arts, who greatly influenced his pupil and gave him a genuine love for the beautiful. Later, the boy studied history and geography under Taunay, who was made subpreceptor. Apparently at about the same time Friar Pedro added Latin and logic to the subjects in which he himself instructed his charge. In 1839 German was begun under Dr. Schuch, but study of other languages was continued. In the same year Araujo Vianna, later the Marquez de Sapucahy, became his teacher in literature and applied science. By now, Dom Pedro could translate with ease Latin prose and verse, could compose in that language, and was studying the comparative grammar of Latin and Portuguese. He was able to read, write, and speak both French and English, and was making good progress in German. His study of piano and other musical instruments was continuing, as were his lessons in art. In fencing he was showing firmness and agility. The next year, after he had passed his fourteenth birthday, he took up philosophy and rhetoric, while continuing other subjects, especially history, Latin, and the Portuguese classics.[40] Though Dom Pedro was

---

[38] Teixeira, *op. cit.*, p. 25.

[39] Vicente de Quesada, *Mis Memorias diplomaticas*, II, 473. Late in life Dom Pedro told Quesada that the Friar had perverted his character through making him wilful. *Ibid.*

[40] Escragnolle Taunay, "A formação intellectual de Pedro II," *Rev. do Inst. Hist. e Geog. Bras.*, vol. 152, p. 891.

fond of all of his studies, he especially delighted in history, geography, and the natural sciences, as his mother had done.

To a considerable extent the textbooks for the royal children were prepared by the teachers themselves. Many of them, in clear, bold script, still exist.[41] One contains extracts from Rollin's *Ancient History,* in French. Another text is a brief manuscript history of Spain, in English, with an introductory note to the teacher, apparently written by Friar Pedro. The teacher, the foreword declares—in harmony with the Marquez de Itanhaén's code—should inculcate in his pupil love and esteem for virtue, "for whosoever is vicious or unlearned can be neither great nor happy." The teacher must also be "well bred, understanding etiquette and the measures of civility relating to all of the variety of persons, times, and places, and keeping his pupil, as much as his age might require, constantly to the observance of these qualities. This is an art not to be learnt or taught by books."[42]

By means of copy for writing, mottoes introductory to exercises of various kinds, and specific precepts to be committed to memory, worthy ideals along all lines were drilled into the children. Such inspirational thoughts were usually phrased in Portuguese, French, or English. Here are some of them:

"Let us think before we speak."

"Let us do unto others that which we wish them to do unto us."

"Greatness includes simplicity, unity, and majesty."

"It is necessary to study to avoid boredom; knowledge is the food of the spirit."

"Of what use are laws without morals?"

"Virtue, health, power, and happiness are the fruits of patience and attention."

At the head of the manuscript "Spanish History" text used by Dom Pedro are the words, "Let the love and practice of

---

[41] They are mostly at the Château d'Eu, France, in the Pedro d'Orléans Bragança Archives, B, XLII, 1065.   [42] *Ibid.*

Virtue be our delight, and the attainment of Wisdom be our constant aim." Heading each subdivision of a long essay of Dom Pedro's on "Political Right" are Francis Bacon's words, "Knowledge is power."[43]

Following the Marquez's code, endless effort was made to impress upon the young prince the essential qualities of a model ruler. A text given him in 1832, before he was seven, informed the little boy that "In proportion as man figures in society, he has obligation to work for his fellow men." Another motto pointed out that, "The source of all the virtues in a king is merely the love of his people." A text given to Dona Januaria, the Princess Imperial, stated that "No one can be happy under a despotic government. Despotism is contrary to the aim of civil society and is opposed to the will of God, who created man free, in order that he might be happy."

A text headed "Sovereigns" reads: "Love your people as your children; taste the pleasure of being loved by them; and so act that they will never reflect upon their peace and joy without remembering that these rich gifts have come from a good king."[44]

One of the most interesting surviving exercises of Pedro II is the essay on "Political Right," written in English, presumably when the Emperor was in his early teens. It is to some extent a study of governments, and shows knowledge of the French Revolution, United States history, and the writings of Burke. In it the youth set forth liberal ideas that had been planted in his mind by tutorial precept and by the reading selected for him. At one point he remarked that "the spirit of moderation should be the spirit of the Legislator." In another, he promised: "I will never separate Justice from Politics. Justice should ever be the Polar Star of all the arts of Government in Civil Society."[45]

Thus, almost from the cradle, Dom Pedro II was trained

[43] *Ibid.*
[44] *Ibid.*
[45] *Ibid.*

in the principles of liberty and in the political philosophy which produced the French Revolution. The training sank deep. When he was a tiny boy of six years he is reported to have declared solemnly—and rather pathetically, "I do not want to be vicious. You tell me that by their vices heads of nations destroy themselves."[46]

In spite of the emphasis placed by Dom Pedro's tutor upon his intellectual and political education, the sessions of study were really short, and effort was made to give him plenty of time for rest and recreation. Long vacations, quite free from lessons, were passed in the mountains or at the fazenda of Santa Cruz. Here he spent much of the time in the open air, riding horseback, or, when he grew older, in hunting, of which he was fond; and he was an excellent shot.

Every effort was made to improve his health; but his physical heritage on his father's side was poor, and he suffered from frequent illness, at times serious. Some of the attacks were caused by infant's diseases, but when he was about seven years old he had a critical case of brain fever and his life was in danger. Recovery, delayed by a stomach malady, was slow. After many months he was still weak, and the Marquez de Itanhaén, in his report to the General Assembly, referred to the Emperor's delicate constitution and nervous temperament. Early in his fifteenth year he was again ill from stomach trouble, attributed to intense application to his books, especially immediately after meals. This assiduity apparently came from his own zeal, and was against the wishes of Friar Pedro. His physicians advised a letting up on his studies and an increase in physical exercise, especially gymnastics and horseback riding.[47]

Dom Pedro had much to do besides learn his lessons. Many duties were placed upon him as head of the state, even under the regency. He was always present when court was held in the

---

[46] Fleiuss, in *Contribuições para a Biographia de D. Pedro II*, Pt. I, p. 62; Calogeras, *op. cit.*, III, 388.

[47] *Ibid.*, pp. 80, 85, 109-11; Calmon, *O rei do Brasil*, pp. 7-22, *passim*.

City Palace. On such occasions he stood with the regency at his right and his sisters at his left, and there was much formality. Members of the diplomatic corps, after having paid their respects to the imperial group, bowed, retreated backwards, and executed three additional bows before disappearing out the door. An American naval officer who attended court in 1831 remarked that the Emperor looked upon these ceremonies with an air of indifference[48]—as was to be expected of a normal small boy to whom the whole was quite familiar.

Dom Pedro was also present for the reviewing of the troops. One account states that on his seventh birthday he was dressed for the event in the grand uniform of the national guard and that four legions of troops passed before him.[49]

At times, at least, it was he who formally received new diplomatic representatives. When the British minister presented his credentials in 1833, the boy ruler, then in his eighth year, made the proper responses in English, on which he had been fully coached.[50]

On his twelfth birthday, December 2, 1837, the little Emperor participated in the dedication ceremonies for the Collegio de Dom Pedro II. This, the national preparatory school, fostered by his interest, played an important part in the educational system of the country. At a meeting held in the palace at Boa Vista on March 9, 1839, Dom Pedro became likewise the patron and protector of the Instituto Historico e Geographico Brasileiro, founded the preceding October.[51]

Because of their colorful and festive character, Dom Pedro enjoyed much some of the formalities in which he was the central figure. To his subjects, the ceremonies meant even more, for the Brazilians delighted in pomp and pageantry. Late in 1836, the royal squadron of the Netherlands, on its way to the

---

[48] Ruschenberger, *op. cit.*, pp. 78-79.
[49] Fleiuss, in *Contribuições para a Biographia de D. Pedro II*, Pt. I, p. 71.
[50] Escragnolle Taunay, "Formação intellectual de Pedro II," *Rev. do Inst. Hist. e Geog. Bras.*, vol. 152, p. 889.
[51] Fleiuss, in *Contribuições para a Biographia de D. Pedro II*, Pt. I, p. 115.

DOM PEDRO II AT ABOUT ONE YEAR
From a crayon portrait by Simplicio
de Sá at the Château d'Eu

DOM PEDRO II IN BOYHOOD
From a miniature at the
Château d'Eu

From a lithograph at the Château d'Eu
DOM PEDRO II AND HIS SISTERS AT THEIR LESSONS IN SÃO CHRISTOVÃO PALACE
Left, Princess Francisca; *right*, Princess Januaria

East Indies with one of the Dutch princes aboard, visited Rio de Janeiro, and the event was marked by a round of dinners, balls, and other social gatherings. Dom Pedro, on his birthday, gave his first dinner party, in the visiting prince's honor. It took place at São Christovão Palace, and, according to the American minister, William Hunter, was a grand affair. The Marquez de Itanhaén wrote the notes of invitation, and all of the diplomatic corps and most of the dignitaries of Church and State were present. "The old courtiers crept out covered with stars and diamonds and the little boy's hand was smothered with kisses." The Emperor, the Dutch prince, and the princesses, Januaria and Francisca, were at the table. In the evening came a court ball at which the members of the royal party danced a quadrille or two by themselves before general dancing began.[52]

A more spectacular celebration took place on Dom Pedro's thirteenth birthday, and was described by an American visitor, Captain Charles Wilkes. On this occasion the Emperor and his sisters rode into the city from São Christovão in a carriage mounted with bronze and gold and drawn by eight cream-colored horses, gaily caparisoned. Behind them came the guards of honor, five thousand military, and the carriages bearing the imperial suite. The streets through which the procession passed were carpeted with leaves from orange trees and with other foliage. Flags were flying and richly colored damask draperies hung from windows and balconies. At one point in the route was a triumphal arch decorated with natural flowers, and with two tiny boys dressed in pink and blue and equipped with wings. From a basket that he carried, each of these cherubs scattered blossoms over the sovereign as the carriage passed under the arch. The procession ended at the City Palace. Here court was held, and the Brazilians who attended went through the usual ceremony of *beija mão*, the kissing of the hands of the three royal children, a custom brought from the

[52] Hunter to Forsyth, no. 49, Jan. 17, 1837, Dept. of State, Despatches, Brazil.

Orient. Each of the guests walked backward as he retired, bowing repeatedly.[53]

When Dom Pedro approached adolescence his tutors tried to guard against such weaknesses and vices as had appeared in his father. The youth was put through a new regimen including cold bathing, horseback riding, and broadened and varied social events. Now, he participated in more balls, soirées, musicales, and the like. It was hoped that by thus meeting many young women of high class and fine character he would develop a wholesome and chivalrous attitude towards all women.[54]

Now also began a broadening of the Emperor's attitude on political questions, through formal dinners at the palace every Sunday with a certain number of government officers, ecclesiastics, and foreign diplomats present. Their conversation was expected to help the youth realize that people often differ honestly on serious matters, and that he would thus develop a spirit of tolerance.[55]

In spite of the careful planning and the devotion of those who had him in charge during his minority, the memory that Dom Pedro had in later life of his childhood was not an unclouded, happy one.[56] And this was natural, in view of the strict, at times irksome, regimen enforced by his tutor, and of the fact that he was made to feel some of the burdens of office even before their full weight was placed upon his shoulders. Furthermore, the very fact that he was monarch of Brazil created isolating formality and aloofness, especially since etiquette was very strict at the court.[57] Though he was fond of many of those about him, and they of him, he missed warmth and intimacy from his elders, who never forgot that he was the Emperor. His position even prevented him from as close association with his sisters as would have been possible had he been

[53] Charles Wilkes, *Narrative of the United States Exploring Expedition during the Years 1838, 1839, 1840, 1841, 1842*, I, 48.

[54] Hunter to Forsyth, no. 80, Aug. 13, 1838, Dept. of State, Despatches, Brazil.

[55] *Ibid.*   [56] Teixeira, *op. cit.*, p. 82.

[57] Prince Adalbert, *Travels in the South of Europe and in Brazil*, I, 312.

a mere noble. He never knew mother love and he was deprived of his father when scarcely out of babyhood. On the whole, his was a rather lonely childhood. But it helped develop the philosophic attitude which enabled Dom Pedro II to bear life's disappointments and tragedies with serenity, and to show understanding, compassion, and forgiveness towards his fellow men.[58]

[58] Monteiro, "A infancia do Imperador," *Rev. do Inst. Geog. e Hist. Bras.*, vol. 152, p. 44.

III

THE REGENCY AND THE BOY EMPEROR

WHILE Dom Pedro's tutors were intent upon training him to be a good man and a good emperor, the Brazilian regency was struggling to hold the country together—to preserve it for him to rule. In the effort much was learned by all.

The provisional regency of three members appointed on the morning of Dom Pedro I's abdication showed a good spirit. It promptly pardoned all political offenders, and likewise all soldiers who had deserted, on condition that they return at once to their respective corps.[1] It also issued, on April 13, a proclamation warning the people against rash action caused by patriotic enthusiasm and love of liberty and urging wisdom and moderation of conduct. "We are free"; declared the Marquez de Caravellas, president of the regency, "let us be just."[2] The influential *Diario do Rio de Janeiro* likewise came out editorially in support of law and order.[3] No trouble was caused by the Portuguese who remained in the country, for they were warned by the envoy of little Queen Maria da Gloria to conduct themselves properly if they wished the protection usually given to strangers.[4] When the Parliament met in regular session in the winter of 1831 it appointed another regency of three, which headed the government for the next four years.

The regency, which was the most troubled period of nineteenth century Brazil, has been correctly called an experiment in republicanism. It was also a "decade of political earth-

---

[1] *Diario do Rio de Janeiro*, April 12, 1831.
[2] *Ibid.*, April 14, 1831.
[3] *Ibid.*, April 7, 1831.   [4] *Ibid.*, April 9, 1831.

quakes."[5] During it, rebellion and civil war were the regulators usually resorted to for internal relations. The unrest and disaffection preceding April, 1831, now developed into turbulence amounting to chronic anarchy. Repeatedly, the infant Emperor was hastily carried from the palace at Boa Vista to some place of greater obscurity and safety. Yet his extreme youth prevented his being blamed for the sad state of affairs. His Brazilian birth, his reported resemblance, in disposition, to his mother, and his utter helplessness tended to rouse loyalty and gallantry, and caused the nation as a whole to rally around him.

Yet the country was in great danger of being torn to pieces: sentiment was strong for local autonomy and in some quarters it was accompanied by frank desire for a republic. However, the liberals decided to content themselves for a time with the existing constitution and to federalize it as opportunity offered. This policy of moderation triumphed. Monarchy and national unity were saved largely by the influence of Evaristo da Veiga, whose *Aurora Fluminense* was the most important newspaper in the country.[6]

Under the regency not only did various troubles of Dom Pedro I's reign continue, but new ones were added. In the northern provinces, especially, Portuguese residents were attacked by mobs, usually without cause. In Pará one of the most restless spots, the soldiers, who were seriously undisciplined, ousted their officers, killed the civil authorities, and precipitated a local war which lasted for some years. Indeed, the disloyalty and general demoralization of the army, which had appeared in the wars for independence, was one of the chief causes for trouble. Even in the capital of the Empire the soldiers mutinied more than once.[7] Here and there republican revolts overthrew

---

[5] Joaquim Nabuco, *Um estadista do Imperio: Nabuco de Araujo*, I, 32, 42.

[6] Oliveira Lima, *Formation historique de la nationalité brésilienne*, p. 201; Oliveira Lima, *O Imperio brazileiro*, p. 26; Nabuco, *op. cit.*, I, 32.

[7] B. Mossé, *Dom Pedro II*, pp. 26-28; Fleiuss, *Paginas de historia*, pp. 49-50.

local governments. In some parts, notably Bahia and Rio Grande do Sul, federalism culminated in separatist movements. The struggle began in the latter province with a mere conflict between the "ins" and the "outs," but it soon became a war for independence which lasted for ten bitter years, partly because the defeated element could escape across the border into Uruguay and rally its forces. Trouble also came from political reactionaries, whose desire to restore Dom Pedro I started civil wars in Alagôas and Pernambuco.[8] Only three of the important provinces—Rio de Janeiro, São Paulo, and Minas Geraes—remained comparatively calm and law-abiding, and thus helped to save the vast Empire from being wrecked.

Even with Dom Pedro I far away, discord continued within the central government. Factional strife was almost chronic in the chamber of deputies. Here were represented three different political groups: the *Exaltados*, made up largely of the federalist element; the *Moderados*, who stood for a constitutional monarchy and were led at first by Evaristo da Veiga; and the *Restauradores*, who wished the return of Dom Pedro I. In 1833, Antonio Carlos, one of the three Andrada brothers, was sent to Lisbon to try to bring back the exile.[9] When the ex-Emperor died the next year, his supporters aligned themselves with the Moderates. This faction was later called Conservatives, and their federalist opponents, Liberals. The disappearance of the Restauradores helped but little to simplify the hard task of the regency, for class friction as well as political differences caused trouble. Those who had assumed control after Dom Pedro I's abdication were mostly inexperienced in governmental matters. The elder statesmen who had sat in the constitutional convention dissolved by him in 1823 felt little sympathy or respect for these upstarts.[10] An effort was made by the regency to follow the cabinet principle of government, keeping the ministry

---

[8] Rocha Pombo, *op. cit.*, VIII, 345-46.
[9] Mossé, *op. cit.*, p. 30.   [10] Nabuco, *op. cit.*, I, 31.

in harmony with the majority party in the lower house; but this worked painfully and discordantly, when it functioned at all.

The least political of Brazil's troubles were soonest ended. Diogo Antonio Feijó, a Liberal priest from São Paulo who was Minister of Justice, bettered conditions in the army by punishment of its seditious members. A national guard was likewise created to maintain law and order and to crush insubordination in the regular army.[11] Thus the supremacy of the civil authority was established.

Meanwhile the federalist element was agitating for a change in the constitution, to reduce the power of the Emperor which Dom Pedro I had so tenaciously defended. In 1834, an amendment known as the *Acto Addicional* was adopted. It provided that there should be only one Regent, and it abolished the rather futile council of state and increased the authority of the provinces by granting them elective legislatures which could be only slightly restricted by veto from Rio de Janeiro. But the moderating power *(poder moderador)* of the Emperor, granted him by Dom Pedro I's constitution of 1824, was not specifically changed. The regency, furthermore, tenaciously made use of this power in various connections.[12]

The person selected as sole Regent, in accordance with the constitutional amendment, was Feijó, the energetic Minister of Justice, who took charge in October, 1835. By now many of the smaller disturbances in the country had been ended. But the revolt in Rio Grande—which developed into a ten years' war—broke out a month before he took office, and he was unable to crush it, with the result that he lost popularity. In 1836, the opposition reorganized into a strongly Conservative group, won the election, and in September, 1837, forced Padre Feijó to resign.

---

[11] The disloyalty of the army during the regency did much to disgust the nation as a whole with it, and to prevent militarism from becoming a national tradition, such as existed in most of the Spanish American republics during the nineteenth century.

[12] José Maria dos Santos, *A politica geral do Brasil*, pp. 15-18.

His successor was one of the founders of the new Conservative faction, Pedro de Araujo Lima, later Marquez de Olinda. Now came a strong reaction. The Regent apparently hoped to gain more respect for law and authority through focussing greater attention upon the Emperor. In 1838 he restored to its old importance the beija mão ceremony, which seems to have fallen into disuse officially. Before a great crowd in the Church of Santa Cruz dos Militares, Araujo Lima knelt at the feet of the thirteen-year-old Dom Pedro II and solemnly kissed the boy's hand.[13] Since, under the *Acto Addicional*, decentralization was being fostered to a degree considered by the new Regent dangerous to the integrity of the Empire, he took steps to reduce the power of the local assemblies through a new interpretation of the *Acto*. This largely nullified the democratic provisions of the amendment.[14]

Aurajo Lima, however, like Padre Feijó, failed to pacify the country. Revolts in various parts of the north, especially in Maranhão, handicapped him in his efforts to end the trouble in Rio Grande do Sul. Matters were worse instead of better, and the Empire was in great peril. This led to an insistent demand that Dom Pedro be given control of the government at once, though according to the constitution he would not be of age until he was eighteen.[15]

The idea of shortening the period of Dom Pedro's minority had, in fact, been broached soon after his father's abdication. José de Costa Carvalho, a member of the first permanent regency of three, was enthusiastically in favor of it. Francisco de Lima e Silva, another member, not only favored the plan, but acted as if it were a definite arrangement. In a letter written to Dom Pedro in December, 1835, shortly after Padre Feijó had been made sole Regent, Lima e Silva told the ten-year-old boy that he would begin to reign when he was fourteen, and offered

[13] C. B. Ottoni, *D. Pedro de Alcantara*, p. 20.
[14] Affonso Celso, *Contradictas monarchicas*, p. 23.
[15] James, *op. cit.*, p. 246.

him good advice against that time.[16] Thus, the defeated Conservatives hoped to prevent their opponents from remaining in power too long. Early in 1837, it was rumored that the Liberals, defeated the year before, planned to prevent the election of a Conservative Regent by shortening the term of minority of the Emperor.[17] The project seems to have been seriously considered; but Padre Feijó, the Liberal, gave place in September to Araujo Lima, the extreme Conservative.

A cautious, but systematic, propaganda for the plan was now begun, largely by the Liberal opposition, though a few Conservatives favored it. In various ways the idea was broached to feel out public opinion and educate the nation to the idea. It was presented in the press, in debates by masonic lodges, and other groups, and was much discussed privately.[18]

In the middle of 1839 a proposal was made in the senate that the regency be given extraordinary powers to combat the growing anarchy and save the Empire from catastrophe. But this failed to meet with favor in the lower house, where Acaiba de Montezuma on August 19 stated that it would be better to give the Emperor control at once. This roused excited opposition, but the idea had now been mentioned publicly in official circles. Early the next year, under the leadership of José Martiniano de Alencar, the *Club da Maioridade* was founded for the express purpose of putting through the plan. Its members were mostly Liberals, but there were a few Conservatives whom the Regent Araujo Lima had alienated. The campaign appealed to popular imagination and rapidly gained momentum.[19] Some of the propagandists of the "majority" idea tried through palace functionaries to influence the Emperor.[20]

---

[16] Pedro d'Orléans Bragança Archives, A, I, 4911; Hunter to Forsyth, no. 25, Sept. 23, 1835, Dept. of State, Despatches, Brazil; Jonathas Serrano, *Historia do Brasil*, p. 352.

[17] Hunter to Forsyth, no. 56, July 7, 1837, Dept. of State, Despatches, Brazil.

[18] Hunter to Forsyth, no. 111, July 31, 1840, Dept. of State, Despatches, Brazil.

[19] Rocha Pombo, "A maioridade, desde quando se cogita da maioridade," *Rev. do Inst. Hist. e Geog. Bras.*, vol. 152, pp. 218-19.

[20] J. M. Pereira da Silva, *Memorias de meu tempo*, I, 7.

Meanwhile, Bernardo Pereira de Vasconcellos circulated in influential quarters the opinion that the Princess Imperial, who was now eighteen, should be made Regent.[21] This opinion was based upon Article 126 of the constitution, which provided that in case of troubled conditions the relative nearest the heir to the throne should assume the authority. But Article 122 stipulated that such a relative must be at least twenty-five years old. Yet the distracted Regent, in the effort to bring peace to the country, seems to have thought seriously of giving Dona Januaria the power—until some government supporters showed their disapproval by pointing out the age requirement.[22] Vasconcellos and others insisted, however, that it would be better to make the Princess Imperial Regent than to proclaim the majority of her brother, who would not be of age for four years. Francisco Alvares Machado, of the lower chamber, in April, 1840, declared that Princess Januaria had the right to rule for her brother, and that the regency of Araujo Lima was holding power illegally.[23]

These efforts did not rouse any serious demand in behalf of Dona Januaria. Instead, the idea of declaring Dom Pedro of age grew, for national thought had been centering upon him as the best hope for the peace and progress of the country. Though he was but little more than fourteen years old, his long, careful training and his reported mature judgment and seriousness of purpose somewhat discounted his youth. In spite of the secessionist movements and other internal disturbances, Dom Pedro had a strong hold on the loyalty and affections of the nation. Time had battled for the boy Emperor; the nine years of experimentation by the regency with popular rule had been disillusioning. Moreover, the turbulent neighboring Spanish-American "republics" had served as grim warnings—rather than as enticing examples—to most intelligent and public-

---

[21] *Ibid.;* Nabuco, *op. cit.*, I, 41.
[22] Moniz, *op. cit.*, pp. 27-28; James, *op. cit.*, p. 246.
[23] Pereira da Silva, *op. cit.*, I, 7.

spirited Brazilians.[24] These were willing to retain their present form of government, headed by a hereditary official who wore a golden crown.

By May, 1840, public opinion seemed to the plotters to make a further step safe. Therefore, on the 13th two members of the senate presented a resolution for immediately declaring Dom Pedro of age and investing him with supreme authority. This created much excitement, though the Marquez de Paranaguá, who presided, at once expressed his approval, and continued to support the project. It was, however, rejected on constitutional grounds.[25]

Shortly afterwards, a project was presented in the chamber of deputies calling for a change in Article 121 of the constitution, to authorize the declaration of Dom Pedro's majority before he was eighteen. This started a debate lasting for more than two months. During it, passions ran high. On July 18, Honorio Hermeto Carneiro Leão, Conservative leader in the lower house, offered a motion to withdraw the measure, which was carried. But this only increased the impatience of those who had favored the plan. Francisco Alvares Machado, the most enthusiastic, now advocated that the Emperor be at once proclaimed of age. Another deputy, Clemente Pereira, referring to the gravity of the situation, declared that it was no longer possible to wait until Dom Pedro was eighteen. "In truth" he added, "*coups d'état* are lamentable, but they are countenanced by all publicists in extreme cases."[26]

These words produced a sensation in the chamber, and great tumult in the crowded galleries. The populace thronged the rooms of the building cheering for the Emperor. Some even invaded the floor of the chamber. The following day the police patrol was doubled in the capital, and guards were stationed in

---

[24] *Ibid.*, p. 6; Hunter to Forsyth, no. 85, Dec. 22, 1838, Dept. of State, Despatches, Brazil. [25] Pereira da Silva, *op. cit.*, I, 8.

[26] Rocha Pombo, "A maioridade, desde quando se cogita da maioridade," *Rev. do Inst. Hist. e Geog. Bras.*, vol. 152, pp. 219-20.

the parks, as if a revolt were threatened. On the 20th a deputy proposed that a committee be appointed to consider and report on the question of proclaiming Dom Pedro of age. This was discussed in the midst of much confusion—for the president was unable to maintain order—and was approved.[27]

Carneiro Leão, seeing that it was impossible to stop the movement for shortening the minority of the Emperor, tried to secure a compromise. He proposed that Dom Pedro be declared of age on December 2, his fifteenth birthday, and that a council of state be created to help the youth prepare for his task and to which he could turn for advice while he was still young and inexperienced.[28] But the extremists—who included Antonio Carlos and Martim Francisco de Andrada, brothers of José Bonifacio—were against delay. On July 21, Antonio Carlos, an able man, but rather hot-headed and unscrupulous, introduced a resolution declaring the Emperor of age, and urged that the question be considered at once. The debate on it began the following day.[29]

The Regent Araujo Lima, who seems to have opposed the plan simply because of the Emperor's youth, was by now much disturbed by developments in the chamber of deputies. He, therefore, called a meeting of leading Conservatives to consider the situation. It included Bernardo Pereira de Vasconcellos, who had voted in the senate against the resolution to declare Dom Pedro of age at once and had wanted Dona Januaria made Regent. Vasconcellos advised that the sessions of Parliament be prorogued until the close of November, to give passions time to cool, and that Dom Pedro be declared of age on December 2. Like Carneiro Leão, he thought that recent developments had made it impossible to meet the constitutional requirements regarding the majority of the Emperor. Peaceful evolution, he

---

[27] *Ibid.*, p. 220; Hunter to Forsyth, no. 111, July 31, 1840, Dept. of State, Despatches, Brazil.

[28] Pereira da Silva, *op. cit.*, I, 9.

[29] *Ibid.*, pp. 9-10; Rocha Pombo, "A maioridade, desde quando se cogita da maioridade," *Rev. do Inst. Hist. e Geog. Bras.*, vol. 152, p. 221.

held, was preferable to revolution. The plan was adopted, and Araujo Lima offered Vasconcellos the portfolio of Minister of Empire, which was accepted. The decree proroguing the Parliament was drawn up on July 22, and countersigned, in his new capacity, by Vasconcellos.[30]

The decree was sent promptly to the house of deputies, and arrived when the debate was well started on Antonio Carlos's motion to declare immediately the majority of the Emperor. The reading of the decree produced a tumult of anger. From galleries and halls came cries of "Calumny! Treason! It's a government conspiracy! . . . Viva Dom Pedro II!" Several deputies tried to get recognition at once. The president of the session declared the meeting prorogued. The mob surged in. Above the tumult sounded the voice of Antonio Carlos de Andrada: "I declare that I do not recognize this act of the government as legal; the Regent has been a usurper since March 11 [Princess Januaria's eighteenth birthday]. . . . He is a traitor. . . . The present ministry is a disgrace." His brother Martim Francisco charged that the move to prorogue was caused by unwillingness to see the Monarch on his throne. The government, he declared, was in the hands of its worst enemy. Others supported these views with impassioned voices.[31]

It was now about eleven o'clock in the forenoon. Those who sympathized with the regency had left the chamber. Soon Antonio Carlos cried, "All who are patriotic Brazilians, come with me to the senate!" The irate Liberals thronged through the streets to the senate building, followed by cheering crowds. Most of the senators had departed promptly after the decree of prorogation had been read. But some, chiefly Liberals, lingered. With them was the Marquez de Paranaguá, the Conservative president of the upper house, who consistently opposed delay. The newly-arrived deputies and remaining senators, with Paranaguá presiding, promptly began to plan the realiza-

[30] Pereira da Silva, *op. cit.*, I, 10-11.
[31] Rocha Pombo, *Historia do Brasil*, VIII, 553-54.

tion of their common aim. They quickly agreed upon a message to the Emperor, to be carried by a delegation made up of five senators and three deputies, including the two Andrada brothers. These eight men set out at once for the residential palace at Boa Vista.[32]

For years Dom Pedro II had followed events in Brazil with anxiety, and even with distress; for he deeply loved his native land, and the keen sense of responsibility natural to him had been sharpened by his education for office. That the nation looked eagerly forward to his assumption of control he was well aware. He also realized his limitations. It is said that a short time before this, a courtier, after referring to the existing jeopardy to peace and to the cause of monarchy, had added: "There is only one arm that can save both—that of Your Majesty. Confiding in such high wisdom, we foresee from now on a future of good fortune." Dom Pedro is reported to have replied by the question: "But can you be certain that with little more than fourteen years of age it is possible to possess wisdom?"[33]

During the past two months, when the majority question had been under debate in Parliament, the youth had apparently been encouraged by palace officials to accept control of the government, if it was offered to him, in order to save the country from even worse disorders than the existing ones.[34] But he was only a boy, deeply absorbed in his studies, and he was certainly in no haste to assume the responsibility of governing his turbulent Empire.[35]

When the deputation of eight from the irregular session of the General Assembly reached the Palace of São Christovão, Dom Pedro received them on the veranda, and Antonio Carlos

[32] Pereira da Silva, *op. cit.*, I, 11-12; Rocha Pombo, *Historia do Brasil*, VIII, 556.
[33] Moniz, *op. cit.*, 172-73.
[34] Mario Behring, "Documentos preciosos," *Collectanea Rabello*, II, 218; Escragnolle Doria, "Quero já," *Revista da Semana*, Feb. 16, 1924; Pereiro da Silva, *op. cit.*, I, 13.
[35] Fleiuss, in *Contribuições para a Biographia de D. Pedro II*, Pt. I, p. 113; Ottoni, *op. cit.*, p. 18.

de Andrada read to him the message which they brought. The proroguing of Parliament, stated the communication, was an insult to the Emperor, besides being an act of treason by the Regent, who had had no legal sanction for his position since March 11. In view of the consequent grave peril of the country, the message requested that Dom Pedro save the throne and the nation by assuming charge of affairs at once.[36]

After listening carefully to the communication, the Emperor asked that the delegation wait while he took time to consider the matter. Apparently he now consulted three of the men who had been closest to him for many years—the Marquis de Itanhaén, his tutor; Friar Pedro de Santa Marianna, his headmaster; and José de Araujo Vianna, his instructor in literature. In any case, he conferred with them at some point after the controversy over the majority had reached a climax, and they all advised him to favor immediate assumption of control. Araujo Vianna, who had voted in the senate, on constitutional grounds, against the immediate declaration of Dom Pedro's majority, now told him that, in view of developments, and of the perilous condition of the country, such action, though revolutionary, had become a measure of public salvation.[37]

Very shortly after Dom Pedro had retired to his apartments to consider the question, the Regent arrived, accompanied by the Minister of Marine. The youth soon returned to the veranda, where both delegations waited, and Araujo Lima informed him that the prorogation of Parliament had been decreed to insure public order, and to prepare properly for his accession to power on December 2, when, he assured the Emperor, it had been the intention to turn the authority over to him. But, added Araujo Lima, meanwhile there had come a great clamor for immediate investiture, and he had resolved to come to the Emperor to say

---

[36] Rocha Pombo, *Historia do Brasil*, VIII, 557-58; *Fallas do throno*, pp. 328, 331-32.
[37] Fleiuss, in *Contribuições para a Biographia de D. Pedro II*, Pt. I, 115; Pereira da Silva, *op. cit.*, I, 13.

that he would be equally prompt to obey him whether he desired to wait until December 2, or preferred to enter at once into the exercise of his powers.[38]

The inexperienced but conscientious youth was thus placed in a very difficult position. He well knew that to assume control before he was eighteen would be a direct violation of the constitution. But even the Regent had planned to have him invested with power on his fifteenth birthday. And those who had directed his education and trained his thinking advised him to save the Empire from possible great disaster by taking up his duties at once. He decided to place his country above its constitution, and ordered that the two chambers be convoked on the morrow so that he might be invested with authority.[39]

In view of the popular demand and of the state of practical anarchy, Dom Pedro's decision was probably wise. That he bore the Regent no ill will because of his original desire for delay is apparent from the fact that for the remaining thirty years of Araujo Lima's life he remained a friend of the Emperor and continued to serve him in various official capacities.[40]

According to agreement, the two houses met in general assembly at ten o'clock the next morning, Thursday, July 23, 1840, in the senate chamber. The galleries and the corridors of the building were packed. The Marquez de Paranaguá, who presided, made the following statement:

I, as organ of national representation gathered in general assembly, declare that His Imperial Majesty the Senhor Dom Pedro II is from now on in his majority, in the full exercise of his constitutional rights. Long live the Senhor Dom Pedro II, constitutional emperor

---

[38] Rocha Pombo, "A maioridade, desde quando se cogita da maioridade," *Rev. do Inst. Hist. e Geog. Bras.*, vol. 152, p. 222; Pereira da Silva, *op. cit.*, I, 12. The accounts regarding Araujo Lima's attitude are slightly contradictory, but this version seems the most probable.

[39] Pereira da Silva, *op. cit.*, I, 12; Behring, "Documentos preciosos," *Collectanea Rabello*, II, 216-18; Escragnolle Doria, "Quero já," *Revista da Semana*, Feb. 16, 1924; *Fallas do throno*, pp. 328-30.

[40] Affonso Celso, *Poder pessoal* (in *Oito annos de parlamento*), p. 188.

and perpetual defender of Brazil! Long live the majority of His Majesty Dom Pedro II! Long live the Senhor Dom Pedro II!⁴¹

The vivas were taken up by the General Assembly and the enthusiastic crowd. The Marquez then appointed a commission to prepare a proclamation for the nation, and another to call upon Dom Pedro at his residential palace to arrange for the taking of the oath of office.

At a little after three o'clock in the afternoon Dom Pedro arrived at the senate building and was escorted to the throne by the officers of the General Assembly and by the commission sent to communicate with him at Boa Vista. Seating himself, he said, "August and most worthy senhores, representatives of the nation, be seated." The Assembly sat down. Then, Dom Pedro, in a clear voice, took the following oath: "I swear to maintain the Roman Catholic apostolic religion and the integrity and indivisibility of the Empire, to observe and enforce the political constitution of the Brazilian nation, and the laws of the Empire, and to work for the general good of Brazil to the extent of my power."⁴²

The proclamation announcing that the Emperor had taken the oath required by the constitution concluded with, "Brazilians, the hopes of the nation have been made a reality. A new era opens. May it be one of union and prosperity! May we be worthy of such a great blessing!"⁴³

There followed three days of celebration such as the Brazilians loved—decorated streets, illuminations, fireworks, shouted vivas, triumphant patriotic music, *Te Deums* in the churches. Congratulatory messages were showered upon the Emperor, and the palace was thronged with delegations and individuals who came to pay their respects. Dom Pedro's attitude was kindly and courteous, but dignified and reserved, and the callers were delighted. Unquestionably the premature assumption of power was approved by the nation.⁴⁴

---

⁴¹ *Fallas do throno*, p. 334.   ⁴² *Ibid.*, p. 338.
⁴³ *Ibid.*, pp. 336-37.   ⁴⁴ Pereira da Silva, *op. cit.*, I, 18-19.

Yet, in some ways the sovereign was but a child. His new dignity perhaps prompted him on December 2, 1840, to begin a diary which shows the naïveté of the average boy of fifteen. In his first entry he remarked that his birth was an historical event for Brazil. Then he solemnly proceeded to mention the coffee and eggs he had had for breakfast, and his round of daily tasks.[45] Though his formal lessons went on, they occupied a smaller share of his time than before; but he continued his education throughout his life.

The coronation, which was delayed until July 18, 1841, to give adequate time for preparation, was the most elaborate and colorful event so far connected with Dom Pedro's career. It took place in the Cathedral of Rio de Janeiro in the presence of the Regent, six bishops, Princesses Januaria and Francisca, and a great number of dignitaries. The Archbishop of Bahia, metropolitan of the Empire, officiated and placed the tall crown upon the boy's head. Dom Pedro wore his father's imperial mantle and the sword which he had flourished when he declared independence at Ypiranga. Several days of festivities followed the ceremonies. Many thousands of additional lights helped illuminate the important streets, which were decorated with blossoms, palm branches, draperies, flags, a temple of harmony, numerous triumphal arches, and other symbolical structures.[46]

As was natural, Dom Pedro's first ministry was made up of Liberal leaders, including the two Andrada brothers. Its initial public act was the granting, in the Emperor's name, of amnesty for all political crimes under the regency. This was in harmony with advice given Dom Pedro on his tenth birthday by Francisco de Lima e Silva of the first permanent regency.[47] Thus, the new Emperor began his reign magnanimously.

The first ministry was short-lived, however, because Antonio Carlos de Andrada, though nominally a Liberal, conducted him-

[45] Pedro d'Orléans Bragança Archives, A, CII, 4990.
[46] *Jornal do Commercio*, July 19, 20, 1841; Pereira da Silva, *op. cit.*, I, 64-65.
[47] Pedro d'Orléans Bragança Archives, A, I, 4911.

CORONATION OF DOM PEDRO II

From a painting at the Château d'Eu

self in a high-handed manner. Hoping to win the next election for his party, he removed fourteen presidents of provinces and many other local officials and replaced them by men on whom he could depend to see that the wished-for election returns were reported in their districts. Thanks to this, the balloting for members of the chamber of deputies, in October, 1840, resulted in a sweeping Liberal victory.

Immediately, however, from many quarters came violent protests against the methods of Antonio Carlos, who seemed merely a new tyrant to take the place of Dom Pedro I. Resentment was so strong that a delegation of leading men of both parties went to the Emperor and advised him to get rid of his cabinet. Accordingly, on March 23, 1841, Dom Pedro signed a decree dismissing it.[48] His next cabinet was Conservative.

Naturally, the chamber elected by means of fraud and violence proved unpopular as well as unrepresentative; it was dissolved in May of 1842. The election held late that year returned a Conservative majority, which was maintained for the next two years.

The committee of public-spirited subjects who asked Dom Pedro to remove his first cabinet also suggested restoration of the council of state to which he could turn for advice; for Carneiro Leão's recommendation of the year before that this be done had not been followed. Therefore, in the address from the throne on May 3, 1841, the Emperor called the attention of the General Assembly to the need. That body responded favorably, and by an act of November 23, 1841, authorized the restoration of the council. To his first council Dom Pedro appointed men of both political parties, and also some who were independent. Two of the Conservatives named were Carneiro Leão and Araujo Lima, the last Regent.[49]

A vivid impression of the Emperor at this time, when he was having his first lessons in practical politics, was given by Prince Adalbert of Prussia, who visited Brazil in 1842. Dom

---
[48] dos Santos, *op. cit.*, pp. 25-27, 84.   [49] Serrano, *op. cit.*, pp. 537-38.

Pedro, then seventeen, was not yet full grown, for he was described as of "small stature." He was "rather stout, with a largish head, blond hair, and well-formed features." His "blue, speaking eye expresses earnestness and benevolence," wrote Prince Adalbert. For his years, he was remarkably advanced in mental vigor and acquirements, and he had the gravity and deportment of a full-grown man. The Prince referred to "the noble spirit of ambition in the youthful Emperor to educate himself more and more for his exalted but difficult station." History was at the time the Emperor's favorite study. But he was also much interested in chemistry, and he disclosed to Adalbert that he had experimented with the daguerreotype. His visitor was much impressed with the youth's skill in copying in oils the portraits of various famous European sovereigns whom he admired; and he was pleased when Dom Pedro gave him one of these samples of his handiwork, a likeness of Frederick the Great.[50]

For some time after his accession to the throne the young Emperor needed much advice which he could not properly get from the council of state. Therefore, he consulted his tutors. To some extent he probably leaned upon Friar Pedro de Santa Marianna, for whom he had deep affection and respect, which he showed by appointing the friar chief almoner of the imperial household, and by having him made bishop titular of Chrysopolis.[51] But Dom Pedro was far more dependent upon his instructor in literature, José de Araujo Vianna, Marquez de Sapucahy. Araujo Vianna was made Minister of Empire in the Conservative cabinet appointed in March, 1841, to succeed that of Antonio Carlos de Andrada. Another member of the same cabinet closely in touch with the Emperor was Aureliano de Souza, later Visconde de Septiba.[52] Since, at the time, there was

[50] Prince Adalbert, *op. cit.*, I, 272-75, 281; II, 89.
[51] Moraes, "Frei Pedro de Santa Marianna, o preceptor de Pedro II," *Rev. do Inst. Hist. e Geog.*, vol. 152, pp. 53-54.
[52] Tavares de Lyra, in *Contribuições para a Biographia de D. Pedro II*, Pt. I, p. 241; Pedro Calmon, "Visconde de Septiba," *Rev. do Inst. Hist. e Geog. Bras.*, vol. 152, p. 59.

no chief minister to serve as a link between the sovereign and the other members of the cabinet, Dom Pedro himself had to invite men to accept the various portfolios and had to confer with them later regarding the performance of their duties. This situation led to charges, beginning early in 1845, that there existed an aulic faction, or palace group—dubbed the *Club da Joanna*—which surrounded the Emperor and tried to exploit his youth and inexperience for selfish ends. There was probably some truth in the accusations, and when they appeared in the press they were accepted by the public as facts. Later a pamphlet called *A facçao aulica* came out, which stated that the palace group, said to be headed by Aureliano de Souza, had a bad influence upon the Emperor. The charges created a stir and led to discussion of the matter in Parliament. Dom Pedro felt hurt by the criticism—the first he had received—and tried to improve the situation by appointing as Minister to Russia one of the three alleged leaders of the faction.[53]

Apparently the attempt to dominate the Emperor continued, however, and led finally to a decree of July 20, 1847, which created the office of president of the council of ministers, or prime minister. Since the president of the council, in consultation with the sovereign, appointed the other members of the cabinet and was in many regards its spokesman, few pretexts were left for close association of individual ministers with the Emperor.

Dom Pedro's training under the Marquez de Itanhaén had taught him to be suspicious of government officers, to investigate for himself, and to draw his own conclusions. As soon as the decree of July, 1847, rid him of the palace faction, he took full control and exercised his moderating power free from outside influence. He was twenty-two years old when he thus secured a position of political independence. From then on he tried to keep aloof from members of the government, except for consultation with the council of state, and to depend upon his

[53] Pereira da Silva, *op. cit.*, I, 130-31, 152-54.

own judgment. Rarely thereafter was he seriously accused of domination by any individual or faction.[54] But throughout his reign he had to pick his way carefully between political attacks and factional intrigues.

By 1847 Dom Pedro had attained his growth and looked much as he did for the next fifteen years. He was distinctly handsome. Though six feet and three or four inches in height, he was well proportioned, and had conspicuously beautiful hands. His hair had turned to a light golden brown, and his full beard was of the same color. He had a fine brow and a frank, open countenance. Though his face was rather stern in repose, and his glance keen and steady, his blue eyes were generally reassuring. He carried himself with imperial dignity, and an air of reserve discouraged familiarity.

He was highly intelligent, tolerant, broad-minded, somewhat blunt in speech, but conspicuously kind-hearted; rather insistent when sure he was right; devoted to his country and its welfare; and extremely conscientious and unwearying in his efforts to serve it.

Ever since his investiture the Emperor had personally opened and closed the sessions of Parliament, by reading the speech from the throne. On these two annual occasions he appeared in state dress, and, as a whole, the senate chamber, where the two houses assembled to hear the message, was a scene of colorful magnificence. Dom Pedro's ceremonial costume included an inner suit of white satin, consisting of a long, gold-embroidered tunic with white frills at neck and wrists, close-fitting breeches, and slippers decorated with rosettes and gold embroidery. At his left side hung a gold sword. Beneath the white lace color was a tippet made from the fluffy yellow plumage of the toucan, an idea copied from the costume of ancient aboriginal caciques. Over the tippet was placed the chain which

---

[54] João Pandiá Calogeras, "O poder pessoal e o lapis fatidico," *Rev. do Inst. Hist. e Geog. Bras.*, vol. 152, p. 428; Capistrano de Abreu, "Phases do segundo imperio," *Rev. do Inst. Hist. e Geog. Bras.*, vol. 152, p. 436.

was the symbol of the Order of the Rose, founded by Dom Pedro I. From the Emperor's shoulders flowed a long, green velvet mantle, lined with yellow silk and embroidered in gold thread with a border of acorns and oak leaves. His high gold crown, surmounted by a cross, flashed with diamonds and other gems. When he entered the senate chamber and departed from it he carried a long staff-like scepter topped with the Bragança device, a golden griffin, and the train of his mantle was borne by a courtier.[55]

On such occasions, according to Ewbank, an American traveler, all deputies and senators except those drawn from the clergy wore an official costume consisting of "white pants with laced seams, coats buttoned up to the chin and half covered with lace, swords, and chapeaux."[56]

Nominally, a new era began for Brazil when Dom Pedro was declared of age. All trace of sedition and disorder did, indeed, disappear from the capital, but serious disaffection and warfare persisted for many years in some other parts of the country. The rebellious spirit existing in colonial times had been fostered and developed by later political crises to such a degree that it was not easily quieted. Matters became even worse for a time.

In February, 1840, the regency had made Major Luis Alves de Lima e Silva president and military commander of the province of Maranhão, where there was civil war. When Lima e Silva learned of the accession of the Emperor to power and of the decree of amnesty, he did everything possible to spread word of it among the rebels. By this policy, combined with use of arms, he brought peace to the province by January, 1841, and was rewarded by being made Barão de Caxias. Later he was raised to the rank of duke.

Unfortunately, early the next year revolt broke out in São Paulo, against the acts of the new imperial government itself.

---

[55] Kidder and Fletcher, *op. cit.*, p. 212; Thomas Ewbank, *Life in Brazil*, pp. 278-79. See frontispiece. [56] Ewbank, *op. cit.*, p. 278.

Changes made in the criminal code and the restoration of the council of state were resented. But the major grievance was the dissolution in May, 1842, of the fraudulently elected lower chamber of Parliament. This action was attributed to the evil influence of the aulic faction upon the Emperor. The Paulistas began to fear for their own rights.[57] Padre Feijó, former Regent, was one of the leaders in resistance and became publisher of *O Paulista,* organ of the revolutionary government. In June, Minas Geraes, inspired by its neighbor, broke out in revolt. Caxias, given full authority to suppress the trouble in these two provinces, did so by the close of August, 1842, and imprisoned Padre Feijó and the other leaders.[58]

It was more difficult to bring peace to Rio Grande do Sul, where revolution and civil war had existed since 1835. There the situation was aggravated by political turbulence in the countries of the Plata basin, where the dictator Rosas of Buenos Aires kept things stirred up. News of the accession to power of the popular young Dom Pedro II and of his decree of amnesty had little influence upon the rebels of Rio Grande. Caxias, who had been trying to end war in the far south before he was sent to Maranhão, returned to Rio Grande do Sul after he had quieted São Paulo and Minas, and by March, 1845, subdued the province. The terms offered the vanquished were generous— full amnesty with personal guaranties in return for surrender of arms and recognition of the Emperor.[59] Late in 1845 Dom Pedro and the Empress—he had been married two years before —visited the province which had been the theatre of ten years of war. They were well received by the recent rebels, who appeared pleased by their sovereigns' courtly manners and gracious words. This visit helped wipe out old resentment among the Rio Grandenses.[60]

[57] F. J. Oliveira Vianna, *Evolução do povo brasileiro,* p. 265; José Francisco de Rocha Pombo, *Historia de S. Paulo,* pp. 109-10.
[58] Serrano, *op. cit.,* pp. 358-61.   [59] Oliveira Lima, *O Imperio brazileiro,* p. 32.
[60] Ewbank, *op. cit.,* p. 62; Oliveira Lima, *O Imperio brasileiro,* p. 32; Pereira da Silva, *op. cit.,* I, 136-37.

But permanent peace had not yet come to Dom Pedro's restless land. New trouble arose in 1847, this time in Pernambuco. At first came attacks by jealous Brazilians on the Portuguese planters and merchants of the province; but there were other local quarrels, as well as considerable feeling against the imperial government, which was looked upon as arbitrary. In 1848, a serious revolt broke out and spread to many parts of the province, but by the early part of 1850 law and order were finally restored.[61] Now began for Brazil a long period of internal tranquillity.

[61] Serrano, *op. cit.*, pp. 364-65; Pereira da Silva, *op. cit.*, I, 185-204, 212; *Fallas do throno*, pp. 439-40, 447.

IV

DOM PEDRO'S BRAZIL IN THE 1840's

THE BRAZIL which General Caxias had restored to peace was an Empire geographically as well as politically. Its eighteen provinces had an area about equal to the present United States of America. This was broken into numerous physiographic units, each with its own climatic characteristics, even though most of the country lay within the torrid zone. In the northwest was the vast basin of the Amazon River, where excessive rainfall made the air steam with moisture under the direct rays of the sun. Here was unconquered jungle, the paradise of the naturalist who semi-occasionally penetrated its outer fringe. The closely-set, bewildering variety of palms and hardwood trees, the bamboos, ceibas, mimosas, tillandsias, bignonias, arborescent ferns, and countless other kinds of vegetation were spangled with orchids and other parasites and were bound together by creepers and by twisted, interlacing lianas. In places the traveler had to cut his way through the walls of living green.

In the northeast, which included the province of Ceará, very little rain fell. Prickly, thorny plants, like the cactus and the agave were conspicuous in the scant vegetation, and droughts, followed by famine, were frequent.

Farther south along the Atlantic, where the rainfall was more generous, the land was again green. The surplus water of the region was carried to the Atlantic by the crooked São Francisco River, which, traversing the provinces of Bahia and Minas Geraes, picked its way between the ridges of the eastern highlands. Near the coast stood lofty mountain islands, picturesque green sentinels guarding the land. The broken character of the shore gave Brazil excellent harbors. Where the coast line ran east and west for a distance, Rio de Janeiro stood, with the best haven of all. It was framed by individual, strangely-sculptured peaks of the Serra do Mar. The Pão de Assucar (Sugar Loaf), sheer and symmetrical, towered on the west at the entrance to the bay; beyond was graceful Corcovado (the Hunchback); and still farther, forming a background for the Palace of São Christavão at Boa Vista, was broad Mount Tijuca with its twin horns. On clear days there could be seen from Rio the slender, purple summits of the noble Orgãos (Organs) Range, rising many leagues to the north. The most impressive of its peaks was the sharply-pointed, spirelike Dedo de Deus (Finger of God), so named by the devout early Portuguese.

Just below Rio de Janeiro the Tropic of Capricorn cut across the continent, marking the lower boundary of the torrid zone. After the coast line again turned southward, for a long stretch the climate was moderated by the existence of high tableland as well as by the fact that here the sun's rays were less direct. In this region was the self-assertive province of São Paulo, where winters were sharp and snow at times fell on the more elevated parts. To the westward of São Paulo lay Matto Grosso, a great interior province broken by mountains and well clothed with sub-tropical forests. Since high ranges shut it off from the Brazilian coastal slope it was drained by long rivers flowing into the Plata. The rugged province of Santa Catharina, to the south of São Paulo, had a good showing of evergreens. Among them were majestic araucaria pines, at times two hundred feet in height, with peculiarly horizontal branches which made the trees look like gigantic candelabra.

Rio Grande do Sul, where chronic turbulence had hastened Dom Pedro's majority, was on the southern frontier. In places it was hilly, but on the whole its surface was rolling or open and flat, like Uruguay and Argentina. Here the climate was temperate, with a moderate rainfall.

In the early years of Dom Pedro's reign wild animals roamed freely in most other parts of the country. Tapirs, jaguars, and monkeys could be hunted in the jungles a few days' ride from Rio de Janeiro.[1] Brilliantly colored birds and butterflies and other winged things were even more abundant than at present.

Brazil was then almost an empty land. Its estimated population in 1845 was between seven and eight million; most of these people lived near the coast. The province of Rio de Janeiro, with approximately 1,400,000 inhabitants, was the most densely settled, and Minas Geraes, with perhaps 1,130,000, ranked next. The largest city, Rio de Janeiro, was credited with a population of 250,000, and Bahia, the original capital of the country, claimed 150,000. The white element—made up chiefly of creoles but including also many Portuguese, and a sprinkling of Germans, Swiss, French, and English—may have numbered a million; and the pure-blooded aborigines, a million and a half. Most of the natives lived in the interior, and many of the tribes, such as the Botocudos, were naked, roving savages. Of *mestiços*, offspring of white and aboriginal blood, there were probably a few hundred thousand. Negroes, most of them found in the deep tropics of the north, and many of them born in Africa, made up the remainder of the population. Probably one half to two-thirds of the inhabitants were slaves. These included some Indians and mulattoes, but were chiefly full-blooded Negroes.[2]

When Dom Pedro began to sway the imperial scepter, slavery was strongly entrenched in the social and economic life of the country. The condition of the bondmen varied, however. Some masters were ferociously cruel, at times driving victims to suicide, though oftener they fled to freedom in the forests and jungles. Yet, on the whole, slaves fared better in Brazil than in the United States of America at the time. The Roman Catholic

[1] Adalbert, *op. cit.*, I, 22-34, *passim*.
[2] Ewbanks, *op. it.*, pp. 323, 430-32; Adalbert, *op. cit.*, I, 269.

Church helped lighten their woes, manumission was in many ways encouraged, and there was no sharply marked color line to handicap freedmen. Church choirs were at times made up of Negroes, and blacks could attain to the highest positions, socially, professionally, and politically.[3]

As in all slave-holding countries, labor was considered degrading. To suggest that a youth of poor but respectable family learn a trade was thought an insult. Work, in the opinion of the proud Brazilian, was the function of the unfree. Indeed, it was the custom in many a family to live entirely on the labor of one or two bondmen, who were at times hired out. Many slaves supported their masters by peddling in the streets. The professions, especially the priesthood, were considered respectable, but the most coveted positions were connected with the army or navy or with the civil service of the Empire, and these tended to be overcrowded. Begging was common, partly because of aversion to honest labor. Brazilian business houses followed the Portuguese custom of having on Saturdays a supply of coppers to distribute to mendicant callers. There was also much begging for religious purposes. Groups of collectors, accompanied by bands of music, passed and repassed through the streets beseeching "Alms for the Holy Ghost!" or for some saint whose festival was being celebrated.[4]

As in most countries at the time, the position of women was hard. Their status was still marked by the patriarchal conception of society prevailing in colonial days. Both law and custom discriminated against them. The father or husband was lord and master. Sons were far more privileged than daughters. Everywhere, to some extent, Moorish tradition still kept women secluded, but this was especially true in the rural sections, where

---

[3] Mary W. Williams, "The Treatment of Negro Slaves in the Brazilian Empire: A Comparison with the United States of America," *Rev. do Inst. Hist. e Geog. Bras.* Tomo especial (*Congresso Internacional de Historia da America*, 1922), pp. 273-92; Ewbanks, *op. cit.*, p. 135; Gilberto Freyre, *Casa Grande & Senzala*, pp. 261-92.

[4] Ewbank, *op. cit.*, pp. 184-85, 196, 250-51, 281.

formerly they had rarely appeared at the table if a man from outside the family was present.[5]

Most of the population made a living by extraction or production of raw materials. From some of the coast provinces north of the capital and from the Amazon basin came woods of many kinds. Minas Geraes was still producing gold, silver, and precious stones in important quantities. Sugar cane, cotton, and tobacco were grown in the provinces of the extreme northeast, notably Pernambuco and Bahia. The plantations on which these products were produced formed complete economic systems of patriarchal type. Rio de Janeiro and São Paulo were noted for manioc, maize, wheat, rye, and rice, and were becoming increasingly important for coffee-growing. The pine trees of Santa Catharina were in demand for masts of ships. The northern province of Ceará produced cattle, although the chief range country was in the south, where in Rio Grande do Sul cattle-raising was the chief industry. Sugar, cotton, and coffee were among the leading Brazilian exports, but hides, horns, tallow, and jerked beef were sent out in considerable quantities.

Good furniture was made to help meet internal needs, as were pottery of various qualities, leather, coarse cotton cloth, and several products from sugar cane. But, in general, expert manufacturing had made little headway. This was natural, for mechanically, the Empire was backward, and the tools and machinery used in all lines of work were either primitive or old-fashioned.[6]

In the towns were one or more market places which carried such commodities as fish, birds of bright plumage, monkeys, flowers, fruits, manioc, coarse clothing, and pottery. Much buying and selling was done through street peddlers who, by shrill cries and quaint jingles and songs, advertised everything from sweetmeats and toys to lottery tickets, laces, silks, and muslins.

[5] Edmundo, *O Rio de Janeiro no tempo dos vice-reis*, pp. 68, 349-67; Gilberto Freyre, *Sobrados e mucambos*, pp. 87-158.
[6] Ruschenberger, *op. cit.*, I, 110-15; Ewbank, *op. cit.*, pp. 185 ff.

Women of the better classes rarely went out to shop. The street merchant came to them, upon receiving a signal from window or balcony.[7]

The country lacked up-to-date means of transportation. Not until many years after Dom Pedro's coronation was the first mile of railroad built. Steamboats which carried freight and passengers along the coast and up and down the rivers offered the best means of getting about. They were supplemented, especially on the rivers, by large sailing vessels, and by *felugas*,[8] *jangadas*,[9] and dugout canoes with awnings made from cattle hides. Freight was usually carried over the rough roads of the interior in heavy ox carts or by strings of pack mules. In the cities, Negro slaves were often yoked to the trucks used for hauling cargoes to and from the docks. Small loads were commonly carried on people's heads, and included objects as diverse as coffins, baskets of live chickens, trays of sweetmeats, and collections of jewels in glass exhibition cases. Travel by horseback or muleback was very common, but where the character of the roads would permit, carriages, or lighter vehicles, generally drawn by mules, were also used. When trails were rough and travelers could afford a more comfortable means of transportation than the saddle, they went in hammocks, swung on poles carried by hired Indians or slaves. *Cadeirinhas*, or sedan chairs, very common in the colonial era, were still in use and were either privately owned or obtainable for hire. They were often Oriental in their magnificence, with carved and gilded tops, and heavily embroidered curtains, and were carried by liveried Negroes.

Comfortable hotels were non-existent in the country districts, but for the accommodation of the wayfarer there were occasional country stores and rough inns. In the remoter sections travelers were forced to ask at private houses for entertainment, which

---
[7] Ewbank, *op. cit.*, pp. 87-88; Kidder and Fletcher, *op. cit.*, pp. 166-69.
[8] Open boats with several sets of oars as well as lateen sails.
[9] Rafts, or floats, supplied with a single sail.

was gladly granted, since news from the cities and the outside world was a rare treat. Furthermore, in rural areas hospitality was a well-established virtue, and hosts took pride in giving their best to the stranger. An offer of money for such food and shelter was commonly looked upon as an insult.

The Brazilians as a whole, though good-natured and friendly, were ignorant and superstitious. Perhaps less than one person in ten could read and write, and most of the others were indifferent to their lack. Education had made some progress since colonial days, but the schools were quite inadequate to the population, and the existing ones were almost entirely for boys. It was thought, as elsewhere at the time, that for girls education was needless or hurtful, or that the weak "female intellect" was incapable of serious development. The few girls who became literate were usually taught at home or by the nuns in the convents, and their book-learning was limited indeed. They did, however, receive much training in plain sewing and in fancy embroidering.

Besides the schools under public control there were numerous private ones, often conducted by foreigners, some of the best belonging to religious orders. The instruction in the village schools seems to have commonly been limited to reading, writing, arithmetic, and the Roman Catholic religion, but the best elementary training of the cities included also geography and Brazilian history, natural history, drawing, advanced arithmetic, elementary geometry, elementary physics, and singing. A small yearly fee was charged for instruction beyond the three R's.[10]

The outstanding secondary school under public control was the Collegio Dom Pedro II, in Rio, of which the Emperor had become protector while still a child. Its course of study, similar in quality to the best academies of the United States at the time, included advanced mathematics, elementary training in most of

---

[10] Primitivo Moacyr, *A instrucção e o Imperio*, pp. 262, 563; Freyre, *Casa Grande & Senzala*, pp. 292-93.

the natural sciences, history, geography, Portuguese literature, French, English, Greek, and Latin. At the end of the year prizes were awarded to those who had excelled, and the winning boys were crowned with wreaths made from the twigs of coffee trees twined with flowers. Those who completed the course were granted the bachelor's degree. But the Collegio was a boarding school with high fees, and was intended for the sons of the upper classes. There were, however, a small number of free scholarships for gifted children of the poor.[11] Like most countries at the time, the Empire seems to have had no free secondary schools.

Instruction in the lower schools was largely by the catechismal method, with emphasis upon memorizing, and laboratory experiments, if they took place, were usually performed by the instructor. School buildings for the lower grades were usually poor and discipline was strict.

The Collegio Dom Pedro II and others of the better secondary schools—most of which seem to have been private—prepared Brazilian youths to enter the institutes of law and medicine and the theological seminaries, with which the Empire seems to have been well provided.[12]

Dom Pedro's Brazil of the 1840's had no liberal arts colleges of the type then found in the United States of America, and no universities. Though the establishment of a university was proposed as early as 1823—by the constituent assembly dissolved by Dom Pedro I[13]—and though it was repeatedly urged later, especially by the Minister of Empire, who had general responsibility for national education,[14] nothing had been done about the matter. The explanation seems to be lack of interest on the part of the leaders in providing at home opportunities for advanced work in the liberal arts and also the conviction that better professional training was supplied by the separate institutes than would be given if these were united under one ad-

[11] Moacyr, *op. cit.*, pp. 276-319.
[13] *Ibid.*, p. 89.
[12] *Ibid.*, pp. 320-455.
[14] *Ibid.*, p. 457.

ministration.[15] Wealthy men who were dissatisfied with the facilities for higher education at home sent their sons abroad for study, especially to the ancient Portuguese university at Coimbra.

Though lacking a university, Brazil had, in connection with its capital, several other institutions which contributed to culture and enlightenment. These were an astronomical observatory, a public library with something over seventy thousand volumes, an Academy of Fine Arts, founded by Dom Pedro's grandfather, and a Botanical Garden, also started by King João. The Garden, six miles out of the city, between Corcovado and salt water, was world famous.[16]

The Brazilian press was free, and all of the larger cities had one or more newspapers. Rio de Janeiro had four dailies in 1846. There were also a few literary and factual magazines. Practically all cultivated people read and spoke French, as well as Portuguese, and great numbers of French books were imported yearly.

The Empire had produced some able literary men. José Bonifacio de Andrada, Dom Pedro's first tutor, who was a distinguished poet of classical style, was dead by now, but other able singers were coming to the fore. Gonçalves de Magalhães, the first prominent Brazilian romanticist, published his *Suspiros Poeticos e Saudades (Poetic Sighs and Longings)* in 1836. One of his best works was an epic, *A Confederação dos Tomayos (The Confederation of the Tomayos)*, a tribe of liberty-loving Indians who lived near Rio de Janeiro in colonial days. This poem, like the novels of James Fenimore Cooper, set forth the virtues of the aborigines. During the 1840's Gonçalves Dias began to write. The fact that in his veins ran aboriginal and Negro blood, as well as Portuguese, gave him a great interest in the darker races, and he wrote about both of them. Like Magalhães, he idealized the red man, and helped give importance

---

[15] *Ibid.* [16] *Ibid.*, pp. 501-35.

to "Indianism" in Brazilian literature. Most of Dias's poems are lyrical, and tell of the natural beauty of his country, glorified by patriotic love. The first notable one, his "Canção do Exilio" ("Song of Exile"), written in Portugal, was set to music and became a favorite song of the nation, and the author, its best-beloved poet.

The low average of intelligence in the country was reflected in religious practices. Roman Catholicism was the established church, but its humbler adherents were characterized by an unusual degree of naïve superstition. Religious relics and votive offerings in abundance were found in the churches, the patronage of various saints was expanded, and the Virgin and Child likewise underwent almost endless metamorphoses through a widening of their functions. An American who visited Brazil in 1846 noted the image of Our Lady of the Cape of Good Hope (Nossa Senhora de Cabo da Boa Esperança), who was believed by the pious to insure a safe voyage around southern Africa in return for a prayer and a coin dropped into her money box.[17] Though Protestant worship was freely permitted, it was illegal for meeting houses to have steeples or bells, which would make them too conspicuous.

Some of the Roman clergy were among the leading thinkers of the country, many members of Parliament were churchmen, and most priests were worldly and tolerant.[18] In 1846 Monsignor Bedini, the papal nuncio to Brazil, in a furious sermon at Petropolis denounced as immoral the marriages that had taken place between Brazilian Catholics and a few of the German Protestants who had settled in the town. The chapel of these Germans in Petropolis was at the time receiving aid from the

---

[17] Ewbank, *op. cit.*, pp. 176-83; Kidder and Fletcher, *op. cit.*, pp. 140-60.

[18] The learned bishop of Rio de Janeiro, José Caetano, one of the early advocates of toleration in Brazil, was described by R. Walsh, the chaplain of the British embassy in Rio, as "not only a tolerant and liberal man, but a man of excellent good sense and knowledge of the world." Bishop Caetano was elected president of the constituent assembly of 1823, which Dom Pedro I dissolved.—Walsh, *op. cit.*, I, 322-23; II, 428.

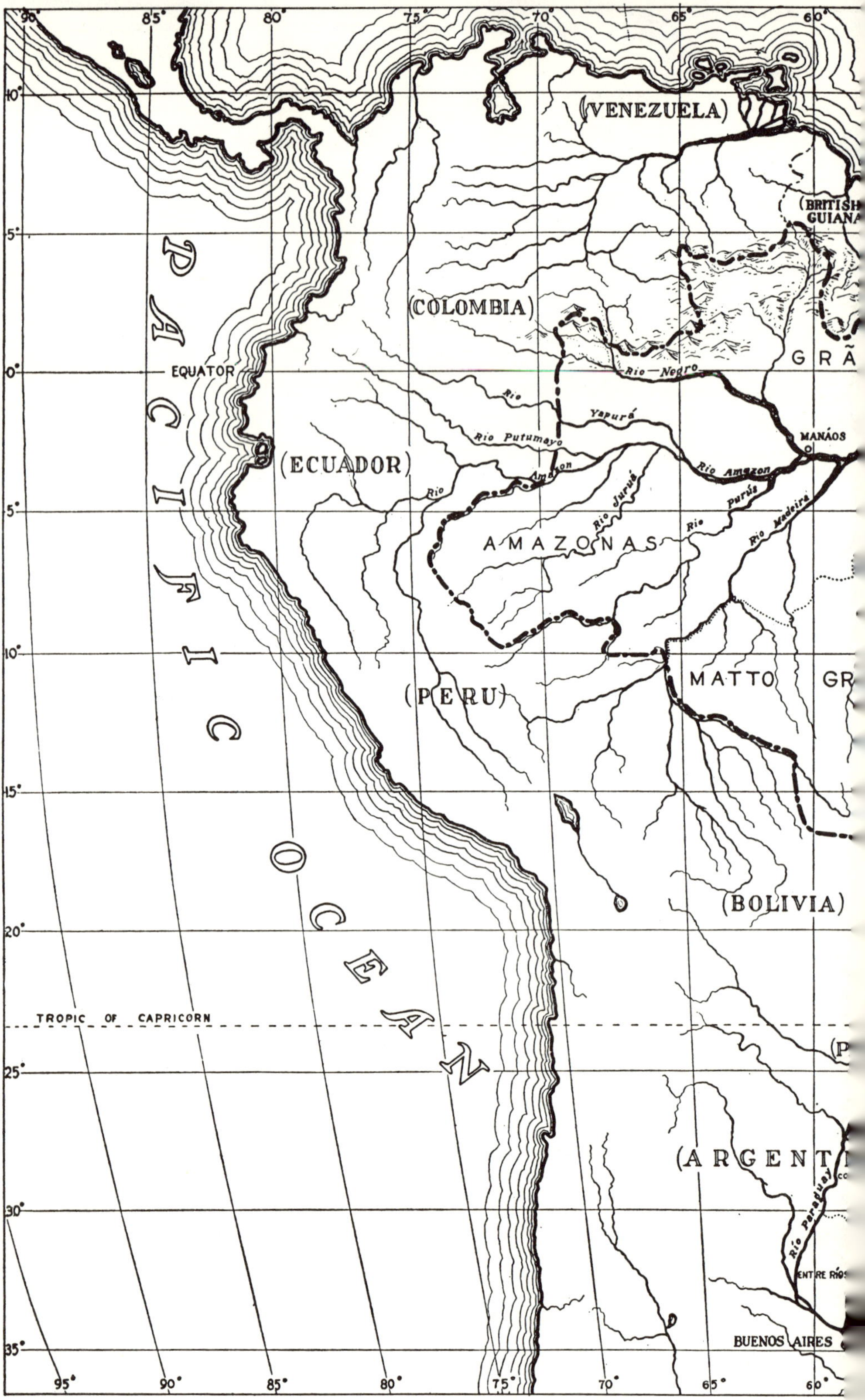

(VENEZUELA)
(COLOMBIA)
EQUATOR
Rio Negro
Yapurá
Rio Putumayo
MANÁOS
(ECUADOR)
Amazon
Rio Amazon
Rio Juruá
Rio Purús
Rio Madeira
AMAZONAS
MATTO
(PERU)
PACIFIC OCEAN
(BOLIVIA)
TROPIC OF CAPRICORN
Rio Paraguay
ENTRE RÍOS
BUENOS AIRES

MAP OF THE BRAZILIAN EMPIRE UNDER DOM PEDRO II

SHOWING PLACES MENTIONED IN THE BOOK

When Dom Pedro II began his rule in 1840, there were only 18 provinces in the Empire, but the two others, Amazonas and Paraná, were organized early in the reign. Boundaries are merely approximate in many cases, for very few frontier limits had been definitely fixed even by the close of the imperial era.

Scale Of Miles

Brazilian treasury, and Bedini's attack caused much resentment in Rio de Janeiro as well as in Petropolis. The conservative *Diario do Rio de Janeiro*, which was looked upon as something of a government mouthpiece, criticized his action as likely to kindle the fires of religious intolerance. "Propositions like those emitted from the Chair of Truth by a priest of the character of M. Bedini," said the *Diario*, "are eminently censurable." And it called upon the bishop to act promptly in the matter.[19]

Upon the Church fell much of the burden of caring for the orphaned, sick, and outcast. The largest hospital in Brazil, and one of the most famous in the world at the time, because of its charity, was the Santa Casa da Misericórdia, (Holy House of Charity) founded by the Jesuit José de Anchieta in 1582. Its doors were open day and night to receive the sick and distressed —male or female, black or white, Moor or Christian. Many thousands of people, including large numbers of foreigners, especially seamen, were cared for every year by the Casa.

The *irmandades*, or lay brotherhoods, of the Roman Church in Brazil did much social service work. These groups were more than mere mutual benefit societies. By means of bequests and of contributions from members, they cared for poor and sick individuals, gave decent burial to paupers, supported masses for souls, and even founded hospitals and churches.[20]

Since disease germs had not yet been discovered, there was but little basis for sanitary regulation in the Empire. Even Rio de Janeiro lacked a sewer system. Garbage was pitched into the middle of the narrow streets, to be disposed of by turkey buzzards, which, indeed, were the chief scavengers in the warmer climates of the world at the time. Clothes were washed in streams by chattering, laughing Negro women and spread on the grass to dry. The water supply for the capital was brought from the nearby mountains by a handsome eighteenth-century aqueduct with two tiers of arches. It was dispensed in various

---

[19] Ewbank, *op. cit.*, p. 393; Kidder and Fletcher, *op. cit.*, pp. 142-43.
[20] *Ibid.*, pp. 136-38; Kidder and Fletcher, *op. cit.*, pp. 107-12.

parts of the city through public fountains, known by the Moorish name of *chafarizes*. The largest of these stood in the praça before the City Palace and dated from the time of Queen Maria I, Dom Pedro II's great-grandmother. It was an obelisk topped with a representation of the imperial crown and had fifteen spouts. This fountain was a favorite social center for slaves and other humble folk, who dallied and gossiped before carrying away on their heads the kegs or jars which they had come to fill.[21]

Brazilian architecture followed Portuguese models of an earlier day. In Rio de Janeiro, Bahia, and some of the other larger cities were churches from the colonial period, with round arches and massive towers, and rich in churrigueresque sculpture, gold leaf, and glazed tiles. The secular public buildings, of heavy stone, were of simple quadrangular style. Private houses ranged from the primitive huts of palm leaves and mud, occupied by the wild Indians and the humblest Negroes or whites, to palatial brick or stone mansions with marble staircases and panelings of rosewood, glazed tile, or other beautiful materials. The homes of the better-to-do were plainly built with thick walls of rough stone covered with stucco, left white, or tinted—generally pink or blue, or decorated with frescoes set in panels. Usually these houses were two-storied, but some of the older city dwellings had three floors, the first being used for stable and carriage house. The street windows of the ground floor were protected by iron grilling; balconies projected from those on the second floor, or ran across the whole front of the building. The roofs were of red tiles, and on some buildings turned upward at the corners in Oriental fashion. In Rio de Janeiro rain was poured from the roofs into the streets by long copper spouts, some of them shaped like fishes. City houses commonly stood flush with the sidewalk, and at times inclosed

---

[21] Max Fleiuss, *Historia da Cidade do Rio de Janeiro*, pp. 193-200; Joh. Bapt. von Spix and C. F. Phil. von Martius, *Travels in Brazil in the Years 1817-1820*, I, 157-58.

a *páteo,* or court, with a small garden and fountain. Windows were closed with wooden shutters; glass panes were exceptional, and were found only in the finer homes. Street doors usually had no knockers, and visitors announced their presence by rapping with knuckles or cane, or by clapping the hands—an Oriental survival also generally used for calling servants.[22]

The "great house" *("casa grande")* of the fazenda or plantation—near which was the *senzala,* the rude quarters for the slaves—tended to be larger and more rambling than city dwellings, though often built in two or three stories. It always included a chapel, and these were occasionally found likewise in urban residences.[23]

Rooms were high and spacious, and where the climate was hot partition walls stopped a foot or so short of the ceiling, to permit free circulation of air. The articles of furniture were few, and were stiffly arranged; but in many elegant homes they were made from native cabinet woods, inlaid or carved in artistic designs. Generally, the wealthier classes followed French styles of furniture and of interior decoration. The hammock, an aboriginal invention, was an exception, for it was used as a bed where the climate was oppressive, and was at times swung across the corners of the drawing room, serving as an additional sofa or settee.

Houses were lighted by candles of wax or tallow, or by lamps which burned oil from whales or from domestic castor beans. Bracket-lamps attached to the outer walls of the houses supplied the narrow streets with uncertain illumination.[24]

In the suburban sections handsome modern villas, set in ample, well-planted grounds, were beginning to appear. Thomas Ewbank, who visited Brazil in 1846, mentioned the variety of tropical fruits found on such an estate near the capital. "After dinner we adjourned outside," he wrote,

[22] Ewbank, *op. cit.,* pp. 85-87; Kidder and Fletcher, *op. cit.,* pp. 162-63.
[23] Freyre, *Casa Grande & Senzala, passim.*
[24] Ewbank, *op. cit.,* p. 87.

and partook of dessert after the manner of Eden. Reclining under venerable tamarind and cinnamon trees, we knocked fruit off them and off wide-spreading mangoes. We ranged among cloves and pimentos, bananas and plantains, oranges and lemons. Here red coffee berries were pendent from the stems of tall and slender bushes; there stands a caja, a species of Indian palm, and near it the caju, yielding a yellow plum, the jaça, with its gourd-like nuts, the patinga, on which grows a scarlet or purple berry of a sweetish acid taste: the favorite mamão, with its egg-shaped treasures hanging like cocoas from the boll. . . .

Among the gorgeous flowers in the more spacious gardens were wont to flit tiny, jewel-like humming-birds, and butterflies of many colors, one of the most common and beautiful of which had unusually large wings of bright, iridescent blue.[25]

The food was such as the Brazilian soil supplied in abundance. The chief fare of the humble was maize or manioc, *carne secca* (jerked beef), and native fruits. Among the wealthy, several courses of nitrogenous foods were served at dinner—eggs, fish, poultry, and red meats. Owing to the cheapness of sugar, *doces,* or sweets, were eaten by all. There were many varieties of these, one of the most common being *goiabada,* made from the guava apple. Since the late 1830's ice, used for refreshments, had been imported from the United States of America.[26] Alcoholic drinks were used temperately. The common beverages were Oriental tea, coffee, cocoa, and in the south, *mate,* made from the leaves of a native shrub related to the common holly.

Dress varied much in materials and style. The clothes of the slaves were of coarse white cotton, but where the climate was very hot the men wore only a breech-cloth. Slaves commonly went barefooted, since shoes, and also neck cloths, were regarded as emblems of freedom. In the arid section of the northeast, the outer garments worn on the ranges by the men were often of leather, because textiles were easily torn by the spiny vegetation. Farther south, in the rural sections, men's

---

[25] *Ibid.*, pp. 75-77. [26] Adalbert, *op. cit.,* I, 279.

winter garb was characterized by high, wide-topped boots, broad-brimmed gray felt hats, and capes usually made of blue wool lined with red. But in the warmer season cotton or linen suits and straw or palm-leaf hats were the fashion. European men's styles prevailed in the cities. For ceremonial occasions officials still wore the three-cornered velvet hat, but the silk "stove pipe" was coming in. Both types of hats were seen in liveries which inclined to be as gorgeous as they were elaborate. Women of the upper classes followed south European styles, characterized by large silk shawls, conspicuous ear pendants, gold neck chains, and fresh flowers as ornaments for their glossy black hair.

The Brazilians were, on the whole, unhurried, light-hearted, and pleasure-loving. Sundays and the more than fifty saint's days and other Church holidays gave ample opportunity for them to indulge themselves in a carefree manner. After attending mass, they spent most of the remainder of the day in amusement and diversion. The remark of a Brazilian lady of the period indicates the difference in attitude towards the Sabbath from that taken in Britain and the United States at the time. "God, in making the world, worked every day till Sunday, and then took his pleasure," said she; "so must we; he would be angry if we did not."[27] Even slaves who were not household servants were given much of the Sunday or holy day for themselves.

Cards, chess, and other table games were favorite indoor pastimes, and dancing was popular when the weather was not too oppressive. The Brazilians loved music and song. Pianos were found in the homes of the well-to-do, and the guitar, among the rank and file. The humble Negroes played the marimba, brought by them from Africa. It was crudely made by attaching steel wires to a wooden frame set in a large gourd, which served as a resonator. Slaves with heavy burdens on

---

[27] Ewbank, *op. cit.*, pp. 130-31; Kidder and Fletcher, *op. cit.*, p. 165.

their heads often carried marimbas and played grave tunes or gay as they passed along the street.

Theatres existed in all of the larger cities, but their performances were usually inferior. The nation indulged in private theatricals, for which the imperial court helped set the fashion. Even churches and monasteries gave dramatic performances for the purpose of raising money, and the regular commercial theatres unmercifully satirized these competing attractions. Auctions, especially of food, were another money-raising device of the religious bodies. These supplied diversion through band-music and elaborate fireworks. Such church programs took place at the feast of the Holy Ghost in May. A boy elected and crowned as emperor of the Holy Ghost presided over the festivities. Sometimes an empress of the Holy Ghost sat beside him. On the Saturday after Good Friday, youths got amusement from "Killing Judas." Effigies, usually representing the fallen apostle, but sometimes made to resemble unpopular local personages, were stoned, whipped, and finally hanged. The three days preceding Ash Wednesday, called the *entrudo*, were a period for practical joking and general hilarity. In addition to playing such tricks as were associated with All Fools' Day, during the entrudo people pelted friend and stranger with fine starch powder and with colored wax shells filled with water, or perfume. Passers-by on the streets were often surprised by such missiles fired from balconies.[28]

The *festas* connected with established national holidays or with the royal family—the acclamation, coronation, and marriage of the Emperor, the arrival of his children, his birthday anniversary, his visits to other parts of the country, his return to the capital—all helped make life more interesting for the nation. These occasions were celebrated by gaily decorated streets, patriotic music, the boom of cannon, processions and pageants.

Such was Dom Pedro's Brazil in the 1840's.

[28] Ewbank, *op. cit.*, pp. 96-102, 111-12, 235-36, 312-19, 349, 394-97; Freyre, *Sobrados e mucambos*, pp. 74-75.

V

THE EMPEROR'S FAMILY LIFE AND GENERAL ROUTINE

THE national disorders under the regency urged the importance of an early marriage for Dom Pedro, to help stabilize the throne and to secure the Bragança succession. Already in 1841, at about the time of his coronation, search for a bride had begun. Since it seemed desirable that Dom Pedro ally himself with the House of Austria from which his mother came, the imperial agent, Bento da Silva Lisboa, was sent first to Vienna to ask in behalf of the Emperor the hand of one of his Habsburg cousins. By now, Ferdinand I was on the Austrian throne, but he and his ministry were unfavorable to Silva Lisboa's proposal, doubtless because they recalled all too well the tragic experience of Ferdinand's sister Leopoldina as wife of a Bragança.

Yet the government at Vienna was not indifferent to the selection of a mate for the young kinsman of the Austrian Emperor. The chief minister, Prince Metternich, helped Silva Lisboa negotiate with Ferdinand II of the Two Sicilies for the hand of his sister Thereza. The effort was successful, and on April 20, 1842, the betrothal contract was signed, in Vienna, with the minister from Naples. Three months later Dom Pedro, after receiving a portrait of the Neopolitan Princess, ratified the agreement. The marriage took place by proxy on May 30, 1843, in the Royal Palatine Chapel at Naples, the Prince Royal of the Two Sicilies, Leopoldo de Bourbon, answering for the groom. Shortly afterwards the young bride left for Rio de Janeiro in the frigate "Constituição," escorted by vessels from the Neopolitan and Brazilian navies.[1]

Princess Thereza's father was Francis I of Naples, of Habs-

[1] Moniz, *op. cit.*, pp. 35-39; Fleiuss, *Paginas de historia*, pp. 375-380.

burg blood, and her mother, Maria Isabel de Bourbon, was sister of Queen Carlota Joaquina of Portugal. Hence, Dom Pedro's bride was related to him on both sides of her family. Because of this kinship, a special dispensation for the marriage had been secured from Pope Gregory XVI.[2] At the time, the Princess was twenty-one years old, and Dom Pedro was seventeen and a half. She was short of stature, somewhat lacking in grace, and was slightly lame in her walk from a physical defect.[3] Her eyes were brown, and her dark hair was worn, according to the fashion, in long ringlets on either side of her face. That face, though frank and kindly, was unquestionably plain. While well-educated, Dona Thereza had no special interest in things of the mind.

Such was the bride of the bookworm youth, whose tutors had stimulated in him a romantic interest in women—the youth who delighted in the novels of Sir Walter Scott, with their beautiful and fascinating heroines, and in the chivalric chronicles of Jean Froissart. After Dom Pedro had seen the likeness of the Neopolitan Princess, he apparently had fitted her into some personal romantic dream. But, alas, the portrait represented Dona Thereza as more attractive than the facts justified.[4]

The vessel bearing the Princess reached Rio de Janeiro on September 3, 1843. Elaborate preparations had been made for her coming. All of the vessels in the harbor, gay with flags, fired salutes. Late in the afternoon Dom Pedro, with his ministers, went aboard the "Constituição" to greet his bride. When he saw her he was disappointed, shocked, and is said to have turned his back upon her.[5] If so, it was to regain his self-control.

---

[2] Mozart Monteiro, "O casamento do Imperador," *Rev. do Inst. Hist. e Geog. Bras.*, vol. 152, p. 66.

[3] Monteiro, "A familia imperial," *Rev. do Inst. Hist. e Geog. Bras.*, vol. 152, p. 85; information supplied by Dr. Manoel A. V. da Motta Maia.

[4] Pedro S. Lamas, *Contribución historica: etapas de una gran politica*, pp. 46-52; Monteiro, "O casamento do Imperador," *Rev. do Inst. Hist. e Geog. Bras.*, vol. 152, p. 65.

[5] Thomas C. Dawson, *The South American Republics*, I, 457.

After he left the vessel he expressed his indignation over the marriage arrangement, and turned to his faithful Dona Marianna for sympathy and understanding. "They have deceived me, Dadama," he is reported to have said, disconsolately; and he wished to repudiate the contract, for he was too young to see that this would bring embarrassing—possibly serious—results. Upon Dona Marianna fell the hard task of convincing him that the marriage contract must stand and be fulfilled.[6] He yielded to his fate, but he was a most reluctant bridegroom.

How much the Princess knew of these developments is not clear, but she certainly noted the Emperor's coolness towards her, and this caused her to weep with distress, for she had apparently liked him at once.[7]

Late the next morning Dona Thereza landed and the program for completion of the marriage ceremonies proceeded. Her carriage and Dom Pedro's became units of the long, elaborate wedding procession which, under leadership of the cavalry band, made a detour through festively decorated streets to the Imperial Chapel beside the City Palace. For more than twelve years the nation had lacked a First Lady, and now, although showers of rain fell, the sidewalks were packed with enthusiastic people, eager to get a glimpse of their new Empress. They shouted loyal greetings to her and with friendly grace Dona Thereza responded.

Dom Pedro was reported by the next day's press as wearing a "smiling and suitable expression"[8]—but the brother of his

[6] Calogeras, *A politica exterior do Imperio*, III, 387-89.
Since the accession of Dom Pedro II to power, Dona Marianna had served in the palace during much of the time. In 1844 the Emperor conferred upon her the title of Condessa de Belmonte. Later, she received from him other honors. In 1855, during a terrible epidemic of cholera morbus in the capital, she turned her house into a hospital, and on October 17 of that year she died of the disease.—Moniz, *op. cit.*, pp. 136-37.

[7] Lamas, *op. cit.*, p. 53; Monteiro, "O casamento do Imperador," *Rev. do Inst. Hist. e Geog. Bras.*, vol. 152, p. 66.

[8] *Jornal do Commercio*, Sept. 5, 1843, quoted in Fleiuss, *Paginas de historia*, p. 384.

bride rode in the coach with him. At the Imperial Chapel the marriage ceremony was repeated, with Dom Pedro making his own responses. Immediately afterwards the Emperor and Empress went to the throne room of the City Palace to receive the throngs who gathered to do them homage, for all of their subjects, whether high or low, were admitted if they came suitably dressed for the occasion.[9]

There were nine days of celebration. During the period a special mass for the bridal pair was held in the Imperial Chapel at the City Palace, with the whole court present. This was followed by the beija mão ceremony in the throne room of the palace. Then came a reception to the diplomatic corps, at which the papal nuncio, as spokesman for the group, extended greetings to the young sovereigns. The theatres presented special programs in honor of the occasion. On the evening of the 12th of September, near the close of the festivities, Dona Thereza and Dom Pedro made the rounds of the capital to view the illuminations, which were truly remarkable, especially the many triumphal arches which spanned the streets. Some of these arches were more than sixty feet high and were set with thousands of lights. Among the decorations on these structures were pictures of the sovereigns and inscriptions and verses in their honor.[10]

Dona Thereza quickly adjusted herself to her new environment and became deeply attached to her adopted land. By her scrupulous aloofness from politics, her generous gifts to charity, her remarkably sweet smile, and her unfailingly friendly manner in public, she soon won the lasting affection of the people. By them, this Neopolitan Princess came to be called "the Mother of the Brazilians." Not a word of criticism has been found against her in the records of the forty-six years she spent in Brazil. During the latter part of the period she was unques-

---

[9] Fleiuss, *Paginas de historia*, pp. 381-84. [10] *Ibid.*, pp. 385-90.

tionably the most popular and most generally respected woman in the Empire.[11]

Dom Pedro tried always to do his duty by the one whom he had unwillingly made his wife, and to show her proper respect. Shortly after they were married, he once went alone to the theatre in Rio when Dona Thereza was in Petropolis, but, informed by Friar Pedro de Santa Marianna that this did not look well, he did not repeat the indiscretion.[12]

His attitude towards the Empress when he came to know her well, and for a long time following, was expressed in the first entry of a diary begun by him eighteen years after his marriage: "I respect and sincerely esteem my wife, whose qualities of character are excellent."[13] Perhaps this calm regard for her was somewhat filial, even in the early years, for she was a woman when they were married, and he was scarcely more than a boy. Her maternal instincts were strong, and she mothered him as she did his subjects. Her popularity with the Brazilians, her loyalty and devotion to Dom Pedro, and her watchful care during his attacks of illness caused him to develop for her an affection which in the last years was deep and tender.[14]

But romantic sentimentality was always lacking in his feeling for Dona Thereza, and he probably carried with him throughout life the memory of the lovely lady of his youthful dreams. Beautiful women, especially those with charm of manner and intellectual sparkle, attracted him at home and abroad. After he had reached middle age his daughter Isabel is said to have rebuked him for having shown undue attention to a young lady at a reception. His enemies tried to use this alleged weakness

---

[11] *Ibid.*, pp. 390-400; Affonso Celso, in *Contribuiçoes para a Biographia de D. Pedro II*, Pt. I, p. 899; Fleiuss, *Paginas de historia*, pp. 390-91; *Rio News*, July 22, 1889; Kidder and Fletcher, *op. cit.*, p. 212.

[12] "O centenario de Pedro II," *Rev. do Inst. Hist. e Geog. Bras.*, vol. 152, p. 540.

[13] Extrahido do diario escripto por S. M. o Imperador o Senhor D. Pedro II, entry for Dec. 31, 1861, Pedro d'Orléans Bragança Archives, A, CXXX, 6373.

[14] Fleiuss, *Paginas de historia*, pp. 392-95.

against him, but there seems to be no good reason for believing that Dom Pedro was ever disloyal to the woman whom he married without seeing her.[15]

His sister Francisca had in May, 1843, been married in Rio to the Prince of Joinville, son of King Louis Philippe, and she left not long afterwards for France, where she became greatly beloved for her beauty and charm. With the downfall of Louis Philippe in 1848, she was forced into exile.[16]

In the following year, a few months after Dom Pedro's marriage, the Princess Imperial, Januaria, became the wife of the Count of Aquila, brother of Dona Thereza. By the marriage contract, the Count became a Brazilian citizen and an admiral in the imperial squadron; and it was stipulated that, since Januaria would be heir to the throne if Dom Pedro had no children, she and her husband should live in Brazil.[17] But before the close of the year Dom Pedro had a disagreement with his brother-in-law, who asked and received permission for himself and the Princess Imperial to be absent from the Empire, and soon thereafter they left for Europe.[18]

By now, however, it was known that the Empress was soon to have a child, and on February 23, 1845, a son was born, who was named Affonso. Crowds of faithful subjects swarmed out to Boa Vista to offer congratulations, and the happy event was celebrated with the customary illuminations and festivities. On July 29 of the next year a daughter arrived, who was christened Isabel. Both parents were fond of children and they delighted in their two babies. But in June, 1847, Dom Affonso died, and their grief was great. The young father expressed his sense of bereavement in a touching sonnet, "Na Morte do meu Primogenito" ("Upon the Death of my First Born").[19] On July 13, 1847, a month after the death of the little boy, came another

---

[15] Suetonio, *O antigo regimen*, p. 168; Quesada, *op. cit.*, I, 172; Moniz, *op. cit.*, pp. 89-96.
[16] Moniz, *op. cit.*, pp. 30-31.   [17] *Ibid.*, p. 29.
[18] Pereira da Silva, *op. cit.*, I, 121, 126, 129.
[19] Teixeira, *op. cit.*, p. 81.

daughter, who was named Leopoldina in memory of her Austrian grandmother. The fourth, and last child, a son named Pedro, was born July 19, 1848. But the hopes raised in the parents by his birth were soon shattered, for this son likewise died in infancy, on January 9, 1850. Dom Pedro, who was now twenty-four, again marked his loss by a sonnet, "Na Morte do meu Segundo Filho," which reveals more intense feeling than the verses written after the death of the First Born. "Twice already I have suffered death," it begins, "for the father dies who sees his son is dead."[20] In the last stanza he epitomized the tragedy of his short life:

> On me has fallen the saddest of fates:
> Father and mother I lacked in tender infancy,
> And now are dead my little sons![21]

The chief residence of the imperial family was São Christovão Palace, which stood on an elevation with majestic Mount Tijuca as a background. It had been added to since the days of King João and was now a large, square structure, partly of two stories and partly of three, built around a court. At the level of the second flood a gallery ran around the enclosure, communicating with the principal rooms. It was in this gallery that Dom Pedro met the Regent Araujo Lima and Antonio Carlos de Andrada on July 22, 1840, the day when the crisis came over the majority question. The most impressive feature of the palace was the double grand staircase on the outside which led upward to the gallery. A description has survived of the interior of the building as it appeared in 1846. The floors of the more important rooms of the dwelling quarters were of fine inlaid native woods. Though the furniture was of French

---

[20] Duas vezes a morte hei ja soffrido,
Pois morre o pai que vê seu filho morto.
Ibid., p. 82.
[21] Coube-me o mais funesto dos destinos:
Vi-me sem Pai, sem Mãi, na infancia linda;
E morrem-me os meus filhos pequeninos!
Ibid.

design, some pieces were of fine local workmanship, wrought from Brazilian cabinet materials. In one of the salons was the side table on which Dom Pedro I had signed his abdication on April 7, 1831. Another room was given local atmosphere by jaguar-skin mats on the floor. The paintings on the walls of the apartments and corridors were religious in theme or concerned Portuguese or Brazilian history. When Prince Adalbert visited Rio in the early 1840's, in place of doors between connecting rooms, there were hangings of imperial green velvet, with motifs from the Bragança coat-of-arms—stars, spheres, and griffins—embroidered in gold.

Near the dwelling quarters were the imposing throne-room and the chapel. In the latter hung a large painting of São Pedro de Alcantara, the Emperor's spiritual patron.

A considerable space in the palace was given to educational interests. A museum, begun before the days of Dom Pedro II, contained collections of Brazilian minerals and birds, classical coins, objects from Herculaneum and Pompeii brought by Dona Thereza, ancient Peruvian pottery, and other interesting exhibits. Near by was Dom Pedro's scientific laboratory, and next to it was a little theatre, where the Emperor and his sisters had amused themselves in earlier years, and which was later used by his daughters and members of the court. But his favorite room had long been the library, to which were constantly added new volumes.[22]

The life of the Emperor was simple, in accordance with his natural inclinations as well as his training. Furthermore, he was by no means rich; his civil list was too small for the demands made upon it. Outside of those functions which convention demanded, there were practically no formal social gatherings at the palace.

For ordinary occasions Dom Pedro was plainly garbed. He adopted early a style of dress to which he clung for the rest of

[22] Ewbank, *op. cit.*, pp. 145-51.

his life—a black suit with frock coat, black cravat, and tall silk hat. On his breast was the diamond star of the Imperial Order of the Southern Cross and in the buttonhole of his lapel, the gold and diamond badge of the Austrian Order of the Golden Fleece. He would not wear white ties even for the most formal occasions, since, he declared, they made the wearers "look like servants who wait on table."[23]

Thanks to the watchful care of his guardians during childhood, by the time the Emperor was fully grown he had developed a sturdy constitution and rugged health and was able to put in a long, strenuous day. As is customary in the tropics, he rose early, at about six o'clock. After prayers in the palace chapel, he generally read the news from a collection of marked papers or press clippings prepared by his secretaries.[24] Items about the provinces he noted with particular care. After this he turned attention to his huge mail, containing petitions, complaints, compliments, political matters and almost countless requests for money and other special favors. The financial appeals of the really needy he never refused.[25] In addition to responses to such special appeals, each Saturday, in accordance with the national custom, alms from Dom Pedro and Dona Thereza were distributed at São Christovão to all who came to ask who were considered worthy.[26]

Breakfast was served at nine or ten, and dinner, the other main meal, usually at four. The daily fare of the imperial family was simple. Dom Pedro, who was rather indifferent to gastronomic pleasures, drank wine only on extraordinary occasions and, in general, ate rapidly and temperately. Elaborate course meals meant little to him, and he was said to be quite satisfied if served with *canja*, the favorite thick soup of the

---

[23] Mossé, *op. cit.*, p. 365; Ernesto Mattoso, *Causas de meu tempo*, p. 116; Frank Vincent, *Around and about South America*, p. 253.

[24] Large numbers of these clippings survive in the Pedro d'Orléans Bragança Archives, division A, portfolio CXXIV.

[25] Oliveira Lima, *O Imperio brazileiro*, p. 247.

[26] Mesquita Pimentel, *D. Pedro II*, p. 90.

country, and *goiabada,* the sweet made from the guava apple.[27] But he was particular about the quality of the dishes set before him, and more than once he sent complaints about tough meats and badly-prepared meals to the *mórdomo* of the Palace, who threatened to dismiss the culinary staff if the situation did not improve.[28] The smell of tobacco was offensive to Dom Pedro. He did not smoke himself and would not permit his subjects to do so in his presence.[29]

His mail being disposed of, the Emperor usually gave attention to government officials and others who had special business with him. Then, he went for a drive to visit schools and other public institutions.

One afternoon each week he held audience for any of his subjects who desired to come. This completely informal function, which he called "receiving the Brazilian family," took place in the gallery of the palace. Humble, barefooted Negroes who had favors to ask or complaints to make were received as readily as the highest aristocrats. To such receptions came delegations of Indians, whom the Emperor welcomed like a father, for he was much interested in his aboriginal subjects.[30] But while aiming to see that none of his people suffered wrong, he did not encourage idle charges or partisan attacks. Once, a caller complained that a member of the cabinet had done him an injustice. The Emperor replied somewhat sharply, "My ministers do not commit injustices," but he quickly resumed his kindly manner and promised that he himself would look into the matter. He did so, found that the man had been wronged, and promptly saw that amends were made.[31]

Once a week, usually on Saturdays, Dom Pedro met with

---

[27] Escragnolle Doria, "Reminiscencias do palacio de São Christovão," *Rev. do Inst. Hist. e Geog. Bras.,* vol. 152, p. 103; Lucy Ellen Paton, *Elizabeth Cary Agassiz,* p. 74.
[28] Pedro d'Orléans Bragança Archives, A, CLXXXI, 8176, Aug. 23, 1878.
[29] Teixeira, *op. cit.,* pp. 128, 244.
[30] Mossé, *op. cit.,* p. 349; Leo de Amaral, *O Imperador,* pp. 75-76.
[31] Mossé, *op. cit.,* p. 349; Fialho, *op. cit.,* p. 90.

his cabinet, in the City Palace during the early years, but later at Boa Vista. When Parliament was in session these meetings generally began at eight o'clock in the evening; at other times, at ten in the forenoon. About the time the cabinet moved to São Christovão a throne room was fitted up in it, after which the monthly receptions to the diplomatic corps were likewise held there. In addition to this gathering many other formal receptions took place in the City Palace or at Boa Vista, on gala days which, except New Year's Day, were anniversaries connected with the history of Brazil or with the imperial family.[32] On such occasions formal etiquette was rigorously observed and no one who failed to be dressed according to court rules was admitted. At such functions Dom Pedro wore the uniform of an admiral or marshal. Following the European custom, people did not speak to him until he had first spoken to them; and he always chose the theme for conversation.[33] During most of the reign Brazilian guests kissed the right hands of the Emperor and Empress at these galas, but after Dom Pedro visited Europe he abolished the beija mão as a ceremony.[34] Despite all of the formality, there was a degree of simplicity and democracy about even such elaborate gatherings, for attendant servants were not numerous, and there were no armed guards at the palace door.[35]

Elizabeth Cary Agassiz, who, with her scientist husband, called on the Empress, in May, 1865, shed pleasing light on private, informal audiences at the palace. One of the gentlemen-in-waiting showed them into a drawing-room where they took seats. Mrs. Agassiz writes:

> It opened into a long gallery and presently we heard some one coming down this entry in great haste walking very fast—as I supposed, an official of some kind to show us to the Empress. But it was the Emperor himself. . . . After about half an hour's chat he asked us to come in and see the Empress and himself, ushered

---

[32] "Dias de grande gala de D. Pedro II," Section of Manuscripts, Bibliotheca Nacional, Rio de Janeiro.
[33] *Ibid.*; Mossé, *op. cit.*, p. 367; Lamas, *op. cit.*, p. 287.
[34] Lamas, *op. cit.*, p. 283.　　[35] Quesada, *op. cit.*, I, 164.

us into a third drawing-room ("veels vithin veels"), where he went to the door and called his wife like any other mortal. In rolled a little lady with the sweetest possible expression, who seemed very kindly and cordial, who invited us to take seats, and, if I may so express myself in the presence of royalty, 'make ourselves generally at home.' Really if we had gone to make a sociable call on some friendly acquaintance at home, there could hardly have been more ease. This royal pair are so truly well bred that it is impossible to feel any embarrassment. Their simplicity and frankness are quite republican, though I am afraid we must admit that their high breeding partook more, perhaps, of the aristocratic element. There is something peculiarly lovable and lovely about the Empress. She looks so sympathetic and motherly. . . . After as long a call as we thought it discreet to make, we paid our parting respects. One thing about the Emperor's way of saying good-bye is very funny, and Agassiz says he supposes it is to save strangers the embarrassment of backing out of his presence. He shakes hands and then rushes out of the room, as if he were going to walk a mile in a minute on some errand of life or death. At first I thought that he had gone for something and would be back again; but it was the last we saw of him.[36]

In the early years of his reign Dom Pedro had more time free from official duties than he did later, and he liked most to spend it with books, in serious study, and in extensive general reading. He was fond of reading aloud and of having others read to him, a habit formed through the efforts of his tutor the Marquez de Itanháen. Though his voice was not as deep as was to be expected in a man of his large frame, it was pleasing, and he read well.[37]

Part of his free time Dom Pedro gave to his daughters, whom he deeply loved, and he enjoyed watching their growth and guiding their development. He oversaw their educations and personally instructed them, at one time or another, in many subjects. He devoted considerable time to teaching both of

[36] Paton, *op. cit.*, pp. 79-81.
[37] Braz do Amaral, "O Imperador e a proclamação da republica," *Rev. do Inst. Hist. e Geog. Bras.*, vol. 152, p. 456; Ewbank, *op. cit.*, 278-79.

them geography and history, and to Dona Isabel, his heir, he likewise gave lessons in government.[38]

The Emperor was fond of strolling for relaxation in the park of the residential palace. A little anecdote is told in connection with this habit. One day when taking his customary walk he suddenly turned backward in the path. To his chamberlain, who had been some distance in the rear, he explained that he had seen a man stealing cocoanuts in a tree ahead and was afraid that if the thief found he was observed he might be startled and fall from the tree and be hurt.[39] Thus, he was not always willing to let his subjects suffer the results of a guilty conscience.

When in the city, Dom Pedro liked also to saunter about the streets occasionally, carrying top coat and umbrella, and stopping now and then to sample the fruits in the shops and markets.

During much of his reign he continued horseback riding for exercise and recreation, and he also went for drives with Dona Thereza in a coach with six or eight horses or mules, accompanied by several cavalrymen. He liked rapid motion, and two of the dragoons preceded the carriage at full gallop, clearing the streets with blasts from their bugles. A favorite route lay along the coast to the west of the Capital, with the Botanical Gardens as destination. On such drives they were often greeted with vivas, which they always returned.[40]

Dom Pedro got much pleasure from the theatre and attended frequently. The sound of the trumpets and of his galloping team informed early arrivals that His Imperial Majesty had come. After his first trip to Europe in 1871, the Emperor gave up the clarions, but he dashed up to the theatre with

---

[38] Docs. II, 20, 25, 30, Section of Mss., Bibliotheca Nacional, Rio de Janeiro: Extrahido do diario escripto por S. M. o Imperador o Senhor D. Pedro II, Jan. 6, 1862, Pedro d'Orléans Bragança Archives, A, CXXX, 6373; Fialho, *op. cit.*, p. 93.

[39] Told to the writer by Lucia Furquim Lahmeyer, librarian of the Historical and Geographical Institute of Brazil, who knew the Emperor.

[40] Kidder and Fletcher, *op. cit.*, p. 234.

the same speed as before. When, in his later years, the weary sovereign dozed and nodded during the dramatic performance, Dona Thereza roused him with a touch of her fan.[41]

The Emperor also enjoyed the festivities and amusements at São Christovão—the amateur theatricals, and the various family anniversaries. In fact, he cared especially for simple, unconventional recreations. Such was a picnic breakfast served in honor of the imperial family at Juiz de Fóra in Minas Geraes in 1853, when a new post road was opened there. The picnic was held in what was later called the Forest of the Empress in honor of the event. Mrs. Louis Agassiz, who visited the spot twelve years later, thus describes the place and the sylvan meal:

> Surely a more stately banqueting-hall could scarcely be found. The throne was cut in the broad buttressed trunk of a huge figueira; the rustic table, built of rough stems, stood under the shadow of great palm-trees; and around was the tropical forest, tapestried with vines and embroidered with orchids. These were royal accompaniments, even though the whole entertainment was conducted with a simplicity in harmony with the scene. Neither gold nor silver nor glass was brought to vie with the beauties of nature; the drinking cups were made from the hollow stems of the wild bamboo tree, and all the service was of the same rustic description.[42]

Part of the warmer season was spent in the mountains near Rio de Janeiro. In 1847, Petropolis, situated about forty miles from the capital, in a high valley among the magnificent Organ Mountains, became the permanent summer residence of the imperial family, and soon also of the Brazilian aristocracy and the diplomatic corps. Dom Pedro was always glad when the time came to move to Petropolis, for here his life was less bound by conventions, and here he had more time to read and study. In Petropolis the days were tolerable and the nights cool, and there was comparative safety from yellow fever. Usually, the court moved up in November or December. The trip in the early days included a steamboat ride of about an hour among

[41] Quesada, *op. cit.*, II, 472.
[42] Louis Agassiz and Elizabeth Cary Agassiz, *A Journey in Brazil*, p. 77.

the picturesque islands of the Bay, as far as Mauá, then a coach ride of about two hours over a macadamized road, to a point in the mountains, from which the party were carried in litters, or sedan chairs, or walked the rest of the way. Later, a train connected Petropolis with Mauá,[43] and, finally, with Rio.

The summer palace, in design resembling an Italian villa and painted yellow and white in later years, was more modest than the homes of many Brazilian planters. Though some of the salons had inlaid floors and frescoed ceilings, in the 1880's the walls of the reception rooms were of white-finished plaster; the floors were covered with straw matting; and the plain furniture was cane-seated. But the building stood in a terraced hillside park filled with luxuriant trees and ever-blooming flowers.[44]

Even at Petropolis Dom Pedro followed a fairly definite routine similar to that in Rio. Because he enjoyed the morning freshness of the mountains, he rose at his usual time, about six o'clock, and for many years he took an early horseback ride, though gradually he abandoned the recreation. At a public bathing establishment a few blocks from the palace he had a cold bath every morning. Accompanied by his chamberlain, he generally walked to the place, with a carriage following, in case of a storm. After his return he read for a while, and then breakfasted with Dona Thereza, looked over his mail, and gave audience to those who wished to see him. Following that, he often visited the schools and hospitals of Petropolis. After a four-o'clock dinner, he generally went for a ride with the Empress or walked about the town or along the picturesque mountain trails. At times he was accompanied on these walks by the Empress and their daughters. On such strolls they habitually occupied the middle of the road, with two members of the imperial suite a short distance in the rear. Since their subjects did

---

[43] Autobiographie de la Comtesse d'Eu, Pedro d'Orléans Bragança Archives, A, CCIV, 9264; John Candler and William Burgess, *Narrative of a Recent Visit to Brazil*, p. 18.

[44] Quesada, *op. cit.*, II, 110-11; Vincent, *op. cit.*, p. 254; John Codman, *Ten Months in Brazil*, p. 118.

not wish to pass them, this practice slowed up vehicular travel in the little mountain city. The sovereigns often paused to give coins to the humble little children whom they met, and to greet friends, and at times they dropped in on neighbors, to chat and to look over their gardens.[45] In the greetings of Dom Pedro, says Pedro Lamas, whose father was Uruguayan minister to Brazil, there was a "certain majesty, which was peculiar to him." The Empress had a more unreserved and spontaneous friendliness.[46]

One diversion of Petropolis in which Dom Pedro often participated was to watch the trains come in from the capital. There were two daily, and he preferred that of the morning. Amidst the brightly-dressed country folk, the straw hats, white parasols, flowers, and fans of the crowd, he loomed, making a large spot of black with his tall hat and frock coat, and the umbrella under his arm. In the gay environment he appeared somewhat austere, but he mingled freely with the crowd, returned all greetings, and chatted with the bystanders here and there.[47]

Social life was simple in the summer capital. Frequently Dona Thereza was at home to callers from five to seven in the afternoon. Contrary to custom in European royal circles, she and Dom Pedro stood while receiving their guests.[48] Dona Isabel and Dona Leopoldina, after they were grown, were usually at home to friends on Sunday afternoons. They and their parents often attended the weekly dances at the Bragança Hotel in Petropolis, generally arriving at ten and leaving at midnight. But normally the Emperor retired at nine o'clock while at Petropolis.[49]

[45] Mossé, *op. cit.*, pp. 364-65; Lamas, *op. cit.*, pp. 55-56.
[46] *Op. cit.*, p. 56; Arrojada Lisboa, "O Imperador em Petropolis," *Rev. do Inst. Hist. e Geog. Bras.*, vol. 152, pp. 167-68.
[47] Lisboa, "O Imperador em Petropolis," *Rev. do Inst. Hist. e Geog. Bras.*, vol. 152, p. 168.
[48] Quesada, *op. cit.*, I, 111.
[49] Lisboa, "O Imperador em Petropolis," *Rev. do Inst. Hist. e Geog.*, vol. 152, p. 168.

Every Saturday Dom Pedro went down to Rio to preside over cabinet meetings, and spent the night there. At about four o'clock the next morning he left for Petropolis, which, after railroad connections were made, he reached about eight. Two hours later he could be found with his family attending mass in one of the local churches.[50]

In late April or early May the family moved back to Rio de Janeiro, in time for the opening of Parliament, and to a busier life.

[50] *Ibid.;* Webb to Seward, no. 8, January 23, 1862, Dept. of State, Despatches, Brazil.

VI

TWENTY-FIVE YEARS OF FOREIGN TROUBLES

WHILE the young Emperor was experiencing domestic joys and sorrows he was also much occupied by disputes with other nations. His training in history and his habitual wide reading of periodicals and the press made him unusually intelligent on international affairs, for the memory which had won praise from his instructors proved to be truly encyclopedic. In all foreign relations touching Brazil, he was, naturally, sensitive and alert, since he was deeply fond of his native land and felt great responsibility for it. Was he not the "perpetual defender" of Brazil? And had he not sworn to maintain the "integrity and indivisibility" of the Empire? Therefore he early adopted the policy of following the details of foreign relations through reading all diplomatic correspondence on important questions.[1] Though opposed to militaristic aggression, he was keen about protecting the rights of the nation and about maintaining its dignity and honor. His was a strong foreign policy, easily misunderstood by other governments.

Long before he came to the throne difficulties had arisen with Great Britain, partly through heritage from Portugal, where British influence was the result of a very ancient, but unequal, alliance. While the Portuguese flag flew over Brazil Great Britain exercised there a position of economic and political preëminence, and after the Empire was established the British authorities were loath to give it up.[2] For more than twenty

---
[1] Quesada, *op. cit.*, II, 472.
[2] Oliveira Lima, *O Imperio brazileiro*, p. 208; Manchester, *British Preëminence in Brazil*, pp. 1-158.

years after Dom Pedro II assumed control Great Britain struggled to maintain her advantage. During this time British officers repeatedly hurt Brazilian sensibilities by the patronizing or arrogant tone of their communications. No one felt these insults more deeply than did the young Emperor.

For ten years the African slave trade was a standing cause for friction between the two countries. Great Britain had closed her territory to the traffic and labored to get other nations to do likewise. She was moved partly by regard for the rights of the black man, partly by the desire to rid herself of the serious competition caused by unlimited cheap slave labor in other countries. In 1826, the British government had secured recognition of Brazilian independence by various states, including Portugal. In return, the Brazilian authorities had signed a treaty pledging abolition of the African slave trade. The treaty was to go into effect within three years after ratification and was to run for fifteen years. Unfortunately, the arrangement conflicted with the Brazilian view that economic welfare depended upon importation from Africa, since only thus could cheap labor be secured. Hence, it caused bitter resentment.[3]

Under the agreement, the trade should have ended by March 13, 1830. Instead, importation increased. The regency tried honestly to stamp it out, through passing a law in November, 1831, providing for punishment of all who engaged in the traffic, and for the immediate freedom of Negroes brought from Africa. But the turbulence and general demoralization which long existed in Brazil made the enforcement of the law almost impossible.

In March, 1845, the treaty of 1826 expired, for Brazil had refused to renew it. The British government now turned to the first article of the agreement, which gave it the right to treat as pirates all Brazilian subjects found upon the high seas engaged in the traffic. On August 8, 1845, Parliament passed the Aber-

[3] Manchester, *British Preëminence in Brazil*, pp. 187-219. It was based upon treaties signed under coercion by João in 1817 and 1818.—*Ibid.*, pp. 160-85.

deen Act which provided that all captures should be tried by British admiralty, or vice-admiralty, courts, instead of by an Anglo-Brazilian mixed commission as stipulated in the treaty of 1826.[4]

This slight upon Brazilian sovereignty and independence raised a storm of indignation throughout the Empire. Dom Pedro II, not yet twenty years of age, felt the situation keenly. British seizures of Brazilian slavers began; vessels that resisted were destroyed. The imperial government, denying the British contention that Article 1 of the treaty of 1826 was perpetual, repeatedly protested, and entered claims for damages. Britain, in reply, offered to repeal the Aberdeen Act if Brazil would sign a new treaty conceding British right of visit and search. Brazil in turn demanded that any such agreement include a provision that indemnities be paid for seizures. But to this Britain would not agree.[5]

Not only did seizures under the Aberdeen Act continue, but, as Joaquim Nabuco put it, the British legation in Rio assumed the rôle of an anti-slavery society.[6] Dom Pedro so disliked the slave trade that he never conferred a title of nobility upon any one who engaged in it,[7] but national pride at first made yielding to pressure unthinkable for him. With the continuance of internal rebellion, it would have been difficult to find troops to police the coast, but for some years he seems not to have tried to stop the traffic.[8] African importations increased rapidly. In 1846, they numbered 19,453; in 1847, they jumped to 50,000. During the next two years they mounted still higher. The British government retaliated in 1850 by ordering cruisers to enter Brazilian harbors and seize vessels fitted out for the slave trade, and this was done for more than a year.[9] As far as Brazil was concerned, Britannia certainly ruled the waves.

[4] *Ibid.*, pp. 244-50.   [5] *Ibid.*, pp. 251, 254-55.
[6] Nabuco, *op. cit.*, I, 241. *Notes on Brazilian Questions*, by W. D. Christie, the British minister, presents the British viewpoint.
[7] Mattoso, *op. cit.*, p. 60.   [8] Mossé, *op. cit.*, pp. 110-12.
[9] Manchester, *British Preëminence in Brazil*, p. 256.

Continued resistance was more than futile; it was embarrassing to the imperial government, for, by permitting the slave trade to go on, the Empire was not only violating a definite treaty with England but was ignoring one of its own laws. Furthermore, the national conscience was asserting itself, and an increasing number of Brazilians took the attitude that the traffic was disgraceful. Obviously, the best way to end British seizure of slavers was to stop the importation of Africans. By 1848, internal disorders of the Empire had abated somewhat, making policing of the coast more possible. In this year a bill declaring the traffic piracy and punishable as such was introduced into Parliament. In 1850, it became a law and was so strictly enforced that within the next few years the trans-Atlantic trade in Negroes virtually ended.[10]

Thus the Aberdeen Act became inoperative. But Brazilian resentment towards it continued long, and tended to increase irritation over later difficulties. Serious ones developed with England soon after W. D. Christie came to Rio as British minister in 1860. Christie was a poor choice for the position, for he had no understanding of the Latin temperament, was hostile to Brazil from the start, and favored a policy of threats and coercion. When he arrived, a deadlock existed in the claims commission which was handling the slave trade cases.[11] New trouble soon developed, through the wrecking of a British vessel, the "Prince of Wales," on a lonely part of the coast of Rio Grande do Sul in June, 1861. The British consul in the region believed, apparently with reason, that Rio Grandenses had stolen the cargo and murdered some of the victims of the accident; and he considered the investigation made by local authorities inadequate. A British gunboat was sent to the scene of the trouble, but the president of the province refused to let its

[10] Nabuco, *op. cit.*, I, 225; Mossé, *op. cit.*, 114-15. The movement against it was perhaps somewhat accelerated by the fact that yellow fever, before unknown in the country, broke out in Brazil in 1849, and was believed by some to have been brought in by slavers.—Pereira da Silva, *op. cit.*, I, 214.

[11] Manchester, *British Preëminence in Brazil*, pp. 274-76.

captain take part in the investigation.[12] Though the Brazilian government promised Christie to bring the guilty to justice, at the end of a year none of those known to have been implicated had been prosecuted. Christie was impatient over the delay and urged his government to bring to bear all possible pressure upon the imperial authorities.[13]

At this point came a more serious incident. Three men from the British vessel "Forte," at the time in the harbor at Rio, had, according to Christie, been arrested without cause by a sentry, while on their way back from a trip to Mount Tijuca, and had been roughly handled and thrown into prison. The Brazilian authorities charged that the Britishers had been drunk and disorderly and had attacked the sentry without provocation. They were not in uniform at the time of arrest, but as soon as it was known that they belonged to the British navy they were ordered released. Accepting Christie's version of the incident, Sir John Russell demanded punishment of the sentry and of the ensign in charge of the post, censure of the chief-of-police of Rio and of the local prison officials for their treatment of the British subjects, and an apology from the imperial government. In addition, he called for restitution and damages in the case of the "Prince of Wales," but he was willing to arbitrate the amount to be paid. He instructed Christie to resort to reprisals in case the Brazilian government refused to meet the demands.[14]

The Marquez de Abrantes, Brazilian foreign minister, wishing to take the matter out of the hands of Christie, tried to shift the discussion to the Brazilian legation in London, but Christie demanded that satisfaction be given in Rio de Janeiro. Abrantes thereupon refused to comply, and Christie ordered reprisals. On December 31, 1862, ships from the British navy blockaded Rio de Janeiro and held in the harbor five Brazilian coastal vessels.[15]

[12] Pereira da Silva, *op. cit.*, I, 305-8; Serrano, *op. cit.*, p. 376.
[13] Manchester, *British Preëminence in Brazil*, p. 278.
[14] *Ibid.*, p. 279; Pereira da Silva, *op. cit.*, I, 308-10.
[15] Pereira da Silva, *op. cit.*, I, 310-12.

At once, the Brazilians were roused by fear and indignation. The capital was in an uproar and the British consulate and legation were threatened by mobs. Troops were called out to help maintain order. A crowd of people carrying the national flag started for São Christovão. On the road they met Dom Pedro, whom they conducted to the City Palace, where he had called a meeting of the ministry. From one of the front windows of the building he addressed the excited throng in the street below. "Calm yourselves, calm yourselves, senhores," he is reported to have said. "You may trust my government and be assured that without honor I do not wish to be Emperor"[16]. . . . "I wish, above all, to show that in danger I am the equal of any other Brazilian citizen!" His words were greeted with wild applause.[17]

Dom Pedro watched the situation with anxious care. He favored firmness, since the honor of the Empire must be upheld, but he was against resort to war. The majority of his cabinet agreed with him. The British, however, had the whip hand, and delay would only make the situation worse for Brazil. Therefore, on January 5, 1863, the imperial government agreed to pay the damages demanded in connection with the "Prince of Wales" case and to arbitrate the "Forte" question. The blockade was then lifted, and the five vessels freed.[18] But the Emperor felt deeply the humiliation suffered at British hands, and was eager to make Brazil respected abroad.[19] In this, he was backed strongly by his cabinet. Accordingly, when, on February 23, the Brazilian minister in London, Carvalho Moreira, paid to Russell the damages for the "Prince of Wales," he accompanied the remittance with an emphatic protest against the seizure of the five vessels and a reservation of the Brazilian right to ask damages for it. Later, he demanded expression of

---

[16] Mattoso, *op. cit.*, p. 61.   [17] Fialho, *op. cit.*, p. 38.
[18] Manchester, *British Preëminence in Brazil*, p. 280.
[19] Notes of Dom Pedro II to the Marquez de Abrantes, Pedro d'Orléans Bragança Archives, A, CXXXIII, 6507.

regret and acknowledgment of the right to compensation for the seizure, the amount of which was to be decided by arbitration. The British government refused to meet this demand, and in June, 1863, Brazil broke off diplomatic relations.[20]

Almost simultaneously, King Leopold of Belgium, who had agreed to arbitrate in the "Forte" dispute, rendered a decision that no offence had been premeditated or intended to the British navy. Later, Great Britain signified willingness to apologize for the blockade of Rio and the seizure of the five Brazilian vessels, but refused to pay damages. This did not satisfy the imperial government, so the apology was not tendered, and diplomatic relations remained severed.[21]

These experiences made the nation realize its helplessness before a strong military power, and a popular subscription for the modernization of the navy was started at once. To it the Emperor, Empress, and princesses each gave a fifth of their annual incomes. A large sum was in hand within six months, and the improvement of the military equipment of the country began.[22]

During the latest crisis with Great Britain, relations also became somewhat strained with the United States of America, now engaged in its terrible civil war. The main subject of contention was Brazil's recognition of the belligerency of the Confederate States through its decree of neutrality, but all differences were aggravated by the man whom the Lincoln government, through Secretary Seward's influence, sent as minister to Brazil. This was James Watson Webb, vain, tactless, impetuous, and astonishingly lacking in common sense. But, though Webb's absurdities kept feelings stirred up between the two countries, there was never any danger of serious trouble as a result.[23] To-

---

[20] Pedro d'Orléans Bragança Archives, A, CXXXIII, 6508; Pereira da Silva, *op. cit.*, I, 312-14.

[21] Manchester, *British Preëminence in Brazil*, p. 281.

[22] Fialho, *op. cit.*, pp. 39-40.

[23] Lawrence F. Hill, *Diplomatic Relations between the United States and Brazil*, pp. 146-58.

wards the close of the civil strife Dom Pedro personally expressed to the American minister the hope that the North would prevail;[24] and after the war ended the imperial government, without waiting for European precedent, promptly repealed the decree of neutrality.[25]

In the Plata basin, however, trouble was developing which proved a calamity to the Empire and the Emperor. For many years Brazil was believed by its neighbors to be pursuing a policy not unlike that which it so fiercely resented on the part of Great Britain. Precedent for meddling in Plata affairs was set, it will be recalled, by Dom Pedro's grandmother, Queen Carlota Joaquina. But during the troubled years of the regency very little attention was paid to developments in the region, even though disturbances in Rio Grande do Sul were aggravated by the ambitious aggressiveness of Rosas, dictator of Buenos Aires, towards Paraguay and Uruguay. In the interest of national security, the regency merely tried to counterbalance Rosas's influence by supporting these two republics.

Soon after Dom Pedro's accession this policy was strengthened.[26] Brazil was the first country to recognize the government of Carlos Antonio López of Paraguay,[27] a friendly gesture much appreciated by the new dictator. In 1844, the Marquez de Abrantes was sent to Europe to call attention to the importance of preserving Uruguayan independence and establishing peace and order in the Plata basin. At the time Rosas was laying siege to Montevideo, Uruguay's capital, aided by the Blancos, the political "outs" of the country. Somewhat later, France and England, to secure redress of grievances from Rosas, blockaded Buenos Aires, but with no definite effect upon the general situation.[28]

---

[24] Webb to Seward, no. 102, Nov. 14, 1864, Dept. of State, Despatches, Brazil.
[25] Hill, *op. cit.*, p. 158.
[26] Soares do Souza to Pimenta Bueno, Oct. 16, 1843, Pedro d'Orléans Bragança Archives, A, CVI, 5121.
[27] Carlos Antonio López to Dom Pedro II, Oct. 8, 1844, Pedro d'Orléans Bragança Archives, A, CVII, 5192. [28] Mossé, *op. cit.*, pp. 79-82.

At this time—in the late 1840's—Brazil was too weak from internal disturbances to risk a trial of strength with Rosas, but it tried to keep Montevideo from falling into the Dictator's hands. Rosas, for his part, wished to force Montevideo to surrender, but not at the price of a break with the strongest country on the continent.[29] At the turn of the decade, however, various influences served to make the Empire take a bolder stand. By now, practically the whole country was at peace; Brazilian financial interests in Uruguay apparently began to work for intervention;[30] and Andrés Lamas, minister of Uruguay at Rio, strongly urged it. This last was directly influential upon the youthful Dom Pedro, and he signified willingness to take up arms against the tyrant of the Plata.[31]

Soon an alliance against Rosas and the Blancos was formed between Brazil, Paraguay, the Colorado government at Montevideo, and the governors of the Argentine provinces of Corrientes and Entre Ríos. The allied troops, commanded by General Urquiza, governor of Entre Ríos, on February 3, 1852, decisively defeated Rosas, who went into permanent exile. The aid given by Brazil in ousting the common enemy produced for a time in the Plata basin a more cordial attitude towards the Empire. But this intervention of Brazil tempted it to further steps in the same general direction.

In fact, very shortly after the imperial government signed the alliance against Rosas it took advantage of Uruguay's weakness and financial need to gain from it a very favorable treaty settling a boundary dispute. A little later, by another treaty, Brazil granted a financial loan to Uruguay, guaranteed chiefly by customs income from the country. Thereafter it was the definite policy of Dom Pedro and his ministry to work for governmental stability in Uruguay, in the interest of a secure south-

---

[29] Juan Manuel de Rosas to Dom Pedro II, Pedro d'Orléans Bragança Archives, A, CXIII, 5574.

[30] J. F. Normano, *Brazil: a Study of Economic Types*, p. 92; Alberto de Faría, *Ireneô Evangelista de Souza, Barão e Visconde de Mauá*, pp. 312-13.

[31] Lamas, *op. cit.*, pp. 108-9.

ern frontier, and of safety for Brazilian subjects who had settled in Uruguay.[32] Such a policy was likely to be abused by his own subjects and was certain to be misinterpreted by his neighbors. Brazil became a "peril" to the Plata countries, "the Minotaur of the South American continent," always ready to devour adjoining territory and to meddle, with ambitious aims, in the internal disputes of its neighbors.[33] The motives and methods of the Empire were very similar—though on a smaller scale—to those later pursued by the United States of America in the Caribbean area, which roused fear of the "Yankee peril" and indignation towards the "Colossus of the North."

In 1854, Flores, a Colorado leader, got control in Montevideo and, anxious to maintain it, asked Brazil for military aid. Consequently, the Empire made an agreement whereby it sent 4,000 troops, known as an "auxiliary army," to the support of Flores. Apparently at about the same time Flores asked that Brazilian forces be sent to occupy Montevideo; but to this Dom Pedro was strongly opposed, and occupation did not take place.[34] However, the granting of the auxiliary army, though disinterested, roused the suspicions of General Urquiza, now political head in the Plata provinces, and, in a letter of July 10, 1855, he protested against the Brazilian policy. The Emperor answered it himself. Brazil's sole aim with reference to the states on its borders, wrote Dom Pedro, was to help secure for them peace and institutional stability. It was, furthermore, his most earnest desire, he said, to make closer the relations happily existing between the Empire and the Argentine Confederation, for which, as well as for all other American peoples, he most ardently desired peace and prosperity.[35] The auxiliary army,

---

[32] Nabuco, *op. cit.*, II, 151-52.

[33] Antonio Pereira Pinto, *Politica tradicional: intervanções do Brasil no Rio da Prata*, p. 29.

[34] Extrahido do diario escripto por S. M. o Imperador o Senhor D. Pedro II, Jan. 1, 1862, Pedro d'Orléans Bragança Archives, A, CXXX, 6373.

[35] Dom Pedro II to President Urquiza, Oct. 26, 1855, Pedro d'Orléans Bragança Archives, A, CXXII, 6060.

which had done very little to better conditions in Uruguay, was withdrawn the next year. In January, 1859, Brazil signed with the Argentine a treaty guaranteeing the neurality of Uruguay.[36] But political turbulence continued in Uruguay, where one of the factions asked aid of Brazil, and Argentine suspicions persisted.[37]

By the early 1860's, the imperial government had become much disturbed over the situation of Brazilian nationals living in Uruguay, many of whom had been robbed, and some murdered, in that anarchic area. Uruguayan political refugees in Rio Grande do Sul likewise gave trouble. The Blancos, now in control in Montevideo, charged in return that *caudillos* (military chieftains) from Rio Grande do Sul meddled in Uruguayan politics. This was doubtless true, for, though the imperial government tried to preserve neutrality towards the civil war raging between the Colorados and Blancos, it was hard to do so because of the distance from the seat of discord and the lack of coöperation from Rio Grande do Sul. Some of the worst trouble-makers in that province had been leaders in the ten-years' war for independence.[38] One of these was General Felippe Netto, who had an impressive army of cowboys. Would these cattle barons remain even nominally loyal if their grievances were ignored by the imperial government?

Recent developments in Paraguay made the situation more dangerous. Carlos Antonio López was dead and had been succeeded by his son, Francisco Solano, vain, stupid, passionate, and ambitious, who had built up the strongest army in South America, apparently with imperialistic aims. López was suspicious of both Argentina and Brazil, with which he had boundary disputes. Toward Brazil he was especially hostile, partly through jealousy, and was definitely expecting war with it. The Blanco

---

[36] Pinto da Rocha, "A politica brasileira no Prata até a guerra contra Rosas," *Rev. do Inst. Hist. e Geog. Bras.*, tomo especial (1917), Pt. V, p. 614.

[37] José Maria da Silva Paranhos to J. J. de Urquiza, April 19, 1859, Pedro d'Orléans Bragança Archives, A, CXXVII, 6265.

[38] P. H. Box, *The Origins of the Paraguayan War*, I, 107-18.

government in Montevideo, on the other hand, was more unfriendly towards Argentina, which was harboring Flores, leader of the Colorados, and was trying to secure aid from López in war against Argentina. López, while not ready to coöperate thus with the Blancos, became increasingly hostile towards Argentina and Brazil. The fact that in April, 1863, Flores landed in Uruguay and was joined by Brazilians from both sides of the border made the situation in the Plata basin even more serious.

Unfortunately for future events, the attitude of the Brazilian government, formerly patient towards the Uruguayan question, changed early in 1864. The influence of the cattle barons on the southern frontier, now very restive, was largely responsible for this. After Flores returned to Uruguay, General Felippe Netto sent one thousand of his cowboys to the Uruguayan border. His object was not clear to the Brazilian ministry. Late in 1863, Netto went to Rio de Janeiro, as representative of the aggrieved ranchers, to agitate for settlement with Uruguay. In the capital he entertained lavishly, including various members of Parliament and other prominent men among his guests.[39]

When Parliament met on January 1, 1864, the Emperor read from the throne an address insisting that Brazilian rights be maintained but favoring preservation of neutrality towards troubles in the Plata region. The report of the Minister of Foreign Affairs, the Marquez de Abrantes, made critical reference to the fact that Brazilians were aiding the cause of Uruguayan rebels.[40] In the recent elections, however, the Liberals had won, and the lower house was now dominated by a group of young, brilliant, and impetuous men, comparable in their attitude to the "War Hawks" of early United States history. Two weeks after the opening of Parliament a new Liberal cabinet was formed, which was headed by the energetic Zach-

---

[39] *Ibid.*, pp. 29-69, 113-18, 155-70; Pereira da Silva, *op. cit.*, II, 4, 7-8.
[40] Box, *op. cit.*, I, 120.

arias de Góes. From the lower house came fiery speeches demanding effective action against the wrongs suffered by Brazilian subjects in Uruguay. When, in the middle of March, the Minister of Marine emphasized the necessity for a strong navy, in view of conditions in the south, he was heard with much sympathy. Meanwhile, behind the scenes, General Netto carried on propaganda calling for the punishment of Uruguay, and the demands were reflected in many of the newspapers. Apparently Visconde de Mauá, a Brazilian financier who had a powerful bank in Montevideo, also exerted pressure. The speeches in Parliament soon showed that members of both political parties favored intervention.[41]

The Zacharias ministry seems to have yielded almost at once to this jingoistic clamor, and before long the Emperor gave way. As constitutional defender of Brazil, Dom Pedro was hit in a tender spot by the charges that his subjects were suffering outrages. Here was an appeal to his sense of duty. Furthermore, the recent humiliation suffered from Great Britain tended to make him, as well as the nation, more impatient and bellicose towards Uruguay. Wounded national prestige could be somewhat healed through a "strong" policy towards the troublesome little neighbor to the south.[42]

The imperial ministry decided to make new demands on the Blanco government at Montevideo, accompanied by a threat of force. These were to be presented by a special envoy. The leader of the faction of moderate Liberals, José Antonio Saraiva, wise, honorable, and open-minded, was chosen for the task. In connection with his mission, troops were ordered to the southern frontier and a strong squadron was sent to the Uruguayan coast. Saraiva's detailed instructions included demands for punishment of the chief offenders, payment of damages for property losses, and guarantees against further wrongs to Brazilian residents. He was also to explain to Blanco authorities that the troops on

[41] *Ibid.*, I, 120-21; Normano, *op. cit.*, p. 92.
[42] Nabuco, *op. cit.*, II, 165-66, 180, 184.

the southern frontier were to help prevent Brazilian aid to Flores, and also—in case the government at Montevideo was unable or unwilling to do so—to protect the lives, honor, and property of the Brazilians.[43]

When Saraiva arrived at the Uruguayan capital, the government there was headed by a new chieftain, Aguirre, a weak tool of the Blanco element, which was now trusting to the armies of López of Paraguay. The Envoy realized that the situation was loaded with dynamite, which could be easily set off by blunt presentation of the Brazilian demands. For Brazil the outcome of war was by no means certain, since the Empire was not trusted by any of the countries of the Plata basin. Therefore, Saraiva ignored his instructions and presented only the first part of the demands, and he did this with studied tact, making no allusion to the Brazilian troops. But, attached to his note was a memorandum on the claims for damages which had been accumulating since 1852. The Uruguayan foreign minister replied by counter-charges and counter-claims, but Saraiva maintained a pacific attitude and decided to try to end the factional strife in Uruguay before pressing further the demands made in his instructions.[44]

Believing that Argentine coöperation was necessary to success, he wrote home for and received authority to try pacific methods. The Argentine government likewise had claims against Uruguay, and with it Saraiva soon came to an agreement for joint efforts to end, by diplomacy, the civil conflict in the little country. To disarm suspicion of aggressive motives, Thornton, the British minister in Buenos Aires, was asked to coöperate with Saraiva and Elizalde, the Argentine envoy. The three diplomats conferred with Aguirre, the Blanco leader, and subsequently with other Uruguayan leaders. But their efforts to secure internal peace for Uruguay finally proved useless, largely

---

[43] José Antonio Saraiva, *Correspondencia e documentos*, p. 3; Box, *op. cit.*, I, 123-24.

[44] Box, *op. cit.*, I, 130-32.

owing to the weakness and indirection of Aguirre, who was dominated by the Blanco "die-hards."[45]

With hope gone for peace in Uruguay through negotiations, Saraiva tried to get President Mitre of Argentina to agree to Brazilian-Argentine joint intervention to force the combatants to lay down arms, to insure freedom and honesty of elections, and to support those who were elected. Because of political troubles at home, the Mitre government would not undertake to coöperate in this, but it consented to independent Brazilian action.

Saraiva thereupon asked for new instructions from his government. The Zacharias ministry, which had been under constant fire from the jingoes in the chamber of deputies for countenancing the pacific activities of the envoy, instructed Saraiva to present an ultimatum to the Blanco government. He did so on August 4, 1864, giving the Montevideo authorities six days in which to accede to the terms stated in the note of the preceding May, and informed it that if the terms were not complied with the Brazilian squadron and the troops on the frontier would be ordered to seek reprisals for any future wrongs done to subjects of the Empire. The Uruguayan foreign secretary now proposed arbitration of the questions at issue, but the Brazilian authorities doubted the sincerity of the suggestion, which they also considered impracticable. Therefore, imperial forces were ordered to act in support of Flores, the leader of the Colorados. "The diplomats," as one writer put it, "had thrown the reins to the soldiers and sailors."[46] Late in August a Brazilian gunboat fired upon a Blanco war vessel, and on September 14 the imperial army began to cross into Uruguay.[47]

Shortly before this land movement took place, there arrived in Rio de Janeiro two young men who were soon to be Dom Pedro's sons-in-law, and one of them was to play an important

[45] *Ibid.*, I, 134-45; Nabuco, *op. cit.*, II, 172-75.
[46] Box, *op. cit.*, I, 152.
[47] *Ibid.*, I, 150-51; Nabuco, *op. cit.*, II, 180, 185-86.

part in the coming war. By now, Dona Isabel was a little past eighteen and Dona Leopoldina, a year younger. They were fine young women of excellent education and high ideals of character. Both were blondes, like their father, and were attractive in appearance. Remembering his own bitter matrimonial disappointment, Dom Pedro had decided to let his daughters see in advance the men whom he had in mind as husbands for them. Consequently, upon his invitation Prince Louis Augustus, Duke of Saxe-Coburg-Gotha, aged nineteen, and Prince Louis Gaston d'Orléans, Comte d'Eu, aged twenty-two, reached Rio on September 2, 1864. They were grandsons of the exiled King Louis Philippe of France, and were well known to Princess Francisca, who had suggested them as husbands for her nieces. The suitors lived in the City Palace, but visited at Boa Vista every day, and Dom Pedro as well as his daughters found them congenial.[48] The father's plans went slightly awry, however. Perhaps influenced by his sister, he had intended Prince Louis Augustus as husband for his elder daughter, and Prince Louis Gaston, for his younger one. But, wrote Dona Isabel many years later, "God and our hearts decided otherwise."[49] Dom Pedro, wishing the happiness of his children, raised no objections. Therefore, on October 15, 1864, the Princess Imperial was married to the Comte, and two months later his cousin became the husband of Dona Leopoldina. The bridegrooms were men of education and character, and both marriages seem to have been happy. Certainly that of Dona Isabel and Prince Gaston—as he was called—was blessed with romantic love. The marriage contract stipulated that, except with the consent of the government for absence, the heiress and her husband must reside in Brazil. The first such permission was secured by them for a honeymoon trip to Europe, which the Princess had never seen.

[48] Alberto Rangel, *Gastão de Orléans, o ultimo Conde d'Eu*, pp. 53-56, 91-96; W. Sloane Kennedy, *Henry W. Longfellow*, pp. 92-94.

[49] Autobiographie de la Comtesse d'Eu, Pedro d'Orléans Bragança Archives, A, CCIV, 9264.

DOM PEDRO II IN MIDDLE AGE
From a painting at the Château d'Eu

DONA THEREZA IN MIDDLE AGE
From a painting at the Château d'Eu

PRINCESS ISABEL
From a painting by Henner, 1881,
at the Château d'Eu

PRINCE GASTON D'ORLÉANS, COMTE D'EU
From a painting by Jaquemart
at the Château d'Eu

Meanwhile, things were going badly in the Plata basin. The Aguirre government, having cast aside the opportunity for internal and external peace, turned again to López of Paraguay. The Blancos, by working on the Dictator's fears of Argentina and Brazil, gained his support. Twice in August, 1864, the López government protested to the Brazilian minister in Asunción against the threatened imperial invasion of Uruguay. A note of the 30th declared that Paraguay could not consent to "the occupation either temporary or permanent by Brazilian forces of the territory of the Republic of Uruguay." Such occupation, it stated, was an attack upon the balance of power of the Plata states, which was the guarantee of the security, peace, and prosperity of Paraguay. The communication concluded: "The government protests in the most solemn manner against such an act, disclaiming at once all responsibility for the ultimate consequences of the present declaration."[50]

Two weeks later, as already stated, Brazilian occupation of Uruguay began. On November 12, López seized, north of Asunción, the Brazilian steamboat "Marquez de Olinda," which was making one of its regular trips up the Paraguay River to Matto Grosso with the new president of the province aboard. The next day the Brazilian minister in Asunción received a note from the Paraguayan minister of foreign affairs declaring diplomatic relations severed between the two countries and the Paraguay River closed to all Brazilian vessels. Late the next month, without the formality of declaring war, López sent 6,000 troops north and occupied Matto Grosso.[51]

He was anxious to strike at Rio Grande do Sul likewise, and, therefore, in a note of January 14, 1865, he asked permission of the Buenos Aires government to send troops across the Argentine province of Corrientes, which separated Paraguay from Brazil at the southeast. The request was at once refused by Mitre, for he and the Argentine nation greatly desired to remain

---

[50] Box, *op. cit.*, II, 212-13; Cecilio Báez, *Resumen de la historia del Paraguay*, pp. 135-37.   [51] Box, *op. cit.*, II, 218-19.

neutral. On March 18 an extraordinary, hand-picked congress called by López authorized continuance of the war which he had begun against Brazil and also declared war against Argentina. Shortly afterwards Paraguayan troops invaded Corrientes.[52]

Argentina and Brazil signed, on May 1, a treaty of alliance for prosecution of the war against Paraguay; and General Flores, who, aided by Brazilian troops, had got control of Montevideo, was obliged to assent to it. The agreement, which was promptly ratified, indicated that the war was directed not against the Paraguayan nation, but against its Dictator, and it pledged the allies not to lay down arms until the existing authorities of Paraguay—meaning López—should have been overthrown. The allies also agreed to respect the "independence, sovereignty, and territorial integrity" of Paraguay, which country, however, if defeated, was to be required to pay the whole cost of the war and to be completely disarmed. The future boundaries of Paraguay were tentatively agreed upon to the mutual satisfaction of Brazil and Argentina, each acquiescing in the extreme claims of the other in the disputed areas. It was a drastic arrangement which would have deprived Paraguay of about two-thirds of the territory claimed by her. Indeed, the Argentine representatives wished to leave the way open for future annexation of the remainder of the country. To this Dom Pedro, who had made a careful study of the draft of the treaty, was opposed, though he seems to have acquiesced in the specific Argentine claims.[53] But apparently Flores was insistent that the pledge regarding Paraguayan independence, sovereignty, and territorial integrity be included in the treaty.[54]

Upon the Brazilian Empire fell the brunt of the conflict with Paraguay, for Uruguay was small and demoralized, and in

[52] *Ibid.*, 260-63; Báez, *op. cit.*, p. 138.
[53] "Questão do Paraguay" (May 12, 1865), Pedro d'Orléans Bragança Archives, A, CXXXVI, 6651; Nabuco, *op. cit.*, II, 417-22.
[54] Box, *op. cit.*, II, 270-71.

Argentina, which was also torn by factional strife, there was, contrary to Brazilian expectations, a strong anti-war sentiment. Uruguay's aid was largely nominal, and the troops sent by Argentina were few in proportion to her population. Neither country had a navy. Though Brazil, owing to her friction with England, had strengthened her fleet, her peacetime land forces numbered only 15,000 men. López, on the other hand, had a well-trained army of more than 60,000, and several fighting vessels on the Paraguayan rivers. All three of the allies were short of money, and within the past year Brazil had experienced a financial crisis that threatened to end in bankruptcy.[55] But the material resources of the Empire and the high character of its ruler made possible foreign loans with which to help finance the war.

What the Brazilians lacked at the outset in military equipment they partly made up for by their hearty enthusiasm for the war, largely stimulated by López's invasion of imperial soil. When word of this event reached the centers of population, more men than could be accepted volunteered for the army. In the whole Empire there was no one more devoted to the war than was Dom Pedro, who never for a moment doubted its justice. When, shortly after the triple alliance was formed, word reached Rio that the Paraguayans had invaded Rio Grande do Sul and occupied the town of Uruguayana, he decided to go at once to the front to inspire his subjects, by his presence and his example, to defend their native soil. The ministry was quite opposed, but the Emperor was determined. "I have resolved to go; *I want to go*," he said. "If not permitted to go as Emperor, I will abdicate and go as a private citizen. Though I may not be permitted to go as a general, the quality of Brazilian cannot be taken from me: I will enlist with a musket as a volunteer of the *patria*."[56] This pronouncement was less indi-

---

[55] Pereira da Silva, *op. cit.*, II, 21-23; Báez, *op. cit.*, 142-43; William Hadfield, *Brazil and the River Plate in 1868*, p. 50.

[56] Nabuco, *op. cit.*, II, 256-57; Pereira da Silva, *op. cit.*, II, 50; *Jornal do Commercio*, April 9, 1871.

cative of the Emperor's actual intentions than it was of his great earnestness. He felt, with what Joaquim Nabuco called a "fanatical intensity," his duty as perpetual defender of Brazil. "The ministry was, therefore, compelled to yield," says Nabuco, "and could only pray to God Almighty that the Emperor might be returned safe and well."[57]

On July 10, 1865, Dom Pedro left for the south, accompanied by the minister of war and by his son-in-law Prince Louis Augustus. The Comte d'Eu and the Princess Imperial had not yet returned from their honeymoon in Europe, but they arrived in Rio a week later and Prince Gaston left shortly afterwards to join the Emperor at the seat of the war. The imperial party went by boat as far as the City of Rio Grande do Sul, where, on July 16 Dom Pedro issued a proclamation to the people of the province intended to stimulate their loyalty and enthusiasm.[58] Two days later he left for Porto Alegre, where he remained until near the end of the month. On July 31, the party began the trip, made mostly on horseback, to the western border of the province. Two weeks later the Comte d'Eu joined the party, and on September 11, the travelers reached their destination.[59] The allied armies were then besieging Uruguayana. At military headquarters Dom Pedro presided over a council of generals, and opposed bombardment of the town, which the Argentine and Uruguayan officers had favored. The siege therefore continued a few days longer until the Paraguayan commander decided to surrender. He appealed to the generosity of the Emperor, who ordered that the prisoners of war, who numbered more than 5,000, be treated with humanity. After the surrender, Dom Pedro visited the sick and wounded Paraguayans and saw that they were given generous care. In preparation for the campaign in Corrientes, a second council of

[57] *Op. cit.*, II, 257.
[58] Pedro d'Orléans Bragança Archives, A, CXXXVII, 6670.
[59] A. Candido Rodrigues, "O maior dos brasileiros," *Rev. do Inst. Hist. e Geog. Bras.*, vol. 152, p. 13; Rangel, *Gastão de Orléans, o ultimo Conde d'Eu*, pp. 115-16.

From a painting at the Château d'Eu
DOM PEDRO II AT THE OPENING OF THE WAR AGAINST PARAGUAY

generals was held, with Dom Pedro, President Flores of Uruguay, and President Mitre of Argentina present.[60] Without question, Dom Pedro's visit to the war zone stimulated allied solidarity as well as Brazilian loyalty in support of the conflict.

Before the Emperor left Uruguayana, Thornton, the British minister, called upon him, by previous arrangement, for the purpose of restoring diplomatic relations between the two countries, which had now been severed for more than two years. The British government had persisted in refusal to pay damages for the seizure of the five Brazilian vessels but was still willing to offer apologies for the incident. In view of the war with Paraguay, the imperial government had decided to waive damages in return for harmony with Great Britain, and the Emperor accepted the apologies tendered by Thornton.[61]

On November 8, Dom Pedro returned to Rio de Janeiro, where he was received with joyful demonstrations of loyalty and affection. After that, until the end of the war, he remained in or near the capital and set for the nation an example of tireless and sacrificial devotion in support of the conflict. He gave a fourth of his civil list to help meet war expenses, and the members of his family were likewise generous. All matters connected with the conflict received his minutest attention, and he wrote countless notes to members of the ministry regarding it.[62] He spent much time in the arsenals and fortresses supervising military preparations, and he boarded and inspected minutely every war vessel and transport before it left for the distant war zone, and shook hands with departing officers and men.[63] With those bereaved by battle he suffered in sympathy, and in certain cases that came to his attention he tried to have the tragic news broken gently.[64]

---

[60] Pereira da Silva, op. cit., II, 50-52, 53; Rangel, Gastão de Orléans, o ultimo Conde d'Eu, pp. 118-19.

[61] Manchester, British Preëminence in Brazil, p. 282.

[62] Wanderley Pinho, ed., Cartas do Imperador D. Pedro II ao Barão de Cotegipe, pp. 19-238; Letters of Dom Pedro to Ferraz and other ministers, Pedro d'Orléans Bragança Archives, A, CXXXVIII, 6702. [63] Mossé, op. cit., pp. 150, 151.

[64] Augusto Tavares de Lyra, Deodoro da Fonseca, pp. 14-15.

By April, 1866, the Paraguayans were on the defensive, but they were fanatically brave and loyal, and López resorted to monstrous cruelties to keep his war machine working. The allied troops, furthermore, soon met with unexpected handicaps: the Paraguayan terrain, broken by streams, lagoons, and jungles, was unfamiliar; cholera carried off large numbers of soldiers; supplies were lacking; and many of the horses died of starvation, forcing the cavalry to become foot soldiers, often without shoes. Worse still, the commanders of the allied troops quarreled among themselves, and the Argentine and Brazilian governments distrusted each other—which added to the delay. Towards the close of 1866 the Brazilian fleet, headed by Admiral Tamandaré, began to attack Humaitá, "the American Sebastopol," which López had built at a turn in the Paraguay River.

Meanwhile, the heavy sacrifices in money and men began to tell on the spirits of the nation, which had expected an early allied victory. Many now regretted Brazilian entrance into the war, and wanted to end it by negotiation with López. Indeed, even early in the struggle the ministry favored such a solution. But Dom Pedro, though he suffered greatly from the strain, was utterly against compromise. When the suggestion was first made he pounded his clenched hand upon the cabinet room table and cried: "Never! We did not provoke the war, and we will not propose the peace! If the sacrifice is enormous, the humiliation would be greater. Now, we must keep on until the end! I will again go to the seat of war, if my presence seems needed there. I will exchange the throne for an army tent, and I wish to see whether there is one single Brazilian who would not accompany me!"[65]

When, early in 1867, an offer of mediation, which had been accepted by Paraguay, came from the United States, it was declined by the Emperor, for the reasons just given.[66]

---

[65] Codman, *op. cit.*, pp. 161-62; Teixeira, *op. cit.*, p. 149; Nabuco, *op. cit.*, II, 422-64; III, 611-13, 643-64. [66] Hill, *op. cit.*, pp. 195-97.

In taking this stand, Dom Pedro was not only influenced by the desire to defend Brazilian prestige, but also by absolute conviction of the wisdom of the war. For, as reports—on the whole, true—spread of the Paraguayan Dictator's cruelties and atrocities to his own people, as well as to the allied prisoners, the Emperor became convinced that López was a barbarous tyrant, a disturber of continental peace, and a terrible enemy of Brazil. Under no conditions except the elimination of López and of his influence, would he agree to lay down arms.[67] Repeatedly he declared that sooner than treat with such a monster he would abdicate his throne.[68]

For a time he stood almost alone in his demand that the war go on: his was the responsibility for prolonging it.[69] Much resentment was felt towards him for this, and for the autocratic methods resorted to for prosecution of the war. The tide of sentiment turned somewhat when news came that, on July 27, 1868, the stronghold of Humaitá had fallen—after eighteen months' siege. Yet, much opposition remained, and in a letter of September, 1868, the American minister, Webb, reported to Secretary Seward that twice the walls of Rio had been plastered with placards calling for revolution and immediate resistance to the one-man power.[70] Hoping to allay internal discontent and to hasten victory, in the middle of this year Dom Pedro had called the Conservative party into power. The slowness of the advance towards Asunción worried him.[71] His energetic direction of the war took on greater drive, if possible. Finally, after heavy losses, the way was cleared to Asunción, which the allied armies occupied early in January, 1869. The capital was almost empty, for the government and much of the population had

---

[67] Wanderley Pinho, *op. cit.*, pp. 33-37.
[68] Webb to Seward, no. 34, May 3, 1867, Dept. of State, Despatches, Brazil; Ottoni, *op. cit.*, p. 43; Mossé, *op. cit.*, p. 177.
[69] *Fallas do throno*, pp. 625-26, 639.
[70] Sept. 23, no. 74, Dept. of State, Despatches, Brazil.
[71] Wanderley Pinho, *op. cit.*, pp. 22, 33-34.

withdrawn to the north, where López busied himself trying to get together another army.

It seemed now that the war would soon end. However, though the ministry agreed with the Emperor that the Paraguayan Dictator must be eliminated,[72] the Duque de Caxias, commander-in-chief of the Brazilian army, was old, weary, and ill, and was inclined to think of the fighting as over and that the time had come to treat with the vanquished. Hence, there was a period of inaction until after Caxias had resigned and returned to Rio de Janeiro.[73]

His place was taken by the Comte d'Eu, Princess Isabel's husband. The Comte, who had been made a marshal in the army in 1865, had ever since the war began repeatedly asked for permission to participate in it, but he had always been refused by the Emperor, who was backed by ministry and council of state. The reason given him for refusal was fear that the imperial soldiers would not follow him as readily as they would a Brazilian, and that he would not be as acceptable to the Argentines and Uruguayans, which might weaken the Alliance.[74] But it seems likely that Dom Pedro and the members of the government also felt that, though the Prince had a fair military record when he arrived in Brazil, he was far too young and inexperienced to be a good risk if given the command called for by his rank.[75] He had been made commander-general of artillery and head of a commission for improvement of the army, but, since neither position sent him to the battle front, he keenly resented his situation and sent many a complaining letter to his father, the Duque de Nemours.[76] Now, when he was not yet twenty-

---

[72] *Ibid.*, pp. 36-37.
[73] *Ibid.*, pp. 37-41; Pereira da Silva, *op. cit.*, II, 106; Rangel, *Gastão de Orléans, o ultimo Conde d'Eu*, pp. 135-36.
[74] Comte d'Eu to Dom Pedro II, Oct. 10, 1866, Pedro d'Orléans Bragança Archives, A, CXXXVII, 6772; Dom Pedro II to Comte d'Eu, Oct. 10, 1866, *ibid.*, CXLVI, 7045A; Comte d'Eu to Joaquim Manoel de Macedo, July 4, 1868, *ibid.*, CXLII, 6954.
[75] Rangel, *Gastão de Orléans, o ultimo Conde d'Eu*, pp. 143-44, 147-50.
[76] *Ibid.*, pp. 119-223, *passim*.

seven years of age, the chief command of the Brazilian armies in Paraguay came to him.

He was appointed on March 22, 1869, and departed promptly for Asunción. Though in his new position he met with some criticism,[77] he was able to rally the Brazilian forces and to win considerable popularity by his friendliness and by the ability with which he directed the Paraguayan campaign. But as the armies advanced north, the handicaps increased, and there was much suffering from lack of food for horses and men. Furthermore, month after month passed and López was still at large, for he had taken refuge in the mountains near the northern frontier of the country. Since the Dictator had been eliminated from power, and the Allies had set up a provisional government, the Comte, mindful of the loss of life, proposed, in October, 1869, that the war be considered finished and that he be permitted to return to Rio on a short leave of absence.[78] To this both the ministry and the Emperor were opposed, and the latter again declared that hostilities should not terminate until López had been captured or had fled from Paraguayan soil.[79] Finally, on March 1, 1870, the war suddenly ended, through the death of López at the hands of a Brazilian corporal.[80]

By now, Paraguay was a complete wreck, with most of its population dead, including practically every able-bodied man. On July 2, 1870, a treaty of peace was signed with the provisional government, and it was agreed that a division of Brazilian soldiers should remain in the country for a time to preserve order. Owing to friction between Argentina and Brazil, the latter sided with Paraguay in the subsequent boundary negotiations, and this finally resulted in Paraguay's retaining more of her territory than had at first seemed likely.

[77] Wanderley Pinho, *op. cit.*, pp. 104-5, 209-13, 217, 219-20.
[78] *Ibid.*, pp. 190-96; Rangel, *Gastão de Orléans, o ultimo Conde d'Eu*, pp. 271, 291.
[79] Rangel, *Gastão de Orléans, o ultimo Conde d'Eu*, pp. 272-92.
[80] *Ibid.*, pp. 296-97.

Brazil, the victor, was also much the worse for the war, despite the fact that it had vindicated its honor in the conventional manner and had gained military prestige. The struggle had cost the country vast sums of money, and about 50,000 lives, and had left many times that number maimed and crippled. During the five years of conflict the settlement of various important domestic questions had been postponed, and material and intellectual progress had slowed up. From the war, furthermore, largely developed the influences that at last proved fatal to the Empire.[81]

It is obvious that the Zacharias ministry made a tragic blunder in presenting the ultimatum of May, 1864, to the Blanco government. Perhaps the Emperor could not have prevented this from being done even if he had wanted to, for the pressure from the interested propagandists and the professional jingoes for armed intervention was very strong. But his sense of responsibility for the security of the Empire caused Dom Pedro himself to be swept away by the popular hysteria, like many a ruler before his day and many a one since. According to the standards by which such things were then judged, his policy in the Plata basin was justifiable. It would have been far better for Brazil, however, if the Zacharias ministry had shown more patience towards the situation in Uruguay and had made greater effort to disarm the suspicions and fears of López. It would also have been wiser if Dom Pedro had consented to negotiate with López in 1867, when the Dictator expressed a willingness to make peace. However, to say these things is to apply the best criteria of the present to a situation of seventy years ago.

Certainly no one suffered more during the war than did the Emperor himself. He was constantly overworked through his activities in furtherance of the conflict. The casualties in the battle area and the grief of the bereaved ones wrung his heart. But, most wearing of all, was his terrible sense of responsibility

---

[81] Mossé, *op. cit.*, p. 174; Nabuco, *op. cit.*, II, 189; Normano, *op. cit.*, p. 176.

for the honor and security of Brazil, especially during the period when, in the face of strong opposition, he insisted that the war go on. A year after the conflict opened, he was described as looking "careworn and somewhat older than his years."[82] When it was over, his youth was also definitely past. His once golden brown hair was now almost white, and his face was furrowed by lines of care.[83] Yet he was only forty-four years of age.

[82] Agassiz and Agassiz, *op. cit.*, p. 58.   [83] Mossé, *op. cit.*, p. 151.

VII

DOM PEDRO'S STRUGGLES WITH A PREMATURE POLITICAL SYSTEM

THOUGH Dom Pedro believed that his natural gifts fitted him better for an intellectual life,[1] which he would have preferred to a political one, he had inherited the Brazilian throne and his strong sense of duty caused him to work ceaselessly for the good of the nation. The established governmental system of the Empire was, however, a distinct obstacle, and his constant struggle with it was depressing.

From the first he was handicapped by a clash between the political facts of the country and its political ideals. Though the Brazilians who were interested in government wanted a democratic system, they lacked the experience and self-discipline needed to make such a system work. The constitution drawn up under the direction of Dom Pedro I showed awareness of this lack; it recognized the facts and ignored the ideals. But the first Emperor had lost his throne through insisting on his constitutional rights, which were intended to compensate for the national inadequacy.

After his abdication, his bitterest enemies, the liberal element, supported the Empire and the infant Dom Pedro II with the definite intention of making the constitution more federal and democratic as soon as possible. This was partly achieved by the *Acto Addicional* of 1834, which abolished the council of state and granted elective legislatures to the provinces. But when, in the face of increasing disorders, the regency turned conservative, it practically nullified the new powers of the provinces. And after the accession of Dom Pedro II the council of state was, by

[1] Pedro d'Orléans Bragança Archives, A, CXXX, 6373.

Conservative initiative, restored, since the youthful ruler needed a disinterested body to advise him. The anarchic realities of the regency period had tended, however, to discount the political theories of the Liberals, and they, through sponsoring the *coup* which prematurely placed Dom Pedro II on the throne, had somewhat spiked their own guns. Therefore, in the early years of the second Empire there was rather general conviction that the political system for Brazil should combine liberalism with authority.

This, the constitution provided: it included an extensive bill of rights, but gave broad powers to the Emperor. It definitely authorized the sovereign to rule and govern as well as to reign. His strength lay chiefly in his moderating power. Under this he had the right to approve legislation; to appoint and dismiss the members of his cabinet, the provincial presidents, and other administrative offices; to prorogue Parliament; and to dissolve the chamber of deputies when the safety of the Empire required it. He also had unrestricted power to select the members of his council of state and to name the senators from triple lists of nominees,[2] chosen indirectly by the electorate.

The chief bulwarks of the Emperor were, in fact, these two bodies. The senate—called by some Brazilians "Siberia" because of its supposed austerity and its cool aloofness towards the problems of the rank and file—was less troubled by partisan squabbles than was the lower house, for its members had life tenure, which gave them a more detached viewpoint. And clashes between the senators and the Emperor were rare, since he tended to choose from the lists of nominees men with whom he thought he could work. But he generally named them from the party in power, in some cases even overlooking personal dislikes. It was complained that he regularly ignored certain names, even though they appeared again and again on the triple lists. In doing so, however, he was within his constitutional rights. In

[2] James, *op. cit.*, pp. 244-45.

one instance, when he created much criticism by ignoring a distinguished Conservative and selecting a Liberal his real reason was that when the rejected candidate and his wife returned from a trip to Europe some time before a considerable quantity of smuggled goods had been found in the packing case of a grand piano which they brought back.[3]

The council of state, composed of about ten members, had more influence upon the sovereign than had any other part of the governmental machinery, for it was of his own choosing and he was bound to consult it on all important matters. Since the council in its consultative capacity was the final interpreter of the constitution, it was to some extent equivalent to a high tribunal, such as the Supreme Court of the United States.[4] It, like the senate, was conservative in its policy, and its interpretations tended to fortify central control and to give prestige to the crown. Undoubtedly it greatly strengthened the moderating power of the Emperor. Both council of state and senate were criticized as strongholds of autocracy, but the council, because of its special powers, was more subject to political attack than was the upper house.[5]

Though after 1847 there was always a president of the imperial cabinet, Dom Pedro had great influence upon his ministers. At the regular Saturday cabinet meetings each one reported on the matters in his department which called for approval of the Emperor. If these were important, and especially if they called for expenditure of money, Dom Pedro often delayed his decision, to give him time to study them or to consult the council of state.[6] He questioned his ministers closely about affairs in their departments, made comments, and stirred up dis-

---

[3] A. Gomes Carmo, "O Imperador: factos, reminiscencias e anecdotas," *Jornal do Commercio*, July 21, 1935; Teixeira, *op. cit.*, pp. 124, 125; Oliviera Vianna, *op. cit.*, pp. 272-78.

[4] James, *op. cit.*, pp. 247-48; dos Santos, *op. cit.*, pp. 84-85; Nabuco, *op. cit.*, III, 11.

[5] T. B. Ottoni, *Circular dedicada aos srs. eleitores e senadores pela provincia de Minas Geraes*, pp. 31-36.   [6] Mossé, *op. cit.*, p. 351.

cussion. Cabinet members therefore called their meetings *sabbatinas*, after the Saturday examinations of students on the lessons of the week.[7] Though Dom Pedro had a natural fondness for asking questions, developed by his teachers, and a Germanic bent for details and thoroughness, he seems to have quizzed his ministers chiefly because he was unwilling to assume that they had performed their full duty, or that they could be expected to do so without careful watching. This suspicion, likewise traceable to pedagogical influence,[8] was probably well justified, on the whole, by his experience with successive cabinets, for the Emperor had high standards of efficiency to which perhaps few of his ministers would have attained without prodding.

Between cabinet meetings, the Emperor sent his ministers notes containing additional information or instructions, or asking questions intended to guard against neglect of details, or for his own enlightenment.[9] Occasionally, especially in emergencies, he performed part, or all, of the duties of a minister. He was driven by nervous zeal for getting things done promptly and properly. When he was in Uruguayana during the conflict with Paraguay, Silva Ferraz, the minister of war who accompanied him, complained to Nabuco, "The Minister disappeared. The Emperor threw himself into everything, even to the smallest details, and confused everything. . . ."[10] The criticism may have been just in the case mentioned, but the fact that the Emperor inclined to be "minister of all of the portfolios"[11] doubtless resulted in greater general efficiency in the administration.

The information secured by the Emperor from his cabinet on the condition of the Empire he supplemented abundantly through making himself accessible once a week to all who wished to see him and through reading the daily papers and the debates in the legislature. "The tribune and the press are

[7] Pimentel, *op. cit.*, p. 90.   [8] See p. 33 of this book.
[9] *Cartas do Imperador D. Pedro II ao Barão de Cotegipe*, edited by Wanderley Pinho, offers many examples of such notes.
[10] Nabuco, *op. cit.*, II, 259.   [11] Wanderley Pinho, *op. cit.*, pp. 5-6.

the best informants of the monarch" was a comment he once made in his diary.[12]

The ministers occasionally resented his countless questions, his watchfulness over their work, and his meddling with it, all of which seemed to show a lack of trust in them. Undoubtedly he was at times over-solicitous regarding the efficiency of his ministers, but, since he was well aware of the common undependability of human beings, he preferred to take no risks.

The members of his cabinet also felt that the Emperor lacked frankness in his attitude towards them. Some even accused him of indirection to a Machiavellian degree.[13] That he often omitted to take them into his confidence is very true. But, in most such cases, to have laid all of his cards on the table would have been against the best interests of the nation, for his ministers were rarely frank with him,[14] and he was forced to meet their methods with similar ones. It might seem that if from the outset he had taken his ministers completely into his confidence, they would have played fair with him; but this is improbable, for a large proportion of the political leaders were moved chiefly by selfish, partisan aims, whereas Dom Pedro was unquestionably the best friend and best servant of the nation. Members of the cabinet at times even made the Emperor the scapegoat for their own faults and mistakes: when criticized for some unwise or unpopular act, they placed the responsibility upon him.[15] Certainly Dom Pedro would have been perfectly frank with all of the members of his government if he had dared do so, and he fervently wished it possible. In the latter part of his reign he remarked in a conversation with his friend the Visconde de Taunay: "Ah! If I could but speak the truth frankly always! Then, things would go better!"[16]

[12] Pedro d'Orléans Bragança Archives, A, CXXX, 6373.
[13] Ottoni, *D. Pedro de Alcantara*, pp. 18, 44; Suetonio, *op. cit.*, pp. 77, 86.
[14] F. J. Oliveira Vianna, *O occaso do Imperio*, pp. 56-57.
[15] *Ibid.*, p. 57.
[16] Max Fleiuss, "O Imperador D. Pedro II no archivo do Conselheiro José Antonio Saraiva," *Annaes do Primeiro Congresso de Historia Nacional*, I, 1512.

The most serious differences between the Emperor and his council of ministers and also between him and the chamber of deputies resulted from the fact that the lower house was not really representative of the nation. A further look at the political system that Dom Pedro inherited should make the problem apparent.

From the first days of the Brazilian Empire the British cabinet system had been an aspiration, especially among political Liberals. The constitution did not provide for it, but Dom Pedro I's unwillingness wholly to concede it had forced his abdication. Under the regency the cabinet system got—in practice, of a sort —a definite foothold. Then came Dom Pedro II, to whom democracy was a political ideal, apparently even in boyhood. In the early part of his reign he definitely stated that he would prefer the position of president of a republic to that of Emperor.[17] But no one knew better than he that the Brazilian nation, largely illiterate and only recently permitted to experiment with self-government at all, was quite unready for the democratic political system of Great Britain, where representative government had existed for more than five centuries. But, in the interest of harmony, he tried to make the best of the existing situation.

Brazil did not even have political parties in the British sense of the term. There was, indeed, during the final crisis of Dom Pedro I's reign a definite line-up on important political issues, and in the period of the regency this was true to some extent, but by the time Dom Pedro II came to the throne these issues had disappeared, or no longer attracted much attention. During much of his reign the Liberals and Conservatives had but a small membership and failed to stand consistently for clear-cut principles of government. They did not to any marked degree represent public opinion or currents of national thought. Though among them were able, public-spirited individuals,

[17] Extrahido do diario escripto por S. M. o Imperador o Senhor D. Pedro II, Dec. 31, 1861, Pedro d'Orléans Bragança Archives, A, CXXX, 6373.

these so-called parties were on the whole factions or clans, interested not in putting into effect constructive ideas, but in gaining political power for selfish ends. Dom Pedro indicated the discouraging situation by his question to the prime minister, Carneiro Leão, in 1853: "But, Senhor Honorio, where are our parties?"[18]

Dom Pedro II as a boy had been taught that a monarch who ignored the constitution was an unspeakable tyrant, heading for his own destruction. But after his accession a highly developed conscience, rather than policy, urged scrupulous observance of the basic law of the Empire. In 1861, he observed in his diary, "I swore to support the Constitution; but even if I had not done so it would be for me a second religion."[19] However, in the direction of authority as well as of liberalism, he interpreted the constitution broadly. The argument of experience caused him soon to regard the "safety of the Empire" proviso connected with the authority to dissolve the chamber of deputies as equivalent to "general welfare and national justice."

Since no literacy test was required for voting—though a small income was—there was little chance that those having the ballot would have used it wisely, even if the vote had been free. But, owing largely to the tradition of political corruption inherited from colonial days, it was not free. Elections for the lower chamber, as well as for other positions, were dominated by local political "bosses," under direction of members of the ministry who were intent upon maintaining their faction in power.[20] An especially crude example of this was Antonio Carlos de Andrada's wholesale removal of local officers in order to put in men who would bring about the desired election returns.[21]

After the Emperor had begun to assert himself as head of

---

[18] Oliveira Vianna, *O occaso do Imperio*, pp. 25-26, 29, 41.
[19] Pedro d'Orléans Bragança Archives, A, CXXX, 6373.
[20] Pereira da Silva, *op. cit.*, I, 126-27, 173-78; Oliveira Vianna, *O occaso do Imperio*, p. 34; James, *op. cit.*, pp. 237-52.
[21] See pp. 58-59 of this book.

the nation, and to control removals and appointments, fraud and coercion—often accompanied by violence—continued at the polls. And since the political "ins" could dominate the elections, they would have held office indefinitely if permitted to do so. The Emperor, however, by dissolution of the lower house, prevented such monopoly of the blessings of office. Though Dom Pedro never used the suspensive veto granted by the constitution, he dissolved the chamber eleven different times, and in a number of instances when he did so the political issues under discussion were very slight, or none existed. In such cases, he generally used his power of removal and appointment before the next election to secure victory for the political "outs." At other times he dismissed his cabinet and selected, to form a new one, a leader of the opposition who saw to it that his faction won in the next balloting for deputies. Thus the Emperor let the unpreventable frauds bring about party changes.[22] But for the sake of harmony he kept up the fiction that the deputies represented the will of the nation. He, furthermore, would not permit the party in power to crush or take revenge upon its opponents. This, as well as his arbitrary dissolutions of the chamber of deputies, at times caused ill will towards him. Such paternal intervention, by its very impartiality, was resented by the faction at the moment not favored by his policy, for the politicians did not understand, or pretended not to understand, the spirit of fair play which motivated the Emperor.

Unquestionably Dom Pedro used his moderating power for the good of Brazil. He tried to act for the nation as it would have acted through the house of deputies if the nation had been intelligent and if the deputies had been fair-minded. He showed this not only in his dismissal of cabinets and dissolution of the lower chamber, but also through his insistence upon freedom of speech and of the press, and in his use of the pardoning

[22] Tavares de Lyra, in *Contribuições para a Biographia de D. Pedro II*, Pt. I, p. 272; Webb to Seward, no. 73, Sept. 24, 1868, Dept. of State, Despatches, Brazil.

power.[23] The Emperor represented the interests of the people far better than did the house of deputies. His assertion of personal authority was, as Manoel de Oliveira Lima expressed it, a "dictatorship of morality."[24] That he made mistakes goes without saying. But these occurred more often in his personal relations, for, though he was rather an expert on human nature, in general, he was not especially keen at reading individual character. Towards the political factions, his attitude was impartial, save where the welfare of the nation was involved. Though he was charged with favoring the Conservatives, whatever preference he showed them was in the interest of preserving internal order and territorial integrity—of holding the Empire together.[25] Though the moderating power could have been used by an ill-willed ruler to destroy all of the liberties of the nation, the constitution nevertheless granted that power. Dom Pedro II exercised it benevolently, and permitted as well—what the constitution did not require—the pretense of a cabinet system.

However, the existence of this make-believe, the antagonism of his ministers, and the fierce opposition attacks prevented the Emperor from using his personal power as fully, freely, and benevolently as he desired. "That he did not do more and better than he did," says Affonso Celso, "was not because he did not wish to do so, or did not attempt to do so, but because circumstances would not permit it."[26] This was basically true. In his situation—handicapped by the indifference or opposition of governmental authorities to what he thought the best policy or procedure—he once likened himself to a man locked in a glass tower, who could see wrongs and injustices done but was helpless to prevent them.[27] His helplessness was often caused by the

[23] Extrahido do diario escripto por S. M. o Imperador o Senhor D. Pedro II, entry for Jan. 1, 1862, Pedro d'Orléans Bragança Archives, A, CXXX, 6373.
[24] Oliveira Lima, *O Imperio brazileiro*, p. 64.
[25] dos Santos, *op. cit.*, pp. 29-32.
[26] Affonso Celso, "O Imperador como estadista," *Jornal do Brasil*, Nov. 24, 1925.
[27] Moniz, *op. cit.*, p. 176; Alfredo de Escragnolle Taunay, *Reminiscencias*, pp. 145-46.

STRUGGLES WITH PREMATURE POLITICAL SYSTEM 137

fact that his only recourse was to remove the offender, which might make conditions worse, in general, through stirring up new antagonisms. Thus, at times, he permitted unworthy men to retain office, hoping that they would resign on their own accord.[28]

He was likewise averse to the removal of efficient men who wronged him. "I am sensitive to the injustices," he once said, "and am hurt by the jibes; but my duty will not permit me, because of personal injuries, to deprive the country of the services of distinguished Brazilians."[29]

Serious trouble occurred at times from the fact that he refused to dismiss officers whom his ministers desired eliminated for partisan reasons. The first notable example of this took place in February, 1844, when he was but little more than eighteen years old. Carneiro Leão, the leading minister in this period, before provision had been made for a president of the cabinet, asked the Emperor to remove from the department of finance a subordinate officer who was politically offensive. Dom Pedro refused, and the ministry resigned in protest. Later, after one of the Emperor's critics, Tito Franco, in his *Biographia do Conselheiro Furtado*, had charged that the change of ministry had been brought about by a purely personal question, Dom Pedro wrote on the margin of Franco's work explaining that he had believed dismissal would be unjust and that he would be thought weak if he yielded to the minister's insistence.[30]

The Emperor did, however, remove officers whom he thought inefficient, and for the public good he occasionally refused to make appointments desired by members of the government. This also caused irritation at times. José de Alencar, in one of his political attacks, referred to the *lapis fatidico* ("fate-

---

[28] Oliveira Vianna, *O occaso do Imperio*, p. 59.
[29] Fleiuss, "O Imperador D. Pedro II no archivo do Conselheiro José Antonio Saraiva," *Annaes do Primeiro Congresso de Historia Nacional*, I, 1512.
[30] Oliveira Vianna, *O occaso do Imperio*, p. 61; Pereira da Silva, *op. cit.*, I, 117-19.

ful pencil") used by the Emperor in making decisions of this sort;[31] and the epithet stuck.

The ministers especially resented Dom Pedro's policy of keeping them in the dark as to his intentions during political crises. Often, they did not know in advance whether he would consent to a dissolution of the lower house, or, if the ministry was to be changed, whom he would choose for the presidency of the cabinet. Such uncertainty did not exist in Great Britain, they declared, quite ignoring the vast difference in the political traditions of the two countries.[32]

Dom Pedro believed the moderating power necessary because of the political inexperience and handicaps of the nation,[33] and for nearly three decades, whenever he considered it to the interest of the nation to do so, he exercised unreservedly this constitutional right if circumstances permitted. Then, in 1868, during the war against Paraguay, came a ministerial crisis which produced far-reaching changes. Zacharias de Góes was at the time head of the Liberal ministry, and developments turned upon the selection of a senator from the province of Rio Grande do Notre to fill a vacancy caused by death of a Liberal incumbent. The abolition of slavery, for which agitation had begun, was somewhat involved, for the Liberals were more favorable to it than were the Conservatives. The nominee for senator who had the largest number of votes was a Liberal, Amaro Bezerra Cavalcanti, who was preferred by the ministry, but the council of state favored Salles Torres Homem, an unusually able Conservative who had been somewhat irregularly placed on the list of nominees. Cavalcanti wished to go further in the direction of emancipation than did Salles Torres Homem.[34]

The chronic resentment felt by the ministry towards the powerful council of state now flared to new heights because of

---
[31] Calogeras, "O poder pessoal e o lapis fatidico," *Rev. do Inst. Hist. e Geog. Bras.*, vol. 152, pp. 424-31.
[32] Ottoni, *D. Pedro de Alcantara*, pp. 29-30.
[33] Behring, "Documentos preciosos," *Collectanea Rabello*, II, 218.
[34] dos Santos, *op. cit.*, pp. 105-6.

the latter's stand regarding Torres Homem; and Zacharias hurried to the palace to protest to the Emperor against the action of the council, which he declared not only illegal but likely to cause disturbing reactions. The cabinet had no authority to pass upon the legality of senatorial elections, however; that was the exclusive right of the senate itself, granted by the constitution. Furthermore, the Emperor's choice of senators from the list of nominees was an exercise of the moderating power in connection with which he was required by the constitution to consult the council of state. Though neither the original constitution nor the acts which reëstablished the council of state, in 1841, stipulated that the Emperor was bound to take the advice of the council, he had almost invariably done so. Hence, it was clear to him that Zacharias was asking for an abrupt change in the policy followed for almost twenty-seven years, a veritable *coup d'état*. He, therefore, refused to support Zacharias, thus standing by the constitution as he had, up to then, interpreted it.[35]

Since the two opposing sides could not be reconciled, Zacharias made the matter a question of confidence and asked that the ministry be dismissed. Dom Pedro, after consulting the council of state, gave the order for dismissal, and on July 16, 1868, he asked a Conservative, the Visconde de Itaborahy, to form a cabinet. He was probably influenced to change parties by the belief that it would not be well to push abolition—much as he would have liked to do so—when the war against Paraguay was at a critical stage. He was also fearful of splitting the country by precipitating a serious constitutional discussion. Furthermore, the Liberals were, by now, divided into three quarreling factions, whereas the Conservatives were united, and they included the chiefs of the land and naval forces and also the leading financiers of the war.[36]

The Liberal chamber of deputies, however, looked upon Dom Pedro's selection of a Conservative cabinet as a *coup d'état*,

---

[35] *Ibid.*, pp. 106-8.
[36] *Ibid.*, pp. 108-10; Pereira da Silva, *op. cit.*, II, 87-90.

and this it deeply resented. On July 17, it passed the following resolution of protest: "The chamber views with deep concern and general surprise the appearance of the present cabinet, begotten outside of its own body and symbolizing a new policy—the fall of its predecessor without a parliamentary question. The chamber, sincere friend of the representative system and constitutional monarchy, laments this singular fact, and has not, and cannot have, confidence in the government."[37] Dom Pedro met the challenge by dissolving the chamber of deputies and calling for a new general election, which of course resulted in a Conservative victory.[38]

But the Emperor did not, by the party change, save the country from serious dissension. The ousted Liberals, unwilling to acquiesce, started a movement to deprive him of his moderating power. The members who went back to their homes made known their resentment through the local press, and those who remained in the capital organized a Reform Club, with an official organ, *A Reforma (The Reform)*. The chief support for the movement came from the Progressive Liberals and the Historical Liberals, but at about the same time a third branch of the faction, the Radical, formed the Radical Club.[39]

During this period feeling against the Emperor ran high among the political "outs"; there was daily talk about his despotism and his generally Machiavellian conduct,[40] and suggestions were even made for drastic resistance to the "one-man power."[41] But this criticism was caused partly by the unusual authority exercised by Dom Pedro in connection with the conflict with Paraguay, such as always characterizes war time.

The Emperor's enemies, looking for weapons to use against him, now turned to the premature, unconstitutional proclama-

[37] dos Santos, *op. cit.*, 110, note 1.
[38] Webb to Seward, no. 73, Sept. 24, 1868, Dept. of State, Despatches, Brazil.
[39] Tobias Monteiro, *Pesquisas e depoimentos para a historia*, pp. 35-37; Affonso Celso, *Oito annos de parlamento*, p. 231.
[40] dos Santos, *op. cit.*, p. 112.
[41] Webb to Seward, no. 73, Sept. 24, 1868, Dept. of State, Despatches, Brazil

STRUGGLES WITH PREMATURE POLITICAL SYSTEM 141

tion of his majority, which, they declared, had injured Brazil's sovereignty, independence, and liberty.[42] His alleged reply to the inquiry as to when he wished to assume headship of the government—"Quero já" (I want it now)—was interpreted as indicating his eagerness for power. This attitude, the critics pointed out, had its natural sequel in his persistent dictatorial rule. He began with "I want it now," declared one opponent, and ended with "I want everything."[43] In view of the circumstances under which the majority was proclaimed, as well as of the extreme youth of Dom Pedro at the time,[44] such charges were of course absurd as well as unjust.

The Emperor did not, however, take revenge upon his detractors, and he rarely replied in public, no matter how false the charge. But in many cases he made answer, point by point, to his critics in their own writings by comments on the margins.[45] These notes were always restrained, and even charitable. In Tito Franco's book, which made a sharp attack upon him, he remarked: "In spite of the injustices done me, I was not roused to anger like the author of this pamphlet; and I believe that if he heard my side, he would, at least, change many of his ideas."[46]

Yet the long, often futile, struggles to get needed measures through a legislature torn by selfish factional strife, as well as the unjust attacks upon him, often saddened and depressed the Emperor. In letters to his friend Gobineau he referred to the difficulties that he experienced and to the "political miasma" of the capital, from which he gladly escaped to Petropolis.[47] The

---

[42] Tito Franco, *Biographia do Conselheiro Furtado*, p. 13.
[43] Wanderley Pinho, *op. cit.*, p. 6; Ottoni, *D. Pedro de Alcantara*, p. 18; Escragnolle Doria, "Quero já," *Revista da Semana*, Feb. 16, 1924.
[44] See pp. 48-56 of this book.
[45] Among the writings containing such notes are Franco's *Biographia do Conselheiro Furtado*, Pereira da Silva's *Historia do Brasil, 1831-1840*, Pressensé's *Les origines*, and Chandordy's *La France en 1889*.
[46] Oliveira Vianna, *O occaso do Imperio*, p. 54.
[47] Letters of Sept. 5, 1872; Nov. 1, 1875; Dec. 24, 1877; Jan. 22, 1878; Aug. 18, 1879, all in Pedro d'Orléans Bragança Archives, A, CLXXXV, 8347b.

entry in his diary for January 10, 1862, is more revealing. "Nothing new," he wrote,

> only I am very sad, though it is necessary to show a cheerful face. Many things trouble me; but it is not possible to remedy them immediately, and that distresses me deeply. If only I could at least generally reveal what I think! But, what for, since so few believe in the existence of the obstacles that I meet in trying to do what I deem proper and wise! There is much lack of zeal, and love of country is mostly mere talk! To see what is desirable to do but not to be able to contribute towards it except slowly, . . . is a torment of Tantalus to a conscientious sovereign; but resignation is indispensable in order that the sovereign's influence may continue to produce—without shake-ups, which are always bad—its disinterested effects, which, though they be not for the public good, are necessary to a constitutional monarchy.[48]

The reaction of the Liberals to his treatment of the Zacharias ministry in 1868 did, on the other hand, seem to produce a change in some of the Emperor's ideas. Never again did he completely ignore the wishes of the cabinet in connection with the naming of senators. But his change was probably more a bowing to an apparently growing popular demand than the result of a conviction that yielding was for the best interests of the nation. At about this time he seems to have begun to think that the results of his struggles with the government were not always worth the efforts that they cost.

The explosion caused by Dom Pedro's resistance to Zacharias's demands was not the origin of the Liberal campaign against imperial authority. Already in the early 1860's a reform program was beginning to take free shape. Now, in 1868, the Liberals were demanding an elective senate with limited terms of office and transfer of the moderating power to the president of the cabinet of ministers.[49] Fusionist Liberal sentiment was further crystallized and was made public on May 4, 1869, by a manifesto drawn up by Senator José Thomaz Nabuco

---

[48] Pedro d'Orléans Bragança Archives, A, CXXX, 6373.
[49] Calogeras, "O poder pessoal e o lapis fatidico," *Rev. do Inst. Hist. e Geog. Bras.*, vol. 152, pp. 430-31.

de Araujo of Bahia, the gifted leader of the new reform Liberals. The document advocated responsibility of the ministry for the moderating power; a sovereign who reigned but did not rule; organization of the council of ministers in accordance with these two ideas; decentralization through granting of provincial and municipal autonomy; the maximum of liberty in industry and commerce, and consequent extinction of monopolies; effective guarantees of liberty of conscience; freedom of instruction; independence of the judiciary; unity of jurisdiction of the judicial power; reduction of the council of state to an auxiliary of the administration, through eliminating its political authority; reform of the senate by abolishing the irremovability guarantee; reduction of the military effectives in time of peace; and an army maintained by volunteers, instead of by recruiting.[50] The manifesto ended with the slogan, "Reform or revolution!"[51]

In November, 1869, the Radical Liberals published a brief, vigorous manifesto similar to that of the Fusionist Liberals, but including the abolition of slavery.[52] Here was a recrudescence of the political spirit of 1831 which had been fatal to Dom Pedro I and had produced the short-lived Acto Addicional.

Such energetic declarations were likely to bring demands for more sweeping changes. These came, inspired partly by the overthrow of Napoleon III of France and the political troubles of Spain. A republican party, developed logically from the Radical wing of the Liberals, announced itself on December 3, 1870. "We are of America, and we want to be Americans,"[53] proclaimed its leaders. But for many years the new group played almost no part in the political life of the Empire.

Meanwhile the movement for reform of elections had been gaining headway in the nation. Early in his region Dom Pedro had realized that the elections, as conducted, were the chief

[50] Nabuco, *op. cit.*, III, 145-50.
[51] *Ibid.*, p. 147.   [52] dos Santos, *op. cit.*, 124-25.
[53] [C. B. Ottoni and others], *Brazilian Republican Address*, p. 20.

cause of the country's political ills,[54] and he had favored laws to wipe out election evils. Over and over again references to the need for free and honest elections rang like a refrain through his speeches from the throne, and numerous laws were passed, but with practically no effect.[55] Loopholes making governmental intervention possible were always found in the measures.

The reformers finally turned to direct elections as a panacea. The Liberals adopted the idea by the close of 1877; there was strong party sentiment in favor of it. Some of the ablest Conservative leaders also came out in support of the plan, but the Conservatives as a whole held back. They had been in power since 1868, so no bill calling for direct elections had been adopted. Finally, early in 1878 there began a train of events leading to a serious political shake-up, and resulting in adoption of the reform so long agitated, and also in further change in policy on the part of the Emperor himself. Developments were started by the fact that Marshal Caxias, who headed the cabinet, was ill and that Barão Cotegipe was filling his place temporarily. When early in December Caxias asked permission to resign in favor of some other member of the cabinet, Dom Pedro went out to Caxias's fazenda and assured himself that the Minister was too ill to carry on the work. On this occasion Caxias again requested dismissal, but advised that the ministry be continued, under the presidency of Cotegipe. Dom Pedro consulted with the president of the chamber of deputies and became convinced that the demand for direct elections was so strong that it must be considered. Therefore, he wrote Caxias conceding release to him and "to the rest of the ministry." This last created a sensation, but Cotegipe at once took the hint and asked for collective dismissal of the cabinet.[56]

Though Dom Pedro had by now abandoned whatever hope

[54] Carlos Magalhães de Azeredo, *Dom Pedro II: traços da sua physiognomia moral*, p. 49.
[55] *Fallas do throno*, pp. 412, 453, 498, 509, 536, 550, 572, 594, 639, 660, 669.
[56] Pereira da Silva, *op. cit.*, II, 183-85.

he once had that purity could be brought to politics through legislation, he conferred seriously with the presidents of the two houses regarding the question of direct election. The Conservatives, hoping to prevent the ascendency of the Liberals, agreed to yield to the demand for the reform. But the Emperor, after this concession had been promised, stated that it was fitting that the Liberals, who had originated the idea and had agitated for it, should now assume leadership. Therefore, he asked the old Conde de Sinimbú to form a ministry. Sinimbú believed, as did the Emperor himself, that the reform should be made by a constitutional amendment. A man of long political experience, he selected his cabinet from various elements to get support in the chambers for the reform measure.[57]

The ministry completed, Dom Pedro dissolved the Conservative lower chamber. The election that followed resulted in a strong Liberal majority. To this body Sinimbú presented a project for calling a convention for the sole purpose of considering the proposed amendment to the constitution. The suggested limitation of power caused an uproar, since some members wished to push other reforms. Finally, however, the resolution passed the deputies. But in the senate, where many wished an ordinary law instead of an amendment, there was sturdy opposition. Sinimbú, therefore, suggested to Dom Pedro that, if the senate continued to hold out, he repeatedly dissolve the lower house until the upper one should submit to the manifest will of the nation. The Emperor agreed. When the senate voted definitely against the calling of the convention, however, the president of the cabinet decided not to resort at once to the extreme measure of dissolution; he preferred to adjourn the house, in order to gain time for careful consideration of the next step. With this in mind, he went to the palace to see the Emperor. "Have you brought the decree of dissolution?" Dom Pedro asked. "No, Senhor," the Minister replied, "I bring a decree of adjourn-

---

[57] Monteiro, *Pesquisas e depoimentos para a historia*, pp. 38-43; dos Santos, *op. cit.*, pp. 140-42.

ment." The Emperor, whose mind had moved with Sinimbú's, was so relieved that he cast reserve aside and embraced the head of his ministry.[58]

When Dom Pedro saw, however, that either the chamber of deputies or the cabinet had to be sacrificed, he gave up his stand for a constitutional amendment, discharged the Sinimbú government, and asked José Antonio Saraiva, also a Liberal, but who favored an ordinary law, to form a new ministry. This, Saraiva did in March, 1880. The bill that was drafted provided in its final form elaborate details covering the creation of electoral districts, qualifications of voters, registration before and after casting the ballot, and other devices intended to guard against fraud. The measure made special effort to define the property requirements and other qualifications for voting called for by the constitution. Dom Pedro had much desired a literacy test,[59] but he did not hold out against the bill, which finally passed both houses and was signed by him on January 9, 1881.

The task for which he was called being accomplished, Saraiva asked the Emperor to dismiss the cabinet. Dom Pedro refused, for he wished Saraiva, whose political honor was above question, to help put the law into effect through remaining in office at least until after the first election under it. The Minister consented and, in consultation with Dom Pedro, prepared for the election. To fix electoral districts and to define election rules, they named a bi-partisan committee of senators and deputies, and they chose as impartial men as could be found for presidents of the provinces, instructing them not to interfere in any way with the elections and not to permit subordinates to do so. Though some irregularity and violence marked the polling for deputies in 1881, the election was probably more honest and free than any held before. To the surprise of the Brazilians, two

[58] Monteiro, *Pesquisas e depoimentos para a historia*, p. 47.
[59] *Collecção das leis do imperio do Brasil de 1881*, vol. I (*Actos do Poder Legislativo*), no. 3029, pp. 1-28; Collecção Saraiva, case 269, no. 14,255, *Inst. Hist. e Geog. Bras.*, Rio de Janeiro.

members of the ministry lost their seats, and the political parties were almost balanced in the lower house. Shortly after the new Parliament met in January, 1882, Saraiva asked prompt dismissal of himself and the rest of the government; and the Emperor reluctantly let him go.[60]

Dom Pedro had no illusions as to what would now happen. On January 10, 1879, he had written his friend the Comte de Gobineau, "The electoral reform is stirring up some interest. Since the two parties think it necessary, it must be done. However, I have no confidence except in the education of the people."[61] Within a few years the elections were about as turbulent and corrupt as ever.[62] The fault was not in the laws, but in the incapacity or unwillingness of the Brazilian politicians to observe and enforce them. Very few men in public life were as honest and conscientious as Saraiva.

But the election law was not without effect. The Emperor's attitude towards his moderating power had changed in the past ten years, and it was about to yield further. After the passage of the election law he proceeded as if the chamber of deputies were representative of the people. No cabinet governed without support of the majority of the lower house; ministries defeated at the polls were obliged to resign.[63] He likewise gave much more freedom to the president of the council of ministers. In fact, from 1881 on the Emperor observed more strictly the letter of the English parliamentary system, to which the Brazilians thought they had a right.[64] And he was apparently glad to be free from the old feeling of responsibility for trying to make the system work equitably. Shortly after he had adopted this more

[60] Fleiuss, "O Imperador D. Pedro II no archivo do Conselheiro José Antonio Saraiva," *Annaes do Primeiro Congresso de Historia Nacional*, I, 1539; Pereira da Silva, *op. cit.*, II, 224-26.
[61] Pedro d'Orléans Bragança Archives, A, CLXXXV, 8347b.
[62] Pereira da Silva, *op. cit.*, II, 245, 283-84.
[63] Ottoni, *D. Pedro de Alcantara*, p. 28; Monteiro, *Pesquisas e depoimentos para a historia*, p. 54; Tavares de Lyra, in *Contribuições para a Biographia de D. Pedro II*, Pt. I, p. 282.
[64] Ottoni, *D. Pedro de Alcantara*, pp. 30, 44.

complete "hands-off" policy he read a work by one of his critics, in which the author asked, "And, after all, what recourse have a people against the abuse of personal power by the Emperor?" In the margin of the book Dom Pedro wrote: "How much I have learned and changed my way of thinking in forty-four years!"[65] He had come to believe it important to the democratic evolution of the government that the nominal representatives of the nation, even when wrong-headed, be permitted to have their way.

[65] Behring, "Documentos preciosos," *Collectanea Rabello*, II, 216-18.

VIII

A VISIT TO THE OLD WORLD

DOM PEDRO had ruled for more than thirty years when he first saw other lands than the vast, undeveloped one of his birth. Though he had long desired to go abroad, internal problems and his policy in the Plata had so occupied his attention that there had been no time for foreign travel. But he had read extensively and had so combined understanding and sympathy with knowledge as to be something of a world citizen, mentally and spiritually, even before he set foot on alien shores.

By 1871 Brazil was at peace within and was free from vexing foreign problems. In February of that year his daughter Leopoldina died of typhoid fever in Vienna, leaving four little sons.[1] This, and the fact that Dona Thereza, long in delicate health, was now ill and needed climatic change and expert medical care, caused the Emperor to plan to go to Europe. He obtained from Parliament permission to absent himself from the country and arranged to have the Princess Imperial act as Regent during his absence.

She and the Comte d'Eu, who were still childless, had been spending their summers in a modest home in Petropolis, about two blocks from the imperial summer palace, and the cooler season in Laranjeiras, a suburb of Rio de Janeiro, at the Isabel Palace. The building was close to the beach, at the head of what is now the Rua de Paysandú. Because of the delicate health of the Empress, Dona Isabel had assumed much of the responsibility for entertaining, and she was known as a charming and gracious hostess. Her careful education for the throne

[1] *Jornal do Commercio,* Mar. 5, 1871.

and the fact that she had been made an extraordinary member of the council of state the year before[2] well qualified her to fill her father's place during his absence.

But the Comte had been made a councilor at the same time,[3] and Dona Isabel was fearful that his position might prove an obstacle to harmonious relations with the ministry; for the Brazilians, though grateful for his services in the war with Paraguay, could not forget that he was a foreigner. The Visconde do Rio Branco, president of the cabinet, talked over the matter with the Emperor, who assured him that there would not be trouble, but the Comte kept in the background while his wife was Regent.[4]

The chamber of deputies wished to vote a large sum for the expenses of the Emperor's trip and to have him escorted to Europe by a Brazilian squadron, but Dom Pedro refused both. His civil list was enough for his expenses, he said, and he wanted to travel simply, like a private citizen, and incognito, untroubled by formal etiquette. It was therefore arranged that he and Dona Thereza should sail on a regular trans-Atlantic steamer, the "Douro," accompanied by only a small suite of ten persons. Among these were Dom Pedro's childhood friend, Luiz Pedreira, now Barão do Bom Retiro, and the Condessa de Barral, former governess of Princess Isabel. The party also included Rafael, the black friend and servant of the Emperor's infancy, whose only services during later years had been to clean his master's boots.[5]

The royal voyagers left Rio on May 25, 1871, with many of the inhabitants at the dock to wave goodbye. For three days the vessel followed the majestic coast of Brazil, much of which Dom Pedro had never seen before. In a little notebook where he scribbled his impressions of sights and events he made occa-

---

[2] Serrano, *op. cit.*, p. 541.   [3] *Ibid.*

[4] Pedro d'Orléans Bragança Archives, A, CLX, 7368; Monteiro, *Pesquisas e depoimentos para a historia*, p. 23.

[5] Mossé, *op. cit.*, p. 206; Fleiuss, in *Contribuições para a Biographia de D. Pedro II*, Pt. I, p. 98.

sional pencil sketches of the mountains and other bits of nature that he wanted especially to remember.[6]

On the 28th the vessel reached Bahia and made a brief stop. Two days later, early in the morning, it anchored at Pernambuco. Dom Pedro went ashore at seven o'clock, attended mass, rode by special train over a new short rail line, visited schools, and had refreshments at the government palace. In the afternoon the "Douro" departed, heading for Lisbon, which was reached on June 12.[7]

The Emperor's sister Queen Maria II da Gloria had died in 1853, after nineteen years of struggle with the rival political factions of the country. Her eldest son, who had succeeded her as Pedro V, was also dead, and her second son, Luiz I, was on the throne. King Luiz came aboard the "Douro" to greet the Emperor, who was dressed in a plain suit and wore a traveling cap like any tourist. The two chatted, using the familiar "thou," and the King offered to excuse his uncle from the usual delay caused by quarantine regulations; but Dom Pedro would not accept, and he spent the several days of quarantine aboard the "Douro," instead of on the Portuguese war vessel which Dom Luiz, as a second resort, wished to place at his disposal.[8] The Emperor also declined the King's invitation to stay in one of the palaces, and, instead, took quarters at the Hotel Bragança. Here he registered as "Dom Pedro de Alcantara," and the Empress as "Dona Thereza Christina," a practice which they consistently followed while traveling abroad.

Promptly after landing, Dom Pedro devoted himself to family duties, one of the first being a visit to the ancient church of São Vicente da Fóra, the Westminster Abbey of Portugal, where many of his ancestors were buried. He later paid his re-

---

[6] Pedro d'Orléans Bragança Archives, B, XXXVII, 1057; Viagem de D. Pedro II á Europa em 1871, manuscript in library of Inst. Hist. e Geog. Bras., in Rio de Janeiro.

[7] Viagem de D. Pedro II á Europa em 1871.

[8] Fialho, *op. cit.*, p. 65; *O Senhor Dom Pedro Segundo, Imperador do Brasil*, pp. 53-55.

spects to the one relative in Lisbon whom he had met before, his step-mother Dona Amelia. Since the death of her only child, Maria Amelia, born after her husband's abdication, the ex-Empress had lived in strict retirement in the Palacio das Janellas Verdes, on the outskirts of the capital. Here she received Dom Pedro of Brazil, who remembered her with affection, though it was forty years since she and his father had departed for exile.[9] There were likewise exchanges of visits with King Luiz and his family.

While blood is thicker than water, intellectual congeniality is often stronger than family ties; and Dom Pedro probably derived more pleasure from a caller received when he was in quarantine, but whom he had never met. This was Alexandre Herculano, the distinguished historian, poet, and anti-clerical, who as a young man had been a volunteer in the armies of Dom Pedro I in the war against Prince Miguel. Dom Pedro II had corresponded with this Portuguese liberal, and now enjoyed with him the first of many intellectual feasts of his trip.[10] Later, Herculano went sight-seeing in Lisbon with the Emperor and Empress.

Most of Dom Pedro's short time there was, in fact, spent in visiting points of interest, since he wished to get as much as possible from his time abroad, for himself as well as for his country. His intellectual curiosity was insatiable, and he hurried from place to place, up and down the steep streets of Lisbon, noting details with meticulous care and asking countless questions like a famished man consuming the last crumb from the loaf on which he breaks his fast. "Good heavens," remarked his chamberlain, Visconde de Nogueira da Gama, in his account of it, "what a dizzy life!"[11] During the few days in Lisbon the imperial traveler visited most of the important places, includ-

---

[9] *Viagem de D. Pedro II á Europa em 1871.*
[10] *O Senhor Dom Pedro Segundo, Imperador do Brasil,* p. 61.
[11] Nogueira da Gama, *Minhas memorias,* p. 184.

ing schools and other public and private institutions. Accompanied by the Empress, he went to the outskirts of the city to view the convent church of São Jeronymos with its slender marble pillars richly carved in Manoelin style antedating the ecclesiastical architecture of Brazil.[12]

On June 22, they left Lisbon. That morning Dom Pedro rose at four o'clock, had his usual cold bath, breakfasted between six and seven, and personally thanked the hotel proprietor for the hospitality. Before eight o'clock the imperial party were at the railroad station, where the Portuguese royal family gathered to see them off for a short visit to other parts of Portugal, and then to Spain.[13]

In Madrid, King Amadeo I called to pay his respects, but not much time was given to formalities, since only one night was spent in the Spanish capital. However, Dom Pedro made the best of the brief opportunity and surprised even hardy travelers by his great activity and his customary attention to detail. Part of this time was spent in viewing the paintings of Velasquez and other masters at the Prado Museum.[14]

The next day they entered France, and on the border were met by the Comte de Gobineau, a warm friend of Dom Pedro, who embraced him affectionately. France was then in a sad condition. The war with Prussia which had eliminated Napoleon III had but recently ended; within the past month the streets of Paris had flowed with blood of civil strife; the victor's armies were occupying various parts of the country; and the French National Assembly at Versailles was struggling to set up a satisfactory government. In the name of this assembly, Gobineau welcomed the Brazilian Emperor to France and offered his services.

---

[12] *O Senhor Dom Pedro Segundo, Imperador do Brasil*, p. 71.
[13] *Ibid.*, pp. 76-79.
[14] Viagem de D. Pedro II á Europa em 1871; Rodolpho Garcia, "Viagens de D. Pedro II," *Rev. do Inst. Hist. e Geog. Bras.*, vol. 152, p. 122.

Dom Pedro and his party traveled rapidly northward with brief stops at the more important cities. At Versailles, Thiers, head of the Republic, received them cordially. At Rouen they met the Empress's sister and brother-in-law, the Count and Countess of Trapani, and others of her relatives. Here, the commander of the German army of occupation offered to place a guard of honor at the door of Dom Pedro's hotel and to serenade him with German military music, but the Emperor refused the intended courtesies, explaining that in France he could not consent to have the music of the conqueror salute him on the soil of the conquered. The hearts of the humiliated and saddened French people went out to Dom Pedro in grateful affection, and were never withdrawn.[15]

Owing to the disturbed political situation, the visit of the Brazilians in France was brief. Having been joined by Dom Pedro's sister Francisca, on June 29 they crossed to London, where they met Dona Januaria and her husband, who were then living in England. The imperial party established itself at Claridge's Hotel on Brook Street, where Queen Victoria, the Princess of Wales, and other members of British royalty called; and the courtesies were returned. Such necessary formalities took considerable time, but by rising early, retiring late, and making his meals short, the Emperor was able to do much else. He visited all of the places seen by the zealous tourist, from the Houses of Parliament and Westminster Abbey to the Kew Gardens and Madame Marie Tussaud's wax works museum.[16] He also went to an agricultural exposition and to the Greenwich Observatory, and did various other less conventional things.

On July 8, accompanied by Nogueira da Gama, he attended services at the Jewish synagogue on Upper Berkeley Street. The congregation rose as he entered, and the rabbi uttered a

---

[15] Mossé, *op. cit.*, p. 393; Garcia, "Viagens de D. Pedro II," *Rev. do Inst. Hist. e Geog. Bras.*, vol. 152, p. 122.

[16] Mattoso, *op. cit.*, p. 116; Condessa de Barral, Diario de viagem dos soberanos do Brasil, Pedro d'Orléans Bragança Archives, A, CLX, 7382.

special benediction. Dom Pedro had studied Hebrew, and when the services were over he greatly impressed the rabbis by taking one of their religious works and reading correctly from it.[17] But some folk in royal and other circles were shocked by this display of friendliness towards the Jews.

He gave an audience to the American minister, Robert C. Schenck, who, as a member of the joint high commission on the "Alabama Claims," mentioned to him the nomination of a Brazilian to the arbitral tribunal. But, wrote Schenck to Bancroft Davis, the Emperor "protested that he had nothing to do with any government affair, that he had left all of that behind him at Rio—that he was during his absence not Emperor of Brazil but only & strictly a private citizen. When I suggested, 'But Your Majesty of course advises, etc.,' he said, 'No, I assure you I have not written one line home about *affairs* since I came away & I do not intend to.'" This attitude rather shocked as well as annoyed the Minister.[18]

After a visit on July 17 to Queen Victoria, who was then at Osborne House, the Isle of Wight, Dom Pedro and the Empress left for the north, making short stops at Kenilworth ruins, Stratford, Birmingham, Liverpool, and other places on the way. In the industrial centers, he went to see the factories; in Lancaster, the penitentiary; in Carlisle, the asylum for the feebleminded, and also the cathedral.[19]

On the 29th the royal tourists reached Glasgow, and from there Dom Pedro and Nogueira da Gama went to visit Ben Lomond. After the customary sightseeing in Glasgow, the party journeyed on to Edinburgh by way of Loch Katrine and the heath-covered Trossachs. The Emperor delighted in these landmarks of Sir Walter Scott, whose writings he had loved in boyhood days, and he made a side trip to Melrose Abbey and to

---

[17] Viagem de D. Pedro II á Europa em 1871.

[18] Robert C. Schenck to John C. Bancroft Davis, Private, July 26, 1871, Davis Papers, Vol. IX.

[19] Condessa de Barral, Diario de viagem dos soberanos do Brasil.

the novelist's home, "Abbotsford." From its gardens he brought away an ornamental bush which was later planted in the palace grounds at Petropolis.[20]

Since Edinburgh was at the time a famous medical center, physicians were consulted here by Dona Thereza, who had usually stayed quietly at hotels or with relatives while her strenuous husband was taking in the sights. She was advised to go to Carlsbad for the water treatment.[21]

On August 4, they started south along the eastern side of the country, stopping here and there—at Durham and York for the cathedrals, at Normanton to visit the mines, and at Cambridge to see the university. Back in London on the 11th, Dom Pedro took a look at the slums. The next day, on the way to Ostend via Dover, he and his party visited Canterbury Cathedral.[22]

In Belgium the Emperor saw the important show places and institutions of various cities, and made a special trip to the battlefield of Waterloo. He was much interested in a school of agriculture near Brussels. In Brussels he attended a geographical congress. Though he stayed at a hotel in the capital, he accepted an invitation to dine with the King of the Belgians.[23]

From Belgium, the travelers started east towards Berlin, stopping at Liege, Aix-la-Chapelle, and Cologne. From the last named, where they visited the Gothic cathedral, a side trip was made on August 20th to Rolandseck and other places. That day they were guests at a formal midday meal, to which the Condessa de Barral referred as "an eternal luncheon, from one o'clock to three!"[24] Returning to Cologne by boat on the Rhine, they went to Düsseldorf and then to Hamburg. In Hamburg a group of German merchants who had been in Brazil serenaded them with military music. During the short stay here, the Con-

[20] *Ibid.;* Dom Pedro to Gobineau, Sept. 27, 1879, Pedro d'Orléans Bragança Archives, A, CLXXXV, 8347b; N. Y. *Herald,* April 17, 1876.
[21] Condessa de Barral, Diario de viagem dos soberanos do Brasil.
[22] *Ibid.*
[23] Viagem de D. Pedro II á Europa em 1871.
[24] Diario de viagem dos soberanos do Brasil.

dessa remarked in her diary that the Emperor had gone to visit a waterfall and "a thousand other things," but they reached Berlin that night.

Before breakfast the next day Dom Pedro went to see the University of Berlin, and afterwards, the museum. That evening there was a reception by the diplomatic corps. Here, and at all other formal functions in Europe, the Emperor wore his customary black cravat, which gentle eccentricity at times caused dismay in court circles, and hasty changes to black—doubtless to his quiet amusement. On the 25th the travelers lunched at Potsdam Palace with the Prince Imperial, where the Emperor occupied the apartments used by Voltaire when he was a pensioner of Frederick the Great.[25]

In Dresden his request to be treated as a private citizen was ignored, and he was met at the railroad station by the King of Saxony, accompanied by military guards in glittering uniforms. "The Emperor revolted against this formal etiquette," remarked the Condessa de Barral in her diary. But he liked Dresden, and greatly enjoyed the music in the royal chapel, and also Raphael's "Sistine Madonna," the Holbeins, and other great paintings in the art museums.[26]

Reaching the Wartburg by way of Leipzig and Eisenach, he and the Empress visited the castle where Martin Luther, under protection of Frederick the Wise of Saxony, completed his translation of the *New Testament*. When the visitors reached the room which had served the reformer as a chapel, his hymn, "Ein Feste Burg Ist unser Gott" ("A Mighty Fortress Is our God") was played in their honor on the ancient organ. At the first majestic notes, the birds in the tree tops around the tower burst into song, and Dom Pedro dropped to his knees and remained so until the hymn was ended.[27]

---

[25] *Ibid.*; Mattoso, *op. cit.*, p. 116.

[26] Condessa de Barral, Diario de viagem dos soberanos do Brasil.

[27] Mary Elizabeth Sargent, *Sketches and Reminiscences of the Radical Club*, p. 303.

Going next to Coburg, the Emperor and Empress had a sad reunion with their son-in-law, Prince Louis Augustus, and his three eldest sons—Pedro Augusto, Augusto Leopoldo, and José Fernando. The youngest of the children, Luiz Gastão, had been born in Vienna the year before.[28]

By September the imperial party were settled in Carlsbad, where Princess Januaria had preceded them. Now came much consultation with physicians, and a short period of quiet and rest for the Emperor. He and Dona Thereza both drank the mineral water, and in addition the Empress took the baths. Towards the middle of the month Dom Pedro and Visconde do Bom Retiro made trips to Nuremberg and Prague. By the 25th Dona Thereza was feeling better and the whole party left for Munich, where, again, they were greeted with a royal reception. Here they spent two days and then went to Salzburg and to Ischl. Near the latter place the Emperor made a special trip to get a close view of the Dachstein glacier. On October 1, they reached Vienna by a Danube steamer.[29]

The visit of more than a week in the Austrian capital was especially enjoyed by Dom Pedro, who met for the first time his cousin the Emperor Francis Joseph and other Habsburg relatives. But, as usual, he stayed in a hotel. The art and music delighted him, and also the intellectuals whom he met at the sessions of the Academy of Arts and of the Geographical Society. In a chemistry class that he attended he showed himself as attentive and eager to learn as any student. Repeatedly he explained to those connected with the institutions he visited, "All of this information will be immensely valuable to me when I have returned home." The Viennese, for their part, were much pleased with the Emperor.[30]

Indeed, before his visit ended he was the most popular royal

---

[28] Condessa de Barral, *Diario de viagem dos soberanos do Brasil.*
[29] *Ibid.*
[30] Manuscript translation from *Fremdenblatt*, Oct. 10, 1871, *Inst. Hist. e Geog. Bras.*, case 26, no. 552.

person in Europe. To the masses, he, and likewise the Empress, made a powerful appeal by the generosity with which they gave alms to individuals and institutions. The people were also attracted by the Emperor's democratic simplicity as well as by his courtesy and kindness. He delighted, while abroad, in ignoring as much as possible the accepted code for royalty; it appealed to his sense of the dramatic to do so. To a considerable extent he was his own servant. He invariably carried his own traveling bag and umbrella; and at hotels he was in the habit of going down stairs bareheaded to inquire for mail. When he attended the exposition in Vienna he ignored the entrance reserved for royalty and, after buying his own ticket, went in by the general door. He was sincerely anxious to remain unknown and to avoid crowds and fuss, but at times his unusual height and distinguished appearance and bearing betrayed him. He won intellectuals by his wide knowledge and his passionate interest in scientific and literary development. He never missed an opportunity to attend learned gatherings and to meet scholars and eminent figures in the field of belles lettres. With practically all intellectuals whom he met he was able to talk in their own tongue, and when that failed he at times resorted to Latin.[31]

Dom Pedro was highly pleased with the cordial welcome given to him and the Empress everywhere, and by the space devoted to them in the press. This desire for attention was not personal, however; it was in the interest of making his beloved Brazil better known and esteemed abroad. His chief personal satisfaction came from his reception by scholars.

After a brief side trip to Pesth, Dom Pedro and his party left Vienna for Italy, where they made short stops in Venice, Milan, and Bologna. On October 24, they embarked for Cairo, Egypt. After leaving the Adriatic their vessel encountered stormy weather, but Dom Pedro remained on deck gazing wist-

[31] Viagem de D. Pedro II á Europa em *1871*; Dom Pedro II's note on margin of Chandordy's *La France en 1889*, p. 168; Castro, in *Contribuições para a Biographia de D. Pedro II*, Pt. I, p. 580; Mattoso, *op. cit.*, p. 117.

fully at the Ionian Islands, Cape Matapan, in the distance, and at Crete with its Mount Ida, of which he got a close glimpse by moonlight.[32] To Greece he was much attached, but that was all he saw of it during this trip.

In Egypt Dom Pedro remarked upon the brilliancy of the stars and had his first view of the Southern Cross since he left the western hemisphere. With the Austrian consul and the Visconde do Bom Retiro, he ascended the Great Pyramid, aided by four sturdy Arabs, and enjoyed from its top the view of the Nile. In Cairo he attended a session of the Egyptian Institute, was elected a member, and joined in the discussions.[33] But his call on the land of the Pharaohs was very brief.

Before the end of October he reëntered Italy at Brindisi, and then spent some weeks traveling in the peninsula. He visited Naples and climbed Vesuvius, to the secret disgust of Nogueira da Gama, who had to accompany him. But he cared less for the natural wonders than he did for the past and present intellectual culture of the country. Long interested in the Italian Renaissance, he greatly enjoyed the opportunity to study its artistic monuments. To Gobineau he wrote that Venice and Florence enchanted him. In Florence he expressed the wish to meet the distinguished journalists, scholars, and artists; and this was arranged.[34] He also visited the studio of the American Hiram Powers, who was then the leading sculptor of the city, and later, in 1873, conferred upon him knighthood in the Imperial Order of the Rose.[35]

In Rome, on November 24, he had an audience with Pope Pius IX, and extended his good offices—but in vain—towards

---

[32] Dom Pedro II to Gobineau, Oct. 28, 1871, Pedro d'Orléans Bragança Archives, A, CLXXXV, 8347b.

[33] Pedro d'Orléans Bragança Archives, B, XXXV, 1087; Nicolas Debanné, "D. Pedro II no Egypto," *Rev. do Inst. Hist. e Geog. Bras.*, vol. 75, pp. 131, 132.

[34] Nogueira da Gama, *op. cit.*, p. 184; Viagem de D. Pedro II á Europa em 1871.

[35] Information obtained from the sculptor's grandsons, Charles W. Lemmi of Baltimore, Maryland, and Hiram Powers of Winter Park, Florida.

smoothing out the difficulties between the Pontiff and King Victor Emmanuel of Italy.[36]

While in Milan, he called on Alessandro Manzoni, then in his eighty-seventh year, with whom he had been in correspondence. When the venerable poet expressed the honor he felt over a visit from the Emperor of Brazil, Dom Pedro replied that it was he who was complimented, in being received by Manzoni, who, he declared, would be remembered long after Dom Pedro de Alcantara was forgotten.[37]

From Italy, the imperial party went to Southern France, where the Emperor engaged in sightseeing as strenuously as before, to the continued resentment of his chamberlain. Though they reached Nîmes late at night, wrote Nogueira da Gama, it was hardly daybreak when he was called upon by Dom Pedro to accompany him through the streets of the city "in an open cart." They returned to the hotel after the others had breakfasted, and there was time for only bread and butter and tea, consumed standing, since the Emperor was calling, "Let's go; let's go; there is no time to waste!" for by now the others were ready to start out.[38]

At Montpellier, he visited various departments of the university, and chatted with the faculty. He was much interested in a class in Arabic which he observed in Marseilles. Here he attended one in modern Greek also, sat on a bench with the students, and joined in the discussion, using contemporary Greek. In Paris, he had failed to find any study being made of the language, and was delighted that Marseilles, founded by the ancient Greeks, was giving attention to it. When one of the students asked for a general holiday for classes, in honor of the royal visitor, the Emperor objected. "No, my friend," he said, "I am not here as a sovereign but merely as a private individual,

---

[36] A. Gallega, *The Pope and the King: the War between the Church and State in Italy*, II, 61.

[37] Manzoni to Dom Pedro II, Oct. 16, 1871, Pedro d'Orléans Bragança Archives, A, CLXI, 7401; Castro, in *Contribuições para a Biographia de D. Pedro II*, Pt. I, p. 581.   [38] Nogueira da Gama, *op. cit.*, p. 185.

and, furthermore, I am not much in favor of these supplementary vacations which always interfere with good studying."[39]

By the latter part of January Dom Pedro was again in Paris, which soon became, and remained for him, the most beloved city in Europe. Here he visited all sorts of places, including the work rooms of the *Moniteur* and the *Monde Illustre,* going through them with characteristic zeal. But he had most pleasure in the company of French scholars. Through the Comte de Gobineau, he met the philosopher Adolphe Franck, whose writings he knew, and he greeted him as an old friend. In one conversation they talked about capital punishment and human slavery. Regarding the latter the philosopher made a rather pointed inquiry. "I understand you," replied Dom Pedro; "the question of slavery occupies still more of my attention than does capital punishment. But, if you will permit me, we will talk about that some other time." Meanwhile, he had been attending Franck's public lectures at the Collège de France, where he refused a place of honor and insisted upon sitting with the general audience.

Some weeks after the conversation about slavery had taken place, Franck read in the press about the passage of the first Brazilian emancipation law, whereby all children born in future of slave mothers should be free. On the same day he took as his theme man's natural right to liberty and the evils of human slavery, and he closed his lecture with words to this effect: "That horrible institution is nearing its end, as regards the New World. Only today it was struck a mortal blow by a sovereign of that region. And the sovereign is in France at this moment; he is in Paris; he is among you, within these walls." The audience turned and, recognizing the towering figure and the benevolent features of the Emperor of Brazil, broke into enthusiastic exclamations.

Dom Pedro quickly found refuge in Franck's office, where he took the professor to task for revealing his presence. "Do

[39] Henri Raffard, *Homenagem do Instituto Historico e Geographico Brasileiro á memoria de Sua Magestade o Senhor D. Pedro II,* p. cxxiii.

you know," he said, "that I consider you a traitor? I so strongly urged, and you so fully promised, that you would not refer to me." But Dom Pedro readily forgave the friendly treason, and shortly afterwards when he visited the French Academy he refused a place of honor and asked merely to be seated by Professor Franck. Franck wrote later, however: "That honor was not a sinecure, for he asked me to tell him the names of all my confrères and the titles of all of their works. The session was ended long before my task was completed."[40]

In February, Dom Pedro and his suite returned to the Iberian Peninsula. During a short stay in Madrid the Emperor attended a session of the Spanish Academy and made an address in Castilian; in Toledo he was fascinated by the Moorish survivals and was also much interested in an old synagogue that he visited.[41]

At the end of the month the imperial party reached Oporto, Portugal, by boat. The waiting crowds were impressed, and perhaps somewhat shocked, by the simple dress of Dona Thereza and Dom Pedro, and by the latter's democratic conduct. The Emperor wished to take a public coach to the hotel, and approached the door of one of them, carrying a satchel in one hand and an umbrella in the other, while under an arm was tucked a parcel. However, the city had made elaborate preparations for the distinguished guests, and these could not well be swept entirely aside. Therefore, the Emperor accepted places for his party in private carriages, but he objected to most of the other formalities, including a guard of honor. That guard followed at a distance as the procession moved off through the flag-decked streets to the accompaniment of salvos from cannon in the fortresses and the music of the Brazilian national hymn. After resting at the hotel, the Emperor attended mass and then visited the mausoleum where the heart of his father was buried; here he prayed for a time. Later came the usual visits to the

---

[40] Mossé, *op. cit.*, pp. 377-84.
[41] Castro, in *Contribuições para a Biographia de D. Pedro II*, Pt. I, p. 582; *Viagem de D. Pedro II á Europa em 1871*; *O Primeiro de Janeiro*, Mar. 1, 1872.

museum of fine arts and other institutions. Dom Pedro also ascended to the tower of one of the churches to view the beautiful fiord-like estuary of the Douro River and the ancient city itself, strongly Moorish in design, resting on the terraced hills. In 1832-1833, his father had defended the place against a sturdy siege by the troops of Dom Miguel. For considerable time Dom Pedro contemplated the scene.[42]

The next day, the Emperor called on Camillo Castello Branco, the romantic novelist, who was ill at his home; and here he met also Guilhermo Braga, the political poet. After chatting with them for some time on travel and on Portuguese and Brazilian literature, he took cordial leave. Referring to the incident, one of the Porto dailies remarked, "If all kings were thus, who would be a republican?"[43]

From Oporto the imperial party went south, making various brief stops. The first was at hilly, picturesque Coimbra with its thirteenth-century university, where the Emperor spent some time browsing in the library, examining the natural history collection, and visiting the various faculties. At Batalha they paused to see the Dominican monastery of Santa Maria da Victoria, established to commemorate the battle of Aljubarrota in 1385, whereby Portugal won independence from Castile. The structure, which had for more than thirty years been a national monument, was remarkable for its intricate and exquisitely beautiful stone carvings. In one of the chapels were the tombs of King João I of Portugal, who led the national troops to victory at Aljubarrota, and his wife Philippa of Lancaster, daughter of John of Gaunt, who had sent five hundred English archers to reinforce the Portuguese army. These two "old, old dead" were remote grandparents of Dom Pedro II.

The royal travelers reached Lisbon on March 7, and were met at the station by their nephew King Luiz and their brother-in-law Fernando, widower of Queen Maria II.[44] Now followed some days of visiting and a little sightseeing. The museum espe-

[42] *O Primeiro de Janeiro*, Mar. 1, 1872.   [43] *Ibid.*, Mar. 3, 1872.
[44] *Ibid.*, Mar. 8, 1872.

cially interested Dom Pedro, and when he departed after examining its collection he shook hands with its officers and urged them to preserve the monuments of the country.[45]

In the middle of March Dom Pedro and the Empress, whose health was now much improved,[46] left Lisbon for home on the British Royal Mail packet "Boyne." With them were their son-in-law, the Duke of Saxe-Coburg-Gotha, and his two older children, Pedro Augusto, aged six, and Augusto Leopoldo, a year younger. In view of the fact that the Princess Imperial had no direct heirs, it was desirable, for the safety of the throne, that these sons of Leopoldina be reared and educated in Brazil. And this was done, under the direction of the Emperor.[47]

On Easter Sunday, March 31, 1872, the imperial travelers reached Rio de Janeiro, which was festively decorated in their honor, and they were given an enthusiastic welcome by their subjects, for the attention and praise showered upon the Empress and Emperor abroad, and especially the great European popularity won by Dom Pedro, was most gratifying to national pride. The Brazilians felt a new appreciation for their sovereign, who, during the past year, had been Exhibit A for Brazil and had made other countries definitely and favorably aware of their own. As the "Boyne" moved up the Bay hundreds of vessels of all descriptions escorted it. The people sang and shouted joyously, cannon boomed from foreign and Brazilian craft in the harbor and from the fortresses on the hills. The next day a grand *Te Deum* was chanted in the imperial chapel, and was followed by a reception in the City Palace.[48] Through the press, individuals and organizations uttered expressions of homage. Happy in the love and loyalty of his people, the Emperor set about benefiting them as much as possible from his educational expedition to older lands.

---

[45] *Ibid.*   [46] Pereira da Silva, *op. cit.*, II, 147.

[47] Teixeira, *op. cit.*, pp. 157-58; Viana, "O principe D. Pedro Augusto: o romance de uma desillusão," *Jornal do Commercio*, Sept. 9, 1934.

[48] Partridge to Fish, no. 46, April 8, 1872, Dept. of State, Despatches, Brazil.

IX

THE EMPEROR'S RELIGIOUS VIEWS AND CHURCH POLICY

SOON after the Emperor's return from abroad the "Church question" developed in Brazil. Towards it he took an attitude which produced bitter attacks from extremists on both sides. In view of his temperament and training, and of his interpretation of his obligations as ruler, his policy was, however, most natural.

His childhood environment had been deeply religious, but the people most influential in it—Dona Marianna, the Marquez de Itanhaén, and Friar Pedro de Santa Marianna—were more intent upon teaching religion as a way of life than as a system of theology. They worked to make their charge a good man and a good king. In the dedication of the small catechism which she prepared for him when he was scarcely out of babyhood, his governess emphasized the duties of the Christian sovereign, and she named piety, justice, and charity as of special importance in a ruler.[1] The Marquez had, in his instructions to the boy's teachers, stressed the same ideas. Though Friar Pedro is a somewhat shadowy figure, he was certainly true to the trust placed in him by the Marquez. It seems likewise clear that by his high personal character he set a fine example for his pupil.

These educators impressed upon Dom Pedro the superiority of Christianity to other faiths. Apparently early in life he read two works which for a time, at least, remained his favorites in the field of religion—Tertullian's *Apologetica*, which defended Christianity against second-century attacks and asserted its unrivalled qualities; and Jacques Bossuet's *Traité de la connaissance de Dieu et de soi-même*, dealing with the nature of

[1] Fleiuss, in *Contribuições para a Biographia de D. Pedro II*, Pt. I, p. 48.

God and of man, and written by the French clergyman for the benefit of his pupil, the son of Louis XIV of France.[2] Though his teachers emphasized the superiority of Christianity, meaning the Roman Catholic faith, this emphasis was apparently free from bigotry and intolerance, for at the time the Brazilian Church showed much breadth of view.[3] In fact, as has been said before, the Marquez definitely stipulated that his pupil must be made to realize the importance of tolerance towards other peoples, regardless of their religion and form of government. Furthermore, he was not to be shielded from facts which might jeopardize his religious views. Instead, he was to be made to see that "religion and politics are in harmony, and that both are in accord with all science."[4]

Dom Pedro, who was tolerant by nature as well as by training, developed the attitude towards religion that his tutor desired. In the early years of his reign he was orthodox according to the teachings of the Church at the time, but open-minded and friendly towards other faiths. Further reading and study and, more especially, travel abroad, stimulated him to greater religious liberalism. Apparently Alexandre Herculano was one of the earliest outside influences in this direction. In 1846, Herculano published the first volume of his history of Portugal, which discredited the story that Christ appeared to Alphonso III in the battle of Ourique. From pulpit and press the historian was denounced for his impiety. Finally, in 1850, he replied in a letter to the cardinal patriarch of Lisbon which he published under the title *Eu e o clero (I and the Clergy)*. This provoked a bitter pamphlet war, which resulted in Herculano's becoming an anti-clerical who differentiated between political Roman Catholicism and the Christian religion. He also championed

---
[2] *Ibid.*, pp. 119-20.
[3] Padre Feijó, the Liberal regent, was so out of harmony with the teachings of the Roman Church that he advocated marriage of the clergy and opposed papal interference in the nomination of bishops.—Hunter to Forsyth, no. 17, Mar. 28, 1835, Dept. of State, Despatches, Brazil.
[4] See p. 32 of this book.

civil marriage, setting forth his views in his *Estudos sobre o casamento civil*, which the Church put on the Index.

Meanwhile, Pope Pius IX had been making a new chapter in the history of the Roman Church. In 1854, he proclaimed the dogma of the immaculate conception of Mary, the mother of Jesus. Ten years later he published his *Syllabus*, which, to many liberals, seemed to declare war against modern civilization and progress.[5] The logical culmination of this trend came in July, 1870, when the Vatican Council proclaimed the infallibility of the pope and the universality of his episcopate. In 1871, Alexandre Herculano attacked the new dogmas, thus aligning himself with the Old Catholics.[6]

Though Dom Pedro II did not meet Herculano until this year, 1871, he had apparently read all of the reformer's writings, had long corresponded with him, and felt for him deep admiration and affection.[7] Judging from the Emperor's policy towards the Church in Brazil and from his utterances regarding religion, by the early 1870's he and Herculano saw eye to eye on the matters under controversy.

Some time before this, Dom Pedro began the study of Hebrew, in order to understand the Old Testament better. This seems to have increased his religious liberalism, especially his appreciation of the Jews. Repeatedly, during his trips abroad he visited the synagogues and found pleasure in the company of the rabbis. Adolphe Franck, the French philosopher, to whom he felt genuine attachment, was a Jew, as was also Benjamin Mossé, who wrote a brief biography of the Emperor.[8]

The New England intellectuals, most of whom were Unitarians, probably also affected Dom Pedro's attitude towards re-

---

[5] "Syllabus. The Syllabus of Pius IX," *Catholic Encyclopedia*; "Syllabus," *Encyclopedia Britannica*.

[6] Antonio de Serpa Pimentel, *Alexandre Herculano e o seu tempo*, pp. 61-137, 219-20.

[7] In the Pedro d'Orléans Bragança Archives are many letters from Herculano to the Emperor.

[8] "Frank (Adolpho)," *Enciclopedia Universal Ilustrada*; B. Mossé to Dom Pedro II, Aug. 9, 1889, Pedro d'Orléans Bragança Archives, A, CC, 9025.

ligion. He was familiar with the writings of most of them, including William Ellery Channing, the leader of the Unitarian movement in the United States, on whose grave he placed a memorial wreath when he visited the United States in 1876. Years later, in one of his marginal notes, he said of Channing, "I shall recommend the writings of this Protestant saint."[9]

Ernest Renan, who had dared to call Jesus Christ "an incomparable man," also probably influenced the Emperor's views. The two met in Paris in 1872, and later corresponded; and Dom Pedro read Renan's writings with much interest.[10]

The Emperor's friendliness towards other faiths led political enemies in Brazil to call him a free-thinker and infidel,[11] but his actions as well as his words disprove the charge. When, in Paris, he learned that a league against atheism had been founded with Professor Franck as its president, he was one of the first to enroll as an honorary member,[12] for he believed that materialism and atheism debased humanity and menaced the social order.[13] He likewise saw danger from neglect of spiritual training in national education.[14]

That religion was not to him merely a means of discipline for the masses is apparent from many utterances during the last twenty years of his life, when his views, having reached their logical maturity, seem to have remained on the whole unchanged. He considered religion important to the good life for himself as well as for others. "I am religious," he said in one of his marginal notes, "because morality, which is a quality of intelligence, is the foundation of the religious idea."[15] He assumed a "First Cause," of the universe and asked the mate-

---

[9] On the margin of Chandordy's *La France en 1889*, p. 21; Sargent, *op. cit.*, p. 303.
[10] Pedro d'Orléans Bragança Archives, A, CLXII, 7439a, 7516, 7623.
[11] Ottoni, *D. Pedro de Alcantara*, p. 18.
[12] Mossé, *op. cit.*, p. 384.
[13] *Ibid.*, p. 385.
[14] Dom Pedro II, note in Chandordy's *La France en 1889*, p. 70.
[15] In Pressensé's *Les origines*, p. 532, Nabuco, *op. cit.*, III, 389.

rialists, "Who created albumen?"[16] "The Creator," he believed, "created everything for a progressive and harmonious development," not as a finished product. He was, therefore, as he said, "an evolutionist with reservations."[17] "I believe firmly in doctrine," he wrote in a long marginal note on religion,

and likewise in what St. Augustine said : *"Credo quod absurdum";* since, more and more each day, the study of facts convinces me of the narrow limits of reason; but, likewise, as regards that gift which God has granted to man, I hold as psychological and physical truths only what reason recognizes as facts; it is difficult for me to accept as truths—as if they were future certainty—what is more or less founded on supposition.[18]

Religious sentiment which is not connected with dogma, or is not *properly* within the realm of reason, I respect, and I have even the good fortune to feel it, though not to an exaggerated degree, thanks to education for which I shall always be grateful to those to whom I owe it. I do not separate religious *faith* from *hope*, because I hope that, through the infinite mercy of God, all men who have performed their duties as fully as human imperfection permits will be rewarded; neither do I separate it from *charity,* to which *intolerance* is repugnant.[19]

The Emperor's breadth of religious view was well illustrated by his attitude towards Dr. Lietpold, his beloved former teacher of German. On the day Lietpold was buried the Empress remarked, "He suffers for having been a Protestant." "What, because of that must my good Lietpold go to Hell?" replied Dom Pedro.[20]

The Emperor was in fact religiously emancipated, as Joaquim Nabuco pointed out,[21] and he reconciled priestly dogmas and scientific hypotheses to suit himself. Though he observed

---

[16] Dom Pedro II to Gobineau, Oct. 4, 1874, Pedro d'Orléans Bragança Archives, A, CLXXXV, 8347b.

[17] Dom Pedro II, marginal note in Pressensé, *Les origines,* 532; Dom Pedro II to Gobineau, Oct. 4, 1874, Pedro d'Orléans Bragança Archives, A, CLXXXV, 8347b; Nabuco, *op. cit.,* III, 389, note.

[18] Nabuco, *op. cit.,* III, 389-90, note.   [19] *Ibid.,* p. 390, note.

[20] Alfredo de Escragnolle Taunay, *Dom Pedro II,* p. 60.

[21] *Op. cit.,* III, 390, note.

churchly forms, he was the captain of his own soul. His religion was largely a personal, subjective matter between himself and the Creator, whose work he, as a student of science, profoundly admired. Indeed, from the wonder and majesty of creation came part of his understanding of and reverence for the unseen forces behind it. After visiting the ruins of Karnak on his second trip to Egypt he wrote in his diary: "I climbed to the top of the Pylon, and there I adored the Lord and Creator of all that is beautiful; and I thought of my two lands, Brazil and France; the one, the patria of my intelligence; the other, the patria of my heart."[22]

In Palestine, which he traversed from end to end on his second trip abroad, giving special attention to the places connected with the life of Jesus, he showed a similar reverent devotion. And later he wrote of the Lord's Prayer: "With what fervor I repeated it when I was in the region where Jesus Christ taught it to his disciples!"[23] It was this innate respect for the supernatural lying back of the visible which caused him to drop to his knees in the Wartburg when the organ began to play Martin Luther's majestic hymn.[24]

Dom Pedro II was, in fact, a deeply spiritual being. But, since he interpreted religious doctrines in his own way, he certainly was not an orthodox Roman Catholic. Joaquim Nabuco calls him a "limited Catholic,"[25] which he doubtless was, but the degree of limitation is not apparent. It seems fairly certain, however, that, like Herculano, he never accepted the new dogmas proclaimed by Pope Pius IX, and that he remained throughout life, at most, an Old Catholic.

Occasionally he expressed frank objection to teaching the new beliefs. One instance of this was told by a protégé who accompanied him on a trip to southern Brazil in 1886. In São

---

[22] Debanné, "D. Pedro II no Egypto," *Rev. do Inst. Hist. e Geog. Bras.*, vol. 75, p. 149.
[23] Pedro d'Orléans Bragança Archives, A, CLXXXV, 8347b; Basilio de Magalhães, "D. Pedro II e a egreja," *Rev. do Inst. Hist. e Geog. Bras.*, vol. 152, p. 408.
[24] See p. 157 of this book. [25] *Op. cit.*, III, 390, note.

Paulo the Emperor visited public schools and questioned the children on different subjects, including Christian doctrine, which formed part of the course of study. A little girl whom he examined on the Creed stated that Jesus was "conceived of the Holy Ghost, born of the Virgin Mary, virgin before his delivery, during his delivery, and after his delivery." Dom Pedro, interrupting the child, turned to the teacher and said: "Do not add anything to the Creed; that prayer is the complete synthesis of our religion. And do not introduce the question of the conception, which is a very recent dogma."[26]

Since the Roman Catholic faith was the state religion, Dom Pedro, as constitutional monarch, was bound to observe and defend it. He, therefore, attended mass regularly, marched in religious processions, and, once each year, in accordance with royal practice, washed the feet of some of Brazil's poor.[27] But he felt no obligation to accept changes made in its dogmas since he took the oath of office. In view of his cosmic tolerance, perhaps his attitude towards the Church would not have been very different if he had been a private citizen, though he might have been less regular in his attendance upon its services. As it was, he conceded to the Church only a minor and secondary place in the Empire, and he showed a definitely critical attitude towards its weaknesses. There seems to have been no basis for the charge, made by his opponents and repeated even as late as 1868, that he was "priest-ridden."[28] On the contrary he strove to keep the clergy subordinate, but he deplored the worldliness and corruption found among a large fraction of them, as he likewise did the superstition of the masses of his subjects.[29]

The Emperor realized that the best hope for a purer re-

---

[26] Teixeira, *op. cit.*, p. 115.
[27] Codman, *op. cit.*, p. 165; C. C. Andrews, *Brazil, its Conditions and Prospects*, p. 85.
[28] Webb to Seward, no. 73, Sept. 24, 1868, Dept. of State, Despatches, Brazil.
[29] "A Fé de Officio de D. Pedro II", *Rev. do Inst. Hist. e Geog. Bras.*, vol. 152, p. 764; Extrahido do diario escripto por S. M. o Senhor o D. Pedro II, Pedro d'Orléans Bragança Archives, A, CXXX, 6373.

ligion among the people was general education, which must come slowly. His marked friendliness towards Protestant missionaries was perhaps inspired partly by the desire to foster a competition which might stimulate the Roman clergy to reform.[30] This was consistent with the financial aid given from the imperial treasury to German Protestant clergy in various parts of the country.[31] The Emperor was, furthermore, favorable to a law permitting civil marriages, especially since there had been some marriages between Catholics and Protestants.[32]

In the late colonial period Gallican tendencies had shown themselves among the clergy of Brazil, largely through the influence of the Portuguese minister Pombal; and after independence was established a considerable fraction of the prelates and priests gave support to regalism, and even desired to keep the Church under tutelage of the State.[33] From the early years of his rule Dom Pedro II kept a hand on the Church, and insisted upon complete independence in filling all benefices and dignities, as was already the practice.[34] No serious objection came to this, and in a campaign against the decadent religious orders, initiated in 1854 by José Thomaz Nabuco de Araujo, minister of justice, the government had the hearty support of the bishops.[35]

In fact, there was no serious friction between Church and State until the early 1870's. Then came a grave crisis over the question of Free Masonry, which had existed in the country since before independence, and had helped bring it about. Contrary to the case in most Spanish American countries, in Brazil Free Masonry was not at first antagonistic to the Roman Church. Dom Pedro I had been a grand master in the order;

[30] Kidder and Fletcher, *op. cit.*, *passim*.
[31] *Ibid.*, p. 142; S. Ballard Dunn, *Brazil, the Home for Southerners*, p. 248.
[32] Kidder and Fletcher, *op. cit.*, p. 142; Wanderley Pinho, *op. cit.*, pp. 222-23.
[33] J. Lloyd Mecham, *Church and State in Latin America*, pp. 310-11.
[34] *Ibid.*, p. 314.
[35] Magalhães, "D. Pedro II e a egreja," *Rev. do Inst. Hist. e Geog. Bras.*, vol. 152, pp. 392-94.

many Masons were found among the *irmandades*, or brotherhoods, largely composed of laymen connected with the parishes; and by the middle of the nineteenth century most Brazilian clergy were members of the lodges. According to Edwin Ryan, it was impossible for any person not a Mason to become a member of the Third Order of St. Francis.[36] Soon, however, the churchmen began to drop out, and their doing so was hastened after Pope Pius IX had, in 1864, formally condemned Masonry in his encyclical *Quanta Cura*, to which the *Syllabus* was annexed. But the Emperor, fully realizing that the papal ban would cause trouble in Brazil, had refrained from issuing the *beneplácito*, the sanction for circulation of the encyclical in the Empire, as was his constitutional right.[37] Technically, therefore, the Brazilian clergy were not aware of Pius's pronouncement against Masonry. But word of the papal fiat spread quickly and tightened the lines between those who resented its assertion of power and those who defended it. Some of the clergy undertook to obey the Pope.

The first serious trouble came in Rio de Janeiro early in 1872. The year before, the first emancipation law for the slaves of Brazil had been passed, largely through the instrumentality of Visconde Rio Branco, president of the council of ministers, and a grand master of the masonic order in Brazil. One of the lodges had a meeting in Rio de Janeiro on March 3, 1872, to celebrate his services in this connection. On the occasion a priest, Almeida Martins, who was a Mason, delivered an address. The bishop of Rio de Janeiro suspended the priest and ordered him to abjure Masonry, which he refused to do.[38] The quarrel was now on in the capital.

A few months later trouble broke out in Pernambuco, when,

---

[36] Oliveira Lima, *O Imperio brazileiro*, p. 167; Edwin Ryan, *The Church in the South American Republics*, pp. 89-90.

[37] Magalhães, "D. Pedro II e a egreja," *Rev. do Inst. Hist. e Geog. Bras.*, vol. 152, p. 397.

[38] Raphael M. Galanti, *Compendio de historia do Brazil*, V, 32; Magalhães, "D. Pedro e a egreja," *Rev. do Inst. Hist. e Geog. Bras.*, vol. 152, pp. 397-98.

in May, 1872, Vital Maria Gonçalves de Oliveira, a youthful Capuchin, assumed office as bishop of Olinda. At about this time a pamphlet, probably of masonic authorship, was published in Rio de Janeiro representing the Bishop as ultramontane and dangerous. Apparently to test him, the Free Masons in the city of Pernambuco announced through the press on June 27 that on the 29th they would commemorate, by a mass in the church of São Pedro, the anniversary of their lodge's founding. Bishop Vital responded by instructing the clergy not to function in any mass announced as masonic; in consequence, the proposed mass was not held. The masonic lodges next published the names of their members who belonged to the religious brotherhoods and to the clergy. The Bishop now exhorted these to abjure Masonry, and he ordered the irmandades to expel all members who insisted upon remaining Masons. His communication was almost wholly ignored. Therefore, in December, 1872, he suspended all of the defiant fraternal groups and placed them under an interdict. The brotherhoods appealed to the Crown against this action; asked that the Jesuits, who were especially hostile, be expelled; and declared that they wanted to obey the Emperor, not the Pope.[39]

The bishop of Pará, Antonio de Macedo Costa, a Sulpician and an ardent reformer, was in strong sympathy with Bishop Vital. In 1872, this prelate began a campaign against the Liberal party in Pará by condemning as errors various views recently published by the party. He denounced the Liberal statement that Jesus Christ was a philosopher, and also the demand made by the political reformers that the Bishop should not interfere with free discussion and liberty of thought. "Free thought!" wrote the prelate, "That is the great slogan of modern impiety."[40]

[39] Galanti, *op. cit.*, V, 33; Magalhães, "D. Pedro e a egreja," *Rev. do Inst. Hist. e Geog. Bras.*, vol. 152, p. 399; *Diario Official do Imperio do Brazil*, June 14, 1873.
[40] "Carta pastoral do Exmo. Bispo do Pará . . . contra os erros de um papel . . . sob o titulo de Protesto do Partido Liberal," *Obras do Bispo do Pará*, p. 16.

By the early part of 1873 various papers in the north were attacking the Roman Church, especially the *Pellicano*, a masonic organ, which the Bishop charged with uttering "all sorts of blasphemies against religion." Therefore, he issued a pastoral letter denouncing Masonry and prohibiting the reading of the *Pellicano*. If those known to be Masons, stated Macedo Costa, did not abandon their Masonry, they must leave the irmandades on pain of suspension. Several of the brotherhoods refused to get rid of their masonic members, whereupon the Bishop suspended them and placed under an interdict the chapels and churches with which they were connected. The fraternal groups appealed to the Crown.[41]

As a whole, the masonic lodges of the country quickly aligned themselves against all attempts at ecclesiastical coercion. On May 10, 1873, Bishop Vital suspended Dean Francisco de Faría of his cathedral, and the Masons, regarding this as an act of ultramontanism, held a meeting in Pernambuco to congratulate the officer upon being deprived of his orders. On the occasion of this demonstration there was considerable mob violence. In an attack upon the Jesuit *collegio*, one of the priests was seriously wounded; the office of the Catholic *União* was wrecked and the printer's type thrown into the street, and a picture of Pope Pius IX was burned publicly. Finally the police were called out to restore order.[42]

Meanwhile, Dom Pedro had been much concerned by the quarrel, and held long sessions of his council of state for consideration of it, and of the irmandades' appeal for redress. The first imperial move was conciliatory. On February 15, 1873, the Minister of Empire, João Alfredo Corrêa de Oliveira, wrote Bishop Vital calling attention to the fact that the irmandades had civil aspects as well as religious, and that, therefore, in trying to control them, the Bishop was usurping temporal

---

[41] Galanti, *op. cit.*, V, 36; Magalhães, "D. Pedro II e a egreja," *Rev. do Inst. Hist. e Geog. Bras.*, vol. 152, pp. 398-99.

[42] Galanti, *op. cit.*, V, 33-34.

prerogatives. Vital replied by calling attention to the fact that Masonry had been condemned by the Pope. The government then turned to the papal internuncio, who advised the Bishop not to antagonize the imperial authority. But the Bishop wrote to the Pope.[43]

Pius replied in a letter of May 29, which showed concern over the "masonic virus"; and though he instructed that patience and mercy precede severity in dealing with the prodigals, he recommended as a final remedy for the trouble the excommunication of Masonry and the dissolution of the refractory irmandades and formation of new ones by the Bishop.[44] The council of state, after long consideration of the appeal of the brotherhoods, decided in their favor. This decision agreed with the views of the Emperor, that the civil rights and dignities must be upheld. Therefore, the Minister of Empire, João Alfredo, ordered the Bishop of Olinda to lift the interdict and leave the Free Masons in peace in the religious groups. Vital refused and, in defiance of the law, published the Pope's letter of May 29, in *A União*, from which it was copied in various dailies.[45]

Meanwhile the situation was becoming increasingly delicate and dangerous, owing to the blind Church loyalty of the more ignorant part of the population and to the resentful defiance of the Masons and their friends. Fanatical Catholics were guilty of disorders, and masonic groups went to extremes in aggravating the fanatics. On July 21, for instance, the Masons of Pernambuco celebrated elaborately the hundredth anniversary of the suppression of the Society of Jesus. The anti-clerical press also continued to denounce fiercely the Jesuits and the Bishop. After the government took action against Vital, two of the irmandades that insisted upon protecting their masonic mem-

---

[43] Mecham, *op. cit.*, pp. 318-19.
[44] *Diario do Rio de Janeiro*, July 11, 1873; Galanti, *op. cit.*, V, 34.
[45] Galanti, *op. cit.*, V, 35-36; Pereira da Silva, *op. cit.*, II, 156-58; *Diario do Rio de Janeiro*, July 11, 1873.

bers celebrated religious festivals without benefit of clergy.[46]

The Crown finally decided to take up the matter directly with the Pope, and appointed as ambassador extraordinary for the purpose the Barão de Penedo, a skilled diplomat. The instructions given Penedo by the Visconde de Caravellas, Minister of Foreign Affairs, were definite and were fully approved by the Emperor. The moderation of the imperial government, wrote Caravellas, had failed to restrain the Bishop of Olinda and bring him to reason. Unfortunately, the Pope, whom the Bishop had consulted, had without knowing the conditions recommended to Vital new acts in violation of the constitution and the laws. The imperial government fully realized the gravity of the conflict, said the Minister, but could not consent to have the constitution and laws annulled by the ecclesiastical power. Other prelates, especially the Bishop of Pará, were defying the imperial *beneplácito*. Penedo must, therefore, explain the situation to the Pope and induce him to cease encouraging the bishops in their obedience, and instead to advise them to conform to the constitution and laws, and to the rules which, from the remotest times, had governed the relations between Church and State. A matter of principle was involved: the imperial government wished to prevent more serious occurrences. To take the attitude that the Bishop had, through the Pope's letter, the arbitrary and unlimited right to dissolve and create irmandades as he claimed to have, would amount to exclusion of the temporal power upon whose sanction the constitutive acts of these associations principally rested.[47] Already, however, the government had planned to bring Vital to trial. The aim of Penedo's mission was primarily to get the interdict lifted and to avert future trouble.

Penedo reached Rome on October 18, 1873, and promptly presented a strong memorandum of the imperial viewpoint, which was submitted for consideration to the College of Cardinals. According to Penedo, the Pope now showed a conciliatory

[46] Galanti, *op. cit.*, V, 35.
[47] Barão de Penedo, *Missão especial á Roma em 1873*, pp. 3-30, *passim*.

attitude. The Brazilian envoy reported to his government that Pius IX's Secretary of State, Cardinal Antonelli, had made known to him the contents of a letter written on December 18 to Bishop Vital under instruction from the Pope. This informed the Bishop that he had badly understood the papal letter of May 29, censured him for his conduct, and ordered him to lift the interdict against the churches in his diocese and to establish again the peace which he had disturbed.[48] Pius likewise expressed through Antonelli the hope that the imperial government, for its part, would try to remove all possible obstacles to the reëstablishment of the desired harmony. A copy of the Secretary's letter was sent to the Bishop of Pará.[49]

There has been question as to whether Penedo's version of the Pope's communication was correct. Considerably later, Macedo Costa charged the Barão with failing to represent the situation fairly at Rome, and also with changing the meaning of Pius's instructions to Bishop Vital. This the Ambassador denied;[50] and it seems likely that he did report correctly his interview with Antonelli—who was a statesman advanced in years, not a prelate—and that Antonelli, influenced by Sanguini, the internuncio of Brazil, who was his nephew, placed upon Pius's orders to Vital an interpretation too favorable to the Empire. It is apparent, moreover, that the Pope himself wished to conciliate the Brazilian government, but he expected imperial clemency towards the bishops in return for his order to lift the interdict. And it is probable that Penedo, in good faith, assured Cardinal Antonelli that no drastic action would be taken against the defiant prelates.[51]

Unluckily for chances of peace, at about the time Antonelli

---

[48] *Ibid.*, pp. 52-54.   [49] *Ibid.*, pp. 57-58.

[50] Antonio de Macedo Costa, *O Barão de Penedo e a sua missão á Roma;* Castro, in *Contribuições para a Biographia de D. Pedro II,* Pt. I, p. 510; Nabuco, *op. cit.,* III, 378-83.

[51] Magalhães, "D. Pedro II e a agreja," *Rev. do Inst. Hist. e Geog. Bras.,* vol. 152, p. 400; Penedo, *op. cit.,* p. 54; Mecham, *op. cit.,* p. 319; Ryan, *op. cit.,* p. 91; F. M. Rudge, "Cardinal Giacomo Antonelli," *Catholic Encyclopedia.*

wrote his letter of December 18 to Vital, the imperial government brought indictment against the Bishop, who was imprisoned a few days later.[52] Visconde Rio Branco, whose views apparently represented those of the whole cabinet, wrote Penedo January 18, 1874, that, because of Vital's defiance of the civil power, and of the excited state of public opinion, the least that the government could do was to bring him to trial.[53] Subsequently the Bishop of Pará was also arrested and imprisoned. When Pius IX learned what had happened, he nullified the letter of December 18 and ordered that it be utterly destroyed.[54] The clergy who acted as substitutes for Vital and Macedo Costa while they were in prison obeyed the Pope and did not lift the interdict.[55] Early in 1874, the council of state by a small majority voted in favor of prosecuting the bishops for violation of the constitution. Among those who opposed such action was José Thomaz Nabuco de Araujo, the distinguished senator from Bahia, who feared that prosecution would injure the prestige and moral influence of the Church and would aggravate the existing conflict.[56] On February 21, 1874, Vital was tried before the imperial supreme court for opposing the decisions of the moderating and executive power granted by the constitution, was found guilty, and was condemned to four years imprisonment with hard labor. The Emperor, urged by Barão de Cotegipe and others, on March 12 changed the sentence to simple imprisonment. On March 24, the Bishop of Pará was imprisoned and on July 1 he received the same sentence from the supreme court; but three weeks later Dom Pedro commuted it as he had that of Vital.[57]

The two prelates were given comfortable quarters in for-

---

[52] Penedo, *op. cit.*, p. 80; Nabuco, *op. cit.*, III, 382.
[53] Penedo, *op. cit.*, p. 65.
[54] Nabuco, *op. cit.*, III, 378-79.   [55] Serrano, *op. cit.*, p. 416.
[56] Nabuco, *op. cit.*, III, 372-73, 394-403.
[57] *Ibid.*, pp. 383-84; Penedo, *op. cit.*, pp. 80 ff.; Macedo Costa, *op. cit.*, pp. 252-53; Galanti, *op. cit.*, V, 36; E. Vilhena de Moraes, *O gabinete Caxias e a amnistia aos bispos*, pp. 20-21.

tresses in Rio de Janeiro and were well treated.[58] But the punishment of church officials as if they were laymen horrified many pious Brazilians. The situation was made worse by the fact that the priests who acted as substitutes for the bishops and also some other clergy who defied the civil authorities were likewise imprisoned. Consequently, anarchy and confusion reigned in the affected dioceses. From press, pulpit, and the houses of Parliament, as well as from private circles, came echoes of this modern struggle between Church and State. The sympathizers with the bishops denounced their trial and sentence as scandalous, bitterly attacked the imperial government, and treated Vital and Macedo Costa as martyrs to the faith. Apparently nearly all of the clergy sided with the two bishops, and some prelates openly declared that the Church was superior to civil authority.

The imprisoned churchmen certainly believed that centuries of precedent gave them the right to regulate and control the irmandades. The opposition, some of whom were Old Catholics with little sympathy for the new dogmas or for the strict views of Pius IX, pointed out that the attack on Masonry was a recent development and that the *Syllabus* which denounced it had never received the Emperor's permission, called for by the constitution, to circulate in Brazil; and neither had the Pope's letter of May 29, 1873, which Vital had published in defiance of this fact. Some supporters of the government talked of separating Church and State, of passing the long-discussed civil marriage law, of secularizing the cemeteries, and even of permitting Protestant houses of worship to carry steeples and other outward signs of their ecclesiastical character.[59]

Dom Pedro II, as was his custom, had given much study and thought to the question, and considered the developments inevitable. He believed that to let the bishops have their way

---

[58] Pereira da Silva, *op. cit.*, II, 166; Mossé, *op. cit.*, pp. 327-28.
[59] "Memoria dirigida a sua Magestade o Imperador pelo Exmo. Bispo do Pará," *Obras do Bispo do Pará*; Shannon to Fish, no. 175, Mar. 1, 1874, Dept. of State, Despatches, Brazil; Nabuco, *op. cit.*, III, 385-87.

would merely invite future trouble with the Church. The constitution must be obeyed. Vital and Macedo Costa had defied the supreme law of the land as well as the order of the Emperor acting in his moderating capacity. They had placed the Roman Pontiff above the Brazilian Constitution, thus flouting imperial dignity as well as the Brazilian nation. They had, in the Emperor's opinion, been guilty of the crime of *lese-majesté*. As perpetual defender of the land he must vindicate national supremacy and stand for punishment of those who held it in contempt. "The moderating power does not compromise," he declared.[60] In a letter to Gobineau of April 4, 1874, he said: "The government has done nothing more than maintain the independence of the temporal power in a matter which was not wholly spiritual. I hope, however, that the energy and moderation of the government will finally end resistance, through making the Roman Curia recognize the true interests of the Catholic Church."[61]

Though he remained firm, he was anxious and harassed. The trouble was perhaps more of a strain through coming so soon after the Paraguayan War. Shortly after the Bishop of Olinda had defied imperial authority by refusing to lift the interdict and by publishing the Pope's letter, Dom Pedro had written to Gobineau, on July 23, 1873, the anniversary of his accession, "33 years are completed since I began to bear my cross."[62] Upon him fell the brunt of the criticism from both sides on the Church question. Many Liberals attacked him for exempting the bishops from actual prison treatment, including hard labor, and declared that the government was afraid to enforce the court sentence. But the Emperor was more concerned by the opposition of the superstitious and deeply pious who were stirring up trouble, to some extent incited by the im-

---

[60] *Collectanea Rabello*, V, 707; Princess Isabel's "Rectification," Pedro d'Orléans Bragança Archives, A, CCIV, 9263.
[61] Pedro d'Orléans Bragança Archives A, CLXXXV, 8347b.
[62] *Ibid.*

prisoned bishops themselves.[63] Mobs of half savage country folk in the provinces of Pernambuco and Parahyba sacked public buildings, burned archives, destroyed the newly-arrived standards for the metric system—an innovation which they distrusted, and also wrecked private property. "Down with the Free Masons! Down with the Government! Long live religion!" they shouted. In many instances Catholic priests led the rioters.[64] But finally they were quelled by imperial troops, and some of the foreign clergy, especially Jesuits, who were leaders in the opposition, were sent out of the country.[65]

But the national split continued. The faithful beset the government with petitions for the release of the prisoners. The Province of Minas alone was said to have sent in 40,000 signatures.[66] Some leading statesmen also desired that the bishops be freed. Another who felt considerable sympathy for Vital and Macedo Costa and was distressed over their plight was Princess Isabel, who had been absent in Europe with her husband during most of the early part of the quarrel. As she later explained, she regretted that the government had not been more patient with the bishops, especially in view of their youth and inexperience,[67] and she seems to have begged her father to release them.[68] But Dom Pedro held out until some time after the Rio Branco government had fallen in the middle of 1875.

The Duque de Caxias, who, like Rio Branco, was a Mason, headed the next ministry. But he soon sent a communication from the new cabinet to the Emperor regarding the ecclesiastical anarchy and general disorder, which the ministers feared might bring disastrous consequences unless the causes were eliminated; and they asked the Emperor to grant amnesty to the bishops.

---

[63] Partridge to Fish, no. 168, April 22, 1874, Dept. of State, Despatches, Brazil.
[64] Partridge to Fish, no. 216, Dec. 14, 1874, *ibid.*
[65] Partridge to Fish, no. 226, Jan. 25, 1875, *ibid.*
[66] Macedo Costa, *op. cit.*, p. 251.
[67] Princess Isabel's "Rectification," Pedro d'Orléans Bragança Archives, A, CCIV, 9263.
[68] Letter of "Ganganelli," in *Diario do Rio de Janeiro*, Sept. 19, 1875.

But Dom Pedro was opposed, and he left for a visit to São Paulo without acting upon the communication.[69]

On September 17, 1875, after his return, the Emperor wrote Caxias a letter which still showed strong feeling towards the actions of the bishops. "The question is serious," he declared, "and therefore I reserve, at least, my personal views regarding it." He saw only two ways of solving the problem, he said—use of constant legal pressure which would make the Roman Curia fear the consequences of the error of the bishops, or separation of State and Church. The latter he had always tried to avoid and he would continue to do so, since the independence and dignity of the civil power did not demand it.[70] However, his council of state advised that he comply and therefore on the same day, September 17, he signed a decree of amnesty for Vital and Macedo Costa.[71] Thus, Church triumphed over State.

Though Princess Isabel apparently was in the council meeting, she probably exercised no more influence than did other members. In any case, it is clear that Dom Pedro released the bishops against his personal inclinations.[72]

Nevertheless, the decree of amnesty, which was soon followed by a lifting of the interdicts by the prelates, was a great relief to the nation as a whole. The *Diario de Rio de Janeiro* remarked pompously two days after the bishops had acted: "The sword of civil authority, brandished against the religious conscience which took refuge in the impenetrable sanctuary, at last recognizes its impotence." This apparently reflected the views of the higher clergy, many of whom were thereafter out of sympathy with the Emperor. But the attack on Dom Pedro by the radical Liberals continued—now because he had given way. A letter in one of the Rio dailies accused Princess Isabel

---

[69] "Declaração em favor da amnistia aos bispos de Olinda e Pará, Archivo Nacional," *Memorias*, I, 470-74; Moraes, *O gabinete Caxias e a amnistia aos bispos*, pp. 44-48, 108-13; Nabuco, *op. cit.*, III, 385-89.
[70] Moraes, *O gabinete Caxias e a amnistia aos bispos*, pp. 55-56.
[71] *Ibid.*, p. 49.
[72] Wanderley Pinho, *op. cit.*, pp. 239-45.

of religious fanaticism, and declared that, through working for the release of the bishops, she had given a preface to her reign. The imperial government, it stated, had been humiliated; in an effort to maintain good relations with Pope Pius IX it had sacrificed the people to Roman voracity. The Emperor, the writer declared, governed Brazil under the shadow of papal influence.[73]

Resentment against the Church continued. In 1879, a bill for its disestablishment was introduced into the lower house of Parliament. Separation was desired by many Liberals, and also by officers of the Church itself—to escape the surveillance of the State.[74] But Dom Pedro, jealous for the dignity of the nation and for the imperial authority, was opposed, and continued his opposition. "Separation would involve serious difficulties," he said, "and the civil power might suffer under it."[75] Therefore, Church and Monarchy, though the loyalty of the one for the other was much weakened, remained united to the end by constitutional ties.

[73] Magalhães, "D. Pedro II e a egreja," *Rev. do Inst. Hist. e Geog. Bras.*, vol. 152, pp. 404-5; *Diario do Rio de Janeiro*, Sept. 19, 1875; Penedo, *op. cit.*, p. 165.
[74] Oliveira Lima, *Formation historique de la nationalité brésilienne*, pp. 244-45.
[75] Behring, "Documentos preciosos," *Collectanea Rabello*, II, 218.

X

TOURING THE UNITED STATES OF AMERICA

DOM PEDRO'S first trip to Europe whetted his appetite for more travel and for another vacation from political duties and official formalities. The long struggle over the religious question was a severe strain. He was tired before it ended,[1] and after it was over he was restless. On November 1, 1875, he wrote to the Comte de Gobineau: "I try to do my duty, but you can imagine how much I resent the little liberty I am able to enjoy."[2] He was planning to go abroad again. In fact, before his return from Europe in 1872 he had begun to think of a trip to the United States of America. And when he learned of the projected Philadelphia Exhibition to celebrate the centennial of American independence he was anxious to make the visit in time for the event.[3] Moreover, the Empress's health had again become worse and she was in need of a change.

By the close of 1875 the way was open. No crisis, foreign or domestic, disturbed the horizon, and Princess Isabel was at home, in good health, and ready to rule during her father's absence. Her popularity had been recently increased by the fact that on October 15 of this year she gave birth to a boy.[4] He had been christened Pedro de Alcantara, and, as his mother's heir, bore the title Prince of Grão Pará. Within the next six years came two other sons, Luiz and Antonio.

The Emperor secured from Parliament permission for absence from the country, and pushed his preparations. Desiring

---
[1] Dom Pedro to Gobineau, Aug. 7, 1875, Pedro d'Orléans Bragança Archives, A, CLXXXV, 8347b.   [2] *Ibid.*
[3] Schenck to Davis, Private, July 26, 1871, Davis Papers, vol. 9; Partridge to Fish, no. 237, Feb. 23, 1875, Dept. of State, Despatches, Brazil.
[4] In 1874 her first child, a daughter, had been born dead.

to travel as a private citizen, he informed the American minister in Rio de Janeiro that he wanted nothing official in his reception in the United States, though he hoped that the reception would be friendly.[5] For Princess Isabel he wrote out long instructions on various political problems, told her not to act without consulting the ministry, and not to send him telegrams except when it was really necessary.[6]

As on his former trip, he arranged to take with him only a small suite. But to his party was added James J. O'Kelly, the Irish-born[7] correspondent of the New York *Herald,* whom its enterprising editor, James Gordon Bennett, had sent to Brazil some months before to write up the Emperor and his voyage to the United States. On the morning of March 26, 1876, they departed, in the English liner "Hevelius." Large throngs were at the dock to bid them farewell. "There was a complete absence of formality and pretentiousness," wrote O'Kelly. "It was not a ruler formally taking leave of the nation he governed; it was rather the parting of a well-beloved father from his family."[8] Several vessels from the Brazilian fleet accompanied the "Hevelius" out of the harbor.

Early on the 29th the liner dropped anchor at Bahia, when the white buildings on the high bluffs were still partly obscured by the morning mists, and it remained there until late afternoon. But harbor regulations in force at the time caused it to be placed in quarantine, and Dom Pedro refused the special permission given him to land.[9] The next stop was at Pará, on the Amazon River, which the Emperor had never before visited. The "Hevelius" was welcomed with skyrockets. People had gathered from all parts of the province to do honor to the im-

[5] Partridge to Fish, no. 310, Feb. 10, 1876, Dept. of State, Despatches, Brazil.
[6] Instructions of Dom Pedro to Dona Isabel, Mar. 26, 1876, Pedro d'Orléans Bragança Archives, A, CLXXV, 7927.
[7] Fernando Ortíz, "Introducción biográfica" to *La Tierra del Mambí,* by James J. O'Kelly, p. xiv.
[8] *Dom Pedro II in the U. S.* (hereafter cited as *Dom Pedro in U. S.*); New York *Herald,* April 16, 1876.   [9] New York *Herald,* April 16, 1876.

perial guests. The Empress and Emperor went ashore for a short time and the crowds gathered about them to kiss their hands in affectionate greeting.[10] Pará was the last stop before New York.

Life aboard ship was pleasant. Most of the imperial party sat at the captain's table, where Dom Pedro showed himself especially good company. Since Dona Thereza, whose lameness had increased with the years, was not well and was not a good sailor, she and her lady-in-waiting, Dona Josephina da Fonseca Costa, spent most of the time crocheting and chatting. The Empress was "sweetly amiable" and a general favorite, wrote the *Herald* correspondent.[11] Dom Pedro was very active, and in high spirits, like a schoolboy on a holiday. He was "about the liveliest and jolliest person aboard," reported O'Kelly; merry and light-hearted, he was "ever ready to laugh at a joke or listen to a song."[12]

But not all of the Emperor's time was spent in mere expression of bonhommie. Much of it was devoted to serious study. Every morning he worked on Sanskrit with Dr. Karl Henning, who was along for the purpose. The lesson began at eleven, and the eager pupil was "as regular as a clock." During the evenings, aided by some of the passengers, he added to his knowledge of English. He read Shakespeare's *Julius Caesar* with an American woman, and wanted to learn "The Star-Spangled Banner." O'Kelly supplied him, from memory, with an incomplete copy which he turned into Portuguese. He spoke English clearly, with a slow, measured enunciation. But he had difficulty in understanding the unfamiliar American pronunciation, and in an effort to master it he associated much with the passengers from the United States, especially with O'Kelly—of whose Irish origin he was probably unaware.[13]

[10] *Ibid.*
[11] *Ibid.;* Pereira da Silva, *op. cit.*, II, 168.
[12] New York *Herald,* April 16, 17, 1876.
[13] *Ibid.,* April 16, 17, 1876; New York *World,* April 17, 1876.

The journalist discussed with Dom Pedro his itinerary for the United States, which the sovereign wished to have extensive.

"Your Majesty means to accomplish a great deal in a short time," remarked O'Kelly.

"Yes, I am always go-ahead."

"In fact, Your Majesty is quite a Yankee."

"Yes. Certainly I am a Yankee," said Dom Pedro. "I always go ahead."[14]

The only visit of a foreign sovereign that the United States had so far experienced was that of King Kalakau of Hawaii. Therefore, the coming of the Emperor of Brazil was an unusual occasion, and the American government determined to err on the safe side and make his welcome official as well as friendly. Shortly after the "Hevelius" entered New York harbor early on April 15, a delegation headed by Secretary of State Hamilton Fish boarded it. The Secretary made a brief address of welcome and then invited the imperial party to go to the city in the government steamer "Alert," on which the American delegation had come. Dom Pedro received the committee cordially, but declined the invitation, because, as he explained later, "The Emperor is in Brazil, I am only a private Brazilian citizen."[15] Then he changed the subject by inquiring of the cabinet officers for General William Sherman and for the poet Longfellow. The New York committee in charge of preparations for welcoming the Emperor, failing to take seriously his request that there be no official reception, assumed that he had accepted Fish's invitation. As a result, the "Alert" received hearty cheers from passing vessels and salutes from the forts in the harbor, while the "Hevelius" with Dom Pedro aboard passed almost unnoticed up the East River to its usual landing place. On its deck, taking in the sights, was the sovereign of Brazil. As the *Times* reporter noted, he wore a black broadcloth suit, but on his head was a silk cap with a leather visor, for he had lost his hat overboard within the last day or two. Beside him stood the plump

[14] New York *Herald*, April 16, 1876.   [15] New York *Times*, April 16, 1876.

little Empress, about a head shorter than he. In her hand was a little satchel which she carried to the landing. Responding to those few who greeted him from the shore, Dom Pedro repeatedly saluted.[16]

At the dock the Emperor and Empress took a common hack and drove through the streets decorated in their honor to the Fifth Avenue hotel where apartments had been reserved for them. Here they received from President Grant a telegram of welcome in the name of the American people. In the evening they saw *Henry V* at Booth's Theatre. Most evenings during their visit in the United States probably found them at a concert or a play, for Dom Pedro patronized even mediocre popular drama, since it gave him opportunity to study the masses. The morning after their arrival, Sunday, he and Dona Thereza worshipped at St. Patrick's Cathedral. But the Emperor spent the rest of the day in an effort to learn as much as possible about American ways of doing things. He visited the office of the *Herald*, and also the News Boys' Lodging House. He was present at the revival services in the Hippodrome, conducted by Ira B. Sankey and Dwight L. Moody, and had a seat on the stage beside the evangelist. Between his knees was his umbrella, with his silk hat perched on the handle. Moody's sermon won his closest attention, and he nodded approval or commented favorably to his secretary, who sat next to him, when the preacher exalted the Christian spirit above denominational differences.[17]

Early Monday morning he started on a round of sightseeing, and, while being driven rapidly down Fifth Avenue, his carriage was run into by an ice wagon and badly wrecked. But no one was hurt; another vehicle was secured; and the Emperor went on his way. He spent much of the day in visiting the

---

[16] *Ibid.; Dom Pedro in U. S.*

[17] New York *Herald*, April 16 and 18, 1876; New York *Times*, April 18, 1876; Chicago *Tribune*, April 18, 1876.

Bellevue Hospital and various kinds of schools. With the idea of special training for nurses, which seems to have been new to him, he was much impressed. Though interested in the noted higher institutions of learning, he wished particularly to see elementary classes, and was taken to Grammar School Number 14. More than a thousand children from the primary grades went through calisthenic exercises, which met his approval, and when several hundred boys sang an animated song he beat time with his umbrella. In reply to his inquiry as to what parts of American society the children of the school represented, he was told that they came from all parts, rich and poor alike; at this situation he expressed pleasure.[18]

In hurrying about New York Dom Pedro showed the skill in avoiding crowds that led one newspaper later to refer to him as "the Artful Dodger." But he attracted much attention wherever he was recognized, for the press had heralded his coming and urged the American public to mind its manners and respect his desire for privacy. All of the leading newspapers had been cordial in their welcome. "It must be confessed," said the New York *Times*," that our people do not entertain a very high reverence for Kings and Emperors, as Kings and Emperors go. A monarch so liberal, enlightened, and practical as Dom Pedro, however, must command the respect of all sensible men."[19] The dailies of Philadelphia, which looked to the Emperor to help make the Centennial Exhibition a success, were especially friendly and complimentary. Dom Pedro, declared the *North American*, deserved "high and rare honors." Throughout his career he had "shown himself to be a gentleman in the fine definition of the word, as well as a man of honor, a friend of progress, and a good ruler."[20]

The Emperor's itinerary included a visit to the Pacific Coast,

---

[18] New York *Herald*, April 18, 1876; New York *Times*, April 18, 1876; Chicago *Tribune*, April 18, 1876.

[19] April 17, 1876. [20] April 17, 1876.

and, since he wished to cross the plains before the hot weather began, he left for the Far West two days after reaching the country. The Empress and part of their suite remained in New York. With him were Bom Retiro, his chamberlain, Dr. Henning, and James J. O'Kelly. The route lay through Chicago and Omaha, over the transcontinental railroad completed less than ten years before. Through the train windows and during brief stops he studied intently whatever he saw. The schoolhouses, which Bom Retiro called "educational palaces," particularly impressed him. The Emperor was also pleased with the sleeping accommodations and the cuisine of the special Pullman car selected for his party, and with the fact that in various hotels he found elevators—modern conveniences which he had apparently not met in Europe four years before. Early in his trip he remarked that to the "Yankees," "time is money."[21] The "Yankees," for their part, were greatly impressed by Dom Pedro's rapid traveling and by the way he made his minutes count at his stopping points.

When the party reached the Far West the Emperor delighted in the snow-crested Rockies. In Wyoming he looked eagerly for buffaloes and Indians. But he was more curious about Mormonism, and stopped in Salt Lake City partly to get more light upon the cult of the Latter Day Saints. The press reported him as saying that, having failed to see the harems of Turkey, he wished to visit the seraglio of Brigham Young. This was a joke, for he met neither the Mormon leader nor any of his numerous wives during a day's stop in Utah's capital. But there were other matters of interest. He tested the density of the water in Great Salt Lake, heard the famous organ in the Mormon Tabernacle, and noted the strange architecture of the building. He bought literature on Mormonism, and asked numerous questions about it. At the Catholic Church in the morning he listened to a sermon denouncing it; in the afternoon he

[21] Pedro d'Orléans Bragança Archives, A, CLXXV, 7934.

and his suite attended a Mormon service and, according to the Mormon *Desert Evening News*, "listened with marked attention to an instructive discourse from Elder John Taylor."[22]

But the Brazilian Emperor was not so favorably impressed as the Mormons would have desired, for, in a letter from San Francisco describing his visit to Salt Lake City, he remarked to his daughter, "I do not see why the Yankees permit polygamy in the center of the United States!"[23] O'Kelly had apparently omitted to mention to him the struggles the United States government had gone through in an effort to eliminate the evil.

After the train entered California it made a stop at Cape Horn on the western slopes of the Sierras to let passengers get out and view the scenery. Here, Dom Pedro was introduced to John McCullough, the Shakespearean actor, and the two were soon in such deep conversation on the drama that they failed to hear the repeated shouts of "All aboard!" Not until the train reached the bottom of the mountain did the conductor realize that the Emperor was missing, and start back to recover him. In the foot hills at Auburn some girls boarded the train and welcomed Dom Pedro with bouquets of California flowers. At Sacramento the special car was detached and run into the railroad yards to escape the crowds waiting at the station and to let him see the machine shops. Persistent "knights of the pencil," however, hoping to get an interview, thrust their cards upon the Emperor's secretary, only to be told that they must be mistaken in their man, since His Majesty did not have the pleasure of their acquaintance.[24]

The overland train with Dom Pedro's special coach was due in Oakland on April 25, and the city had planned a hearty welcome for him at the dock. But, with the coöperation of the railroad officials, he was able to dodge it. At Livermore his car was detached and brought by another engine to the Oakland

---

[22] April 24, 1876; New York *Herald*, April 23, 1876.
[23] April 26, 1876, Pedro d'Orléans Bragança Archives, A, CLXXV, 7934.
[24] New York *Herald*, April 27, 1876; *Daily Alta California*, April 26, 1876.

wharf, well ahead of the train schedule. A special boat carried him and his suite to San Francisco, and they were in their apartments at the Palace Hotel by the time the overland train rumbled into Oakland, where it received the planned "royal ovation," with waving handkerchiefs and flags, cheering crowds, military bands, and shrieking whistles. But Dom Pedro was not able to escape all formalities. Before evening Leland Stanford, James A. Fair, Governor Irwin, and other state celebrities called at the hotel to pay their respects; and in the evening he held a public reception.[25]

During his three additional days in the San Francisco Bay region Dom Pedro rose at about five in the morning and hurried from place to place. But he took time to enjoy the theatre. Between acts of an afternoon performance of "King Lear," with John McCullough in the title role, a tiny girl presented the imperial guest with a basket of flowers. Dom Pedro paid her with a kiss, and the audience applauded lustily.[26]

He went out to the Cliff House, where he viewed the Pacific Ocean for the first time, and crossed over to Berkeley to visit the youthful State University. The Bay of San Francisco, with its Golden Gate, impressed him favorably, but he remarked in a letter to Princess Isabel—and correctly—that in beauty it did not approach the harbor of Rio de Janeiro.[27] In San Francisco he studied factories for making silk, ice, and furniture; he visited the old Franciscan Mission Dolores, Chinatown, and a Chinese theatre; he fingered with special pleasure the volumes in Hubert Howe Bancroft's historical library; and at the Emanuel Synagogue on Sutter Street he was received by two rabbis with whom he discussed the Hebrew tongue. When the scrolls were taken out of the Ark to show him he unrolled one and began to read, translating as he went along.[28]

[25] *Daily Evening Bulletin,* April 25 and 26, 1876.
[26] New York *Herald,* April 29, 1876.
[27] Pedro d'Orléans Bragança Archives, A, CLXXV, 7934.
[28] *Daily Evening Bulletin,* April 29, 1876; *Daily Alta California,* April 27, 28, and 29, 1876.

TOURING THE UNITED STATES OF AMERICA 195

Whether the Emperor liked the hearty, energetic Californians is not apparent, but they unquestionably were much pleased with him. Before his departure, one of the leading San Francisco dailies referred to him as "one of the men, who, in our time, have given respectability to the trade of king,"[29] which, in view of the intensified republican pride of that centennial year, was a genuine compliment.

Early in the morning of April 29 the imperial party started East in the special Pullman attached to the overland train. During the stop at Sacramento they visited the capitol in company with Governor Irwin. In the mountains, because of obstructions on the tracks, there were two long, tedious delays of many hours, which Dom Pedro accepted philosophically. But the loss of time cut the visit planned for Chicago to a few hours, which were spent mostly in studying the water-supply system, from which the Emperor wanted especially to get ideas to introduce at home. After another short stop, at Pittsburgh, the Brazilian travelers reached Washington in the forenoon of May 7, and went to the Arlington Hotel.[30]

That evening Dom Pedro studied the northern skies at the Naval Observatory in the company of the Brazilian minister, Carvalho Borges, and Professor Newcomb. The next morning before breakfast he was at the Smithsonian Institution, wearing an "old-fashioned plug hat." Later in the day came his call at the White House—which some petty critics declared should have preceded his trip to the Far West[31]—where he was received by President Grant and Secretary Fish. Several times he visited the Capitol, where the pages besieged him for autographs. Refusing invitations to the floors of the chambers, he always took a seat in the diplomatic gallery. When the chaplain of the House began his prayer the Emperor respectfully rose to his feet, but, said the Washington *Evening Star*, "finding it

[29] *Daily Alta California*, April 29, 1876.
[30] New York *Herald*, May 1, 4, and 5, 1876; Washington *Evening Star*, May 8, 1876.   [31] *Dom Pedro in U. S.*

was the custom for the members to worship in a recumbent position with their heels on their desks, he sat down again."[32]

At the time of Dom Pedro's visit the exposure of administrative corruption was well under way, and the press was airing the scandals involving the "Whisky Ring," and Blaine, Bristow, and Belknap. The trial of Belknap was going on in the Senate, and the sovereign of Brazil followed with interest the snatches he got of it. Perchance he gained a little sad consolation over the fact that such things could happen even in a country with a long tradition of self government. Early in the afternoon of May 9th he left for Philadelphia, where Dona Thereza and the remainder of the party had preceded him and were settled in quarters at the Continental Hotel.[33]

The Centennial Exhibition was formally opened the following day. Dom Pedro, with the Empress on his arm, arrived early for the ceremonies, which were held out of doors. The crowd greeted them with cheers and applause, and when they mounted the steps of the platform the orchestra struck up the Brazilian national anthem. General Joseph Hawley, head of the Centennial commission, in a short speech presented the Exhibition to President Grant, who was on the platform. After Grant had replied, the audience cheered, and the Emperor rose and waved his hat. Both he and the Empress played active parts in the formal opening of the Exhibition. By pulling a golden cord Dona Thereza inaugurated the Women's Section in its special pavilion, and Dom Pedro shared with President Grant the honor of starting the thousands of wheels in Machinery Hall by moving a handle on one of two master Corliss engines. Observers noted that in performing this ceremony the Emperor was a few seconds ahead of the President. The Corliss engine itself was a great attraction to Dom Pedro, who was fond of machinery; and in connection with it he made one of the best Centennial jokes. On learning the number of revolutions

[32] May 8, 1876.
[33] Washington *Evening Star*, May 8 and 9, 1876.

made per minute by the Corliss he remarked, "That beats our South American republics."[34]

In the evening of May 10 came a brilliant reception at the home of George W. Childs of the *Public Ledger*. "Miss Grundy" noted in her press column that the Empress wore an apricot-colored silk gown draped with exquisite white lace, and that her earrings and necklace were of large solitaire diamonds. Dom Pedro in his customary black "Prince Albert" seemed to enjoy himself thoroughly, through avoiding political topics and talking mostly about American literature and literary figures. He asked for James Fenimore Cooper's daughter, Susan Augusta, who was conducting a school in New York for poor children; and also wished to see Harriet Beecher Stowe, who, unfortunately, was then in Florida.[35]

On the morning of May 11 the Emperor of Brazil was one of the earliest arrivals at the Exhibition grounds, though he had already visited the United States Mint. The display of Brazilian products collected under his direction was complete. After studying the exhibits in Machinery Hall, he went to Wilmington, Delaware, to see the iron foundry and the shipbuilding works; but he was back in time for the reception given that evening by the British minister, Sir Edward Thornton, whom he had first met eleven years before during the war with Paraguay.[36]

Since the Centennial Exhibition was not yet complete, the Emperor decided to take another trip and return later to study the exhibits when they were all in place. Therefore, after a few days in Philadelphia, he left with the Empress and his suite, going first to Baltimore, where he arrived about noon and occupied apartments at the Carrolton Hotel. The rest of the day was spent in going through the Academy of Sciences and various other places. One of the last was the City Hall, which had been

---

[34] Baltimore *Sun*, May 12, 1876; *Public Ledger*, May 11, 1876; Baltimore *Weekly American*, May 13, 1876.
[35] *Dom Pedro in U. S.*
[36] *North American*, May 12, 1876.

ablaze with lights at three o'clock and where Mayor Latrobe, whom the Emperor had met the day before in Philadelphia, awaited his coming. But swarms of curious people were also there, so the carriage with the royal guest turned away after almost reaching the building, and it did not come back until five, when the crowds were gone and the lights had been turned off. Dom Pedro noted with apparent amusement the hasty relighting of various parts of the building through which the Mayor escorted him.[37]

The next day, accompanied by the Brazilian Minister, he went down Chesapeake Bay in the steamship "Kent" to Annapolis, and returned the same way. He carried Homer's *Iliad* and Osgood's *Middle States*, but was too busy studying the sights and asking questions about the harbors and the Bay to make much use of the books. The vessels in the harbor saluted. At the Naval Academy the cadets went through maneuvers for his edification, and he praised them in return. Though he was interested in the guns and practiced working some of them, he cared more for the astronomical observatory at Annapolis. Through the State House he was escorted by Governor John Lee Carroll, who showed him the portrait of his grandfather, Charles Carroll of Carrollton, by Sully. Dom Pedro had heard of this signer of the Declaration of Independence and created secret merriment by remarking "Ah! that is Carroll the First."[38]

After the return to Baltimore, following luncheon at the Governor's Mansion, the Emperor visited Walter's Art Gallery and the Peabody Institute, and also the Academy of Music, newly erected, of which Baltimore was especially proud. Here Dr. J. Hall Pleasants explained the various features of the building, and vocal music was rendered to show the acoustics. Dom Pedro applauded heartily. Earlier in the day Dona Thereza, with Bom Retiro and Dona Josephina, had done sightseeing on her own account. In the evening she accompanied

---
[37] Baltimore *American and Commercial Advertiser*, May 13, 1876.
[38] Baltimore *Sun*, May 15, 1876; *Dom Pedro in U. S.*

the Emperor to Ford's Opera House, where they both were so charmed with Mary Anderson in "The Lady of Lyons" that they asked her to come to their box after the play. That box was renamed "The Imperial."[39]

On Sunday, May 14, the Brazilian travelers left early for St. Louis, making a few short stops on the way. The first was at Cincinnati, where during part of a day Dom Pedro followed a varied program which included visits to an art museum, a factory for making surgical instruments, and a pork-curing plant. The party reached Louisville on May 16, where the Empress went to a hotel. The Emperor, with two members of his suite, took a special train to see Mammoth Cave. He found his unusual height a handicap in getting about there, but during the three hours allotted he explored the cavern as far as Green River. Later he remarked that Mammoth Cave, like much else he had seen in America, was not pretty, but magnificent.[40]

The next forenoon the Brazilian tourists reached St. Louis, where Dom Pedro seems to have been franker in his criticisms than before, possibly because his English was increasing in fluency. When he saw the customs house, then being built, he expressed surprise that a sensible people should erect such a massive and costly structure on a mud foundation, and he added that an iron building would have done very well and would have been much cheaper. Informed that the American people built for remote posterity, he was reported to have replied: "But an iron building would last 400 years, and you do not mean to tell me that there will be any custom houses in 400 years."[41] Did the philosophical sovereign of Brazil foresee a golden age when tariff walls should be no more?

He disapproved also of St. Louis's insane asylum, for its lack of proper heating and bathing facilities, and its system of personal restraint. It would be better, he pointed out, to place violent patients in separate cells and have them free from

[39] *The Sun*, May 15, 1876.
[40] *Dom Pedro in U. S.*   [41] *Ibid.*

shackles. In this regard, he said, the Brazilian system was superior. He also criticized the poor house when he learned that some insane people were grouped with the paupers. But he was frankly pleased with the schools of St. Louis, and likewise with the factories, where the Visconde do Bom Retiro left large orders for agricultural machinery to be sent to Brazil.[42]

May 18 found Dom Pedro and his party steaming down the Mississippi on the "Grand Republic," bound for New Orleans. During the voyage of almost a week the strenuous Emperor had a much-needed physical rest. In some of his leisure he read his Homer, but he also asked questions of anyone from whom he thought he might get an answer; and he disseminated information to the members of his party. He was pleased with the activity of the American people, and remarked: "Brazilians say too much 'Bye and bye, bye and bye'; your people say 'Today, today.'"[43] When the boat stopped at ports on the river, crowds invaded it and frankly stared at the imperial visitors until the warning bell caused them to hurry away. Dom Pedro had remarked upon landing in New York that he was willing to let people stare at him as much as they wished, but that he did not like for them to waste his time or to get in his way. Now, he had some free hours and apparently welcomed the opportunity to study these river folk from the interior of the country.[44]

When the boat reached New Orleans on the afternoon of the 24th, a large crowd was waiting on the dock to get a glimpse of royalty, and it was with difficulty that the Brazilians were able to land and depart in public hacks for the St. Charles Hotel. Shortly after he reached the city Dom Pedro submitted to an interview from the reporter of the New Orleans *Times*. Boiler explosions on Mississippi River steamboats were still of frequent occurrence, and his interviewer credited him with saying that he was meditating building a chapel to his patron saint when he got home for saving him from such a calamity. The

[42] *Ibid.*   [43] *Ibid.*
[44] *Ibid.;* New York *Herald*, April 17, 1876.

pride of New Orleans at the time was the jetties at the mouth of the Mississippi, recently completed under the direction of Captain Eads; but in the interview Dom Pedro did not mention them. Instead, he expressed a desire to gain information on other matters—the commerce of the port; the best methods of combatting yellow fever; the colored schools; how far good relations had been established between white and colored; and whether the two races seemed capable of living together.[45]

He was not favorably impressed with New Orleans and missed there the energy and bustle of the North and West. He also remarked that grass was growing in the streets and that the city lacked a good system of street cleaning. He saw a number of colored schools, but apparently did not say what he thought of them. Twice he held at the hotel conferences with physicians on the best methods of combatting yellow fever, but he seemed to learn nothing new. He visited various commercial houses in the city, and also went for a distance into the country to see some large sugar plantations. On a trip to view Lake Pontchartrain, he amused himself by fishing for crabs from the levee. During his short stay in New Orleans he also found time to attend services at a Jewish synagogue, and to enjoy a philosophical discourse with Professor Fontaine, whom he invited to spend an evening with him. Finally, on the afternoon of the 27th he went with Bom Retiro and O'Kelly in a steam yacht to see the famous jetties, explained to him by Captain Eads, with whom he was delighted. He was properly impressed with the engineering feat and was interested and surprised that private American citizens should carry out such important public works at their own risk. Returning the next morning to New Orleans, he and his party left the same day by train via Mobile and Memphis for Washington, which they reached June 2.[46]

In Washington Dom Pedro visited schools and saw various

[45] New Orleans *Times*, May 25, 1876.
[46] *Dom Pedro in U. S.*; New Orleans *Times*, May 26, 27, 28, and 29, 1876; *Daily American*, June 2, 1876.

other points of interest omitted in his first visit. One of these was Mount Vernon, where he laid a wreath on the tomb of the Father of his Country and expressed surprise that the place should appear so neglected. Both he and the Visconde do Bom Retiro contributed towards the fund for the Washington Monument, and he had his chamberlain order a block of Brazilian marble from São Paulo to be set in the inner walls of the shaft. At Dom Pedro's request the Washington fire department gave a special demonstration of its methods. Wearing a "Brazilian slouch hat" and carrying a huge silver-handled umbrella to protect himself against the spray from the hose, he wandered up and down the sidewalk, a pleased spectator.[47]

Before night the party, which had been joined by the Duke of Saxe-Coburg-Gotha, was on its way north. They visited Niagara Falls on June 4, and were photographed with the Falls as a background. The Emperor was impressed with the cataract and spent some time studying it. With a number of the men, dressed in yellow oilskin suits—which caused Dona Thereza to poke fun at their appearance—he went under the Horseshoe Falls. The next day the main party left for a trip into Canada and the Duke returned to New York.[48]

Going by train to Kingston, they took a boat here for a voyage among the Thousand Islands. The Emperor was disappointed in the scenery, but enjoyed the trip. He climbed to the hurricane deck and talked with the captain, chatted freely with the passengers, and told them that there were much grander rapids in Brazil than those in the St. Lawrence. But he admired the skill with which the vessel was handled in the rapids and expressed a wish that there were such pilots in Brazil. Later, he amused himself by getting into an argument with an old farmer whom he tried to convince that Brazil was more fertile than Canada. At Montreal, where the imperial travelers disembarked on June 6, there was the usual whirl of sightseeing. The

---

[47] *Dom Pedro in U. S.; Evening Star*, June 3, 1876; Raffard, *op. cit.*, p. cxvii.
[48] *Dom Pedro in U. S.*

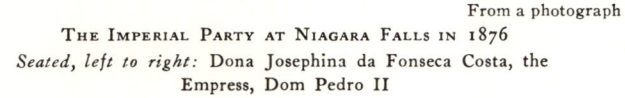

Dom Pedro as Represented by a Contemporary Cartoon
From a reproduction in the *Revista da Semana*, Nov. 28, 1825

The Imperial Party at Niagara Falls in 1876
Seated, left to right: Dona Josephina da Fonseca Costa, the Empress, Dom Pedro II 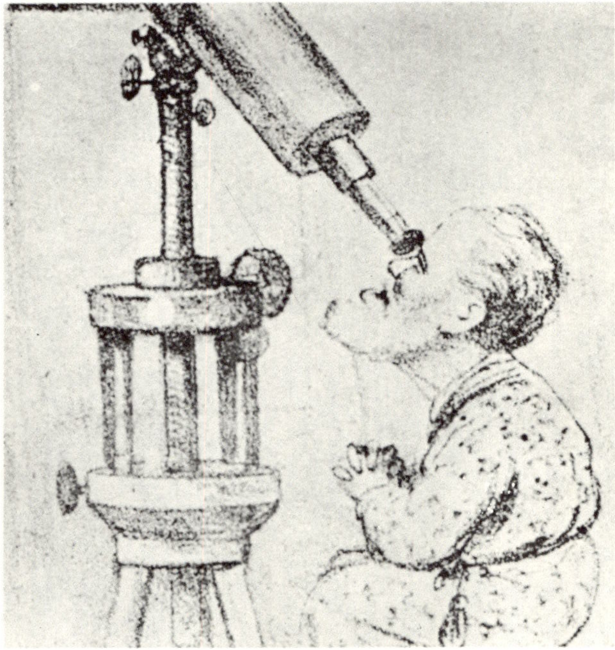
From a photograph

next morning Dom Pedro created a sensation among the butchers by visiting the meat market and examining their wares, but he devoted more time to the museums, churches, and educational institutions. Early in the afternoon of the same day the party took the train for the United States.[49]

That evening they had a sail on Lake Memphremagog, on the border between Canada and Vermont; then took the night express going south. The next day, June 8, was spent in visiting mills in Lowell and in neighboring industrial cities. They reached Boston that night and went to the Revere House.[50]

Dom Pedro liked Boston best of all cities in the United States, and Boston liked the Emperor. He visited, at the outset, the historical landmarks—Old South Church, Faneuil Hall, and Bunker Hill Monument—seeing them before breakfast the first morning. He reached the Monument at six o'clock and the keeper, roused out of bed, asked for the fifty cents entrance fee. The Emperor, who in personal matters was only slightly money-conscious, had come without funds; but he borrowed a half dollar from his hack driver and ascended the shaft for the view. A few hours later came Richard Frothingham, the historian, who, seeing Dom Pedro's signature in the visitor's book, asked the guard how the Emperor looked. The irritated guard, putting on his glasses to see the handwriting, muttered, "Emperor! That's a dodge; that fellow was only a scapegrace, without a cent in his pocket."[51]

Later that forenoon Dom Pedro went to the Public Library and the State House. At the latter place he asked to see the papers, "directing that the witches should be burned," and when told that the victims of the delusion were hanged, and shown the warrants for their execution, he remarked that it was "all the same."[52]

---

[49] *Ibid.;* Toronto *Globe,* June 7 and 8, 1876; Montreal *Gazette,* June 7, 1876.
[50] Montreal *Gazette,* June 8, 1876; Boston *Daily Advertiser,* June 9, 1876; Boston *Post,* June 8, 1876.
[51] Andrews, *op. cit.,* p. 83; Boston *Journal,* June 10, 1876; Sargent, *op. cit.,* p. 302.   [52] Boston *Journal,* June 10, 1876.

He inspected a Cunard liner, a grain elevator, and the Navy Yard at Charlestown, returning to Boston on the street car. The State Prison, because of its small, poorly-ventilated cells, was disapproved by him, as were prisons generally throughout the country.

Since he wished to see the Boston fire department in operation, a special alarm was rung, which brought out the horses and engines. He also examined the equipment of the hook and ladder company, and went on a cruise in the city fireboat, during which all of the hoses were brought into action to show how fires were fought on the waterfront. The speed and efficiency of the whole system surprised and pleased him.[53] At West Somerville he saw the Robinson wireless electrical train signals operate and asked the inventor to correspond with the Brazilian government with a view to introducing the system there.[54]

The educational facilities probably interested him more than did the mechanical inventions. After visiting all grades of schools from the kindergarten up, he listened to a detailed description of the city educational system, given by the president of the board of school commissioners. He frankly expressed his enthusiasm for the Boston schools, and, in fact, for the public school system and facilities in the country as a whole. Out at Wellesley he was pleased to see the girls rowing on Lake Waban. Here, Mr. H. F. Durant showed him the buildings of the new college for women which he had founded, and which was about to open its doors. At Harvard University he was delighted with the laboratory facilities, and had conversations with some of the most learned professors.[55]

The equipment at the Harvard Medical School was perhaps equally stimulating. In fact, health betterment in Brazil was a matter near his heart, and he gathered new medical ideas wher-

---

[53] Boston *Journal*, June 12, 1876; Boston *Daily Advertiser*, June 12 and 14, 1876; *Dom Pedro in U. S.*

[54] Boston *Daily Advertiser*, June 15, 1876.

[55] Boston *Daily Advertiser*, June 12 and 13, 1876; Sargent, *op. cit.*, p. 302.

ever he could. Hence, he visited the Massachusetts General Hospital and also accepted the invitation to attend the annual meeting of the State Medical Society. The organization elected him an honorary member, and invited him to join its discussions, but he declined, saying that he was "not a medical, but a social, physician."[56]

Since he was anxious to help the handicapped at home through education, he usually inspected special institutions for such individuals whenever opportunity came. At the Boston City School for the Deaf, he talked with Alexander Graham Bell, one of the teachers, on the problems involved in his work.[57] Finding it difficult to remember that people in temperate zones did not rise as early as those in the tropics, he startled the authorities at the Perkins Institution for the Blind by ringing its bell at seven-thirty one morning and asking for the sightless deaf-mute, Laura Bridgman. He was disappointed to learn that she was no longer there, but asked for and received a detailed account of the methods used in teaching her. He inspected all departments of the school, examined classes in arithmetic and geography, heard several musical selections played by blind students, and asked that some ciphering and writing boards and types be sent to him for use of the blind in Brazil. He was aware of the work of founding and developing the school done by Dr. Samuel Gridley Howe, who had died six months before, and he became suddenly much interested in Howe's son-in-law and successor, Michael Anagnos, when he learned that the new director was a Greek. In a few minutes he was deep in discussion with him over the comparative qualities of ancient Greek and modern.[58]

The Americans whom he met, or had met, meant far more to the Emperor than the institutions visited. He had become attached to Professor Louis Agassiz when the scientist made a

---

[56] Boston *Journal*, June 13, 1876; *Dom Pedro in U. S.*
[57] Catherine Mackenzie, *Alexander Graham Bell*, p. 118.
[58] Boston *Daily Advertiser*, June 13, 1876.

trip to Brazil many years before. Agassiz was now dead but Dom Pedro visited his grave to lay a memorial wreath upon it; and he took pleasure in meeting again, at her home, the scientist's widow, Elizabeth Cary Agassiz, and in making the acquaintance of Agassiz's son Alexander, who was one of the first to call.[59]

Dom Pedro knew most of the New England writers through their works, and with a few he had corresponded. He had translated into Portuguese Whittier's "The Cry of a Lost Soul," and had sent the poet mounted specimens of the Brazilian bird from which the verses got their name.[60] For the Quaker poet he had developed a deep affection, and was anxious to meet him. Mrs. Agassiz, accordingly, had an afternoon reception arranged for the Emperor at the Radical Club headquarters, to which Whittier and a number of other distinguished men were invited. Of the guest of honor's arrival, Mary Elizabeth Sargent wrote: "Sending up his card, His Majesty followed it with the quickness of an enthusiastic school-boy; and his first question, after somewhat hastily paying his greetings, was for Mr. Whittier."[61] He made to embrace the poet, Brazilian style, but the shy Quaker substituted a cordial handshake; then the two sat in a corner and talked like old friends for a half hour. After the conversation became general, he chatted about what he had seen around Boston, and explained his deep interest in getting new ideas by the remark, "You know, I'm a Doctor of State Diseases."[62]

Sipping his coffee, he noted the hour and exclaimed, "It is five o'clock, Mrs. Sargent; not my fault, only my misfortune."[63] Rising, he put his arm around Whittier and drew him down stairs. In taking leave of him, he apparently managed to include the Brazilian hug. Then, standing erect in the waiting barouche, he waved his hat in a final goodbye.[64]

[59] *Dom Pedro in U. S.; Daily Advertiser,* June 12, 1876; Sargent, *op. cit.,* p. 301.
[60] Sargent, *op. cit.,* p. 301.   [61] *Ibid.,* p. 302.
[62] *Ibid.,* pp. 302-3.   [63] *Ibid.,* p. 303.
[64] *Ibid.;* Charlotte F. Grimke, "Personal Recollections of Whittier," *New England Magazine,* N. S., VIII, 473.

After he had gone a young lady who had helped serve ices to the guests, much impressed, remarked, "The other gentleman thanked me, but the Emperor rose."[65]

For Longfellow, who was his favorite American poet, Dom Pedro had an unusually deep affection, and he enjoyed a dinner given by him at his Cambridge home. Invited to name those he most wanted to meet on the occasion, the Emperor mentioned Emerson, Lowell, and Holmes. Lowell was out of town and could not be present, but the others came. Alexander Agassiz and William Henry Appleton, the publisher, completed the list. Longfellow thought the gathering "very jovial and pleasant."[66] After the meal was ended, he and Dom Pedro paced up and down the veranda and talked. This part of the visit was long remembered by the poet, whom Dom Pedro later invited to come to see him in Brazil, so that they might walk and talk on *his* veranda.[67] But Longfellow thought himself too old to make the trip. In his journal at the time of Dom Pedro's visit, the poet described the Emperor as a "modern Haroun-al-Raschid wandering about to see the great world as a simple traveller, not as a king. He is a hearty, genial, noble person, very liberal in his views."[68]

For a few days after leaving Boston and its environs the Emperor made brief visits to several other points in New England and New York. He and his suite were sightseeing in Albany one morning slightly after six o'clock, before most of its inhabitants were up. At Saratoga he sampled various mineral waters and rode on the lake in Frank Leslie's steam yacht. At New Haven, he was shown around Yale University under arrangements made by the historian George Bancroft,[69] who entertained him at Newport.

At Vassar College, then eleven years old, he was especially

---

[65] Sargent, *op. cit.*, p. 303.
[66] Samuel Longfellow, *Life of Henry Wadsworth Longfellow*, III, 262.
[67] Longfellow to Dom Pedro II, July 12, 1878 (?); Pedro d'Orléans Bragança Archives, A, CLXIX, 7728; Mendonça to Dom Pedro II, July 2, 1880, *ibid.*, CLXXXIII, 8285.
[68] Longfellow, *op. cit.*, III, 261.   [69] *Dom Pedro in U. S.*

attracted by the astronomical observatory, and surprised Professor Maria Mitchell by his appearance, as well as by his familiarity with the instruments. She wrote in her journal: "I had imagined the Emperor of Brazil to be a dark, swarthy, tall man, of forty-five years; that he would not really have a crown upon his head, but that I should feel it was somewhere around, handy-like, and that I should know that I was in a royal presence." The white-haired, blue-eyed Dom Pedro, whom she guessed to be about sixty-five—fourteen years older than he was—proved to have such a "very pleasant, even chatty, manner" that she apparently forgot at the time that he had ever swayed a scepter. She was astonished at his inquiry whether Alvin Clark had made the glass of the equatorial. "He seemed much more interested in the observatory than I could possibly expect," she wrote. "I asked him to go on top of the roof, and he said that he had no time; yet he stayed long enough to go up several times."[70]

By June 20 the Brazilians were back in Philadelphia at the Continental Hotel. Dom Pedro had traveled about nine thousand miles since he landed in New York. "When he goes home," remarked one editor, "he will know more about the United States than two-thirds of the members of Congress."[71]

The *North American* had said of him two months before, "No ruler anywhere has, as a ruler or as a man, ever deserved so well from the United States as Pedro II; and we shall not regret if the appreciation of that fact is clearly manifested."[72] Apparently one result of this hint was the large arch spanning Chestnut Street in the Quaker City, with the greeting "Welcome Dom Pedro" illuminated by gas jets.[73]

Probably most Americans could by now locate Brazil, and also knew who the imperial traveler was; and they had rid themselves of any original impression that Dom Pedro hurried

---

[70] Phebe Mitchell Kendall, *Maria Mitchell: Life, Letters, and Journals*, p. 190.
[71] *Dom Pedro in U. S.*   [72] April 17, 1976.
[73] *Brazilian American*, December, 1925.

about the country with crown on head and scepter in hand, like an animated King of Diamonds. His matter-of-fact attitude and frank criticism were taken good-naturedly, and his frequent praise warmed American hearts. Enthusiasm for him was great. He was probably the most popular foreigner that has ever been in the United States. Whatever he did was of interest. People were fascinated by his strenuous qualities, and by his tendency to turn up unexpectedly. While still in Brazil, James J. O'Kelly, alluding to him as a "will-o'-the-wisp," had remarked, "Now you see him, and now you don't."[74] The secret of his charm was partly that the nation recognized in him some of its own qualities. Thus, an editorial referred to him as "Our Yankee Emperor."[75] Apropos of the national political campaign one admirer wrote, "As for our part, we nominate Dom Pedro and Charles Francis Adams for our Centennial ticket for President and Vice-president. We are tired of common people and feel disposed to go in for style."[76]

With his customary thoroughness, the Emperor proceeded to study the Exhibition. To avoid the crowds, the heat, and afternoon storms, he went to the grounds early, at times arriving before seven, and spent several hours there daily. Afternoons were generally given to visits in various places in the city arranged by George W. Childs. He accepted an invitation of the Academy of Natural Sciences to attend its meeting, and heard Dr. Leidy talk on various classes of rhizopods. One day, after spending some time at the Exhibition, he gave a new demonstration of what the Philadelphia *Public Ledger* called "imperial celerity," through an out-of-town visit by special train. During it he saw Lehigh University and the zinc and iron works in and near Bethlehem, Pennsylvania. At the University were a number of Brazilian students, who were delighted to see him. "The young men gathered about him," said the admiring *Ledger*, "as they would around a father, and he seemed like a

---

[74] New York *Herald*, Jan. 28, 1876; *Dom Pedro in U. S.*
[75] *Dom Pedro in U. S.* [76] *Ibid.*

father in his conduct to them."[77] At the metal foundries he wished to see every detail of operations, and he visited the scorching furnace rooms at the Bethlehem Iron Works and observed with minute attention the Bessemer process of making steel, with which he was already familiar in theory. He had dinner on the train and was back in Philadelphia in time for his evening engagements. Later, a Brazilian protégé aptly likened him to "a library on top of a locomotive."[78]

During these busy days Dom Pedro was finding much pleasure and profit in the Exhibition. The high light of his visits to it was the incident which connected him with the history of the telephone. The obscure inventor, Alexander Graham Bell, was exhibiting his device in the hope of rousing interest and securing financial aid. On a hot Sunday, June 25, he waited anxiously in the electrical exhibits room, since he had to leave for Boston that night in order to teach his classes at the Boston School for the Deaf the next day. Presently, in came the judges, headed by Sir William Thomson, and accompanied by Dom Pedro. Bell heard one of the men say that the exhibit next to his would be the last they would study that day; and his heart sank. When they turned to depart, they paused to let the Emperor precede them.

Dom Pedro, however, did not lead the way out of the building, for at that moment he recognized the teacher from the Boston School for the Deaf. He went up to him with outstretched hand, saying heartily, "How do you do, Mr. Bell? And how are the deaf-mutes of Boston?" Though anxious to get away, the judges could hardly hurry the Sovereign of Brazil. While they waited, Alexander Graham Bell explained the situation to Dom Pedro, and referred to his need to leave Philadelphia that night. The Emperor's intellectual curiosity

---

[77] Philadelphia *North American*, June 23 and 24, 1876; Philadelphia *Public Ledger*, June 27 and 28, 1876.

[78] Philadelphia *Public Ledger*, June 27, 1876; Teixeira, *op. cit.*, p. 128.

and his understanding kindness brought him at once to the rescue. "Ah!" said he, "then we must have a look at it now." Taking Bell's arm, he turned to the telephone. The judges came up, and demonstration of the invention began, with the young man's quoting into the mouthpiece from Hamlet's soliloquy. The others listened in turn to messages uttered by Bell five hundred feet away, and repeated his words. "To be, or not to be," said Dom Pedro, as the doubt in his face changed to conviction. The telephone became one of the sensations of the Exhibition, and after it was put on the market the Emperor of Brazil was one of the first to make practical use of it.[79]

To gain greater pleasure and benefit from the Exhibition, Dom Pedro arranged four evening *conversaziones* in his apartments at the hotel. The first came on June 22, with about thirty-five guests present representing various countries. At the next meeting the group was larger. The time was spent in informal conversation on various particularly interesting features of the exhibits.[80]

When the special centennial program of July 4 began, Dom Pedro waited expectantly from his seat on the platform. The Vice-president of the United States presided. The original manuscript of the Declaration of Independence—which was given three times three cheers by the audience—was read by Richard Henry Lee of Virginia, whose grandfather had moved the creation of the committee which drew it up. Then, the chairman announced that the next item on the program would be a hymn written for the first centennial of American independence by Antonio Carlos Gomes, the most distinguished Brazilian composer, at the request of the Emperor of Brazil "who dignifies this event by his gracious presence." The assemblage at once called for Dom Pedro, who finally rose and went to the speaker's stand, and received an ovation. The hymn, dedicated

---

[79] Mackenzie, *op. cit.*, pp. 122-24, 158.
[80] *North American*, June 24 and 26, 1876.

to the American people, was then played twice by the orchestra and it met with prolonged applause.[81]

After a day or two more in Philadelphia, the imperial tourists left for New York, to spend a short time there before leaving the United States. In New York, Dom Pedro visited various institutions he had not before seen, among them, Sing Sing Prison. A special meeting of the American Geographical Society was held on July 10, with the Emperor and Empress present. Dom Pedro, who was loudly applauded when he arrived, had a seat on the platform. To him, the gathering was hail and farewell. Bayard Taylor began the tribute by saying: "I am sure that no distinguished stranger ever came among us who, at the end of three months, seemed so little of a stranger and so much of a friend to the whole American people as Dom Pedro II of Brazil." He then read as a godspeed the third stanza from Whittier's "Freedom in Brazil," composed when the Emperor took the initiative resulting in the emancipation act of 1871.

> And thou great-hearted ruler, through whose mouth
>   The word of God is said,
> Once more, 'Let there be light!'—Son of the South,
>   Lift up thy honored head;
> Wear unashamed a crown by thy desert
>   More than by birth thy own.
> Careless of watch and ward, thou art begirt
>   By grateful hearts alone.
> The moated wall and battleship may fail,
>   But safe shall justice prove;
> Stronger than greaves of brass or iron mail
>   The panoply of love.

Taylor's eulogy finished, the Society by applause and acclamation elected the Emperor a member. Dom Pedro responded with an expression of thanks for the honor and for the kind welcome of the American people.[82]

---

[81] Philadelphia *Public Ledger*, June 26, July 5, 1876.
[82] New York *Herald*, July 11, 1876.

TOURING THE UNITED STATES OF AMERICA 213

Two days later, on July 12, the Brazilian visitors left for Europe on the Cunard liner "Russia." The day was excessively hot, and Dom Pedro wielded a fan as he stood on the deck with the Empress before the boat started. They were enjoying a goodbye surprise in the form of Gilmore's famous orchestra, which had followed them to the dock to play national anthems and other airs of various countries. The music continued after the vessel had got under way, and the last patriotic strains heard by Dona Thereza and Dom Pedro were those of "Yankee Doodle."[83]

[83] *Ibid.*, July 13, 1876.
During his second trip to Europe Dom Pedro spent more than a year there, returning to Brazil in September, 1877. He visited the countries seen on his first trip, and also traveled in Ireland, Denmark, Sweden, Finland, Russia, Turkey-in-Europe, Asia Minor, Palestine, and Greece. The last named he studied in detail, and to Egypt he gave much more time than when on his first visit, and ascended the Nile as far as the Second Cataract. (Garcia, "Viagens de D. Pedro II," *Rev. do Inst. Hist. e Geog. Bras.*, vol. 152, p. 124; Debanné, "D. Pedro II no Egypto," *Rev. do Inst. Hist. e Geol. Bras.*, vol. 75, pp. 132-49; Dom Pedro-Gobineau correspondence, Pedro d'Orléans Bragança Archives, A, CLXXXV, 8347b; Livro de visitas de segunda viagem de S. M. o Imperador á Europa en 1877, *ibid.*, A, CLXXVIII, 8102.)

XI

DOM PEDRO AS TEACHER OF THE BRAZILIAN NATION

IF I were not an emperor, I should like to be a school teacher. I know of no calling greater or nobler than that of directing young minds and of training the men of the future."[1]

Thus wrote Dom Pedro in the last years of his reign when vacationing in Cannes. In reality, he was both a sovereign and a teacher, for the Brazilian nation was his school. And it was badly in need of education, general and special. When he came to the throne the great majority of the people were illiterate, and the nation's experts in the fields of scholarship and the fine arts were few indeed. Since the Emperor was, intellectually, perhaps the most emancipated person in the country, and likewise the most cultivated, he was well qualified to be its instructor and its leader in things of the mind. The educational backwardness of the nation was a matter constantly in his thoughts. But in his efforts to remedy it he was much handicapped by the indifference of politicians, and the distractions of war, and by an almost constant shortage of money in local and national treasuries. Nevertheless, under Dom Pedro's leadership considerable intellectual progress was made. His ablest assistant in this work was perhaps his life-long friend the Visconde do Bom Retiro,[2] who was for some years Minister of Empire.

The Emperor exercised educational leadership variously— by his public utterances; as member and protector of numerous educational institutions and organizations; by recommendations based upon study of specific problems at home or abroad; by

[1] Mossé, *op. cit.*, p. 331.   [2] Pereira da Silva, *op. cit.*, I, 254.

careful inspection of schools and of other educational factors; through actual classroom teaching; and also by direct, personal encouragement to large numbers of talented young men.

Not only did he call the attention of Parliament to the educational needs of the nation through his addresses from the throne, in which such appeals rang again and again like a refrain, but he bluntly prevented needless expenditure of money on himself, because its lack for educational purposes was so palpable. When, after the war with Paraguay, he learned of a movement to secure by public subscription funds for erecting an equestrian statue of him, he promptly headed it off by a letter to the officer in charge of education. "I wish," he wrote, "that the money from the subscription be applied to the construction of more primary school buildings and to the improvement of other establishments for public instruction."[3] His admiring subjects responded enthusiastically, and their gifts made possible the construction of several new schools in Rio de Janeiro.[4] Considerably later, he was most emphatic in his opposition to the suggestion of the ministry that money be appropriated for a badly needed renovation of the City Palace. "What," he exclaimed, "to think of a palace for me when we have not enough schools and school buildings!"[5]

It has been already mentioned that when he was less than twelve years of age he was made protector of the Collegio Dom Pedro II, the national preparatory school, but this was merely the first of many educational institutions to which he became a loyal friend. Another early one, of which Dona Thereza was a patron also, was the Sociedade Amante da Instrucção, founded in 1829 to help educate orphans and other unfortunate children. Both he and the Empress gave money to the Society and en-

---

[3] Mossé, *op. cit.*, pp. 343-44; "Traços biographicos de D. Pedro II extrahidos das collecções do *Jornal do Commercio*," *Rev. do Inst. Hist. e Geog. Bras.*, vol. 152, p. 644.

[4] Mossé, *op. cit.*, p. 342; Roure, in *Contribuições para a Biographia de Dom Pedro II*, Pt. I, p. 627.

[5] Quesada, *op. cit.*, I, 112, 330; *Jornal do Brasil*, June 16, 1925.

couraged it by attending its meetings. To them both the pupils were deeply attached.[6]

At his own expense Dom Pedro established schools for the children of the employes at São Christovão Palace and at the imperial fazenda of Santa Cruz, thus setting an example for others.[7] He likewise took a leading part in creating other elementary schools. Momentum in educational progress was especially noticeable after 1870, partly because more money was available, but perhaps more through the influence of the Emperor's trips abroad, notably his visit to the United States. But after his first trip to Europe he had some good school buildings erected in Rio de Janeiro, with gardens around them, for girls as well as boys, and he required that examinations be made stiffer. He also had a polytechnic school organized in the capital with engineering taught on Belgian lines.[8]

Since elementary education, except in Rio, was in charge of the provinces, the Emperor had no direct control over it. Consequently, there was a lack of uniformity in educational progress in the country as a whole which he much regretted. But he was largely responsible for the several hundred per cent increase in the number of primary schools in Brazil during his reign. The gain was especially notable in the capital, where education was under national control. Here, the sixteen primary schools of 1846 had grown by 1889 to one hundred and eighteen.[9] But the population had also grown, and when Dom Pedro's reign ended the educational facilities were still far from adequate and most of the population remained illiterate.

American influence was most noticeable in the organization of special educational institutions, such as the elementary night

---

[6] Zeferino de Faría, "O Imperador e a Sociedade Amante da Instrucção," *Rev. do Inst. Hist. e Geog. Bras.*, vol. 152, pp. 592-98.

[7] Affonso Celso, *Contradictas monarchicas*, p. 15; Codman, *op. cit.*, pp. 103-5.

[8] White to Evarts, Mar. 22, 1879, Dept. of State, Despatches, Brazil; Fialho, *op. cit.*, pp. 69-70.

[9] Pedro d'Orléans Bragança Archives, A, CXXX, 6373; *Collectanea Rabello*, I, 130.

school for men in the capital, the school for the blind, normal primary schools, and the agricultural school of São Bento das Lages, founded in 1877 largely through the Emperor's efforts.[10]

Most of the schools, however, even those of primary rank, were intended for boys. Though Dom Pedro gave his daughters excellent educations, he was little concerned with the education of girls in general. In his indifference he reflected the attitude of the Latin nations. After he had been abroad and had seen that Brazilian women were far behind those of England and the United States in education and general intelligence, he showed more interest in the schooling of Brazilian girls, but he had no special zeal for the emancipation of their minds.

To secondary education, which was the concern of the central government, the Emperor gave much attention. He took special interest in the Collegio Dom Pedro II, and even penetrated occasionally to its kitchen, to sample the food and assure himself that the boarding students were properly cared for. A note in his diary for 1862 outlines a plan for reforming the Collegio's course of study. "Lack of zeal, lack of a sense of duty," he wrote, "is our principal moral defect." The aim of the new curriculum was partly to remedy this.[11] The next year he emphasized the need for more scientific training in the secondary schools, including astronomy with telescopic observations. Whether or not the Collegio was thoroughly reformed during this period is not apparent. But, if it was, it reverted to its former condition, for ten years later the Emperor declared in his diary that its examinations were a disgrace to the history of Brazil.[12]

Adequate schools for training in law, medicine, and theology existed in Brazil throughout Dom Pedro's reign, but there were not enough technical institutes. The Emperor urged that such

---

[10] Castro, in *Contribuições para a Biographia de D. Pedro II*, Pt. I, p. 535.

[11] Pedro d'Orléans Bragança Archives, B, CCCV, 1055; Viriato Corrêa, "Pedro II, o democrata," *Rev. do Inst. Hist. e Geog. Bras.*, vol. 152, p. 114.

[12] Pedro d'Orléans Bragança Archives, A, CXXX, 6373; *ibid.*, B, XXXVII, 1057.

schools be provided for different parts of the country, with courses of study suited to the community; and a few were established. His interest in this plan grew greater towards the close of his reign. So did his desire to provide university opportunities, still wanting in the Empire, with the result that Brazilian youths were entirely dependent upon Coimbra and other foreign institutions. But nothing came of his efforts. In his last address from the throne on May 3, 1889, he again called attention to the need for technical schools, and also for two universities—one in the south and the other in the north—to form cultural centers and to give educational impulse to the rest of the country.[13]

Part of Dom Pedro's purpose in visiting schools, which he did regularly throughout his reign, was to stimulate general interest in education and to see for himself the quality of work done, in order to have weak spots removed. He was present regularly at the assemblies and examinations of the Collegio Dom Pedro II,[14] and he and his family attended its commencement exercises. He often went also to various schools, high and low, to distribute prizes and other special honors.

He liked best, however, to drop in at any and every educational institution, to sit beside the teacher, watch the work, and participate in it. But he wanted the teaching to go on, as scheduled, after his arrival, and was opposed to special speeches and programs in his honor.[15] If he did not approve of the method of instruction, he said so frankly. Often he heard the little ones read, and questioned the classes in the subjects studied.[16]

One of Dom Pedro's protégés, Mucio Teixeira, who was with him in São Paulo in 1886, describes an incident connected with a visit to a primary school. When they arrived, a little

[13] *Fallas do throno*, p. 870; "A Fé de Officio de D. Pedro II," *Rev. do Inst. Hist. e Geog. Bras.*, vol. 152, p. 763.
[14] B. F. Ramiz Galvão, "A patria e o livro," *Collectanea Rabello*, I, 130.
[15] Teixeira, *op. cit.*, p. 121.
[16] Lamas, *op. cit.*, p. 55; Barão de Teffé, "Reminiscencias de D. Pedro II," *Collectanea Rabello*, I, 27.

girl, coached for the purpose, came forward and began to recite a speech of greeting. But the Emperor interrupted her with, "No, no, my girl, I do not like discourses." The child stopped, mortified. Noting this, he said, "Well, well, if you would like to talk, come here; come and talk with me." Then, caressing her, he began to ask her questions on her school work. But the pupil, her embarrassment increasing, remained silent. To encourage her, the Emperor said, "I see that you have a bright mind. Do not be afraid. Show me that you are intelligent, for I am very fond of children. I have grandchildren of your age."[17]

Another purpose of the Emperor in visiting schools and examining the pupils was to find gifted boys, who might, with opportunity, become leaders of the nation. For he fully recognized that the greatness of a country is the greatness of its people, and that the world would judge Brazil by the numbers doing superior work in the productive arts, the professions, scholarship, and government. So he was ever on the lookout for promising human material to be made by education into the nation's élite. Many were the protégés thus acquired—how many, perhaps Dom Pedro himself hardly knew. To all, he gave encouragement and sound advice, and he helped a considerable number from his private funds. Much of his civil list was spent for such purposes. On the whole, he was well paid for his efforts, because many distinguished Brazilians came from these imperial protégés. Some of the best known were Benjamin Franklin Ramiz Galvão, who became editor of the *Revista do Instituto Historico e Geographico Brasileiro;* Francisco Varnhagen, the historian; the poets, Gonçalves Dias and Magalhães de Porto Seguro; the romanticist, Joaquim Manoel de Macedo; the composer, Carlos Gomes; and the painters, Victor Meirelles and Pedro Americo. Ramiz Galvão got the elements of education in the school maintained by the Sociedade Amante

[17] Teixeira, *op. cit.*, pp. 121-22.

da Instrucção. At the age of eight and a half, through appeal to the Emperor by his grandfather, he was admitted free to the Collegio Dom Pedro II. After that, the Emperor followed his career closely and lent a helping hand here and there. For some years Ramiz Galvão was tutor of Princess Isabel's sons, and even gave lessons in Greek to his imperial patron.[18]

Pedro Americo, who was seatmate of Ramiz Galvão at the Collegio Dom Pedro II, happened to get the Emperor's attention through drawing a picture of him one day when he was visiting their class in arithmetic. The sketch was given to Dom Pedro, who asked Americo whether he would like to study at the National Academy of Fine Arts. The boy was delighted with the opportunity, and began work there, with the Emperor paying his bills. At the Academy, which in recent years had been much improved, he made good progress, and his benefactor arranged for the continuation of his art studies in Europe.[19] Pedro Americo justified this faith by becoming the best artist of the Empire. Among his canvases in the galleries of the Academy of Fine Arts in Rio is an especially fine one of the Emperor in ceremonial dress, with the tall imperial crown on his head and the scepter in his hand.

Gonçalves Dias, in whose veins was blended the blood of aborigines, Negroes, and whites, showed unusual lyrical gifts. Twice, the Emperor at his own expense sent the young man to Europe, but he doubtless felt fully repaid by the poet's beautiful, homesick "Song of Exile" ("Canção de exilio"), which won the lasting affection of the nation.[20]

Dom Pedro surrounded himself with poets and other writers, some of whom were pensioners at the palace. His aim was to help them, by encouragement and by freedom from financial

---

[18] B. F. Ramiz Galvão, "Gratas reminiscencias," *Rev. do Inst. Hist. de Geog. Bras.*, vol. 152, 859-61.

[19] Ramiz Galvão, "A patria e o livro," *Collectanea Rabello*, I, 29; Pedro Americo to Dom Pedro II, Jan. 6, 1862, Pedro d'Orléans Bragança Archives, A, CXXXI, 6381.   [20] Teixeira, *op. cit.*, pp. 48-49.

worries, to do their best work. Often he himself criticized their products and suggested improvements, at times supplying a new line for a poetical translation. Cardoza de Menezes, one of these protégés, left a pleasing picture of his sessions with the Emperor at São Christovão Palace, in connection with the translation of La Fontaine's *Fables*. This was in the later years of the reign. The conferences began at five in the afternoon in the library, when the Emperor seated himself beside a small table on which were some books, a jar containing a fruit preparation, two glasses of water, a sugar bowl and a lamp of rape oil. Adjusting his tortoise-shell-rimmed pince-nez glasses, Dom Pedro began carefully to compare the translation with the original, stopping now and then to discuss a point. At intervals he would mix a cool, sweet drink and offer it to the poet. Then the books were closed and the two, while sipping the beverage, discussed literature and drama.[21]

The Emperor not only encouraged talented Brazilians to write, but at times defended their publications against what he considered unfair criticism. An instance of this is Gonçalves de Magalhães's Indian epic, "A confederação dos Tomayos," now considered one of the finest examples of Brazilian literature. When first it appeared, José de Alencar, then a young journalist, attacked it anonymously, and others followed his lead. Dom Pedro asked another writer to answer Alencar, and this was done. Later, he, himself, wrote, over the signature "Another Friend of the Poet," a series of letters for the *Jornal do Commercio* in reply to the continued attacks. The next year, 1856, he showed the persistence of his faith by financing the publication of a de luxe edition of the epic.[22]

Perhaps no protégé gave Dom Pedro more pleasure through his success than did Carlos Gomes, who, at the Emperor's re-

[21] *Ibid.*, pp. 46-50, 56-57; Max Fleiuss, "D. Pedro II e as letras patrias," *Rev. do Inst. Hist. e Geog. Bras.*, vol. 152, pp. 895-96, 901.
[22] Fleiuss, "D. Pedro II e as letras patrias," *Rev. do Inst. Hist. e Geog. Bras.*, vol. 152, pp. 895, 897-99; Affonso Celso in *Jornal do Brasil*, June 16, 1825.

quest, wrote a Centennial hymn for the American people in 1876. After Gomes had completed a course at the Academy of Fine Arts in Rio, he went to Europe on a pension from the Emperor, and studied in Rome. Here he completed and staged his most famous opera, "Il Guarany," which was well received in Italy and London. After its first presentation in Rio, Dom Pedro called Gomes to his box, warmly congratulated him, and handed him a certificate of membership in the Order of the Rose and a diamond-studded badge of the order. Appropriately, the composer once remarked, "If it weren't for the Emperor, I would not be Carlos Gomes."[23]

Through encouragement of reading, Dom Pedro helped spread intellectual enlightenment. To those who would use and appreciate them he lent and gave books and periodicals from his own extensive library.[24] He was also responsible for inspiring the Imperial Public Library with new life. In 1870, he nominated as its head his protégé Dr. Ramiz Galvão, a true lover of books, who filled the position for twelve years. Often the Emperor would drop in at the Library, to look over new acquisitions and to suggest other purchases. In 1873, he placed Ramiz Galvão in charge of a commission to visit various European public libraries and archives to study their organization, and to get track of documents relating to Brazil to be copied for the national archives.[25] Through the improvements resulting from the work of the commission, the institution, renamed the National Library, became an important center of culture in the country.

To foster an interest in studying the southern skies, he had an astronomical observatory erected in Rio de Janeiro, and gave some money for buying instruments. He was anxious to have it

---

[23] Antonio Carlos Gomes to Dom Pedro II, May 22, 1867, Pedro d'Orléans Bragança Archives, A, CXL, 6850; Fialho, *op. cit.*, p. 85, note; Max Fleiuss, "D. Pedro II," *Rev. do Inst. Hist. e Geog. Bras.*, vol. 152, p. 1112.

[24] Ramiz Galvão, "A patria e o livro," *Collectanea Rabello*, I, 29.

[25] *Ibid.*; Lecture by Ramiz Galvão, *ibid.*, p. 130.

develop into an institution of great distinction, but the dream was never realized.[26]

To make Brazil better known at home as well as abroad, the Emperor encouraged and aided various foreign scientific expeditions which visited the country. One of the most famous was that headed by Professor Louis Agassiz of Harvard University, whom Dom Pedro received with kindness and enthusiasm. At the Emperor's request, Agassiz gave, in Rio de Janeiro, a course of lectures on a variety of scientific subjects. They were presented in French and were open to the public. The imperial family regularly attended the sessions. In this connection, Mrs. Agassiz wrote of Dom Pedro that "it is worthy of note, as showing the simplicity of his character, that, instead of occupying the raised platform intended for them, he caused the chairs to be placed on a level with the others, as if to show that in science at least there is no distinction of rank."[27]

The circumstances under which women were admitted to the lectures show, however, the Emperor's attitude towards their intellects as well as reveal the general status of Brazilian women. The first topic to be treated by Professor Agassiz was glacial phenomena in Brazil, and his wife, anxious to hear the presentation, planned, as a matter of course, to attend. But when she spoke of going people stared and informed her that "certainly no ladies would appear." Elizabeth Cary Agassiz was indignant as well as disappointed, and she and her husband spoke to the director of the program regarding the matter. He expressed himself as sympathetic, but said that the Emperor would have to be consulted. Therefore, Agassiz asked Dom Pedro, who looked rather doubtful and said that his countrywomen were so ignorant that they would not know what the professor was talking about; still, he had no objection and would

---

[26] Pedro d'Orléans Bragança Archives, A, CXVI, 5725; *Jornal do Brasil*, June 9, 1925; "A Fé de Officio de D. Pedro II," *Rev. do Inst. Hist. e Geog. Bras.*, vol. 152, p. 763.
[27] Agassiz and Agassiz, *op. cit.*, pp. 96-97.

think about it. But he was puzzled as to procedure and asked the scientist about sending the women invitations. "Not at all," said Agassiz, "let them come with their husbands and fathers, as they do with us, and make part of the audience, and if Brazilian ladies are so ignorant as Your Majesty represents them to be, the sooner you put them in the way of learning something, the better for them and for their children."[28] After some further discussion, it was agreed that women might come escorted by their men folk, and a few strong-minded ones did appear.[29]

Obviously, Dom Pedro II was no feminist. But it should be recalled in this connection that in June, 1865, when the incident took place, the modern women's rights movement was less than twenty years old; that Vassar College had not yet opened its doors; and that, in the whole world, there were not more than a few dozen women having college degrees.

The Emperor's conventional attitude towards the "female intellect" did not, however, in any way prevent him from capitalizing all possible chances for general enlightenment. He even made use of the modest services of the American Protestant missionary, J. C. Fletcher. Moved by philanthropy as well as by a desire to stimulate commerce with the United States, Fletcher, in 1855, held in Brazil an exhibition of American products secured by donations from artists, publishers, manufacturers, and merchants. In this, he had the coöperation of the Visconde do Bom Retiro, who set aside for the display a large hall in the national museum. The Emperor examined in detail everything in it, from the books published by D. C. Appleton and Company to samples of farm machinery, and he was free in criticism and in praise. One of the results of the exhibition was the adoption of American models for Brazilian schoolbooks.[30]

In fact, all gatherings to foster intelligence roused Dom

[28] Paton, *op. cit.*, pp. 82-83.   [29] *Ibid.*, p. 83.
[30] Kidder and Fletcher, *op. cit.*, pp. 237-48.

Pedro's interest and had his support. In December, 1873, he wrote Gobineau: "They are beginning to have here political lectures on subjects of general interest, and I hope that the habit will become acclimated."[31]

At his suggestion, for a time literary soirées were held once or twice a week at the Collegio Dom Pedro II. Here, authors read unpublished translations and original works in prose and verse. Dom Pedro attended regularly, took part in the discussions, and sometimes read from his own translations.[32]

The intellectual factor to which the Emperor gave his earliest and most continuous support was the Instituto Historico e Geographico Brasileiro, of which at its first session, he, then thirteen, was made protector. Ever afterwards he was its constant friend, and gave it money, furniture, books, and manuscripts, and also ample quarters in the City Palace. Through his initiative, the Institute made a collection of unpublished material relating to Brazil. In the effort to rouse more interest in studies connected with the geography, ethnology, and history of the country, he began soon after his accession to offer through the Institute a gold medal for the best writing on such topics.[33] Partly in consequence, many valuable studies were published, mostly in the *Revista* of the Institute.

His most valuable help to the Institute came, however, from his presence at gatherings of its members. He first went to a regular meeting on December 15, 1849, when he was twenty-four years old. After that, except when he was ill, excessively busy, or was out of the country, he was present at the fortnightly sessions of the organization—which came in the late afternoon or early evening, and he actually attended more than five hundred of them. He probably used the Institute at first to help him to forget somewhat the loss of his second son, which came

---

[31] Pedro d'Orléans Bragança Archives, A, CLXXXV, 8347b.
[32] Fleiuss, "D. Pedro e as letras patrias," *Rev. do Inst. Hist. e Geog. Bras.*, vol. 152, pp. 896-97; Teixeira, *op. cit.*, pp. 131-32.
[33] *Rev. do Inst. Hist. e Geog. Bras.*, III, 557-59.

in January, 1850, three weeks after he first attended a regular session. But, though he enjoyed the meetings, his reason for being there was chiefly a desire to keep up the interest of the members, as a means of intellectual stimulation and of scholarly activity. To Dom Pedro, the Institute was one more aid towards educating the nation.[34]

José de Alencar, in an article in the *Correio Mercantil* for November 26, 1854, paid tribute to the loyalty of the small group of scholars in the face of a tropical storm. "In the hurricane which descended upon the city, tearing up trees and causing other damage, what dilettante," he asked, "would be capable of leaving his sheltering roof to defy such severe weather? Nevertheless, at the very hour when the blasts of wind were most violent some men made their way through the streets of the city, one by one going to meet in the sessions room of the Historical Institute. A little later His Majesty arrived, and the meeting began with seven members present."

Stimulated by the interest of the Emperor—who, says Oliveira Lima, seemed a Germanic god[35] to the members—the Institute was much more of an academic workshop than it would have been without him. By questions, comments, and suggestions, he helped hold the members down to serious work. And this work had nothing to do with his own glorification.

On one occasion a member proposed appointment of a commission to prepare a comprehensive biography of him. Immediately he protested. "Biography?" he said. "Do not think of that." But he added, "Besides, it would be most simple. At the top of a sheet of paper write the date of my birth and of my accession to the throne. At the bottom, the date of my death. Leave blank the intervening space for that which the future will speak. It will proclaim what I did, the intentions

---

[34] Fleiuss, *Paginas de historia*, pp. 470, 484-85; *Rev. do Inst. Hist. e Geog. Bras.*, vol. 26, pp. 461, 851.

[35] Manoel de Oliveira Lima, "O Imperador e os sabios," *Rev. do Inst. Hist. e Geog. Bras.*, vol. 152, p. 147.

which dominated me and the cruel injustices which I had to endure in silence without ever being able to defend myself."[36] The scholar in him saw that real history was dependent upon a perspective which only time could give.

After each session of the Institute the Emperor spoke personally with those present, thus fostering the solidarity of the organization. Before he left for Europe because of ill health in 1887, he counseled the members to keep on working.[37] By then, the Institute had become the most distinguished of its kind in Latin America. For this, Dom Pedro II was largely responsible, as he was also for making Brazil the most liberal and enlightened of the Latin American countries of his day.

[36] Moniz, *op. cit.*, p. 177.
[37] Quesada, *op. cit.*, II, 442-43; Affonso Celso, in *Collectanea Rabello*, I, 125.

XII

PROMOTION OF INTERNAL PROGRESS

DURING Dom Pedro II's reign of nearly fifty years Brazil became in many ways a modern, progressive nation. Some of the advancement was the consequence of general world development, but other agents also played a part, as is clear from the progress made by the Empire in this period in comparison with many other backward lands. Though it is an exaggeration to say, as does one Brazilian historian, that the country owes all of its progress to Dom Pedro II,[1] nevertheless, its debt to him is great; for he was unquestionably the chief factor in national advancement during his reign, and had a share in every part of it. Perhaps he achieved as much by direct, personal effort as by influence on his ministry and on Parliament, through the speeches from the throne, or otherwise. But these speeches, in which his ideas usually prevailed, were often like a voice crying in the wilderness, far in advance of the reforms for which they asked. Largely because of the selfish indifference of the nation's representatives, and of lack of money—owing partly to official extravagance and dishonesty—many of the calls for betterment were disregarded and the response to others was much delayed.

The long period of insurrectionary disturbances which continued for nine years after Dom Pedro's accession to the throne prevented the government from undertaking serious work of internal progress until about 1850. Later, it was interrupted for several years by the troubles in the Plata, especially by the Paraguayan War. But soon afterwards progressive development was resumed, and it was quickened and expanded through

[1] Fleiuss, "D. Pedro II," *Rev. do Inst. Hist. e Geog. Bras.*, vol. 152, p. 1107.

stimulus from the Emperor's trips in foreign lands. After his visit to Europe in 1871-1872 he made the Visconde de Itaúna, who had accompanied him, Minister of Agriculture, Commerce, and Public Works.[2]

Believing that pastoral and tillage agriculture afforded the best bases for permanent national prosperity, he was anxious for its improvement, but he was handicapped by tropical inertia and traditional indifference among the agrarian population as well as in the members of the government.[3] For many years he urged, in vain, the establishment of an imperial institute of agriculture. Since adequate public funds did not appear, in 1863 he wrote the Marquez de Abrantes, then Minister of Finance, offering one hundred *contos*[4] from his private income to aid in starting the project.[5] He had planned the institute, in accordance with the best existing examples, to include a model farm, a center for distributing useful seeds and plants, facilities for introducing improved agricultural instruments, and a research department which should publish the results of experiment. At its head he desired men of "intelligence, experience, and good will." Six years later, an agricultural school was opened, at Juiz de Fóra in Minas Geraes, under private auspices. Later, it was taken over by the imperial government, but apparently it fell far short of the Emperor's ideals.[6]

For the semi-arid, cattle-raising northeast, especially Ceará, where droughts were frequent, the Emperor felt much concern. Here loss of life on a large scale, from famine, at times was threatened. In severe cases private and provincial aid was not enough, and appeals came to the central government. The weight of responsibility was then heavy upon the shoulders of

[2] Fialho, *op. cit.*, p. 69.
[3] Extrahido do diario escripto por S. M. o Imperador o Senhor D. Pedro II, Pedro d'Orléans Bragança Archives, A, CXXX, 6373.
[4] One hundred thousand milreis, at par the equivalent of about $50,000 in money of the United States of America.
[5] Pedro d'Orléans Bragança Archives, A, CXXXIII, 6507.
[6] *Ibid.*, CLVI, 7075. Information furnished by Clarissa Rolfs of Gainesville, Florida, who obtained it from the son of the one-time director of the school.

the Emperor, who suffered with his people. The worst drought of his reign began in Ceará in 1877. Private aid was sent from various parts of the country, and likewise appropriations were voted from national funds. Yet, the needs of the afflicted section continued. Finally, in cabinet session the Secretary of the Treasury announced: "Your Majesty must know—and I say it with sorrow—that we cannot longer succor the province of Ceará; there is not sufficient money in the treasury." The Emperor bowed his head and wept. Then, straightening up, he replied firmly: "If there is no more money, sell the crown jewels in order that no Cearense shall die of hunger."[7] Aid was secured without this, however, and in 1880 the drought was ended by abundant rains.[8]

To prevent the recurrence of such a calamity, an irrigation system, based on storage reservoirs for rain water, was discussed. Before the three-years' drought had ended, largely through Dom Pedro's efforts an English engineer, J. J. Révy, was commissioned to survey the arid area and to plan an extensive irrigation system. Shortly afterwards he began work on the project, but his progress was slow, partly because of lack of funds.[9]

Brazilian manufacturing fostered by protective tariffs, of which Dom Pedro made a study, progressed well in the latter half of the nineteenth century, but large-scale industrialization of the country did not begin until the twentieth century, during the World War. The delay was natural, since cheap, agricultural land was abundant, and capital for expensive machinery was wanting. The popular inertia of which the sovereign complained was also a deterrent. But, aided by the encouragement of the Emperor and other progressive spirits, new mechanical devices were adopted here and there. A stimulus in this direction was the national exposition planned by the sovereign and opened on his birthday in 1861, with himself and his family

[7] *O Imperador e os Cearenses*, pp. 36-37.   [8] *Fallas do throno*, p. 786.
[9] *Rio News*, Nov. 15, 1884; J. J. Révy to Dom Pedro II, Dec. 2, 1889, Pedro d'Orléans Bragança Archives, A, CCI, 9056.

present. It was the first effort of the kind in the Empire and was aimed to encourage the nation by showing the progress already made in manufacturing and industry.[10]

The visit of Dom Pedro to the United States stirred him to greater efforts towards the mechanical modernization of his people. One result of his seeing American factories and his assiduous study of the exhibits in Machinery Hall at the Centennial was the orders for Brazil of various kinds of machinery, not all of which was agricultural. It was reported that these purchases amounted to two million dollars,[11] which may have been an exaggeration; but Dom Pedro was certainly responsible for introducing many mechanical inventions into the Empire.

Commerce, which had to be fed by agricultural and industrial activities, was a matter of much concern to him, partly because of the need for more money from customs duties to swell the national income.

As an aid to economic development, the Emperor favored the establishment of banks and other institutions of commercial credit, nineteen of which existed in the country in 1889. But the history of Brazilian banking and currency, like that of most young countries, showed over-expansion of credit, extravagance, financial instability, depreciated paper money, and recurrent economic crises.[12] In the 1850's, after internal peace was gained, the Emperor favored easier credit, to encourage the development of agriculture, industry, and commerce. Being rather inexperienced at the time, he probably was overconfident in this regard, which caused him, owing to the bad state of the finances in 1858, to be charged with encouraging commercial speculation and gambling.[13]

---

[10] "O Fé de Officio de D. Pedro II," *Rev. do Inst. Hist. e Geog. Bras.*, vol. 152, p. 763.   [11] *Dom Pedro in U. S.*

[12] Normano, *op. cit.*, pp. 171-77; Pereira da Silva, *op. cit.*, I, 263-66; II, 21-23, 192-200.

[13] Pereira da Silva, *op. cit.*, I, 268-69; Extrahido do diario escripto por S. M. o Imperador o Senhor D. Pedro II, Pedro d'Orléans Bragança Archives, A, CXXX, 6373.

However, though Dom Pedro cared little for money, and was, in fact, lacking in financial-mindedness, he fully realized that extravagance and unsound business methods were bad for the country, morally as well as economically. Repeatedly, in his messages from the throne, he urged economy, and emphasized the importance of balancing the budget.[14] He sought also to have the finances of the country in charge of those best qualified for the task, quite regardless of his personal attitude towards them.

An incident which occurred during the financial crisis of 1858 illustrates this. Limpo de Abreu, Visconde de Abaeté, was forming a new ministry to help the country out of its difficulties, and Dom Pedro instructed him to ask the author of the financial articles signed "Veritas" which had been appearing in the *Jornal do Commercio* to become Secretary of the Treasury. According to Mucio Teixeira, the Prime Minister, embarrassed, delayed carrying out the instruction. When the Emperor asked him whether he had done so, Limpo de Abreu said, "Senhor, if Your Majesty knew who 'Veritas' is—" The Emperor interrupted him with, "That's all right; I know; I know." He was quite aware, he said, that "Veritas" was Francisco de Salles Torres Homem, who, in his pamphlet *Timandro* had cruelly attacked him and the Empress and their daughters. "But," he added, "I never place my personal feelings above the interest of my people. We are going through a most severe economic and financial crisis. This man seems qualified to lessen, if not to conquer, it. Go and invite him in my name to come to me."[15]

The following day Salles Torres Homem was made Secretary of the Treasury, and soon he placed the finances in a sounder condition. It was clear that the Emperor's tolerant attitude had challenged him, for when he presented himself at the sovereign's call he remarked, "Senhor, for great crimes there are great amends."[16]

[14] *Fallas do throno*, pp. 537, 564, 574, 594, 611, 866.
[15] Teixeira, *op. cit.*, pp. 152-53; Pereira da Silva, *op. cit.*, I, 270.
[16] Teixeira, *op. cit.*, p. 153; Pereira da Silva, *op. cit.*, I, 271-73.

In the 1850's, commercial and industrial corporations began to spring up like mushrooms; one hundred and sixty were organized in that decade.[17] The Emperor welcomed them because of their economic significance, but he was aware of their evils, especially their selfish control of prices, for the suffering from poverty in the remoter country districts, especially those of the north—a matter of serious concern to him—was partly the result of monopolistic abuses. These called for correction. In Bahia the evil was especially bad in 1860, and in his message from the throne on opening Parliament he called for a revision of the laws relating to corporations. It was necessary, he added, to regulate, protect, and foster institutions that aided the less favored members of society, especially those that protected them from fraud and usury.[18]

Another type of wrong-doing which gave the Emperor much concern was that perpetrated by the courts of justice themselves, especially in the out-of-the-way parts of the Empire. Courts were corrupt and the laws were not respected or enforced. The bill of rights of the constitution was often ignored. Life, liberty, and property were unsafe. Often the guilty went free, and at times the innocent were punished severely on trumped-up charges. High officers who stole public funds commonly squared themselves by merely returning the money. The Emperor, anxious to remedy the situation, called again and again in his addresses from the throne for reform of the penal code and the judiciary. But adequate laws were never passed.[19]

To prisons and penitentiaries he gave special study, and did much to better them, for he believed that the offender against the law should not be suppressed, but regenerated. This view, and also the injustice of the courts, tended to turn him against capital punishment, but it was a personal experience that caused

---
[17] Ortigão, in *Contribuições para a Biographia de D. Pedro II*, Pt. I, pp. 290-91.
[18] *Fallas do throno*, pp. 523, 534, 549, 550.
[19] *Rio News*, Oct. 5, 1886; *Fallas do throno*, pp. 564-65, 650, 668-69, 709-10, 742, 774, 814, 820, 837, 856, 866-67, 871.

him definitely to oppose it. All death sentences by judges had to have his indorsement before execution could take place, and in early years he had occasionally given such sanctions. One was for the hanging of a man for murder, in a case when the circumstantial evidence appeared to be very clear. Many years later another man, on his death-bed, confessed to the crime. Never again would Dom Pedro sign a death warrant; and he tried, but in vain, to have capital punishment legally abolished. Death sentences were thereafter commonly commuted to life imprisonment. The Emperor also used his pardoning power extensively and was, consequently, charged with abusing it.[20] It is impossible to say whether this was true, though Dom Pedro's kindness makes it seem likely.

In view of the lack of respect—on the parts of individuals, corporations, and courts—for the established law, Dom Pedro perhaps had more hope of removing or reducing by non-legislative means two of the existing evils. He looked to broader production to help break up the monopolies, and therefore was especially anxious to foster agriculture and industry. He believed that crime in individuals and courts would be abated by advancement in civilization. To bring about this transformation he not only counted on the establishment of more schools and the functioning of a more conscientious and exemplary clergy, but also on the extension of rapid means of communication and transportation.[21]

In fact, this last was one of his greatest interests, and to his energy and persistence is largely due the fact that whereas in 1840 Brazilian messages, passengers, and freight were moved entirely by eighteenth-century methods, in 1889 when his reign ended the Empire was as well supplied as most modern nations with steamboats, railroads, telegraphs, and telephones. By 1889

[20] Dom Pedro II, "O Fé de officio," *Rev. do Inst. Hist. e Geog. Bras.*, vol. 152, p. 764; Frank Bennett, *Forty Years in Brazil*, p. 133; *Rio News*, Dec. 24, 1883; Ruy Barbosa, *Quéda do imperio*, II, 205-25.

[21] *Fallas do throno*, pp. 549, 700, 870.

twelve thousand miles of telegraph lines were in operation. Telegraphic communication between Brazil and Europe was also arranged, by a submarine cable to terminate in Portugal, and opened in 1874. The first telephone was installed in the Empire in 1880, four years after Dom Pedro had helped rouse practical interest in Alexander Graham Bell's invention.

But the Emperor was most concerned with the building and extension of railroads, since these had greater cultural possibilities than did electric wires, and since they also fostered economic development. Encouraged by government laws guaranteeing a fair interest on their investments, capitalists began building railroads in the 1850's. The earliest line, begun in 1852, was to connect Rio de Janeiro with Petropolis. Its first section was opened to traffic in 1854, and other parts were built within the next few years, but not until 1883 were the cog tracks up the mountain completed. In 1855, a line to unite São Paulo with Minas was begun, and was later known as the Dom Pedro II Railroad. It was started by a private company, but, owing to the mountainous character of the country it was to traverse, proved too expensive for the available capital. Therefore, in 1865 the imperial government undertook its completion. However, work on it as well as on other lines went but slowly during the next few years, because of the Paraguayan War, and in 1870 the country had a total of less than seven hundred miles of railway. As soon as financial recuperation had made headway after the conflict was over, Dom Pedro began urging further railroad building on Parliament. There followed a period of rapid railway expansion, fostered to a considerable extent by government aid, and by the end of the reign about six thousand miles of road were in operation, and much more track-laying was planned or was under way.[22]

[22] *Ibid.*, pp. 478, 499; Extrahido do diario escripto por S. M. o Imperador o Senhor D. Pedro II, Pedro d'Orléans Bragança Archives, A, CXXX, 6373; Fleiuss "D. Pedro II," *Rev. do Inst. Hist. e Geog. Bras.*, vol. 152, p. 1107; Ortigão, in "*Contribuições para a Biographia de D. Pedro II*," Pt. I, p. 308.

The need for immigration was one of Dom Pedro's constant concerns. Repeatedly he called the attention of the landed proprietors and of Parliament to the situation and asked their coöperation.[23] For the sake of the economic development of the country it was desirable that unoccupied land be settled by industrious foreigners who might be encouraged to come to the country. Dom Pedro and his government likewise looked to Europe to supply the chronic lack of laborers in the Empire, as well as to provide a surplus of workers which would make it easier to bring about the emancipation of the slaves, for which he was anxious. In spite of the efforts of Dom Pedro himself and of his father and grandfather,[24] in the middle of the nineteenth century the number of foreigners in the country was still comparatively small. The suppression of the African slave traffic at this time increased the need for immigrant labor. In some of the provinces, notably São Paulo, individuals and colonization societies somewhat successfully fostered immigration. Agents were sent to Europe, especially to Germany, to spread information about Brazil, and financial aid was given the immigrants for traveling expenses and also for their support during the period of adjustment in the new land.[25] Subsequently, public aid was given. But some of the foreign colonies failed, much dissatisfaction existed here and there among the foreign-born, and their numbers remained quite inadequate. Dom Pedro II readily saw that sufficient immigration could not be secured unless those who came to the country were contented in their new home. Many of the newcomers had special grievances. Some were brought to Brazil under contracts, which companies or individual planters failed to keep. Helpless colonists were given poor land, or land too far from markets or from transportation systems, or were robbed by local officials of titles to land

---

[23] *Fallas do throno*, pp. 430, 440, 476, 502, 514, 522, 535, 536, 551, 573, 627, 639-40, 681, 690, 775, 814, 849, 860, 870-71.

[24] Clemente Brandenburger, "Immigração e colonização sob o segundo reinado," *Rev. do Inst. Hist. e Geog. Bras.*, vol. 152, pp. 481-82.

[25] *Ibid.*, pp. 483-87.

that they had earned. In his speeches from the throne, and in other connections the Emperor called for action that would prevent such injustices. It was partly to attract foreigners that he asked for more and more railroads. It was also his desire for large-scale immigration, as well as his liberalism and sense of fair play and justice, that caused the Emperor to try to improve respect for the law and to secure complete religious freedom and civil marriage.[26]

After the Paraguayan War ended, immigration, fostered by a law passed in 1871, began to increase. Nevertheless, the immediate need, especially for farm hands, continued; but the efforts to fill the need did also; and the stream of foreign-born steadily swelled, until, in May, 1889, the Emperor reported that in the previous year one hundred and thirty-one thousand immigrants had arrived in Brazil.[27]

Contribution of people from Europe and also of the Negroes brought to the country illegally from 1840 to 1850 added considerably to the Empire's population. The natural gain in the Brazilian element was also notable. By 1872 the estimated population of the country was ten million; in 1889 it was believed to have reached sixteen million, which was twice the estimate of 1845.[28]

Most of the immigrants were from southern Europe, Italians being greatly preponderent, and most of them went to the province of São Paulo, which from 1884 to 1889 received more than one hundred and sixty-five thousand.[29]

Some of the ablest people in the Empire, especially the Paulistas, had an aboriginal strain, usually dating from early colonial times. But by 1889 most of the pure-blooded indigenes were found in the remoter regions of the Empire, especially the

---

[26] *Fallas do throno*, pp. 514, 522, 535, 536, 639-40; Dunn, *op. cit.*, pp. 215-16, 265-66; *Rio News*, Mar. 5, 1883; Nov. 24, 1885; Jan. 5, 1886.

[27] *Fallas do throno*, pp. 681, 870-71; Brandenberger, "Immigração e colonização sob o segundo reinado," *Rev. do Inst. Hist. e Geog. Bras.*, vol. 152, p. 487.

[28] Fleiuss, "D. Pedro II," *Rev. do Inst. Hist. e Geog. Bras.*, vol. 152, p. 1109.

[29] Alfredo Ellis (Junior), *Populações paulistas*, p. 70.

Amazon Valley, and played little part in the nation. There were about two or three million pure-blooded Negroes, and several million people in whom white and Negro blood was blended. In fact, perhaps most people whose families had been in the Empire for several generations had an African strain. The largest proportion of whites was found in the south, where European immigration had diluted the Negro element of the population.

In general, the ex-slave as well as the free-born Negro was treated with as much justice as were whites, and some men with an African strain rose to positions of distinction in private and public life. Dom Pedro encouraged blacks as well as whites to excel. People of Negro blood at times received imperial honors, including titles of nobility. There was no serious stratification on racial lines in Brazilian society.

The number of nobles in the Empire perhaps hardly exceeded a thousand at any time,[30] and their titles were not hereditary. It was the aim of Dom Pedro to make the honor a reward for actual service, to use it as an inducement to striving after worthy ideals. This fact was generally recognized by the nation, and titles of nobility, as such, were not awe-inspiring. The Emperor sought also to keep other honors on the same high plane.

The only apparent unpleasant result of his trips abroad was the number of requests for decorations of one sort or another for foreigners. He was irritated by the fact that these were not made, as they should have been, through Brazilian diplomatic channels, but directly to him, by people whom he had met in Europe and who desired honors for their friends. The implication of cheapness connected with some such requests annoyed him much, since those for whom they were made had not received equivalent honors from their own governments. He even criticized his dear friend the Comte de Gobineau for

---

[30] Serrano, *op. cit.*, pp. 543-69.

making such requests for others, explaining his jealous desire that such honors be given only to persons for distinguished individual merit.[31]

According to an incident reported by the Barão de Penedo, in this connection Dom Pedro II even ignored the wishes of the Prince of Wales. The future King Edward VII, after hearing a famous British pianist at a concert in the Brazilian legation in London, expressed to Penedo the desire that the Emperor decorate the man with the Order of the Rose. Upon learning of this, Dom Pedro suggested that England first confer upon him the Order of the Bath, which remark was interpreted by some as a joking reference by the Emperor to the pianist's supposed lack of personal cleanliness.[32]

The Emperor gave much attention to improving conditions in urban sections as well as in country districts. To his influence is credited part of the work done towards embellishing parks and avenues of Rio de Janeiro. Through a contract granted to a company founded in London by the Barão de Mauá in 1854, gas illumination was substituted for oil in the square before the City Palace and in a number of the main streets of the capital. In 1870, a sewer system was introduced into Rio. As a result of the enterprise of Americans from the United States, a line of horse-cars connecting the capital with the Botanical Garden began operations two years before.[33]

These cars were the cause of serious disorders in Rio de Janeiro in January, 1880. Aiming to increase income, the government headed by Sinimbú arranged for a small tax, in addition to the fare, from all passengers. The plan met at once with deep resentment from the public, and soon traffic on the roads was entirely stopped by rioting mobs, who burned some

[31] Dom Pedro II to Gobineau, July 24, 1872, Feb. 7, 1881, Pedro d'Orléans Bragança Archives, A, CLXXXV, 8347b.
[32] J. M. M. F., "D. Pedro II," *Rev. do Inst. Hist. e Geog. Bras.*, vol. 152, p. 758.
[33] Mossé, *op. cit.*, p. 363; Fleiuss, "D. Pedro II," *Rev. do Inst. Hist. e Geog. Bras.*, vol. 152, p. 1107-8; Fleiuss, *Historia da Cidade do Rio de Janeiro*, p. 190.

of the cars and used others for barricades for street fighting. The troops called out to restore quiet killed some and wounded many. It proved impossible to collect the tax, and the incident made the ministry so unpopular that it soon resigned.[34] Dom Pedro was much upset by the events. "The affair distresses me deeply," he wrote to Gobineau. "It is the first time since 1840 that such a thing had happened in Rio. I had presided over the government for almost forty years without there having been need for firing upon the people."[35]

Though the health record of Brazil was unusually good for a tropical country, the Emperor devoted considerable study and thought to bettering it, especially to combatting the epidemics which repeatedly afflicted the nation. He tried in vain to get Pasteur to come to the country and fight yellow fever.[36]

Because of the general backwardness of medical science during the period, not much headway was made and the epidemics continued. When they appeared, private charity was usually supplemented by material help from the government. The Emperor at such times occasionally showed a reckless disregard for his life in an effort to see that everything possible was done for his people, and to give them the comfort of his presence. This was illustrated in 1855, when large numbers of the lower classes were being wiped out by cholera morbus. Accompanied by members of his ministry, he visited many of the public hospitals of the capital, inspected them minutely, and stopped here and there by the beds to talk with the sick or to give them alms.[37]

The Emperor visited various parts of the country for the

[34] Mattoso, *op. cit.*, p. 14; Pereira da Silva; *op. cit.*, II, 205-7.

[35] Dom Pedro II to Gobineau, Jan. 3, 1880; Pedro d'Orléans Bragança Archives, A, CLXXXV, 8347b; Pereira da Silva, *op. cit.*, II, 205-7.

[36] *Fallas do throno*, pp. 447, 498, 501, 519, 535, 581, 626, 761, 826, 838, 848, 858-59, 870-71; Pereira da Silva, *op. cit.*, I, 253; J. M. M. F., "D. Pedro II," *Rev. do Inst. Hist. e Geog. Bras.*, vol. 152, p. 764; Dom Pedro II-Louis Pasteur Correspondence, *Inst. Hist. e Geog. Bras.*, case 396, no. 18, 405F.

[37] Alfredo Nascimento, "Magna nominis umbra," *Rev. do Inst. Hist. e Geog. Bras.*, vol. 152, pp. 635-36.

purpose of inspection as well as to foster and preserve loyalty to the throne. His first trip, made to the south after the ten-years' civil war in Rio Grande do Sul had ended, has already been mentioned.[38] It lasted from early October, 1845, to the latter part of April, 1846, and was the longest excursion that he made within the Empire. On the same trip he spent some time in the provinces of Santa Catharina and São Paulo. Late in 1859 and early in 1860 he was absent in the north for three and a half months, visiting Espirito Santo, Bahia, Sergipe, Alagôas, Pernambuco, and Parahyba. Later, he made one or two trips into Paraná and São Paulo. His second visit to Rio Grande do Sul was a purely military errand in connection with the war against Paraguay. He made several short excursions into Minas Geraes and was also quite familiar with the province of Rio de Janeiro. On his first trip to Europe he touched at Bahia and Pernambuco again, and on his way to the United States in 1876 he saw Pernambuco a third time, and made a slight acquaintance with the Amazonian province of Pará.[39] The only provinces on which he failed to set his eyes were the interior ones of Goyaz, Matto Grosso, and Amazonas, and later he much regretted that he had never visited them.[40]

On the longer trips, except that made to Rio Grande do Sul during the Paraguayan War, Dona Thereza accompanied him and they went by boat, escorted by an imperial squadron. In every province, he visited many parts and examined rural establishments, public works, factories, hospitals, schools, and churches. For recreation on such trips he viewed historic sites or structures, or scenes of natural beauty, in which he delighted. Everywhere he tried to learn whether public officers did their

[38] See p. 64 of this book.
[39] Garcia, "Viagens de D. Pedro II," *Rev. do Inst. Hist. e Geog. Bras.*, vol. 152, pp. 115-22; Letters from Dom Pedro II to Gobineau, Sept. 7, 1875, June 15, 1880, May 8, 1881, Pedro d'Orléans Bragança Archives, A, CLXXXV, 8374b; Teixeira, *op. cit.*, pp. 110-28; Mattoso, *op. cit.*, pp. 64-78.
[40] Goffredo de Escragnolle Taunay, "A morte do Imperador," *Rev. do Inst. Hist. e Geog. Bras.*, vol. 152, p. 195. Ceará, Piahuy, and Maranhão he seems only to have glimpsed from the deck of the "Hevelius" on his voyage to the United States.

duties, and how his subjects fared. If he discovered injustices and inefficiency he tried to remove them. In many places he investigated the colonies of immigrants, because of complaints of the poor treatment which they had received. When, on his first trip to Paraná, he discovered that the foreign-born settlers had been given bad land, he had the officer who was responsible for the wrong punished. Where he thought criticism desirable, he gave it. Where he and the Empress noted need they tried to fill it: both of them distributed money with generous hand, for alms or for other benevolent purposes. During his first visit to the south he started a school for poor girls at Porto Alegre by giving 12,000 reis for the purchase of the site and by encouraging adequate public subscriptions to meet the other expenses for it.[41]

An anecdote which the Brazilians are fond of telling about Dom Pedro is concerned with one of his trips. While he and his party were stopping overnight at a farmhouse the Emperor learned that the owner was much troubled by a debt which he lacked the money to pay, and he acted upon the knowledge. Somewhat later, when saying goodbye to his host, he remarked: "You have forgotten to lock up an important paper which I saw in the drawer of the bureau in my room. It should not be lost." The paper was the creditor's receipt for payment of the debt from Dom Pedro's private funds.[42] Dom Pedro II was the father, as well as the sovereign, of the Brazilian people and desired the happiness of each individual.

Nevertheless, after he had ruled as emperor and patriarch for nearly fifty years many glaring national weaknesses still existed. Manoel de Oliveira Lima implies that if the Emperor had been more resolute and vigorous in the execution of his plans for reform and progress conditions would have improved more rapidly.[43] This seems possible, but hardly likely. As has

---

[41] Garcia, "Viagens de D. Pedro II," *Rev. do Inst. Hist. e Geog. Bras.*, vol. 152, p. 117.   [42] *Dom Pedro in U. S.*
[43] Oliveira Lima, *Formation historique de la nationalité brésilienne*, pp. 213, 215.

been shown, Dom Pedro was remarkably energetic and persistent in the pursuit of his duties as head of the State. Had he been more so, the resentment shown towards him by members of the ministry and other officers would have probably been greater, and his influence, therefore, less. In view of climatic handicaps, national weaknesses inherited from colonial days, suspicion felt towards an hereditary ruler, and the limitations of a premature political system, it is probable that Dom Pedro II accomplished about all that he could. Had he been willing and able to set up a military dictatorship, he could doubtless have speeded up progress along many lines—for a time; but this method would have failed in the end, through his quickly sharing the common fate of New World dictators—overthrow by revolution. The fact that he was a crowned ruler in the Americas would have made his overthrow more prompt. His father, who was only fitfully dictatorial, was on the Brazilian throne for less than nine years.

Obviously, in weighing the achievements of Dom Pedro II as Emperor of Brazil, one should not compare him with the rulers of the advanced countries of northwestern Europe but with those of Spanish America, where the heritage of handicaps was, on the whole, similar—popular ignorance, institutional corruption, and inexperience in self-government.

As a matter of fact, Dom Pedro, while respecting personal liberty and political democracy to a degree unknown at the time in any of the other countries to the southeast of the Rio Grande, fostered in Brazil perhaps as great progress as was achieved during his reign by even the most favored, climatically and otherwise, of these Latin American lands.

XIII

AMONG THE INTELLECTUALS

THROUGHOUT his life Dom Pedro was an avid student, partly to qualify himself better as head teacher of his nation and to render other service to it. But he turned to intellectual matters also as a rest from the "miasma of politics," and for escape from the worries and disappointments connected with his position. Most of all, he studied because he delighted in doing so: his chief interest was things of the mind. "I was born to occupy myself with letters and science," he wrote in his diary on December 31, 1861.[1] This natural bent, which he inherited from his mother, was well developed by efficient teachers during his early boyhood, and when he ascended the throne the habit of study was already fixed.

Thereafter, he devoted as much time as possible to exploring ever further the fields of knowledge. His enemies charged that he neglected the duties of office for his books and laboratory, but this was not true. He always gave first place to his responsibilities as a sovereign. Furthermore, much of his reading aimed at gaining ideas for bettering some department of national administration. The time for books came in the evening and during the summer at Petropolis, when Parliament was not in session. Often he read far into the night, and in later years occasionally fell asleep in his chair, to be discovered the next morning by the servant who came to wake him for his bath.[2] He was not a

[1] Extrahido do diario escripto por S. M. o Imperador o Senhor D. Pedro II, Pedro d'Orléans Bragança Archives, A, CXXX, 6373.
[2] João de Rego Barros, "Reminiscencias de ha 50 annos, de um cadete de primeiro regimento de cavallaria," *Rev. do Inst. Hist. e Geog. Bras.*, vol. 152, p. 93.

rapid reader, though an extensive one; he took time to reflect, to underline and sideline passages, and to write marginal comments. His memory was exceptionally good; he was alert, unusually thoughtful, and showed clarity and breadth of mind in considering questions; but he was not intellectually brilliant. What he achieved in the field of scholarship came largely from persistence. After his youth was past and official duties became more heavy and complicated, he found that he needed more rest, and he regretfully reduced the amount of time given to books.

Though less than fifteen years old when he came to the throne, he had already received a good general education, perhaps equal to that of the average monarch of his day. Thereafter, he read extensively and thoughtfully, and also studied systematically under a tutor. Probably hardly a year passed during the next fifty without some time being given to such study. Soon after his accession he took up higher mathematics, but he cared more for laboratory science, and devoted considerable time to trying new experiments which he had seen described in foreign scientific journals. At first, he was especially interested in chemistry, but later physics, especially electricity, seems to have fascinated him even more. In the case of both sciences, he cared most for their application to human progress. Thus, as a boy he experimented with making daguerreotypes; when he visited the United States he showed himself familiar with the Bessemer process of making steel; he followed hopefully attempts to travel by balloon; and he insisted upon having Alexander Graham Bell demonstrate his telephone at the Philadelphia Exhibition. To Gobineau he wrote in 1881 that the electrical exposition in Paris occupied his mind "enormously," and afterwards he added, "My almost poetic enthusiasm for the sciences constantly increases."[3]

[3] Sept. 15, and Nov. 4, 1881, Pedro d'Orléans Bragança Archives, A, CLXXXV, 8347b; Kidder and Fletcher, *op. cit.*, p. 232.

While still a youth he became interested in astronomy, and in 1846 he had a telescope set up at São Christovão Palace and began to make observations himself. With the director of the Imperial Observatory in Rio he kept in close touch, and frequently visited the place. His fondness for star-gazing caused a cartoonist to portray him clad in bathrobe with his eye to a telescope. That he had a good knowledge of astronomy is quite clear, but there seems to be no sound basis for crediting him—as was done—with having discovered new heavenly bodies.[4]

The biological sciences attracted him early. Botany was a favorite study in childhood, and later his interest spread to related fields. He wrote to Gobineau when the latter was in Stockholm, as minister from France: "Give attention to Linné whom I love much, and give me details about his life which may not be generally known."[5] He would, indeed, have found the eighteenth-century scientist a kindred spirit, since they both were intellectually inquisitive and enthusiastic for knowledge. That he studied Linnaeus and other systematists to advantage seems clear from Professor Louis Agassiz's remark that a collection of fishes from Rio Grande do Sul which the Emperor classified and sent him "would do honor to a professional naturalist."[6] With the French naturalist Quatrefages he carried on a correspondence for twenty years or more.[7]

Dom Pedro was one of the first to show interest in the work of Pasteur, and to become a benefactor of the Pasteur Institute in Paris. In recognition, the Institute placed a bust of him in its salon of honor. After meeting Pasteur in Paris, he became an eager student of the scientist's experiments and began a correspondence with him regarding them. He was hopeful that the scientist might discover a vaccine against yellow fever. At first he was skeptical over inoculation against rabies, but by early

---

[4] Teixeira, *op. cit.*, p. 32; Quesada, *op. cit.*, II, 447.
[5] June 18, 1872, Pedro d'Orléans Bragança Archives, A, CLXXXV, 8347b.
[6] Elizabeth Cary Agassiz, *Louis Agassiz, his Life and Correspondence*, pp. 640-41.
[7] The letters of Quatrefages to Dom Pedro are in the Pedro d'Orléans Bragança Archives at the Château d'Eu, France.

in 1888 he had become convinced of its efficacy and had founded in Rio a Pasteur Institute for treatment of the affliction.[8]

That the Emperor knew considerable about geology is clear from the books he read on the subject and from the fact that he was elected corresponding member of the Royal Imperial Geological Institute of Austria. Among the geological works with which he was familiar was *Études synthéthiques de géologie experimentale*, by Gabriel Auguste Daubrée, with whom he exchanged letters for some time.[9] His knowledge of geology helped develop interest in earthquakes, and in May, 1875, he prepared for a member of the French Academy of Sciences a detailed description of a tremor which had taken place in Brazil.[10]

Though Dom Pedro's independent researches were not deep enough in any field to justify calling him a scientist, his methods and attitude were scientific. He showed painstaking industry in gathering information, a detached viewpoint towards it, and suspended judgment towards what it seemed to show. When discussing with James J. O'Kelly the question of whether other worlds are populated, he remarked: "People are too ready to theorize, and I am in the habit of recommending young men to observe much but to theorize little." Later, he added: "The theory of Darwin is undeniable, but I do not agree with the deductions of some of Darwin's followers. I often recommend young men to read Darwin's work because I am a partisan of truth, and the more I read the more I am convinced that all truth is one and that all science meets in the point of truth. Therefore, no obstacle should be thrown in the way of the development of any science."[11]

[8] Dom Pedro II-Louis Pasteur Correspondence, *Inst. Hist. e Geog. Bras.*, case 396, no. 18, 405F; Pasteur to Dom Pedro II, April 14, 1888, Pedro d'Orléan Bragança Archives, A, CXVIII, 8907.
[9] Pedro d'Orléans Bragança Archives, A, CXXVI, 6214; Notes of Dom Pedro on margin of Pressensé, *Les origines*, p. 138.
[10] Pedro d'Orléans Bragança Archives, A, CLXXII, 7823.
[11] New York *Herald*, April 17, 1876.

It was, indeed, as a patron of science, and not as an investigator, that Dom Pedro rendered service to it. Recognizing this, Charles Darwin wrote: "The Emperor has done so much for science that every scientific man is bound to show him the utmost respect."[12]

Like his mother, Dom Pedro found geography fascinating, and not only had he a wide familiarity with it, but he took much interest in all efforts to add to the geographical knowledge of the world. Exploring expeditions roused his enthusiasm. Referring to a recently-made long journey from east to west across Africa, he wrote Gobineau in 1881: "The deeds of today console a little for the wretchedness of the epoch, and I maintain that society has gained much, in general, since the Middle ages."[13] Such attempts to learn more of the earth and its inhabitants inspired his support and applause. To Baron Nordenskjiöld, the Arctic explorer, he sent in 1879 a letter of congratulations and good wishes.[14] In fact, Dom Pedro wrote messages of encouragement to pioneers of progress in many fields. He was a big brother in the world fraternity of seekers after knowledge.

Fascinated by results of the efforts to push back the frontiers of history into the remoter past, he followed eagerly reports of new archaeological excavations. During his visit to Greece, he met at Mycenae Dr. Schliemann who had begun work there and was on the verge of the find which led him to think the place was ancient Troy. The Emperor, enthusiastic over the prospect, spent some time at the ruins discussing archaeology with Schliemann, who, in recognition of Dom Pedro's friendly encouragement, dedicated to him the American edition of the report on the excavations at Mycenae.[15]

[12] Francis Darwin (ed.), *The Life and Letters of Charles Darwin*, II, 404.
[13] Sept. 15, 1881; Pedro d'Orléans Bragança Archives, A, CLXXXV, 8374b.
[14] Pedro d'Orléans Bragança Archives, A, CLXXXIII, 8281.
[15] Dom Pedro II to Gobineau, Nov. 11, 1876, Pedro d'Orléans Bragança Archives, A, CLXXXV, 8347b; Escragnolle Taunay, "A formação intellectual de Pedro II," *Rev. do Inst. Hist. e Geog. Bras.*, vol. 152, p. 892; Fleiuss, in *Contribuições para a Biographia de D. Pedro II*, Pt. I, p. 118.

When traveling in Brittany on his second visit to Europe, he was attracted and challenged by the megalithic monuments. "I can find explanations for the dolmens," he wrote Gobineau, "but not for the immense alignments of menhirs."[16]

The remains of Egypt's great past seem to have interested him most of all. During the several weeks he spent in the Nile Valley in the winter of 1876-1877, he made thoughtful comments in his diary and raised questions on what he saw, evidently with the idea of having them considered by the Egyptian Institute, of which he was a member. While appreciating the magnificence of the architecture, he expressed regret that the Egyptian artists had had a "dogma" imposed upon them, and remarked that "if they had enjoyed more liberty, their ability would certainly have produced works of first rank."[17]

Shocked at the traces of "incredible vandalism" on the ruins of Karnak and Abydos, he commented that "the Khedive might squander a little less on his palaces and spend a little more on the conservation of these monuments."[18] Upon his return to Cairo, at a meeting of the Egyptian Institute on January 13, 1877, he indignantly denounced the crimes committed by tourists against these records of the past, and appealed for their protection. Apparently he was the first person of prominence to do this, and his interest did much to save the remaining vestiges of ancient Egypt.[19] At the time of Dom Pedro's second visit to the Nile Valley, Heinrich Karl Brugsch, who deciphered demotic writing, was at the head of the government school of Egyptology in Cairo. With him and also with Mariette-Bey the Emperor carried on an assiduous correspondence.[20]

Dom Pedro was familiar with the views of the leading

---

[16] June 29, 1877, Pedro d'Orléans Bragança Archives, A, CLXXXV, 8347b.

[17] Debanné, "D. Pedro II no Egypto," *Rev. do Inst. Hist. e Geog. Bras.*, vol. 75, pp. 135-37.

[18] *Ibid.*, p. 137.   [19] *Ibid.*, p. 132.

[20] *Ibid.*, pp. 144-45; Escragnolle Taunay, "A formação intellectual de Pedro II," *Rev. do Inst. Hist. e Geog. Bras.*, vol. 152, p. 892.

philosophers and sociologists, but for history he had a special fondness, and his grasp on it was extensive. Apparently he was not very familiar with the Far East, but on the past of Western Asia, Egypt, Europe, and the Americas he was exceptionally well informed, and he constantly added to his knowledge of these fields by reading new works regarding them. This historical lore he found of much practical value, and he frequently drew upon it to support his views in discussing governmental problems and policies with his ministry. In the light of past events he followed foreign political developments. To Gobineau he wrote in March, 1880, "What did I tell you about Russia? It would appear that it has returned to the time of the Ivans. That country needs two or three Peters the Great."[21] Some months later, in another letter, he mentioned the new territorial acquisitions of Greece and the increased need for settling the menacing Eastern question. The next year he thus commented to the pessimistic Comte on European affairs: "The picture presented by Europe certainly does not edify me, but I do not fear, or, rather, hope, like you, for the invasions of the Barbarians." He was anxious that the African question not embroil France with Italy, where he desired to see a literary and scientific renaissance.[22]

Dom Pedro's most remarkable intellectual achievement was in the field of linguistics. He could read at least fourteen languages and could speak eight or nine of them. During his minority, in addition to his native Portuguese, he studied French, German, English, and Latin, and then, or later, gained conversational knowledge of them. He could use French almost as easily as he could Portuguese. His grasp of English is shown by the fact that he translated poems of Longfellow, Whittier, Byron, and Shakespeare into his native tongue. He knew Latin sufficiently to converse in it in Europe. After he ascended the throne he began to study Castilian and Italian, and learned to

[21] Pedro d'Orléans Bragança Archives, A, CLXXXV, 8347b.
[22] Ibid.

speak them. He was fond of translating from the Italian, and turned Manzoni's "Cinque Maggio" into Portuguese. During winters spent in southern France he familiarized himself with Provençal.

Shortly after he was voted of age he began classical Greek with Felix E. Taunay, and continued to study and read it the remainder of his life. Benjamin Franklin Ramiz Galvão told an experience he had with the Emperor's knowledge of Greek. At the time he was tutor of Princess Isabel's sons, and Dom Pedro, who had turned Aeschylus's "Prometheus" into Portuguese prose, too busy to versify it, as he had planned to do, told Ramiz Galvão to undertake the task. Somewhat disconcerted by the assignment, the tutor began the work, and in the conferences with the Emperor over it he found him a highly critical and meticulous translator.[23] At some time during the earlier part of his reign Dom Pedro gave much study also to modern Greek and acquired some speaking knowledge of it.[24]

Besides encouraging members of the Brazilian Historical and Geographical Institute to study the aboriginal languages, Dom Pedro himself devoted considerable attention to the tongues of the closely related Tupís and Guaranís of southern Brazil. A brief study of his, "Quelques notes sur la langue tupi," which was unsigned, was included in an article on Brazil published in the *Grande Encyclopédie*.[25] It is probably an exaggeration to say, as does one writer, that Dom Pedro understood Tupí "perfectly";[26] but he doubtless had a fair grasp of it. In 1879, a cacique and some of his men from a tribe in Paraná came to Rio to complain to the Emperor against the treatment they had received from police authorities in the interior. They were given quarters in the National Museum, but were unable to explain

---

[23] Ramiz Galvão, "A patria e o livro," *Collectanea Rabello*, I, 29.
[24] Rafford, *op. cit.*, p. cxxiii. See p. 161 of this book.
[25] Aurelio Lopes, "D. Pedro II e os seus livros," *Rev. do Inst. Hist. e Geog. Bras.*, vol. 152, p. 590; Rodolpho Garcia, "D. Pedro II e as linguas americanas," *Rev. do Inst. Hist. e Geog. Bras.*, vol. 152, pp. 126-31.
[26] Amaral, *O Imperador*, p. 75.

their errand because no one could understand them. Through the press, the Emperor learned of their presence and their plight, and went to see them, and he was reported to have conversed with them naturally and easily.[27] Apparently he knew the speech of the Guaranís from Matto Grosso less well, for he seems to have failed to make himself understood by a delegation of them who visited Rio in 1885.[28]

To get a better understanding of Hebrew literature, especially the poetry of the Old Testament, and of the origins of Christianity, Dom Pedro began the study of Hebrew at Petropolis some time before the war began with Paraguay. He received his first lessons from a Swedish Jew named Akerblom and continued them under Dr. Koch, a Protestant minister who was tutor of the Countess of Barral's children. After Koch's death he went on with his Hebrew studies under Dr. Karl Henning, who came to Rio in 1874 and accompanied him to the United States and Europe in 1876. His last tutor in Hebrew and other tongues was Dr. Christian Frederick Seybold, a specialist in Oriental languages, who was also interested in Tupí.[29] By 1871, as has been already stated,[30] Dom Pedro was sufficiently familiar with Hebrew to read at sight from the scrolls in a London synagogue. That the reports of such feats were not the result of mere flattery is apparent from the statement of the Protestant missionary J. C. Fletcher: "I have heard him read the Hebrew, without the points, as fluently as if he had been a Jew."[31] He translated portions of the Old Testament from Hebrew into Latin, including the books of Isaiah, Ruth, the Psalms, Job, the Song of Songs, and Ecclesiastes.[32] The last, and most original, work connected with this study that

---

[27] Teixeira, op. cit., pp. 109-10.   [28] Rio News, Nov. 5, 1885.
[29] Dom Pedro II d'Alcantara, Poésies hebraïco-provençales du rituel Israélite Comtadin, p. xi; Rodolpho Garcia, "D. Pedro II e as linguas americanas," Rev. do Inst. Hist. e Geog. Bras., vol. 152, p. 130.
[30] See p. 155 of this book.
[31] Kidder and Fletcher, op. cit. (9th. ed.), p. 233.
[32] Mossé, op. cit., p. 346.

the Emperor did was published in Avignon in 1891 under the title *Poésies hebraïco-provençales du rituel Israélite Comtadin*. It is a collection of chants used by the Jews of Southern France in connection with family fêtes.[33] On the left-hand page of the little book is the Hebrew original transcribed by the Emperor, and on the right-hand page, his translation in Provençal or in modern French. The introduction, written by him, shows considerable familiarity with Jewish observances.[34]

After having made a good start in the study of Hebrew, Dom Pedro, about 1875, began on Arabic—apparently by himself, for he wanted the light that it would shed upon Hebrew, as well as the pleasure of reading the Arabic literature in the original. Soon he received aid from Baron Gustave de Schreiner, Austrian minister to Brazil, who offered his services. When the Emperor was in the United States in 1876 he was still in the earlier stages of his studies and remarked in an interview that he found Arabic very difficult because of the many conjugations, and in general the elaborateness of the grammar. "I make slow progress for that reason," he is reported as saying, "but I mean to master it yet."[35] Later he took lessons in Arabic with Dr. Seybold, and he finally became so proficient that he began to translate the *Thousand and One Nights* from the original into the Portuguese, which had never been done before; but the work was uncompleted when death came.[36]

The Emperor also acquired some knowledge—probably only a smattering—of Persian and Babylonian. As already stated, he did some serious studying of the hieroglyphics of Egypt when he was in that country. But he devoted more time

---

[33] The volume, which contains fifty-nine pages, is rare. The present writer consulted the copy in the Biblioteca Nacional at Rio de Janeiro. There is a copy in the Library of Congress.

[34] In a footnote to the work (p. xiii) Dr. Seybold, his tutor in languages at the time, stated that the work was the personal production of the Emperor.

[35] *New York Tribune*, July 12, 1876.

[36] Gustave de Schreiner to Dom Pedro II, Nov. 8, 1875, Pedro d'Orléans Bragança Archives, A, CLXXIII, 7871; Dom Pedro II d'Alcantara, *Poésies hebraïco-provençales*, p. xii.

to Sanskrit, the last language of which he made serious study. Apparently his first tutor in it was Dr. Henning, with whom he was studying it on his trip to the United States. Later he continued under Dr. Seybold.[37]

During his last years, Dom Pedro began work on a plan for a common tongue, regarding which he consulted Max Muller. The philologist in his reply expressed much interest in the project and approved of the basic principles adopted by the Emperor for his *lengua catolica*.[38]

Dom Pedro found considerable time for pure literature as well as for the study of linguistics. He was apparently well read in the classics of all of the languages with which he was familiar, and was also acquainted with the best products of contemporary writers. To certain classics—some gems from ancient Greece and Rome, Dante's *Divina Commedia*, and de Camões's *Os Lusiads*—he turned again and again. Outside of modern Portuguese and Brazilian works, he followed most closely contemporary French writings, reading critical essays on them in the *Revue des deux mondes* and other journals as well as the works themselves.

His letters to Gobineau gave much space to literary comment and criticism, and pointed out what he regarded as faults in the Comte's own writings as well as in the writings of others.[39] But he recognized the ability of the eccentric Frenchman before many others did, and he encouraged him to keep on with his work. "When," he asked in September, 1872, "will your *Pleïades* glitter before my eyes?"[40] And after the romance had appeared he pronounced it the best-written of Gobineau's works, and added: "Here you treat very important questions with all of the spirit and the stamp of originality which I rec-

---

[37] Teixeira, *op. cit.*, pp. 105, 200; New York *Herald*, April 16, 1876.
[38] Max Muller to Dom Pedro II, June 29, 1890, Pedro d'Orléans Bragança Archives, A, CCII, 9114.
[39] Dom Pedro II to Gobineau, June 18, 1872, Pedro d'Orléans Bragança Archives, A, CLXXXV, 8347b.
[40] *Ibid*.

ognize in you."[41] The Comte's *Renaissance* likewise won the Emperor's commendation, for its clear picture of the period and of the personalities who played a leading part in it.[42]

In their letters the Emperor and Gobineau exchanged opinions upon recent scholarly and literary works. Quatrefages and his works Dom Pedro defended against his friend's criticisms. Though he greatly admired Hugo, he noted his decline. "What did I tell you about Victor Hugo's new novel?" he remarked to Gobineau, referring to *Quatre vingt-treize*. "What a fall from the heights of the tower of *Notre Dame de Paris!*" Later, he added whimsically, "I regret not having known personally the *Bug-Jargal* of literature. Monsters reconcile us to humanity."[43]

Though aesthetic qualities in literature made a strong appeal, he was apparently unwilling to place them above moral and spiritual values. There was much of the Puritan about this descendant of the Habsburgs and the Braganças. Hence, his admiration for the writings of the New England school, and his personal fondness for Longfellow and Whittier, to whom he became attached through reading their poems long before he met them.[44]

Dom Pedro possessed some literary ability, as his original writings and his translations from many tongues show. His version of "King Robert of Sicily," from *Tales of a Wayside Inn*, in Portuguese metrical rhyme was considered by Longfellow himself to be the best of several translations that had been made of the poem.[45] Like many Brazilians, he began to write original verse in his early youth, but his productions, though usually correct in form, showed no special imaginative power or other artistic merit. Of this, the Emperor was well

---

[41] July 16, 1874, *ibid*.
[42] Dom Pedro II to Gobineau, Sept. 4, 1877, *ibid*.
[43] April 4, 1874, *ibid*.
[44] Kidder and Fletcher, *op. cit.*, pp. 243-44, 245, 250. Samuel T. Pickard, *Life and Letters of John Greenleaf Whittier*, II, 450.
[45] Kennedy, *op. cit.*, pp. 92-94. A manuscript copy of Dom Pedro's translation exists in the library of the Instituto Historico e Geographico Brasileiro, case 302, no. 15, 148.

aware, and repeatedly he said of these writings, "But it is not poetry."[46] In early 1889, some months after his return from his third trip to Europe, the three sons of Princess Isabel published in his honor a volume of his verses—mostly translations, and he thanked them in metrical lines ending with

> Verses made by me in youth
> Have only the merit of sentiment.[47]

He wrote verse simply because he could thus more adequately express his feelings. His best poems, all of which are sonnets, reflect the deepest sorrows of his life and are "sad as the voice of the ocean." Some show much delicacy of feeling and nobility of soul. Among them are those on the deaths of his sons,[48] "Na Morte da Imperatriz" ("On the Death of the Empress"), "Aspiração," ("Aspiration"), and "Aos Vindouros" ("To Those Who Come Later"). These and various others of his poetical compositions have been published,[49] though they were written without any thought of their appearing in print. A few of the Emperor's sonnets may be classed with the best work of Brazil's minor poets.[50]

Dom Pedro's prose writing shows vigor and charm. The best of his letters to the Comte de Gobineau, in chatty, informal

---

[46] Affonso Celso, in *Jornal do Brasil*, June 16, 1825.

[47] Versos feitos por mim na mocidade
  O merito só tem do sentimento.
      From a handwritten copy in the Pedro d'Orléans Bragança Archives.

[48] See pp. 89-90 of this book.

[49] The poems named, and also a number of translations, appear in Teixeira's *O Imperador visto de perto*, pp. 80-101. Some are in the *Rev. do Inst. Hist. e Geog. Bras.*, vol. 152, pp. 773-79. Various verses written after the banishment were collected by "Um Brasileiro" and published under the title *Sonetos do Exilio*. Some verses written in 1852 are printed on page 595 of Kidder and Fletcher's *Brazil and the Brazilians*. The volume of Dom Pedro's verses published in 1889 by his grandsons, Pedro, Luiz, and Antonio, is rare. A copy exists in the Oliveira Lima Library of the Catholic University of America.

[50] Süssekind de Mendonça's charge that the best verses credited to Dom Pedro were written by Franklin Doria, Barão de Loreto (*Quem foi Pedro II*, pp. 61-77), does not seem worthy of consideration. It is likely, however, that the Emperor, like other writers, asked for and profited by criticisms from others.

French, have these qualities. The same is even more true of some of his letters in Portuguese to Herculano and others.[51] Through the initiative of Roquette Pinto of the National Museum of Brazil, some of the letters to Gobineau were published in August, 1929, in *A Ordem* of Rio de Janeiro and the *Diario Nacional* of São Paulo. Georges Raeders likewise contributed some to the *Jornal do Commercio* for October 20, 1835. Other prose writings by Dom Pedro, some of them mere bits, have greater literary merit than his letters, and are worthy of note for their nobility of sentiment as well as for their simplicity and clarity of expression. Some of the best of these are the marginal notes, already quoted, in which he expressed his religious views.[52]

No relationship outside of his family circle gave the Emperor as great pleasure as his association with distinguished minds through correspondence or through personal contact; for, in spite of his devotion to books, he was at times intellectually lonely and longed for comrades of the mind and spirit. Occasionally he asked members of the government whether they had read certain articles in the *Revue des deux mondes*, or in similar publications. When the ministers were not familiar with the matter referred to they were at times embarrassed or offended, and suspected him of trying to show off his own knowledge or to expose their ignorance.[53] Though he may have wished thus to stimulate them to more extensive reading, he was perhaps chiefly interested in exchanging ideas on what he had read, since he delighted in discussion. But not many of his own subjects were well enough educated to satisfy his needs in this regard. Though his letters to obscure strugglers in various fields of research were prompted chiefly by the desire to en-

---

[51] Drafts of many such are in the Pedro d'Orléans Bragança Archives at the Château d'Eu. Typed copies of many of his letters to Gobineau are likewise there. The originals are in the library of the University of Strassburg.

[52] See pp. 169-71 of this book.

[53] José Verissimo, "D. Pedro II," *Jornal do Brasil*, Dec. 8, 1891.

courage, his pleasure in writing to them was whetted by the contact with other delvers into the unknown. Long before his first trip to Europe Dom Pedro had many such correspondents, a number of whom have been mentioned in other connections. With some of them, such as Agassiz, Quatrefages, Pasteur, and Gobineau, he exchanged letters for many years.

More than one foreign intellectual received from the Emperor material aid as well as moral encouragement. When the Comte de Gobineau was financially embarrassed after he had turned to sculpture, Dom Pedro came to the rescue by buying, for a large sum, his marble figure called "Mima."[54] Likewise, when Lamartine, the French historian and statesman, appealed for aid, it was the Emperor of Brazil who made the most generous response, through subscribing for five thousand copies of Lamartine's work at a total cost of one hundred thousand francs.[55]

Most of Dom Pedro's personal contacts with intellectuals came during his visits to European cities, especially those of Italy and France. He met many through the Comte de Gobineau, who, on the Emperor's second trip to Europe, traveled with him through Russia, Turkey, and Greece, and was later with him for some time in Italy. One person whom he came to know in Rome at this time was Madame de Latour, an artist married to an Italian diplomat. Her charm and brilliance attracted him much, and he wrote to Gobineau: "I already esteem her infinitely. She is a lady of true merit. . . . I thank you for making me acquainted with a so distinguished lady, whom I am impatient to see again."[56]

In cities where he made stays of some length the Emperor had receiving hours and most heartily welcomed scholars, artists,

---

[54] This is in the former São Christovão Palace, now the National Museum of Brazil.

[55] Kidder and Fletcher, *op. cit.*, p. 233.

[56] Letter dated Florence, Feb. 27, 1877, Pedro d'Orléans Bragança Archives, A, CLXXXV, 8347b; Gerald M. Spring, *The Vitalism of the Comte de Gobineau*, p. 177.

and literary people. Thus he came to know practically all famous people of Italy and France.[57]

Victor Hugo, however, remained aloof, and when informed that Dom Pedro II desired to meet him, responded crustily that he did not visit any one. "That is no obstacle," said the Emperor; "Victor Hugo has over me the sad privilege of age, and also the superiority of genius. I will therefore call on him first." And he did, on neutral ground, the senate office in Versailles, suggested by the novelist. The two got on excellently, and the Emperor cast aside all formal etiquette and asked the staunch old republican's permission to call on him alone, without even his chamberlain present, which was readily granted.

A few days later he did so, at nine o'clock in the morning. This meeting was delightfully informal. When he greeted his host Dom Pedro said, "Monsieur Victor Hugo, encourage me. I am a little timid." And after he was seated near the novelist he remarked, "Sitting beside Victor Hugo, I feel that I am for the first time upon a throne."

Shortly before this, Hugo's *L'art d'être grandpère*, had been published. After expressing his admiration for the book and quoting some verses from it, Dom Pedro inquired for the novelist's grandchildren, whereupon Jeanne and Georges were called in. Asked to give the caller an embrace, the little girl hugged Dom Pedro so heartily that Victor Hugo asked laughingly:

"Well, do you want to give yourself the luxury of strangling an emperor?"

In response to Dom Pedro's request, the novelist told how he put in an average day, and remarked, smiling,

"After luncheon, at about one o'clock, I go out and do something that you would not be able to do—clamber aboard the omnibus!"

"Why not?" objected his guest; "it is something that would

---

[57] Mossé, *op. cit.*, pp. 372-73; Dom Pedro II to Gobineau, April 4, 1877, Pedro d'Orléans Bragança Archives, A, CLXXXV, 8347b.

suit me perfectly, 'the imperial!' "—presumably an allusion to the name of an omnibus in Paris.

When they talked of government and the Emperor explained his attitude towards his office,[58] Victor Hugo dubbed him "the grandson of Marcus Aurelius." At one point in the conversation the host remarked,

"Fortunately, we have no monarch in Europe like Your Majesty."

"Why?" asked Dom Pedro.

"Because then there would not be a single republican."

The Emperor laughed heartily, and when he was leaving, with an autographed copy of *L'art d'être grandpère*, he neatly returned the compliment. The novelist went with him to the door, remarking, "I am accompanying Your Majesty to the borders of my empire."

"The empire of Victor Hugo is the universe," replied Dom Pedro.[59]

Some days later the Emperor came, like a simple Brazilian citizen, to dine at Hugo's home.[60]

These meetings of the writer and the ruler were doubtless enjoyed by both, but the association was a passing thing, for Victor Hugo did not become one of Dom Pedro's numerous European correspondents.

The foreign intellectual with whom the Emperor had the most intimate and confidential contact was the Comte de Gobineau who was made one of the small inner circle of his friends almost as soon as the two met early in 1869, when the Comte arrived in Brazil as minister from France. On the day the new diplomat was expected to reach Rio, the Emperor, who knew him through his writings, instructed the Minister of Foreign

---

[58] See p. 296 of this book.

[59] Mossé, *op. cit.*, pp. 417-19; Heitor Moniz, *O segundo reinado*, p. 15; Oliveira Lima, "O Imperador e os sabios," *Rev. do Inst. Hist. e Geog. Bras.*, vol. 152, pp. 147-48; J. M. M. F., "D. Pedro II," *Rev. do Inst. Hist. e Geog. Bras.*, vol. 152, pp. 752-54.

[60] J. M. M. F., "D. Pedro II," *Rev. do Inst. Hist. e Geog. Bras.*, vol. 152, p. 754.

Affairs that Gobineau, if he desired to do so, was to be permitted to call at the palace before the official reception.[61] Soon it became the accepted thing for the Comte to visit Dom Pedro once or twice a week for the sake of the enjoyment the two had in each other's company. During the year he was in Rio, Gobineau spent part of every Sunday, at least, at São Christovão. The two differed on many questions. The Comte held that the Germanic was the superior human type, and he thought badly of the Latin element and was depressed over the racial mixture in Brazil; Dom Pedro, broad-minded and tolerant, saw good in all mankind. The Comte was partial to ancient Persian culture: the Emperor championed that of classical Greece. The Comte considered art superior to science: Dom Pedro gave science the first place. These differences in viewpoint lent opportunity for the arguments and discussions which the Emperor so enjoyed. The Comte likewise found pleasure in them, and he wrote his friends that there were only two things in Brazil for which he cared—the Sugar Loaf Peak which guarded Rio harbor and Dom Pedro II. After Gobineau had returned to Europe the Emperor keenly felt his absence and tried to keep up the discussion by correspondence, but he often ended his letters with a sigh for their Sundays of happy memory.[62]

The continued contact by letter benefited both, however. The Comte's comments on European happenings in various fields kept the Emperor in closer touch with trans-Atlantic developments, and the Emperor's missives enabled the emotional Frenchman to sail his craft on a steadier keel. Dom Pedro was, as he told Gobineau, "very personal" in his affections, and never forgot those who loved him and whom he loved.[63] He urged that the Comte, when he felt lonely, should write to one who was sincerely attached to him.[64] "I find you so melancholy," he

[61] Wanderley Pinho, *op. cit.*, p. 59.
[62] Letters of Gobineau to Dom Pedro II, Pedro d'Orléans Bragança Archives, Div. A, *passim*; letters of Dom Pedro to Gobineau, *ibid.*, CLXXXV, 8347b.
[63] Dom Pedro II to Gobineau, Aug. 27 and Nov. 1, 1875, *ibid.*
[64] Sept. 7, 1879, *ibid.*

said in a later letter. "I should like very much to go and talk with you and bring you a little of my optimism. Be assured, at least, that your friends wish you to be happy."[65]

Other letters to Gobineau from this period show the Emperor's hopeful interest in all progress. Late in 1879 he remarked, "Nothing new here. Write me often; let me breathe a little the atmosphere of the fine arts, and believe that, though my body begins to feel its fifty-four years, my spirit is always young. How I miss those Sundays!"[66] Some months later he remarked, "I have never known ennui, and science has the charm for me of which you are aware, although I am also enthusiastically fond of the fine arts."[67] In a letter of the next month he mentioned the need for more serious attention to popular education to help solve the vexing problems then besetting the world; but he added, "Meanwhile, I am not bored with my century, as you are; and the theory of evolution is basically sound."[68]

Dom Pedro's sense of duty made impossible for him a carefree joy in life, but he experienced the serene happiness of intelligent, constructive living, such as broadly-trained, well-balanced minds may feel.

In recognition of his intellectual interests and achievements, scores of learned societies in many parts of the world made him a member. Most of all he prized election as foreign associate of the French Academy of Sciences, to which, in writing to fellow members he referred affectionately as "our Academy." Probably few experiences in life gave him greater pleasure than this tribute from French scholars.[69]

He was, naturally, proud of his intellectual accomplishments, especially since these were the fruits of persistent industry during very scant periods of leisure; and the pride was justifiable. The charge, made by some of his opponents, that

[65] May 8, 1881, *ibid.*
[66] Oct. 1, 1879, *ibid.*
[68] April 24, 1880, *ibid.*
[67] Mar. 13, 1880, *ibid.*
[69] Raffard, *op. cit.*, pp. cxxvii-cxxxvi.

he was a vain poseur, was, of course, as false as it was stupid, for Dom Pedro II was humble and honest in his attitude towards learning. His knowledge of natural science was deep enough in some fields to have enabled him to gain temporary distinction through formulating new theories or championing obscure ones, if he had been willing to use cheap methods and to accept cheap publicity. But this would have been against his nature as well as in conflict with his intellectual and ethical standards. Therefore, he kept an open mind and followed the advice that he gave to Brazilian youths—"to observe much but to theorize little."[70]

The Emperor's learning was broad rather than deep, since, from his mother, he inherited a bent towards unlimited interest in the world about him; and, furthermore, Brazil needed leadership in all lines of progress. Had he been able to spend his life in intellectual pursuits, he would probably have specialized in some science, but would have worked in many other fields of knowledge as well. As it was, he was able to secure only the wide scholarship permitted by his sense of duty to his country and by his scant leisure. There has been considerable discussion of whether he was a savant. The answer depends largely upon one's definition of the term. In any case, he deserves to be classed with the most learned people of the nineteenth century and with the best-educated rulers of all time.

[70] See p. 247 of this book.

XIV

SLAVERY AND ABOLITION

AS A progressive intellectual, Dom Pedro would naturally have been opposed to slavery, regardless of his training. But it was probably his teachers who turned him against it in early boyhood. As he grew older he fully realized that the system hurt the Empire, since it demoralized both master and slave.[1] But, in working to abolish it, he could not, as a constitutional monarch, move too far in advance of public opinion. Though slaveowners in Brazil did not foster the delusion that servile bondage was part of the "divine plan"—as did some in the United States, still a large proportion of them believed it necessary, especially since the supply of free labor was very limited. So long as this was true, abolition of slavery would be disastrous to agriculture and, in general, to the economic stability of the country. The Emperor fully realized this, and therefore favored gradual, carefully-planned, emancipation.[2]

He emphasized this in a conversation with Hector Varela, a writer from the Plata basin. "Do you think," he said,

that there is in Brazil, any one—any one of my compatriots—who more ardently wishes abolition than I do? There is not one; and those who know best what I think are the very ones who are in the lead in the noble movement for emancipation. . . . Some of those who attack me with such distinct injustice think that I retard the most happy hour of my reign, that in which I can announce to the world that now not a single slave exists in my country, and that the last one of those unfortunates is as free as I. But you know very well that *immediate abolition*, today, this moment, could not be

[1] New York *Herald,* April 17, 1876.
[2] Agassiz and Agassiz, *op. cit.,* p. 66; Mossé, *op. cit.,* pp. 182-83; Evaristo Moraes "Pedro II e o movimento abolicionista," *Rev. do Inst. Hist. e Geog. Bras.,* vol. 152 pp. 323-24.

[264]

decreed without considering something besides the generous and noble impulses of the heart, in which all share. It must *be prepared for* so that sudden liberation given the slaves will not greatly hurt important interests which must be respected.[3]

Therefore, he worked hard to promote immigration of laborers from Europe and to encourage voluntary manumission. He set an example in 1840, the year of his accession, by freeing all of the slaves he had inherited. And twenty-four years later he followed the same principle by giving his daughter Isabel as a wedding present the freedom papers of the slaves who would have come to her as part of her dowry.[4] Apparently these were government bondmen. Two years after this, in 1866, when the Benedictine establishment in Rio emancipated sixteen hundred of its blacks, the Emperor went personally to the monastery to congratulate the abbot and to bestow upon him as a commemorative gift a gold case with the imperial initials set in diamonds.[5]

Since Brazilian leaders as a whole took a just and enlightened attitude towards abolition, sentiment in favor of it spread rapidly towards the middle of the nineteenth century, and voluntary liberations increased, especially after the outbreak of civil war in the United States. The press now became more outspoken against slavery, and in 1862 the *Correio Mercantil* published a series of particularly able articles in favor of abolition.[6]

At this time, perhaps at least one fourth of the population of the Empire was in servile bondage, most of the unfree being in the provinces of Bahia, Rio de Janeiro, Minas Geraes, and São Paulo. National sentiment was probably ripe for gradual emancipation by legislative enactment. But Dom Pedro and the ministry delayed pushing the matter, apparently because of foreign complications. In June, 1861, new troubles began with

[3] Teixeira, *op. cit.*, pp. 147-48.
[4] *Ibid.*, p. 146; P. A. Martin, "Slavery and Abolition in Brazil," *Hisp. Amer. Hist. Rev.*, XIII (May, 1933), 173.   [5] *Jornal do Commercio*, June 12, 1866.
[6] Christiano Ottoni, *O advento da republica no Brasil*, p. 9.

England over the wrecking of the "Prince of Wales" on the coast of Rio Grande do Sul, and for nearly two years serious tension continued between the two nations. Before this crisis was past trouble developed with Uruguay, which soon roused the hostility of Francisco López. Then, just at the time the fratricidal struggle in the United States was ending with the anti-slavery element victorious, Brazil entered the Triple Alliance for the unfortunate war with Paraguay.

The Emperor continued, however, to encourage emancipation, and he definitely favored the freeing of all government slaves who asked to enlist in the army. A considerable number of state-owned blacks on the imperial fazenda at Santa Cruz took advantage of it, after which Dom Pedro had their families emancipated and provided educational opportunities for their children. In all, about six thousand crown slaves won freedom through offering to fight against Paraguay.[7]

Although much absorbed and harassed by the war, the Emperor did not want the question of gradual emancipation to await the end of the conflict. He was anxious to have a beginning made towards it, and, therefore, late in 1865 he asked Pimenta Bueno, a learned jurist, to prepare a project for emancipation. Early the next year this was submitted to Araujo Lima, the Marquez de Olinda, then president of the council of ministers, who declared that to raise the question of emancipation would "open the door to a thousand misfortunes." Other members of the ministry agreed that so far as possible the government should avoid controversial questions during the war, in order to maintain national solidarity. Therefore, the Olinda cabinet opposed the plan.[8]

About six months later support came to Dom Pedro in the form of a petition from a French abolition society, urging him seriously to consider freeing the slaves of Brazil. The message

---

[7] Mossé, *op. cit.*, p. 185; Teixeira, *op. cit.*, pp. 146-47.

[8] Serrano, *op. cit.*, pp. 423-24; Moraes, "Pedro II e o movimento abolicionista," *Rev. do Inst. Hist. e Geog. Bras.*, vol. 152, pp. 325-26; Mossé, *op. cit.*, p. 194.

bore many distinguished signatures, including Guizot's.[9] Though the Emperor had not yet been abroad, he was very sensitive to foreign criticism and was most anxious to have Brazil and himself thought well of in other countries. Shortly after the petition arrived, the Olinda cabinet gave way to that of Zacharias, which was more willing to consider emancipation. The French abolitionists' message was presented before this ministry, which decided to consider it as a public document and answer it officially. Apparently Dom Pedro himself worded the reply, written August 22, 1866, though it was signed by the Minister of Justice. Public opinion, it stated, was favorable to emancipation, and action upon it was a matter of form and opportunity. The government planned to consider this measure which "the spirit of Christianity demanded" when the war with Paraguay was ended.[10]

But without waiting for it to end the Emperor took up the matter with Zacharias, who, early in 1867, presented to the council of state the project for emancipation drawn up by Pimenta Bueno. This provided for emancipation of babies who should be born of slave mothers after a given date, and it aimed at total abolition by December 31, 1899. The council of state, meeting at São Christovão, with the Emperor presiding, expressed itself in favor of emancipation through the method named, "when circumstances permitted." The strongest advocate of abolition among those present was José Thomaz Nabuco de Araujo. Visconde do Rio Branco, aiming at the Emperor, criticized the apparent pressure on the government to speed up the reform.[11] But a committee, headed by Nabuco, was appointed to study the question of abolition; and in his speech from the throne on May 22, 1867, the Emperor asked Parliament to consider means for emancipating the slaves which

[9] Mossé, *op. cit.*, pp. 195, 267; Joaquim Nabuco, *O abolicionismo*, p. 63.
[10] Mossé, *op. cit.*, p. 196; Fleiuss, in *Contribuições para a Biographia de D. Pedro II*, Pt. I, pp. 418-19.
[11] Moraes, "Pedro II e o movimento abolicionista," *Rev. do Inst. Hist. e Geog. Bras.*, vol. 152, pp. 326-27.

would respect the rights of the owners and would not seriously upset agriculture.[12] This was the first time that the government had brought the problem before the legislative body.

The report of the committee of the council of state on emancipation followed the same general lines as the plan of Pimenta Bueno. It provided for liberation of all children who should be born to slave mothers; for freeing of slaves belonging to religious orders and to the government; for the registration of all slaves; and for the creation of an emancipation fund; and it prohibited sale of slaves at auction, and the separation of slave families.[13] The plan represented the wishes of the more liberal abolitionist element in the government. But the majority of the council were opposed to action before the war was ended.[14] Therefore, in his address from the throne of May, 1868, the Emperor merely said that "The servile element has been the object of assiduous study, and when opportunity offers the government will submit a suitable proposal for your wise consideration."[15] The Conservative ministry, headed by the Visconde de Itaborahy, which came into power two months later, refused to touch the question. Therefore nothing was done officially for the next two years to hasten emancipation. But sentiment in favor of it gained momentum. Demands for abolition became more numerous from platform and from press; the Radical Manifesto of 1869 indorsed it; and the Liberal pronouncement of the same year declared abolition to be an imperious and urgent demand of civilization.[16]

Furthermore, though the war with Paraguay delayed government action, feeling against slavery was fostered in connection with the conflict. Argentina and Uruguay had freed their few African bondmen some time before, and the Brazilian soldiers

---

[12] *Fallas do throno*, p. 627.
[13] Moraes, "Pedro II e o movimento abolicionista," *Rev. do Inst. Hist. e Geog. Bras.*, vol. 152, p. 328.
[14] Mossé, *op. cit.*, p. 197.   [15] *Fallas do throno*, p. 640.
[16] dos Santos, *op. cit.*, p. 125; Oliveira Vianna, in *Contribuições para a Biographia de D. Pedro II*, Pt. I, p. 808.

were somewhat mortified to find that their allies looked down upon the Empire because slavery still existed there. The fact that in 1869 the Comte d'Eu, who was a strong abolitionist, induced the provisional government at Asunción to free the Paraguayan slaves further impressed the Brazilians with the backward condition of their country in this matter.[17]

Early in 1870, as soon as hostilities ended in Paraguay, the Emperor wanted the plan for abolition taken up, but he was opposed by his ministers, all but two of whom voted against even mentioning the matter in the address from the throne.[18] Dom Pedro was, however, very reluctant to delay further. His attitude was shown by a reply he made when the Barão de Cotegipe, a member of the cabinet, remarked that the emancipation question was like a stone rolling down a mountain, and warned, "We must not precipitate it lest we be hurt." "I shall not hesitate to expose myself to the stone even though I be hurt," said Dom Pedro.[19] To his ministry he urged the need for faith, without which nothing could be accomplished. He considered it absolutely necessary to persist in the idea of emancipation, but aimed to limit the program for it—not to go too fast. He was anxious to apply to the future children of the slaves connected with the palace—who belonged to the Empire—the principle of free birth, but his cabinet held that he had no authority to do so. If such was the case, said the Emperor, he would dispense with the services of the slaves and send them to the arsenals; if he had the right to free them, he would do so, even at his own expense.[20] However, things soon began to move towards abolition.

While the ministry held out, the lower house helped force the issue, through appointing a committee to draw up a plan of

---

[17] Luis da Camara Cascudo, *O Conde d'Eu*, pp. 106-8.
[18] Moraes, "Pedro II e o movimento abolicionista," *Rev. do Inst. Hist. e Geog. Bras.*, vol. 152, pp. 329-31.
[19] Moniz, *A côrte de D. Pedro II*, p. 69.
[20] Moraes, "Pedro II e o movimento abolicionista," *Rev. do Inst. Hist. e Geog. Bras.*, vol. 152, pp. 331-32.

emancipation. In August, 1870, the committee reported a project rather similar to that of Pimenta Bueno. According to it, all children born after promulgation of the law should be free, but they should serve their mothers' masters until they were twenty-one years of age.[21]

By the next month the Itaborahy cabinet could no longer maintain itself. There was a feeling that the Liberal senator José Tomaz Nabuco de Araujo should head the new ministry. Dom Pedro, however, thought that a plan for emancipation sponsored by the Conservatives would be more acceptable to the wealthy slaveholding element, and he, therefore, asked Pimenta Bueno to form a new government. But it soon was evident that the new cabinet head could not combat the opposition which developed in the lower house and even in the government. The Emperor gave him authority to remove the refractory ministers and appoint others in harmony with the reform; but Pimenta Bueno, discouraged, asked to be released, and suggested that the Visconde do Rio Branco, another Conservative, be appointed to his place.[22]

Since Rio Branco opposed the Emperor's efforts for emancipation three years before, he had been on a diplomatic mission to Asunción and was there when the Paraguayan slaves were freed. His experience seems to have converted him, and he now favored action. As he was both courageous and able, Dom Pedro asked him early in March, 1871, to form a new cabinet and to tackle the servile problem; and he consented. Late in May the Emperor left for his first trip abroad, satisfied that Rio Branco was equal to the task.[23] The Visconde set energetically to work, and soon introduced into the lower house a bill for gradual emancipation, based on the recommendations of the Nabuco committee. In both chambers it met strong opposition,

---

[21] Mossé, *op. cit.*, p. 199.
[22] Moraes, "Pedro II e o movimento abolicionista," *Rev. do Inst. Hist. e Geog. Bras.*, vol. 152, pp. 332-33.
[23] Mossé, *op. cit.*, pp. 202-05; Camara Cascudo, *op. cit.*, p. 110.

but it also had valiant defenders. In the house of deputies Joaquim Nabuco, the talented son of José Antonio Nabuco de Araujo, was a devoted and able champion of the measure, but no one fought for it more valiantly than did Rio Branco himself. Finally, on September 27, the bill passed the senate, and on the next day it was signed by the Princess Regent. It provided for creation of a fund with which to buy the liberation of slaves, and declared free the following classes of bondmen: those belonging to the nation; those for use of the crown; those abandoned by their masters; those to whom title through inheritance was vague; and all children born thereafter to slave mothers. But these children must be apprenticed to their masters until they were twenty-one years old, unless their mothers preferred to hand them over to the government at the age of eight, in which case the master should receive a small indemnity. All bondmen, and likewise the freeborn babies, must be registered.[24] When the law was passed there were about 1,700,000 slaves in the Empire.[25]

As a whole, the population of the capital, which had followed developments with intense interest, rejoiced greatly over the passage of the bill. During the last debate before the final vote was taken in the senate the populace showered blossoms upon Rio Branco and other abolitionists. After the session was ended, the American minister, James Rudolph Partridge, who had watched developments from the diplomats' gallery, descended to the senate floor and picked up some of the blossoms scattered there. "I shall send these flowers to my country," he said, "to show how you achieve here by law what there cost so much blood."[26] To no other Brazilian, however, did the event

---

[24] Nabuco, *Um estadista do Imperio: Nabuco de Araujo*, III, 614-43; *Collecção das leis do Imperio do Brazil, 1871*, tomo 31, Pt. I, pp. 147-51; Mossé, *op. cit.*, pp. 207-9.

[25] Mossé, *op. cit.*, p. 233.

[26] Monteiro, *Pesquisas e depoimentos para a historia*, p. 34; Alfredo de Escragnolle Taunay, *O Visconde do Rio Branco*, pp. 75-94; Escragnolle Taunay, *Reminiscencias*, pp. 30-31; Mossé, *op. cit.*, pp. 207-9.

mean so much as it did to Dom Pedro, who was in Egypt when the news reached him. "Never have I seen the Emperor so joyful!" wrote Bom Retiro.[27]

But the Rio Branco Law—which was ignored here and there, especially in the remoter parts—did not satisfy the more radical abolitionists, who considered it timid and incomplete. They wished to hasten emancipation by additional enactments. Therefore, agitation continued, and anti-slavery writings and organizations increased. José de Patrocinio, the son of a slave, wrote for the *Gazeta de Noticias* fervent and brilliant articles in denunciation of servile bondage. In 1880 came important developments. The *Gazeta da Tarde*, the first frankly abolitionist journal, was founded in that year. Further momentum was gained for anti-slavery sentiment in July, 1880, in connection with the return of the Emperor's protégé Carlos Gomes, after his opera "Il Guarany" had been played with marked success in Europe. Patrocinio and another abolitionist leader collected money which they gave to Gomes for buying the freedom of a slave. In the opening scene of a pageant in Gomes's honor, the composer, who was a popular idol, formally manumitted the bondman. To this, the audience responded with a wildly enthusiastic ovation.[28]

A few months later, on the ninth anniversary of the Rio Branco Law, the Brazilian Society against Slavery was founded, with Joaquim Nabuco as its president. In 1883, about a dozen anti-slavery societies united as the *Confederação Abolicionista*, which now became the spearhead of the abolitionist movement, and was especially active in encouraging slaves to forsake their masters and in helping them to escape to safety. At a public gathering in a theatre in Rio de Janeiro, the Confederação presented an abolitionist manifesto, which was received with great

---

[27] Mossé, *op. cit.*, p. 210.
[28] Moraes, "Pedro II e o movimento abolicionista," *Rev. do Inst. Hist. e Geog. Bras.*, vol. 152, pp. 334-35; *Rio News*, June 15, 1883; Serrano, *op. cit.*, p. 426; Nabuco, *O abolicionismo*, pp. 72 ff.

enthusiasm by the more than two thousand people who were present. But it caused panic among conservative slaveholders.[29]

In 1880, likewise, was founded in Ceará a society for the express purpose of liberating the slaves of that province. One of the subscribers to its funds was the Emperor himself. Among abolitionists, Ceará had been in especially bad repute because it sold slaves to the south, thus separating families. Francisco Nascimento, the leader in the emancipation society there, had been a sailor and consequently had much influence with the *jangadeiros* (boatmen) who carried the blacks out to the slave-trading coastal steamers anchored in the harbor of Fortaleza, the capital of the province. Assembling the boatmen, he appealed to them not to transport slaves for southern trade. They promised, and the pledge was kept. In January, 1881, a steamer waited in the harbor four days, during which the jangadeiros maintained their abolition strike; then it departed without its human cargo. In August of that year a new strike of boatmen permanently closed the port to the traffic, even though the civil authorities intervened and removed some of the abolitionist leaders from public office. Indeed, this meddling increased the zeal of the reformers, who now started a journal, *O Libertador,* for spreading propaganda. Soon a plan was launched in Ceará for emancipation by municipalities, and by the middle of 1883 all slaves had been freed in six of them. To prevent the work of liberation from being undone, the abolitionists placed a ban upon the introduction of slaves into free political units and into the province. The goal was reached on March 25, 1884, when the remaining 19,588 bondmen of Ceará were emancipated. To southern abolitionists the province now became the "Land of Light," and by fugitive slaves it was sought as a place of refuge.[30]

---

[29] Serrano, *op. cit.*, p. 426; Mossé, *op. cit.*, p. 213; Evaristo de Moraes, *A campanha abolicionista (1879-1888)*, pp. 33-36.

[30] José de Patrocinio, *L'affranchisement des esclaves de la province de Ceará au Brésil*, pp. 11-15; *Rio News*, Mar. 24, April 5, 1884.

From Ceará the movement for complete emancipation quickly spread to other parts. Amazonas, which had but few bondmen, completed liberation in July, 1884. Even in Pernambuco and Bahia, where slavery was of more economic importance than in most of the other tropical provinces, able leaders spread abolitionist sentiment. Rio Grande do Sul likewise began in 1884 to emancipate by political units, leading off with its capital, where more than three thousand blacks were given liberty.[31]

Meanwhile, abolitionists connected with the central government had been trying to secure further legislative concessions. Many were disappointed because the Rio Branco Law of 1871 had not fixed the date for final emancipation. Joaquim Nabuco, the leader of the group, on August 24, 1880, introduced into the lower house a resolution proposing that complete emancipation be achieved by January 1, 1890, the year in which the fiftieth anniversary of Dom Pedro's rule would be celebrated. But the majority of the cabinet emphasized the fact that existing legislation would ultimately end slavery, and they refused to consider Nabuco's plan. In the next election Nabuco and two other reform deputies lost their seats.[32] But the abolition idea had by now seized upon the popular mind and it made steady progress.

The spread of anti-slavery sentiment and legislation, however, roused the indignation of many slaveowners, and strengthened the resistance of the pro-slavery organizations which began to appear. From the first, the question had cut across party lines, though most of the support for emancipation came from the Liberals. As usual, both sides blamed the Emperor. Some of his opponents who favored servile bondage laid upon him the responsibility for the origin and progress of the abolition movement. The republicans, in particular, who tended to sup-

---

[31] Monteiro, *Pesquisas e depoimentos para a historia*, pp. 58-62; dos Santos, *op. cit.*, p. 152; Moraes, *A campanha abolicionista (1879-1888)*, p. 279.

[32] Patrocinio, *op. cit.*, p. 8; Mossé, *op. cit.*, pp. 213-15; Carolina Nabuco, *A vida de Joaquim Nabuco*, p. 84.

port slavery, denounced him for taking the initiative resulting in the Rio Branco Law, which they declared should have come from the country, not from the throne. Instead of guaranteeing the rights and defending the interests of the public, they said, he had been inspired by vainglory roused in him by foreign abolitionists. Here, declared his enemies, was another instance of his absolutist methods.[33]

The abolitionists, on the other hand, were impatient because the Emperor did not do more to wipe out slavery. They were greatly fortified by the publication, in 1883, of Joaquim Nabuco's *O abolicionismo*, a penetrating indictment of human bondage and an eloquent demand for total emancipation. Some of the reformers criticized Dom Pedro for declining the invitation of the Confederação Abolicionista to attend a meeting to celebrate the freeing of the slaves in Ceará. As he explained to the officers of the organization, he remained away because he feared that his presence at the gathering would be misinterpreted by those who were not in favor of abolition, but he offered to contribute to an emancipation fund if the Confederação started one.

He did not, however, wholly approve of the methods used by some of the reform groups, for he wished everything done legally; and, while lauding voluntary manumission, he regretted the fact that anti-slavery radicals encouraged bondmen to flee from their masters. But early in 1884 he tried to stimulate spontaneous manumission through more general distribution of titles and honors to those who freed their slaves.[34]

By now, abolition sentiment was so strong that the question almost forced itself upon the government. Therefore, when the Lafayette cabinet fell the Emperor decided to name as his next prime minister a man who would undertake to carry out the abolition ideal with moderation and prudence. Accordingly, he

[33] Pereira da Silva, *op. cit.*, II, 282; André Rebouças, *A questão do Brazil*, sec. 22.
[34] Patrocinio, *op. cit.*, p. 19; *Rio News*, Jan. 24, 1884.

asked Manoel P. de Sousa Dantas, a Liberal who was known to be an abolitionist, to form a government; and he promised Dantas his support in connection with the parliamentary fight which would probably result.[35] But he warned the Minister against too hasty action, adding, "When you try to run I will pull on your coat tails."[36]

The new cabinet agreed upon a plan recognizing that emancipation should be based upon the following points: the age of the slaves; failure of the owner to register slaves; change of legal residence; purchase of freedom by emancipation funds; voluntary manumission by the owners; and forfeiture of slave property. The plan drawn up by the ministry prohibited the sale of slaves, called for establishment of agricultural settlements for freedmen, and for the increase of the emancipation fund provided for in the Law of 1871 by addition to all imposts. Presentation of the project in the lower house, however, raised a storm of protest and produced an attack upon the Emperor, who was considered responsible for the move. The fact that the finances of the country were in bad shape helped add to the resentment. Many wanted that problem considered before taking up another one which might make the economic situation worse. To clarify the question, a test vote was taken and the Dantas project was defeated by a narrow margin. The Prime Minister then asked for a dissolution of the house of deputies, and the Emperor complied on September 3, after the budget had been voted.[37]

Discussion of emancipation in Parliament helped stimulate agitation for it elsewhere. Abolitionists petitioned the government, held meetings in public parks, and paraded the streets of Rio de Janeiro and other cities carrying banners with anti-slavery pictures and slogans and asking for money to foster the movement. The propagandists now openly urged slaves to

[35] Pimentel, *op. cit.*, pp. 95-96.   [36] Serrano, *op. cit.*, p. 430.
[37] *Annaes da Camara dos Deputados do Imperio do Brazil*, 1884, Vol. IV, Projecto No. 48, in appendix, p. 115.

leave their masters, and offered them refuges if the authorities attempted to restore them to their owners. In many cases, however, police and other minor public functionaries sympathized with these demonstrations.[38]

The pro-slavery element in the cities, made up largely of bankers, manufacturers, and merchants, was likewise roused by the new developments. In the capital they formed the *Club de Lavóura e Commercio*, with the aim of defeating the project introduced by Dantas. Their support came largely from the delegates to the provincial legislatures, Conservative members of Parliament, and most *fazendeiros*, who greatly feared the loss of their labor supply. The press gave much space to the discussion and reflected the conflicting viewpoints.[39]

In the election for a new house of deputies the agents of the ministry were unusually active; there was much fraud and violence, and various seats were later contested. Early in March the new Parliament met in extraordinary session to consider the slavery problem. Though the Liberals were in the majority in the lower chamber, many of them were hostile to the ministry and to the plan for emancipation. There was some question as to whether the government would be able to maintain order in the face of the growing excitement over the servile question. Therefore, on May 6, 1885, Dom Pedro dismissed the cabinet and called upon José Antonio Saraiva to form a new one. This was done, and the house passed an emancipation bill less liberal than that of Dantas. But Saraiva and his ministry soon became convinced that they could not get the coöperation of the lower chamber for other important measures. Therefore, he asked for collective dismissal of his cabinet. The Emperor, somewhat reluctantly, consented. Then, after talking over the problem with the presidents of the two houses and learning as much as he could about the temper and inclinations of the two parties as

---

[38] Pereira da Silva, *op. cit.*, II, 280-81; Martin, "Slavery and Abolition," *Hisp. Amer. Hist. Rev.*, XIII (May, 1933), 185-87.

[39] Pereira da Silva, *op. cit.*, II, 281-82.

then represented in Parliament, he asked the Conservative president of the senate, the Barão de Cotegipe, to form a cabinet; and the Barão did so.[40]

Following this imperial *coup*, the senate passed the emancipation bill on September 28, 1885, and Dom Pedro promptly signed it. The measure called for a new registration of slaves; set the purchase price for emancipation; made more specific provision for a manumission fund; and provided for the freeing of all slaves who had reached sixty years, and of all others when they attained that age. Because of the labor shortage, freedmen who had just reached sixty must work for their masters for three years. Those who were older were to be cared for by their former masters. Unregistered slaves must be freed. Change of a bondman's domicile to another province without good reason also gave him his freedom. The law, furthermore, contained provisions for increasing the immigrant labor supply.[41]

Though the Cotegipe Law seemed an important step towards total emancipation, agitation for complete abolition continued, partly because many masters failed to register slaves. Abolitionists likewise resented the delay in passing the bill, and its limitations—especially its failure to fix the date for complete abolition. Joaquim Nabuco, who was again in Parliament, and other anti-slavery men persisted in demanding that the date be named, but the ministry held out against this.[42]

Dissatisfaction therefore increased, and abolition activities continued to gain momentum. Voluntary emancipations grew rapidly, and emancipation leaders collected large sums for purchasing freedom. Those who contributed to the manumission fund in Rio de Janeiro were listed in the *Livro de Ouro*—the *Golden Book*, which included the names of the members of the

---

[40] *Ibid.*, pp. 282-301.

[41] *Collecção das leis do Imperio do Brazil, 1885 (Actos do poder legislativo)*, tomo 32, Pt. I, pp. 14-18.

[42] Affonso Celso, *Oito annos de parlamento*, pp. 130-31; *Rio News*, April 15, 1887.

imperial family and of many nobles.[43] The Emperor's gifts for such purposes were generous and unfailing. When he traveled in São Paulo in 1886 he gave at least five hundred milreis in every municipality where such funds were being collected. In one place he bought the freedom of a slave whom he saw on the street. He also officiated by request at the formal emancipation of other slaves.[44]

Late in February, 1887, however, the Emperor was withdrawn from the abolition controversy through becoming seriously ill. The immediate cause for the trouble seemed to be congestion of the liver, which was accompanied by fever; but for some time he had shown symptoms of diabetes.[45] After some weeks improvement came, but not recovery. The imperial patient remained physically weak; his memory was faulty regarding current affairs; he was irresolute, and slow of speech. Lack of frankness in the official reports of his condition led to popular fears, which were aired in the press, that his mind was really impaired.[46]

With the aim of improving his health, a trip to Europe was prescribed, and Princess Isabel, who, with her husband, was then in Paris, was called home by cable to take charge of the government. She reached Rio on June 7, and her father and mother, accompanied by their eldest grandson, Dom Pedro Augusto, left for Lisbon the 30th of the month.[47] With brief stops, they went from here to Paris, where Dom Pedro's accompanying physician, the Conde de Motta Maia, arranged a medical consultation. The French doctors confirmed the diag-

---

[43] Mossé, *op. cit.*, p. 221; Pimentel, *op. cit.*, pp. 97-98.

[44] Teixeira, *op. cit.*, pp. 112, 116-17, 121.

[45] Olympio da Fonseca, "Molestia do Imperador," *Rev. do Inst. Hist. e Geog. Bras.*, vol. 152, pp. 186-88; Rangel, *Gastão de Orléans, o ultimo Conde d'Eu*, p. 358; Manoel A. Velho da Motta Maia, *O Conde de Motta Maia*, pp. 77-79.

[46] Rangel, *Gastão de Orléans, o ultimo Conde d'Eu*, pp. 358-59; *Rio News*, May 24, June 5, June 15, 1887.

[47] Rangel, *Gastão de Orléans, o ultimo Conde d'Eu*, p. 359; Fonseca, "Molestia do Imperador," *Rev. do Inst. Hist. e Geog. Bras.*, vol. 152, pp. 186-88; *Rio News*, July 5, 1887; Escragnolle Taunay, "Dom Pedro Augusto de Saxe Coburgo Gotha," *Jornal do Commercio*, Sept. 30, 1934.

nosis of the Brazilian ones regarding diabetes, which, however, seemed to be a light intermittent case. The Emperor's chronic physical weakness was caused by this and by malaria. Rest and a course of treatments were prescribed.[48]

Dom Pedro, however, did not wait to get better before proceeding to take intellectual advantage of being again in Europe. He visited places of interest in Paris and attended learned gatherings with all his former enthusiasm. From France he went to Switzerland for a short stay. A sketch of a waterfall in his diary and edelweiss blossoms pressed between its pages suggest his enjoyment of the visit. Next, to Germany, where, at Baden-Baden, he swam and took health baths and gymnastic exercises. Soon his strength began to return and his memory to improve. His grandson, Prince Pedro Augusto, who was not naturally optimistic, reported that his memory was almost normal. Nevertheless, the rumors regarding his weakened mental condition persisted in Brazil, where the report was made through the press that, according to the view of one of the Emperor's physicians, he would not be able to resume his position on the throne.[49]

From Baden-Baden he returned to Paris, but late in the autumn he went to southern France, where he spent the next five months, mostly in Cannes. During this period, he received many visitors, read widely, translated poetry, composed verses, and studied languages with Dr. Seybold. He and the Empress also took much interest in Cannes and its philanthropic institutions, to which they gave liberally; and they received in return the admiration and affection of the people.[50]

[48] Diary of Dom Pedro II, 1887-1888, Pedro d'Orléans Bragança Archives, B, XXXVI, 1056; Fonseca, "Molestia do Imperador," *Rev. do Inst. Hist. e Geog. Bras.*, vol. 152, p. 189; Garcia, "Viagens de D. Pedro II," *Rev. do Inst. Hist. e Geog. Bras.*, vol. 152, p. 125; Motta Maia, *op. cit.*, pp. 85-92, 102, 207-10.

[49] Rangel, *Gastão de Orléans, o ultimo Conde d'Eu*, pp. 364-65; *Rio News*, Sept. 15, Oct. 15, 1887; Motta Maia, *op. cit.*, pp. 92-97.

[50] Fonseca, "Molestia do Imperador," *Rev. do Inst. Hist. e Geog. Bras.*, vol. 152, pp. 189-90; Mossé, *op. cit.*, pp. 400-5; Fleiuss, *Paginas de historia*, p. 398.

While Dom Pedro was in Europe trying to regain his health, in Brazil came new developments connected with slavery. After the second abolition law was passed in September, 1885, various projects for accelerating abolition were introduced into Parliament, but Cotegipe's ministry opposed them, and for two years no headway was made towards new legislation. After the parliamentary session for 1887 had closed without setting the date for total emancipation, a number of the anti-slavery deputies were indignant over the situation, and one of them, Antonio da Silva Prado, a member of the cabinet, returned to his home in São Paulo and headed an abolitionist campaign there. Since he and his family had already freed their numerous slaves, his words had weight, and his friends began to liberate their bondmen. Emancipation in mass followed in parts of the province. Some newspapers now excluded slave advertisements, and some lawyers refused cases that supported slavery. Agitation against the evil soon showed a momentum beyond the fondest hopes of most of the anti-slavery element. Increasing numbers of blacks fled from their masters and hid in the forests or received protection from the abolitionists. The agitation spread to the province of Rio de Janeiro, where, in some sections, large-scale desertions took place. Demands for immediate emancipation grew, regardless of the demoralization to agriculture which was certain to result in spite of the marked growth in immigration. But troops from the regular army were being called out to help the local authorities capture the fugitive slaves.[51]

Abolition sentiment had also been growing at São Christovão Palace, where Dona Isabel was living during the absence of her father; and from it a measure of propaganda was being spread through a small paper, the *Correio Imperial*, published by the Princess's three sons with their mother's aid. In it were numerous anti-slavery articles, mostly written by Franklin Doria,

[51] Affonso Celso, *Oito annos de parlamento*, pp. 130-31; Mossé, *op. cit.*, pp. 227-30; *Rio News*, Oct. 5 and 24, 1887.

whom the Regent made Barão de Loreto, and by their tutor, Barão de Ramiz Galvão.[52]

The Princess, having read and thought much about the subject of slavery, had decided that the government must keep pace with public sentiment. It is probable that her husband and her confessor and, especially, a recent utterance of Pope Leo XIII against slavery, reported in *O Paiz*, helped strengthen her stand. She, therefore, conferred with Cotegipe over the matter, and finally became convinced that further legislative progress towards total emancipation would be impossible with him as president of the cabinet. Yet she thought it wrong as well as dangerous to hold out longer against public demands for action. The deadlock ended in March, 1888, when the Prime Minister, owing to differences with the Princess on this and some other matters, resigned. Dona Isabel then asked João Alfredo Corrêa de Oliveira, a Conservative from Pernambuco, to form a new government. João Alfredo, like Antonio da Silva Prado, had been campaigning for abolition in his home province.[53]

By now, the slavery question was clamorous for attention. In various sections voluntary emancipation was making rapid headway; a portion of the press was demanding total liberation by governmental action; and the army was showing unwillingness to go in pursuit of runaway slaves. When, late in 1887, regular troops began to be employed thus, the *Club Militar*, made up of army officers stationed at Rio de Janeiro, had drawn up a petition to the Princess Regent asking that troops be not used for this purpose, which they considered ignominious. But the Cotegipe government had forbidden presentation of the communication.[54]

[52] *Correio Imperial*, 1887-1888. A file of the paper exists in the library of the Instituto Historico e Geographico Brasileiro in Rio de Janeiro.
[53] Autobiographie de la Comtesse d'Eu, Pedro d'Orléans Bragança Archives, A, CCIV, 9264; Nabuco, *A vida de Joaquim Nabuco*, pp. 216-20; *Rio News*, Aug. 5, 1888.
[54] Monteiro, *Pesquisas e depoimentos para a historia*, pp. 170-71; Ottoni, *O advento da republica no Brasil*, p. 61; Oliveira Vianna, in *Contribuições para a Biographia de D. Pedro II*, Pt. I, pp. 811-12.

The ministry of João Alfredo, supported by the Princess Regent, favored immediate and total emancipation. Parliament had also become strongly abolitionist.

In the face of this situation, the pro-slavery element, made up chiefly of the more conservative planters, was disconcerted and demoralized. By one means or another, more than a million slaves had become free since 1871. About six hundred thousand remained in bondage,[55] but the prospects of keeping them there were far from bright when Parliament met in 1888.

The people of the capital well understood the significance of João Alfredo's appointment to head the government, and when Parliament met on May 3 the streets leading to the senate building were filled with expectant, enthusiastic crowds. "The Princess Regent," says the *Rio News*,[56] "was received with the wildest applause, and her carriage was literally covered with flowers." In her speech from the throne she said regarding abolition,

> The extinction of the servile element, through the influence of national sentiment and of private liberality, in honor to Brazil, has peacefully advanced so that it is today the proclaimed hope of all classes, with admirable examples of self sacrifice on the part of owners. When private interest itself comes spontaneously to assist in relieving Brazil of the unhappy inheritance which agricultural needs have maintained, I trust that you will not hesitate to remove from the national law the only exception in it to the Christian and liberal spirit of our institutions.[57]

On the same day Joaquim Nabuco, in a speech placing the issue above party lines, urged immediate emancipation. On May 8, Rodrigo da Silva, acting for the government, took the next step. The atmosphere was charged with emotion and the hand holding the paper trembled as he read the following resolution: "I. From the date of this law slavery in Brazil is declared extinct. II. All dispositions to the contrary are re-

---

[55] Mossé, *op. cit.*, pp. 233-34.　　[56] May 5, 1888.
[57] *Rio News*, May 5, 1888; *Fallas do throno*, pp. 859-60.

voked."[58] There was no provision for compensating slave-owners. A few years before, proposals to indemnify them would doubtless have been considered seriously, but now the moral indignation over the institution was so great that it would not permit delay for financial matters. A committee appointed to pass upon the Rodrigo resolution quickly reported in its favor. The debate was brief, and the project passed the house of deputies on May 9, 1888, by an overwhelming majority.[59]

When the vote had been taken, the crowds in the galleries, hysterical with joy, shouted vivas and rained flowers down upon the legislators. Throngs even invaded the floor of the chamber, making it difficult for the president to keep order. In the senate, Cotegipe, in opposition, warned that abolition would overthrow the monarchy, but the upper house, at a special meeting on Sunday, May 13, quickly disposed of the resolution by voting its adoption with forty-three members in favor and only six against it. Here, also, the action was hailed by shouts from the crowds and showers of blossoms. On the same day the Princess Regent signed the measure, in the City Palace, surrounded by thousands of people who crowded in. When she had finished, there was an explosion of vivas and bravos. Many wept for joy.[60]

As a whole, the press of the country showed emphatic approval, as did also the people. From all parts of the Empire came word of rejoicings and of festas to celebrate the removal of the hated blot from the national escutcheon.[61]

While the country was rejoicing over total abolition, the Emperor was dangerously ill in Milan. It was a new attack, however, for the quiet winter in Cannes had so improved his

---

[58] *Collecção das leis do Imperio do Brazil, 1888*, tomo 35, Vol. I, Pt. I, p. 1; Monteiro, *Pesquisas e depoimentos para a historia*, p. 191.

[59] *Annaes do Parlamento brasileiro: Camara dos Srs. Deputados*, 1888, I, 43-61.

[60] Mossé, *op. cit.*, pp. 235-44; Affonso Celso, *Oito annos do parlamento*, p. 142; Serrano, *op. cit.*, pp. 428-29.

[61] *Jornal do Commercio*, May 14, 15, 1888; *A Provincia de São Paulo*, May 15, 1888; *Diario de Noticias*, May 14, 1888; *Rio News*, May 5, 1888.

health that he wished to visit the Orient and Egypt. His physicians opposed this idea, but permitted him to leave early in April for a visit to Italy. On the 29th, he and his party reached Milan, after a tour of various Italian cities. From Milan, on the afternoon of May 2, Dom Pedro went for a sail on Lake Como, where he became chilled. When he returned that evening he felt bad, and soon pleurisy developed. Dr. Semmola, director of the school of medicine in Naples, was called at once, but the Emperor grew worse, and on the 6th Dona Thereza asked that special prayers for him be said in one of the churches. On the 11th his condition was so serious that medical experts were summoned from Paris and Padua. Late in the following afternoon, however, a cablegram to Princess Isabel reported that he was better and out of danger.[62] A message with the names of four physicians attached, sent to her on the day she signed the emancipation bill, stated that the fever was almost gone and that a nervous condition which had afflicted the patient was also abated.[63] But Dom Pedro did not make good progress, and a turn for the worse on May 22 seemed to bring a fatal end very near. From Paris, word of his critical condition was spread throughout the world, and in the churches of Italy, Portugal, and Brazil prayers were offered for his recovery. His physicians, with but little hope, had him inhale oxygen and gave him injections of ether and caffein. The archbishop of Milan heard his confession and administered the sacrament and extreme unction. He was very weak and his voice was almost gone.[64]

Dona Thereza now decided that she must tell him the great news from home, which had arrived some days before. When he heard it, his face again became animated and he asked faintly,

"Are there, then, no more slaves in Brazil?"

[62] Motta Maia, *op. cit.*, pp. 111-22, 216, 224; *Jornal do Commercio*, May 13, 1888.
[63] *Jornal do Commercio*, May 14, 1888.
[64] Fleiuss, *Paginas de historia*, p. 394; Fonseca, "Molestia do Imperador," *Rev. do Inst. Hist. e Geog. Bras.*, vol. 152, pp. 191-92; Mossé, *op. cit.*, pp. 258-59; Motta Maia, *op. cit.*, pp. 122-24, 225-26.

"No more," replied the Empress; "the law was passed May 13; slavery is abolished."

"Thank God!" said Dom Pedro. "Telegraph immediately to Isabel and give her my blessing, and my deep gratitude and congratulations to the nation and the chambers."[65] The message, signed "Pedro and Thereza," was sent at once.[66]

After the Emperor had uttered it he lay still, and those around his bed thought the end was at hand. But soon he murmured, "Oh! What great people! What great people!" ... And he wept.[67]

From then, he grew better, though slowly. When he was well enough to be moved he was taken to Aix-les-Bains for convalescence, and after about two months his health was perhaps as good as it ever was again. The word that slavery was ended in Brazil had probably helped snatch him from death's door. That event, he told Dr. Semmola, was the greatest happiness of his life.[68]

On August 5, 1888, he and the Empress embarked at Bordeaux on the French steamer "Congo" for Rio, which they reached on the 22nd, and were received with unusual demonstrations of loyalty and affection.

According to one contemporary writer, when the members of the government went aboard the vessel to welcome the royal pair, the Minister of Empire, in the name of the group, greeted the Emperor on his happy return to a land free from slavery, and Dom Pedro replied, "Yes, yes, but if I had been here, what was done would not have been done."[69] Since the Emperor was inclined to be blunt in speech, he may have said this as the result of a passing feeling, for he doubtless regretted that eman-

---

[65] Mossé, *op. cit.*, p. 259.

[66] Telegram from Milan, May 22, 1888, Pedro d'Orléans Bragança Archives, A, CCVI, 9316.

[67] Mossé, *op. cit.*, pp. 258-60.

[68] Fonseca, "Molestia do Imperador," *Rev. do Inst. Hist. e Geog. Bras.*, vol. 152, p. 192; Motta Maia, *op. cit.*, pp. 125-42, 227-31.

[69] Suetonio, *O antigo regimen*, pp. 156-57.

cipation had not been made easier for the slaveowners. And if he had been in control in May, 1888, he would probably have striven hard to secure some compensation for them. But he would have soon given way to the pressure of public opinion, as had his daughter; for, in spite of his regard for the rights of the planters, he had yielded on the question in 1885, when national sentiment was far less insistent than it was three years later.

He was back in time to close the session of Parliament which had voted away human bondage. When reading the address from the throne, which had been prepared before his arrival, he turned from the manuscript and interjected a reference to the law of May 13, saying that it had consoled him in his homesickness for the patria and had helped lessen his physical sufferings.[70]

Dom Pedro was, after all, chiefly responsible for the ending of slavery in Brazil, for he had done much to educate public sentiment against the system, and he had taken the initiative resulting in the first two emancipation laws. These had given such momentum to the anti-slavery movement that when Parliament met in May, 1888, total abolition was almost inevitable. While he did not wholly approve of the way it was done, the wiping out of servile bondage, for which he had longed nearly fifty years, gave the Emperor much satisfaction and happiness. This feeling he expressed in a sonnet, called "13 de Maio," written in celebration of the first anniversary of the event. In the final stanza he offered hosannas to the Creator for the fact that at last his efforts were ended and that he was ruler of a people who were free.[71]

[70] Monteiro, *Pesquisas e depoimentos para a historia*, p. 198.
[71] The verses are published in Teixeira, *op. cit.*, p. 96.

XV

INCREASING DISCONTENT TOWARDS THE MONARCHY

THOUGH the nation as a whole was proud and happy over the emancipation law of May 13, 1888, many of the slaveowners were resentful. They received no compensation for their losses and were faced by shortage of labor. The lack was especially serious in the tropical north, which was avoided by European immigrants, who by the late 1880's were pouring into the southern provinces in fairly adequate numbers. In general, total abolition was a hard blow to the Brazilian planters, many of whom were ruined financially. The worst victims were those who had failed to see that slavery was doomed and to plan accordingly. They now demanded indemnification, blamed the monarchy for their plight, and began to work for its overthrow. This is what Cotegipe, in opposing immediate emancipation, had predicted would happen.[1]

The stand of the Emperor in the quarrel with the bishops over Free Masonry had roused the hostility of the clergy as a whole. Now, another important conservative element in the population, which might have given strong support to the throne, had been estranged.

There were likewise many individuals who were disappointed because various old evils, such as judicial tyranny, corrupt elections, and crimes against persons and property, continued to flourish in the land. And for these they blamed the monarchy, though the trouble, as the last half century of Brazilian history has fully proved, was caused by weaknesses within the nation itself.

[1] *Rio News*, June 5, 15, 1888; Oliveira Lima, *Formation historique de la nationalité brésilienne*, 246; Serrano, *op. cit.*, pp. 451-52. See p. 284 of this book.

In fact, the crown was made the scapegoat for all sorts of national sins and shortcomings. This was largely because it was an exotic, unique in the western hemisphere, where all other governments were nominally republics. Such shibboleths as "liberty" and "democracy" counted for more in the dictator-ridden Spanish-American states than did the enlightened rule of Dom Pedro in Brazil, for the whole American psychology was against monarchical rule, and the competition of the eighteen republics of the western hemisphere was hard for the Empire to withstand.

Even before the Church and abolition questions had arisen many Brazilians recognized that the future of the Bragança throne was uncertain. As early as 1863 James Watson Webb, the American minister at Rio, wrote to Secretary of State Seward as follows:

> The Emperor of Brazil is personally popular; not so the Empire; and it is admitted by the nearest to the throne, that although in the event of his death now his daughter *might* succeed him, it is too probable that if he should live to be fifty, he will be the last Emperor, and Brazil will become a Republic—and this, too, without a struggle. Such is the advance of liberal, and even Democratic principles, that the best people in Brazil calmly look forward to the day, when, by a slight change in their Constitution, the Empire will noiselessly glide into a Republic.[2]

Though Webb, who was not distinguished for clarity of thought or sound judgment, had perhaps secured his impression from talks with a few disgruntled individuals, his report is, nevertheless, of significance. During the next twenty-five years various undermining influences besides those mentioned had begun to work against the continuance of monarchy in Brazil.

One of these was the Princess Imperial herself. Dona Isabel was personally charming, intelligent, conscientious, and able, and, among a considerable fraction of the population, was decidedly popular. Some Brazilians, however, lacked enthusiasm

[2] Webb to Seward, no. 55, Nov. 7, 1863, Dept. of State, Despatches, Brazil.

for her because she failed to show the broad tolerance and understanding kindness which they especially admired in her father. Others were definitely hostile. The slaveowners blamed her, as Regent, for uncompensated emancipation; and religious liberals who sided with the crown in the quarrel with the bishops were distrustfully aware that she was less broad-minded in Church matters than was Dom Pedro, and that she had shown considerable sympathy for the bishops. Moreover, during the Emperor's absence in 1887-1888 she had further aggravated the religious liberals by opposing a bill permitting Protestants to have steeples and bells on their meeting houses.[3]

The very fact that Dom Pedro had to look to a daughter, instead of to a son, as his successor was, in itself, unfortunate, for the Brazilians distrusted the Princess Imperial's husband. Though the Comte d'Eu was devoted to his adopted country and had gained popularity through his part in the Paraguayan War, he was not long in favor. As time passed he became disliked and feared by many Brazilians. He realized from the first that his position was delicate, but he apparently lacked tact and foresight, and he failed to grasp—or ignored—Brazilian political psychology. He seems not to have tried to gain the affection of the rank and file of the people. Quiet and home-loving, he avoided the festas and parades and other characteristic pastimes of the Brazilians, and they soon became aware of it. This seeming aloofness, aggravated by early deafness, led to a popular suspicion that he was proud. And by refusing to join the Masonic order, to which many prominent men belonged, he threw away an opportunity to win for himself support and friendship in influential circles. A limited income and heavy expenses, especially for medical services for the Princess, forced him to strict economy. This, and the fact that he showed little of the warm-hearted generosity in financial matters found in the

---

[3] Autobiographie de la Comtesse d'Eu, Pedro d'Orléans Bragança Archives, A, CIV, 9264; P. A. Martin, "Causes of the Collapse of the Brazilian Empire," *Hisp. Amer. Hist. Rev.* IV (Feb., 1921), 23, note 41.

Emperor and Empress, led to the circulation of stories, probably false, intended to prove him avaricious. Actually, in view of his limited income, he seems to have been rather liberal with his money.[4]

Of far more concern to the Brazilians than the Comte's alleged personal qualities was their belief that he meddled in the government, and that he influenced his wife in political matters. This was true to some extent, and, furthermore, it was expected by some before the two were married that he would, in an unofficial way, help her to rule the Empire. Princess Francisca assumed this[5] when she corresponded with the Emperor regarding husbands for his two daughters. Apparently Dom Pedro took a similar attitude, though he had supervised Princess Isabel's education for the throne and had personally instructed her in government, and though she possessed superior ability and character. The dominant idea was, seemingly, that, being a woman she, like Victoria of England, would need in her governmental duties husbandly help behind the scenes. Presumably the imperial leaders forgot the spinster Queen Elizabeth, who managed very well without. In any case, when, in 1870, the Princess Imperial was made an honorary member of the council of state the Comte was given the same position,[6] and there seemingly was no objection on the part of any of the other councillors to the arrangement. It is true that Prince Gaston was not invited to the sessions when serious matters of policy were up for discussion,[7] but at other times he did attend and expressed his opinion like the others,[8] though his deafness was a handicap in his attempts to follow the discussion.[9] Repeatedly he offered his views to the Emperor on

---

[4] Camara Cascudo, *op. cit.*, pp. 60, 110-28; Oliveira Vianna, *O occaso do Imperio*, p. 190; Francisco T. Barroso, "O Conde d'Eu," *Jornal do Commercio*, Oct. 6, 1935.
[5] Rangel, *Gastão de Orléans, o ultimo Conde d'Eu*, pp. 53-54.
[6] *Camara dos deputados, organisações e ministeriaes*, p. 428.
[7] Rangel, *Gastão de Orléans, o ultimo Conde d'Eu*, pp. 312, 319, 336.
[8] Consultas do Conselho de Estado, Imperial Archives, Rio de Janeiro.
[9] Rangel, *Gastão de Orléans, o ultimo Conde d'Eu*, p. 309.

governmental matters, especially with reference to the army, and he and Dona Isabel seem to have discussed Brazilian politics together.[10]

He probably occupied no more important place in the government than most princes in his position; his influence upon the Emperor and the Princess Imperial was certainly slight; and it was always exercised with the good of the nation in mind. But those who disliked him exaggerated the part he played in governmental affairs and tended to blame him for unpopular policies.[11]

The suspicion and criticism of him were largely stimulated by his foreign birth and connections. If he had been a Brazilian national, many of his faults, alleged or actual, would have been overlooked.

The Empress, it is true, had shown that alien birth need not be a permanent handicap. By her friendliness and generosity she had won and retained the people's affections, and by her scrupulous avoidance of politics she prevented development of even the slightest distrust towards her.

In the Comte, however, the combination of personal unpopularity, alien birth, and what seemed like meddling in the government was most unfortunate. Moreover, his heritage of French provincialism would have made such a conquest as Dona Thereza had won difficult for him, even if he had seen the importance of gaining it—and, if in order to do so, he had been willing to play a rôle as wholly private as did the Empress.

The political adventures of the Comte's family, especially of Louis Philippe, who had ascended the throne of France following the overthrow of the Bourbon line in 1830, likewise influenced the hostile Brazilians, who made capital of it. Even in the early years after Dona Isabel's marriage, members of the opposition feared, or pretended to fear, French meddling in

[10] *Ibid.*, pp. 113 ff., *passim;* Pedro d'Orléans Bragança Archives, A, *passim.*
[11] Pedro d'Orléans Bragança Archives, A, CLXXII, 7826; Mattoso, *op. cit.*, pp. 159-60.

Brazil. They expressed resentment over the visits which she and the Comte made to Europe, and some even criticized her sharply because she was attended in childbirth by the surgeon from whom she had received treatments in Paris which made it possible for her to become a mother.[12] As time passed, because of the Comte's supposed influence upon the government, and especially upon the Princess Imperial, enemies referred to him in the press as the "third sovereign," or the "French sovereign,"[13] the implication being that this foreigner of the house of Orléans would succeed Dom Pedro as ruler of Brazil. Such false and malicious propaganda was used persistently, and when, in 1888, Dom Pedro was believed to be dying in Milan a circular, signed "Desmoulins," was issued, warning the nation of the danger before it.[14]

More influential than the Comte's unpopularity in undermining the throne was the growth of republicanism, which became more rapid after the fall of the Zacharias cabinet in July, 1868; for many who had hoped that liberty and democracy might be combined with monarchy were now disappointed with what was regarded as the Emperor's dictatorial action. The movement was also aided by interest in the philosophy of Auguste Comte, which began to develop in Brazil at about this time.[15] Soon republican clubs were formed, and in December, 1870, appeared a party newspaper, *A Republica*, which presented in its first issue a *Manifesto Republicano*. The new organizations agitated for reforms, especially at their congresses or conventions. One of these, held in 1875 in São Paulo, where the republican movement was especially strong, issued a proclamation denouncing the *Syllabus* of Pope Pius IX and calling for separation of Church and State, civil marriage, and civil

---

[12] Propaganda circular, Jan. 23, 24, 1868, Pedro d'Orléans Bragança Archives, A; Dom Pedro II to Conde d'Eu, Arez de Maio, *ibid.*, CLXXXV, 8359; Rangel, *Gastão de Orléans, o ultimo Conde d'Eu*, pp. 314-15, 319.

[13] Camara Cascudo, *op. cit.*, pp. 59-60.

[14] Desmoulins, *Pedro II e Isabel I*.

[15] Oliveira Vianna, *O occaso do Imperio*, p. 97; dos Santos, *op. cit.*, pp. 212-14.

registration of births and deaths. That these early Brazilian republicans got their inspiration from the United States of America is apparent from the pseudonyms attached to some of their press articles—Hamilton, Madison, Jefferson, and Theodore Parker. In 1876, the party nominated a candidate for Parliament who won many votes, but fell short of election.[16] The republicans gained their first seats in the lower house in 1884, when one was elected from Minas and two were from São Paulo.[17]

Though the party as a whole was not favorable to abolition,[18] the emancipation laws of 1885 and 1888 greatly accelerated their movement, through bringing recruits from the monarchists. By November, 1889, the republican clubs in the Empire numbered two hundred and thirty-seven, but they were usually small groups, mostly found in the south. There were fifty-six in Minas, forty-eight in São Paulo, thirty-two in Rio Grande do Sul, thirty in Rio de Janeiro, and a thin scattering elsewhere. At the same date the Empire was reported to have seventy-four republican newspapers, most of them being likewise in the south, but the majority of such papers were short-lived, and probably many were counted after they were defunct.[19]

Dom Pedro himself was partly responsible for the growth of the sentiment against the crown. Apparently since early manhood he had believed that a republic was the ideal form of government, and this view was strengthened by his visit to the United States, during which he remarked, "Were I not a monarch, I should be a republican."[20] Eleven years later he said of Brazil in one of his marginal notes, "for me it would be

---

[16] Castro, in Fleiuss, *Contribuições para a Biographia de D. Pedro II*, Pt. I, pp. 561-70; dos Santos, *op. cit.*, pp. 206-10.
[17] Pereira da Silva, *op. cit.*, II, 283-84.   [18] dos Santos, *op. cit.*, pp. 208-9.
[19] Castro, in *Contribuições para a Biographia de D. Pedro II*, Pt. I, p. 570; Oliveira Vianna, in *ibid.*, p. 831; Oliveira Vianna, *O occaso do Imperio*, pp. 114-15; Ottoni, *D. Pedro de Alcantara*, p. 52.
[20] Moniz, *A côrte de D. Pedro II*, p. 167.

better if it were a republic, if I could be president."[21] He well knew that some presidents had more real authority than he, and he also knew that, with more power to make things go, he could achieve much more for his country. But since his people were largely illiterate and were inexperienced in the real principles of democracy, he considered monarchy under the existing constitution, with its moderating power—which served as an emergency brake—best for them. The political careers of the so-called republics of Spanish America had made him believe that without preparation for self-government, Brazil would, if the monarchy were set aside, soon be dominated by unscrupulous military dictators. He was anxious for his country to qualify through education for truly popular rule, regardless of how such government might be classified politically.

Meanwhile, he benevolently permitted the anti-monarchist propaganda to follow its course. After the early 1870's, republicanism was openly indorsed in the schools, but Dom Pedro was undisturbed by that fact. He heard such principles advocated by the teacher of a class that he visited in São Paulo, and he merely remarked on departing that if Brazil became a republic he wished to be its first president. He even chose an ardent republican as teacher of mathematics for the two elder sons of Dona Leopoldina. This was Benjamin Constant Botelho de Magalhães, a member of the faculty of the military academy in Rio de Janeiro and one of the leaders in the spread of positivist philosophy in the Empire. When the instructor was first asked to tutor the princes he refused, on the ground that he did not want pupils to whom he must show deference. The Emperor assured him that he could treat the two boys like any other students, but Benjamin Constant raised another obstacle—his republican views. These, Dom Pedro replied, had nothing to do with mathematics. Benjamin Constant declared, however, that circumstances might arise making him feel obliged to point

---

[21] "Como o Imperador rebatia os seus criticas," *A Noite*, June 23, 1925.

out to the princes the superiority of republicanism. "That won't hurt," said the Emperor; "you might be able to convert them." The instructor yielded and accepted the task.[22]

Though Dom Pedro's intelligence favored republicanism and popular rule, his feelings at times inclined to dictatorship, owing perhaps to the tradition established in his family by a thousand years of rule in Europe. Occasionally these two bents conflicted, as was shown by a conversation he had with Victor Hugo. During it, he used the expression "my rights," but he quickly took it back by adding, "I have no rights; I have nothing but a power resulting from chance; it is my duty to use it for good, for progress, for liberty."[23] Thus, the democrat in him dominated the dictator.

Furthermore, believing as he did in liberty, he defended the right of the republicans to a place in the life of Brazil. Repeatedly, he showed friendliness towards people connected with the republican press. When the office of one of the papers was wrecked by a mob, he was among those who condemned the act, though many believed that the hostility of the ministry to the publication was basically responsible for what had happened.[24] In 1870's, when the wife of the editor of *A Republica* died, Dom Pedro, knowing that the propagandist lacked money enough for a proper funeral, sent him anonymously two contos of reis for the purpose.[25] While the poet Mucio Teixeira was enjoying the friendship and financial aid of the Emperor he was also a contributor to the republican paper *O Paiz* and was a close associate of other republican leaders; and Dom Pedro was well aware of this relationship with the enemies of the crown.[26]

The Emperor was, furthermore, opposed to banning the

---

[22] Tobias Monteiro, "A tolerancia do Imperador," *Rev. do Inst. Hist. e Geog. Bras.*, vol. 152, p. 155; dos Santos, *op. cit.*, pp. 212-13.
[23] Affonso Celso, in *Jornal do Commercio*, July 26, 1925.
[24] Pereira da Silva, *op. cit.*, II, 163-64.   [25] Teixeira, *op. cit.*, p. 155.
[26] *Ibid.*, pp. 35, 110-11, 125-30, 133-37, 243-44.

republicans politically; he insisted upon treating them as he did other political groups. Shortly after the party made its appearance, Pimenta Bueno, Visconde de São Vicente, then head of the cabinet, told the Emperor that the invariable rule must be adopted of never having any republicans in office.

"Senhor São Vicente," said Dom Pedro, "let the country govern itself as it thinks best and consider right whoever may be right."

The Minister replied that the Emperor was not justified in holding such a view; that the monarchy was a dogma of the constitution which he had sworn to maintain; that it was not incarnated in his person.

But the incorrigible Dom Pedro retorted laughingly, "Well, São Vicente, if the Brazilians do not want me for their Emperor, I will go and be a professor."[27] And thereafter he urged the appointment of republicans to office whenever he thought one the best qualified for a given place. Even as late as April, 1889, he wrote to João Alfredo, then president of the cabinet, a sharp note calling attention to an able republican who, he thought, had been ignored in considering men for a certain position.[28]

After the first deputies were elected by the party in 1884, attacks on the monarchy and predictions of its downfall began to be heard in Parliament. On September 6, 1888, about two weeks before the return of Dom Pedro from Europe, following his serious illness, Joaquim Nabuco declared in the lower house that the monarchy was "in a phase of complete tolerance,"[29] apparently meaning by this that the nation felt no real preference for it. In November, the Comte d'Eu, writing to his father, remarked upon the inertia of the government while republican manifestations were multiplying on all sides. When, in the latest session of Parliament, a republican deputy from Minas had refused to take the oath of allegiance, said the

[27] Nabuco, *Um estadista do Imperio*, III, 191-92.
[28] Letter of Dom Pedro II to João Alfredo, printed in *Selecta*, April 12, 1919.
[29] Oliveira Vianna, *O occaso do Imperio*, p. 65.

Comte, the chamber had at once dispensed with the requirement.[30]

Most of the republican leaders were not, however, planning any move against the Emperor. They had tacitly agreed, as Oliviera Vianna put it, to wait with patience, mixed with affection and veneration, the liquidation of Dom Pedro's career by death before changing the form of government.[31]

Accompanying the elections in São Paulo early in 1889 there were noisy demonstrations by the republicans, with the singing of "The Marseillaise," but the candidate of the party was defeated at the polls.[32] At about the same time there was much activity in the province in behalf of decentralizing the imperial government. On March 4, 1889, Dom Pedro, referring to events in São Paulo, pointed out in remarks made to André Rebouças, the abolitionist, the weakness of the republican position: "I am a republican," he said, "everybody knows that. If I were an egoist, I would proclaim a republic in Brazil to obtain the glories of Washington. But I would only sacrifice the country to my vanity, for, of course, the small provinces have not the necessary leaders. There would be general misgovernment, which would end by separation."[33]

Even though the Emperor realized that the country was not prepared for republican rule, he did practically nothing to combat the movement against the throne, and for this he was openly criticized by loyal subjects.[34] Perhaps partly because of the criticism, the government decided to have the Comte d'Eu make tours through the provinces with the aim of promoting loyalty to the crown. The arrangement suggests that the ministry quite underestimated the extent of the Prince's unpopularity. Why Dona Isabel, accompanied by only her suite, did not go instead of her husband is not clear, though the conservative

[30] Rangel, *Gastão de Orléans, o ultimo Conde d'Eu*, p. 373.
[31] *Contribuições para a Biographia de D. Pedro II*, Pt. I, p. 875.
[32] Rangel, *Gastão de Orléans, o ultimo Conde d'Eu*, p. 374.
[33] Rebouças, *op. cit.*, sec. 7.   [34] *Rio News*, June 10, 1889.

attitude towards woman's position was perhaps the reason. The Comte went first to São Paulo, a hotbed of republicanism, where he visited Santos and Campinas. Here, the federalist Ruy Barbosa attacked him in his *Diario de Noticias*, as an invader, pretended that the visitor was quite indifferent to the sufferings of the Paulistas from yellow fever, then raging, and declared, "We need not be slaves to the third sovereign!" This was followed by an even more insulting pamphlet and handbill issued by others. The handbill, addressed to the "Fluminenses," as the inhabitants of Rio de Janeiro were called, and signed "Paulistas," referred to the Comte d'Eu as "an individual hated by all good patriots," who had proved himself a despot even in Santos by giving telegraphic orders to the Minister of Empire. The old Emperor, it stated, was about to die; the Fluminenses must be prepared for the imminent struggle. This was practically a call to revolution.[35]

Shortly after his return from São Paulo the Comte left, on June 12, in the packet "Alagôas" for the north. In the same vessel went Antonio da Silva Jardim, a republican propagandist, with the aim of nullifying any influence the Prince might exert in favor of the monarchy. Some feared that, in consequence, clashes and bloodshed would take place between republicans and monarchists at the points where the boat stopped; and there was trouble, but nothing very serious. The Comte visited several provinces, going as far as Amazonas, and was, on the whole, well received, though in some places he was greeted by republican hymns and other signs of hostility. At Belem, Pará, as spokesman for the government, he delivered an address which showed recognition of the fact that the fate of the Empire was at stake. "The Brazilian monarchy has no selfish interests or special ambition," he told his audience. "If it becomes convinced that the Brazilian nation wishes to dispense with its serv-

[35] Rangel, *Gastão de Orléans, o ultimo Conde d'Eu*, pp. 374-77. One of the handbills is preserved at the Château d'Eu, in the Pedro d'Orléans Bragança Archives, Div. A.

ices, it will be the first to avoid putting obstacles in the way of the national will and the first to help in the transformation which is the most desirable for the interest of the country." But he asked for fair play for the monarchy and a careful consideration of what it had meant to the country during two generations.[36] In the middle of September the Prince returned to Rio, apparently somewhat encouraged by his trip to the north.[37]

During his absence things had not been going well in the capital. Though Dom Pedro was by no means at death's door, some of the ills that beset him in 1887 were incurable, and he was in decidedly bad health. His friend the Visconde de Taunay,[38] a member of the senate, remarked in his diary that at the opening of Parliament on May 1, 1889, the Emperor was feeble, walked with unsteady step, and did not read well the address from the throne.[39] His poor health gave a handle to the enemies of the monarchy, and on May 17 a resolution was introduced in the chamber of deputies calling for a committee to investigate whether the Emperor was competent to rule. The next day Ruy Barbosa's *Diario de Noticias* published a long editorial favoring such investigation. The old charge that Dom Pedro neglected his duties of state for his books was repeated, but with the implication that his mental powers were failing, making him weak-willed and vacillating. The authority formerly exercised by him, it was said, was now in the hands of others.[40] The Conde de Motta Maia was especially mentioned in this connection. A cartoon in *Revista Illustrada* for June 1, 1889, represented the physician with the imperial crown on his head and in his hand the "fateful pencil" used to symbolize the Emperor's personal power.

---

[36] Rangel, *Gastão de Orléans, o ultimo Conde d'Eu*, pp. 376-84; *Rio News*, June 17, 1889; Silva Jardim, *Memorias e viagens*.

[37] Rangel, *Gastão de Orléans, o ultimo Conde d'Eu*, p. 384.

[38] Alfredo de Escragnolle Taunay, son of Dom Pedro's teacher of art, Felix Emilio Taunay.   [39] Escragnolle Taunay, *Pedro II*, p. 66.

[40] Barbosa, *Quéda do imperio*, II, 457-503; Oliveira Vianna, in *Contribuições para a Biographia de D. Pedro II*, Pt. I, pp. 878-79; *A Provincia de São Paulo*, Nov. 14, 1889.

It is evident that by 1889 Dom Pedro was, mentally as well as physically, rather old for his sixty-three years, but even with that he was perhaps more alert than were many of his critics. He discussed intelligently with Taunay the message of May 1 from the throne—with which the latter was disappointed because it said nothing about civil marriage and liberty of cults, and he assured the Visconde that it was the best that could be had under the circumstances; but he was rather discouraged over the present ministry.[41]

The most serious handicap connected with the Emperor was the fact that he seemed to be detached from current events, and to lack to some degree awareness of significant political developments. Writing in his diary before Parliament met, Visconde Taunay had mentioned this.[42] But Dom Pedro's remoteness from the present was perhaps caused less by mental deterioration than by the fact that his illness had put him out of touch with things and had, to some extent, kept him so. After his health broke in 1887 his physicians forbade him to read newspapers from the capital dealing with imperial politics, though there was no ban on the provincial or foreign press.[43] Then came his fifteen months of absence in Europe. And after his return he was subjected to a medical regimen which probably withheld from him knowledge of political matters which might have caused him worry. To prevent late evening sessions of the ministry which would rob him of his rest, the hour of meeting was changed to two in the afternoon. But, in general, his week included the same activities as when he was in his prime— walks and rides, reading aloud to his family, visits to the Petropolis railroad station and to public institutions, and audiences for those who wished to see him.[44] Whatever the reason for his failure to do so, it is quite clear that he did not fully grasp the danger to the crown in the recent rapid growth of republican sentiment.

[41] Escragnolle Taunay, *Pedro II*, pp. 66-67.   [42] *Ibid.*, p. 63.
[43] Rangel, *Gastão de Orléans, o ultimo Conde d'Eu*, p. 359.
[44] *Ibid.*, p. 373; Motta Maia, *op. cit.*, p. 172.

The Emperor was probably quite right in his view that the address from the throne was the best that could be obtained, for the ministry of João Alfredo had become so weak that it could not count upon a working majority in the chamber of deputies. Repeatedly during May its president asked for dismissal, but Dom Pedro hesitated to comply because he wished to be certain that such a step was necessary. After consultation with his council of state, on May 31, however, he thought it would be unwise to dissolve the chamber; therefore, he agreed to accept the resignation of the cabinet.[45]

In view of the growth of republicanism and of the demand for federalization of the provinces, the Emperor and his advisers considered it best to try to maintain the Conservatives in power, since they were favorable to a strong central control, which might be needed to keep the country from disintegration. Therefore, Dom Pedro turned first to Saraiva, in whom he had unusual faith, and asked him to form a government. In the discussion taking place between the two, the venerable statesman came out definitely in favor of federation without imperial control, and stated that the presidents of the provinces and the senators should be elected free from any interference from the central authority.[46] According to Coelho Rodrigues, who quoted, on hearsay, part of the conversation which is supposed to have taken place, Saraiva's reason for his policy was that the birth of a republic in Brazil was near at hand, and inevitable, and that it was necessary to prepare for it.[47]

Dom Pedro then asked Saraiva whether, in view of the state of affairs as he saw it, he thought a third reign—that of Isabel—no longer possible. "The kingdom of Her Highness is not of this world," the statesman is said to have replied.[48]

"Well, Senhor Saraiva," said Dom Pedro, "organize the

---

[45] *Rio News*, June 17, 1889.   [46] *Ibid*.
[47] A. Coêlho Rodrigues, *A republica na America do Sul*, p. 8.
[48] *Ibid*. This reply, couched in biblical language, was a tribute to the unselfish generosity of the Princess in standing for total emancipation, even at the risk of her throne (dos Santos, *op. cit.*, p. 181, note 2).

ministry and govern as well as you can; I shall not put obstacles in the way."[49]

But Saraiva, because of his advanced age and uncertain health, felt that he could not undertake the task.[50] The Emperor tried in turn two other Conservatives, neither of whom found himself able to form a ministry that could command a majority in the lower house.[51] Dom Pedro then tried the Liberals. Acting on Saraiva's advice, he asked Affonso Celso de Assis Figueiredo, Visconde de Ouro Preto, to organize a government; and on June 7 Ouro Preto consented to do so.[52]

The new Prime Minister was a leading commercial lawyer and an accomplished politician of considerable experience. He was brilliant, but impetuous, and was considered by some proud and haughty. As Minister of Finance nearly ten years before, he had become unpopular through placing a tax on street-car passengers.[53] Ouro Preto's was no light task, for he faced a discontented nation and a minority which was bitterly hostile to the dynasty.

In the formation of the cabinet considerable effort was made to conciliate the disgruntled. Ruy Barbosa was offered the portfolio of empire, but he refused it.[54] At the suggestion of Dom Pedro, influenced by his advisers who aimed to win more support from the military, a new precedent was set by selecting as heads of the departments of war and the marine men who had had practical experience in the fields of their new authority. Barão de Ladario, an admiral in the Brazilian navy who had been trained on vessels of the United States, was made Minister of Marine, and Visconde de Maracajú, an adjutant general in the imperial army, was given the portfolio of war. Neither of them was in Parliament. The members of the new government, as a whole, had fair ability, but there were no highly distinguished figures among them.[55]

[49] *Ibid.*, p. 9; *Rio News*, June 17, 1889. [50] *Rio News*, June 10, 17, 1889.
[51] *Ibid.*, June 10, 1889. [52] *Ibid.*, June 17, 1889.
[53] *Ibid.*, June 10, 1889. See p. 239 of this book.
[54] *Ibid.* [55] *Ibid.*

In discussing with the Emperor the problems before the new government Ouro Preto told him that he planned to combat republican propaganda by showing that the existing form of government was elastic enough to satisfy every demand of enlightened public opinion; but he believed that there must be sweeping liberal reforms in the political, social, and economic order. In response to the Emperor's wish for a specific outline of the measures which the minister thought necessary, the Visconde gave him the program of the congress of the Liberal party which had recently met in Rio. This called for a large number of reforms, including guarantees of personal liberty; freedom of religious worship; civil marriage; better educational facilities; expansion of rapid transportation; reduction of tariffs; laws to facilitate the acquisition of land; formation of credit establishments to help commerce, industry, and—especially—agriculture; temporality of the senate; reform of the council of state, making it merely administrative; complete local self-government for the municipalities; and increased autonomy for the provinces through permitting them to nominate lists of candidates for their vice-presidents and presidents from which the national government should select the officers.[56] Obviously, this last provision did not give the provinces the complete autonomy and federalization which Saraiva favored, and which many others demanded.

When, on June 11, Ouro Preto presented before the chamber of deputies the list of new cabinet members and the ministerial program, there was an outburst of oratorical resentment. João Manoel de Carvalho, a priest who was a Conservative, indignant over the change to a Liberal ministry, went over to the republicans. His speech, ending with, "Down with the monarchy! Long live the republic!" met with considerable applause.[57] But consternation was apparent in some sections of

[56] *Ibid.*, June 17, 1889; Visconde de Ouro Preto, *Advento da dictatura militar no Brazil*, pp. 213-21.

[57] João Manoel, *Reminiscencias sobre vultos e factos*, p. xiv; *Rio News*, June 17, 1889.

the house, for this was the first time that such outspoken political heresy had been uttered in Parliament.

With eloquent indignation Ouro Preto made reply. *"Viva a republica?"* said he.

No! No! and, again, No! For it is under the monarchy that we have obtained the liberty which other nations envy us, and under which we can maintain it to a degree satisfactory to even the proudest people! *Viva a monarchia!*—the only form of government to which the immense majority of the people are attached, and the only one that can make for its happiness and greatness! Yes; long live the Brazilian monarchy, so democratic, so self-denying, so patriotic that it will be the first to conform itself to the votes of the people and will not place the slightest obstacle in the way if they, through their competent instruments, show a desire for change of institutions.[58]

Ouro Preto's words, which were very like those uttered by the Comte d'Eu under government instructions at Belem some weeks later, brought enthusiastic and prolonged applause. But Antonio de Macedo Costa, bishop of Pará, who was present, remarked that the incident gave an idea of what the French Convention was like.[59]

In the debate that followed Ouro Preto's speech, among specific criticisms of the ministry was the fact that the holders of the portfolios of war and the marine were not members of Parliament. Before the day's session ended, a resolution of want of confidence in the new government's program was introduced, and it was quickly passed by a vote of seventy-nine to twenty.[60]

The ministry, hoping to win the confidence of the country, immediately sent to the presidents of the provinces a circular letter giving the program of reform, explaining that the present chamber was composed largely of enemies of the government, and expressing the hope that the new election would bring in

[58] Ouro Preto, *op. cit.*, p. 222; Affonso Celso, *Oito annos de parlamento*, pp. 66-67.
[59] Affonso Celso, *Oito annos de parlamento*, p. 67.
[60] *Camara dos deputados*, p. 247.

the elements necessary to carry out the program.[61] On June 15, the Emperor dissolved the chamber of deputies and called a meeting for November 20 of the one to be elected.

Two days later the non-partisan *Rio News,* referring to developments, predicted a radical change in the form of government, though how soon could not be easily foreseen. "Were the Brazilian republicans as resolute and courageous as they are declamatory," remarked the editor,

> the republic would be declared before the year closes; but, as they are not, the course of events depends largely upon accident. It is entirely within the bounds of possibility that the apathy and temporizing policy thus far dominant in imperial circles will lose the empire almost without a struggle, and at a moment when least expected, while, on the contrary, a prompt change from this negative policy to one of vigorous repression, attended by a generous grant of political privileges and reforms, would postpone the inevitable change for many years to come.

On July 15 came an incident which seemed a test of the regard in which the Emperor was held. As he and his family were leaving the theatre that night there was a disturbance at the entrance, accompanied by vivas for the republic. A few minutes later, as his carriage was entering the Praça da Constituição, a shot was fired, presumably aimed at him. Immediately there was great commotion. But the bullet had missed its mark, and Dom Pedro, quite calm, smilingly said to the excited people about him, "Be prudent; it is nothing." Investigation disclosed that the attempt on his life had been made by a Portuguese youth, Adriano do Valle, who had been roused by the republican propaganda and was apparently drunk when he fired the shot. The Emperor interceded for him and he escaped serious punishment, but spent some time in the house of correction.[62]

From all parts of the Empire came expressions of indignation over the attempted assassination, and of affection and

---

[61] *Cearense,* June 15, 1889.

[62] *Jornal do Commercio,* July 17, 1889; Monteiro, "A tolerancia do Imperador," *Rev. do Inst. Hist. e Geog. Bras.,* vol. 152, p. 160; Rebouças, *op. cit.,* sec. 22.

loyalty for Dom Pedro. Special services of thanksgiving were held in the churches; crowds swarmed to the palace at Boa Vista to show their happiness at their sovereign's escape; and when his carriage passed in the streets people rained flowers upon it from upper-story windows.[63]

Similar demonstrations took place in Minas when the imperial family visited there about a week later. At the stations where their train stopped they were received by large crowds, bands of music, and showers of blossoms. According to the press, the people showed "delirious" enthusiasm in their welcome.[64] Apparently, the republicans were more noisy than numerous. The demonstrations of popular affection and loyalty helped reassure the Emperor that the throne was secure for himself and his daughter.

The elections for the lower house, which took place on August 31, resulted in a sweeping victory for the Liberals; only one republican deputy secured a seat, and but four or five Conservatives. Doubtless, the attack on Dom Pedro was partly responsible, but the fact that the Ouro Preto ministry had arranged long-term, low-interest loans to help the planters had also caused a favorable reaction among them.[65] The thwarted opposition, however, charged that the government had won through meddling with the elections, expenditure of much money, conferring of honors upon individuals, and similar methods. The new congress was born corrupt, its enemies declared.[66] If such methods were used to an uncommon degree in 1889, it was because the Ouro Preto government realized that the situation was desperate, and that a Parliament which would grant extensive constitutional concessions was necessary to preserve the dynasty and to save the nation from possible anarchy.

---

[63] *Jornal do Commercio*, July 17, 1889.

[64] *Ibid.*, July 23, 24, 26, 1889.

[65] *Rio News*, July 1, Nov. 18, 1889; Adams to Blaine, no. 9, Sept. 9, 1889, Dept. of State, Despatches, Brazil.

[66] Ottoni, *O advento da republica no Brazil*, pp. 103-4; Affonso Celso, *Contradictas monarchicas*, pp. 34-35.

The attitude of the powerful Ruy Barbosa doubtless influenced the Prime Minister. Not only did the radical leader refuse a place in the government, but he reprinted in his paper an article from a less responsible Paulista daily which denounced the program of the ministry for failure to include federation. The caption of the article was "Federation or republic!"[67]

Though Dom Pedro would have gladly had Saraiva, with his policy of complete federalization, head the government in June, he certainly thought that Ouro Preto's compromise plan, reserving some control to the central government, would be better for the country. He realized, however, that the moderating power must soon be given up by the crown. The question was, to whom should it be yielded? Shortly after the lower house was dissolved, he revealed one possibility that he had in mind, to Salvador de Mendonça, who was returning to his post as consul-general in New York, and Lafayette Rodrigues Pereira, who was likewise going to the United States, as special envoy to negotiate a commercial treaty. When the men took leave of him the Emperor instructed them to study carefully the American supreme court, as an institution which might help the Empire, and upon their return he would have a conference with them about it.

"Things are not going well with us," he added, "and it seems to me that it would be better if we could create here a tribunal like the North American one and transfer to it the attributes of the moderating power of our constitution. Give every attention to this point."[68]

As regards the whole problem of the crown and Brazilian welfare, he took the attitude expressed by him two years later, on the margin of Carvalho's *Emperio e republica dictatorial:*

I should have desired, I repeat, that the civilization of Brazil had made possible the immediate admission of the republican system,

---

[67] *Diario de Noticias*, June 7, 1889.
[68] Levi Carneiro, "O Imperador e o federalismo," *Rev. do Inst. Hist. e Geog. Bras.*, vol. 152, p. 383.

which, to me, is the most perfect possible in human affairs. . . . I wanted only to contribute towards a social state in which the republic could be "planted," so to speak, by me, and could bring forth fruit in proper season. Provided that it was a natural product, the rights of my daughter and grandsons would not have deterred me.[69]

This attitude on the part of an hereditary ruler towards his throne had few parallels in recorded history.

[69] Quoted in dos Santos, *op. cit.*, p. 182. The copy of Carvalho containing the note is in the possession of the Instituto Historico e Geographico Brasileiro in Rio de Janeiro.

XVI

THE MENACE OF MILITARISM

WHILE the Ouro Preto ministry was planning to save the monarchy by liberal and sweeping reforms, the factor which became directly responsible for destroying the throne was gaining strength. This was disaffection among the military.

In most of the Spanish American countries at the time, *caudillismo*—political dominance by army chieftains—was the rule. Brazil was, however, spared this affliction through most of the imperial era. Though Dom Pedro I was high-handed and despotic in various regards, this attitude was not inspired by consciousness of military support; and he finally abdicated because even the palace guard deserted him. During the regency, the regular army proved a broken reed because of its insubordination, forcing the government to call upon the militia to restore order. In fact, by the time Dom Pedro II came to the throne the army was held in low esteem because of its tradition of indiscipline.

As a result of the war with Paraguay, however, the problem of indiscipline took on new and complicated aspects; thus helping prepare the way for the "military question," which later harassed the government. One of the causes for this was a quarrel between two of the generals, Osorio and Caxias, with the Liberals championing the one and the Conservatives siding with the other. Thus, militarism entered Brazilian politics. The appointment of the Comte d'Eu to take Caxias's place probably aggravated somewhat the situation, through increasing discontent among the soldiery.[1]

[1] Wanderley Pinho, *op. cit.*, p. 78; Monteiro, *Pesquisas e depoimentos para a historia*, pp. 116-22.

[310]

More important, however, in fostering egotistical disaffection in the army was the fact that for several years a large portion of its members were stationed in the Plata region, the countries of which furnished an excellent school for self-love among the military. Though Rosas had been eliminated from Argentina, to some extent his spirit still lingered; and caudillism was rampant in Uruguay. Francisco Solano López of Paraguay, with his Napoleonic apings, was admired by some of the imperial soldiers. Furthermore, in this atmosphere where the science of killing human beings in mass was exalted, it was natural that the Brazilian forces should acquire a new and exaggerated sense of their own importance. This happened, and soon showed itself among the returned troops, especially among the officers, in swaggering and arrogance. Such self-esteem led the soldiers to think that they had not received enough credit for their services in the war, and, therefore, to decide that the government was hostile to them. This attitude was soon reflected in the faculty and students of the military academy in Rio de Janeiro.[2]

During the latter part of the Paraguayan War the imperial authorities had feared indiscipline in the army.[3] This fact, and the need for the strictest economy because of the heavy war debt, made it desirable, when the conflict ended, to discharge most of the standing forces. The Comte d'Eu realized the situation and, fearing the dissemination of republican propaganda based on ideas gained in the south by the veterans, he advised that the regular army be greatly reduced and that the national guard be prepared to take its place.[4] But the Emperor is said to have opposed the reduction of the army,[5] and this report was probably true, for if the sovereign had really desired to follow this advice he probably could have done so. Though

---

[2] Monteiro, *Pesquisas e depoimentos para a historia*, pp. 117-20.
[3] Wanderley Pinho, *op. cit.*, pp. 172, 192.
[4] Monteiro, *Pesquisas e depoimentos para a historia*, p. 304; Louis de Orléans Bragança, *Sous la Croix-du-Sud*, p. 14.
[5] Monteiro, *Pesquisas e depoimentos para a historia*, p. 304.

Dom Pedro's early training had developed in him distrust of public officials, this did not seem to include army officers; and he apparently saw no danger from them. Moreover, after the trouble with Great Britain, connected with the "Prince of Wales" and the "Forte," it was his policy to keep the army and navy in condition, "in order to be prepared for any eventuality," hoping thus to avoid wars.[6] This was the policy of all rulers of his day who were civilized enough to oppose war. Others, who, like López, had not advanced this far deliberately prepared for conflict, and, like him, they often went down to destruction. Furthermore, Dom Pedro was probably influenced by the customary attitude that the "prestige" gained by victory in war called for a larger military establishment, as an indication of the country's enhanced importance among the nations of the world. In any case, the Brazilian regular army was not cut down to the degree that it might have been.

Therefore, the soldiers did not have enough to keep them busy and, influenced by the politico-military notions which they had brought from the south, they began to mix in governmental matters. This was dangerous, in view of the strength of the military organization, and of its clannishness, which soon became much pronounced in the army. Its members could not separate their party politics from their soldierly code: in their political interests and activities they showed their military psychology with its extreme emphasis upon what they called "honor."[7]

The fact that the Emperor was not especially interested in the army, and did not feature it or cultivate its favor—though he wished the soldiers treated justly—increased the likelihood of difficulty after the Paraguayan War. The army seems to have been, on the whole, poorly organized, in spite of the serv-

---

[6] "A Fé de Officio de D. Pedro II," *Rev. do Inst. Hist. e Geog. Bras.*, vol. 152, p. 764.

[7] Oliveira Vianna, in *Contribuições para a Biographia de D. Pedro II*, Pt. I, p. 845.

ices of the Comte d'Eu towards bettering this. The pay was low—but the pension system was fairly liberal; promotion came slowly, and, unlike the situation in most Spanish American countries at the time—where generals were so numerous as to be a joke—the proportion of officers to enlisted men was small. These facts became grievances in some quarters.[8]

Not until 1883, more than ten years after the war ended, however, did anything develop to show to a serious degree the new temper of the army. Then, a proposal in the senate for changing the plan of reform in the military service and for compulsory contributions from the soldiers for a *monte-pio* (a pension or insurance) created strong resentment. At the military school a directory of resistance against the plan was formed, and the president of the organization, Lieutenant-Colonel Senna Madureira, attacked the project in the *Jornal do Commercio*. The Minister of War, Candido de Oliveira, therefore, ordered that no discussion through the press by members of the army should take place without his permission. But the proposal for the monte-pio was dropped, and this encouraged the military to further opposition.[9] The talk about "honor" increased among army officers, as did insubordination among the privates. According to the Minister of War, the discipline was the "worst possible."[10]

In 1886, the prohibition of the Minister of War was twice violated—by Colonel Cunha Mattos, then in Rio de Janeiro, and by Senna Madureira, who had been given charge of the military school in Rio Grande do Sul. Both officers were censured, and Cunha Mattos was imprisoned for eight hours. In response to the rebuke, Senna Madureira protested violently that he was a victim of injustice, and asked that the matter be considered by a court martial, all of which was contrary to the

---

[8] Serrano, *op. cit.*, p. 452; Andrews, *op. cit.*, p. 215.
[9] Serrano, *op. cit.*, pp. 452-53; dos Santos, *op. cit.*, p. 190.
[10] Oliveira Vianna, in *Contribuições para a Biographia de D. Pedro II*, Pt. I, p. 850.

rules of military discipline. His request was ignored and he was criticized in Parliament when the subject came up for discussion. This further roused the officer, and a number of his colleagues in Rio Grande sided with him and sent to the government a collective protest against the attitude of the Minister of War. To this protest, General Deodoro da Fonseca, commandant and vice-president of the province, publicly assented. And in November, 1886, he wrote Cotegipe, then head of the cabinet, that the army officers were not bound by the prohibition, and that their protest was justified. The military, he said, must not be the subject of offenses and insults.[11]

This attitude of defiance caused the government to deprive of their positions the officers who were involved and to order them back to the capital. When Deodoro da Fonseca arrived in Rio he was given an ovation at the dock by the students of the military school.[12]

This former commandant in Rio Grande do Sul, a man of wide military experience and great influence, was a trouble-maker. His character, says Oliveira Lima, was based on a mixture of pride and vanity.[13] Even before Senna Madureira sent his second letter to the press Deodoro was apparently encouraging rumors among the soldiers in Rio Grande that there were disorders in the capital, caused by opposition to the ministry. Therefore, in October, 1886, Cotegipe sent him a telegram branding the reports as false.[14] But this did not give pause to the Commandant, who almost immediately championed Senna Madureira. In fact, the adulations of the disgruntled who rallied around him so increased Deodoro's self-esteem that, following his recall to Rio de Janeiro, he was quite ready to lead a movement of protest there.

[11] Monteiro, *Pesquisas e depoimentos para a historia*, pp. 124-30; Oliveira Vianna, in *Contribuições para a Biographia de D. Pedro II*, Pt. I, pp. 852-55; dos Santos, *op. cit.*, p. 190.
[12] dos Santos, *op. cit.*, p. 190.
[13] Oliveira Lima, *O Imperio brazileiro*, p. 155; Tavares de Lyra, *op. cit.*, pp. 4-8.
[14] Oliveira Vianna, *O occaso do Imperio*, p. 158.

Shortly after his arrival in the capital a meeting of military officers was held in one of its theatres—with Deodoro da Fonseca as chairman and Senna Madureira as secretary—to consider the legality of ministerial prohibitions. The gathering decided that army officers, in common with other citizens, had the right to express their opinions in the press. A report of this was published in the *Jornal do Commercio* of Rio de Janeiro.[15] Deodoro, authorized to take up the matter with the Emperor, wrote him an energetic letter on February 5, 1887, and another on the 12th, asking for justice to the military. As a result of the first communication, the government seems to have seriously considered dismissing the General; but it became fearful of the results of such action and, instead, on February 12 dismissed the Minister of War, Alfredo Chaves, who had censured the army officers and who now stood out for punishment of Deodoro. The action was taken with the consent of the Emperor, who was already ailing and was, two weeks later, laid low with the illness which permanently impaired his health.[16]

This yielding of the government encouraged another move on the part of the military, and soon Deodoro da Fonseca and the Visconde de Pelotas, formerly a general in the army and now, as a member of the senate, an ardent champion of the army, published a boldly worded manifesto calling for cancellation of the notes of censure against the two officers. The document had been written by the editor of the *Diario de Noticias*, Ruy Barbosa.[17] The ministry decided to close the incident by giving way, and, therefore, an understanding was reached with the senate leaders, one of whom, Silveira Martins, a friend of Pelotas, presented a resolution calling for virtual cancellation of

---

[15] Serrano, *op. cit.*, p. 453; Monteiro, *Pesquisas e depoimentos para a historia*, pp. 137-38.

[16] Oliveira Vianna, in *Contribuições para a Biographia de D. Pedro II*, Pt. I, pp. 855-56; Monteiro, *Pesquisas e depoimentos para a historia*, p. 141; *Rio News*, Feb. 15, 1887.

[17] Serrano, *op. cit.*, pp. 453-54; Monteiro, *Pesquisas e depoimentos para a historia*, pp. 149-50.

the notes. With this, Cotegipe, in the name of the government, complied. He later explained this retreat by the fear that refusal might produce scenes of violence which would aggravate the Emperor's illness.[18]

Cotegipe was perhaps right about the alternative to yielding, but if Dom Pedro had been well enough to handle the situation it is not likely that he would have weakened before the arrogance of the army officers, any more than he did before the defiance of the bishops fifteen years before. He placed the civil authority first. But he seems to have had no voice in the government after he fell ill on February 28, and on June 30 he sailed for Europe leaving Dona Isabel in charge.

As was to be expected, the retreat of the ministry before the demands of the military simply made the military more unreasonable and rebellious. The whole psychology of soldiers, and their tendency to place their professional honor above all else, created wide solidarity in military circles. Naval officers took sides with the army against the government; indiscipline grew among the rank and file of the enlisted men; and friction occurred almost daily. The ministry was so subjected to insults that some of its members had their homes guarded at night by loyal soldiers.[19] The police were attacked by rioting members of the army or marines, and attempts to punish the offenders led to new difficulties.

In March, 1888, an officer of the marines was arrested by police in Rio, which occurrence caused the Naval Club there, supported by the military officers, to demand dismissal of the chief of police. Barão de Cotegipe, now thoroughly afraid of the dictatorial military group, resisted. The Princess Regent, however, showed an unexpected sympathy with the Naval Club, owing to the influence of her nephew, Prince Augusto Leopoldo, Princess Leopoldina's second son, who was a marine officer and

---

[18] dos Santos, *op. cit.*, p. 195; Ottoni, *D. Pedro de Alcantara*, pp. 56-57; Oliveira Vianna, in *Contribuições para a Biographia de D. Pedro II*, Pt. I, p. 862.

[19] Ottoni, *D. Pedro de Alcantara*, p. 55.

made himself the mouthpiece of his disaffected companions-in-arms. His reports led to the belief that it would be perilous not to yield again to the demands of the military and dismiss the chief of police. Accordingly, a family conference seems to have taken place at São Christovão Palace at which it was agreed that the Comte d'Eu was to visit the Naval Club. Apparently the impression he gained from doing so confirmed Prince Augusto's views. In any case, the Regent continued to sympathize with the Naval Club. This fact and the ministry's stand on emancipation now caused the ministry to resign in a body. Seemingly, the removal demanded by the Naval Club did not follow, but the government of João Alfredo, which came in on March 10, in the following November dismissed the chief of police of São Paulo, who, in defense of public order in the city, opposed the officers of the seventeenth infantry stationed there. This surrender, declared the *Rio News*, was "disgraceful and pusillanimous in the highest degree."[20]

Already, several years before, military leaders had begun to join in the discussion of the slavery problem, and during the abolition agitation of 1885 some of them had frankly declared themselves in favor of immediate emancipation without indemnity. As already stated, early in 1888, after João Alfredo was made head of the cabinet, the Military Club expressed its opposition to using the soldiers for pursuit of fugitive slaves.[21]

In January, 1889, the João Alfredo government took advantage of a boundary quarrel between Paraguay and Bolivia to send, under a command of General Deodoro, a considerable portion of the soldiers then in Rio out to the frontier in Matto Grosso to observe developments over the territorial dispute. The soldiers suspected that the order was given primarily to get them out of the capital, and they departed grumbling and irritable. Out in the lonely wilds, with Corumbá as headquar-

---
[20] dos Santos, *op. cit.*, pp. 195-96; *Rio News*, Dec. 5, 15, 1888.
[21] Monteiro, *Pesquisas e depoimentos para a historia*, p. 112.

ters, their animosity towards the government increased, and they talked of settling scores when they got back.[22]

Meanwhile, the regular troops left in Rio showed no signs of mending their ways, but continued to riot in the streets and otherwise to get into conflict with the civil authorities. It was clear therefore that the trouble was something more serious than political factionalism. Various radical papers, particularly *O Paiz* and the *Diario de Noticas,* had made things worse by coming out for the army, and were active in publishing propaganda which helped spread sedition.[23] On July 10, 1889, Marshal Floriano Peixoto, writing to a fellow officer, referred to the need for a military dictatorship to purge the country of its evils. Though, as a Liberal, he could not, he declared, wish for his country a government by the sword, yet there was one who knew how to purify the blood of the social body, which, like the Brazilian, was corrupt.[24]

Apparently some of the politicians who were opposed to the monarchy had hoped to capitalize through a foreign war the disaffection of the military. The Missions Territory was in dispute between Brazil and Argentina, and early in 1889 serious trouble seemed to threaten between the two countries. There was talk of war, which, according to André Rebouças, was favored by Quintino Bocayuva, one of the most prominent republican agitators. If the Brazilian army was victorious, Quintino reasoned, it would proclaim a "military republic"; if the Empire lost, the events of 1870 in France would, he hoped, be repeated.[25] This dream faded, however, late in May, 1889, when the Argentine government agreed to arbitrate the dispute, a

---

[22] dos Santos, *op. cit.,* p. 196; Affonso Celso, *Oito annos de parlamento,* p. 160.

[23] Ouro Preto, *op. cit.,* p. 32.

[24] Monteiro, *Pesquisas e depoimentos para a historia,* pp. 118-19. Oliveira Vianna's account in *Contribuições para a Biographia de D. Pedro II,* Pt. I, p. 845, gives the date of Floriano's letter as July 10, 1887, but this seems to be a misprint.

[25] Mary W. Williams, "The Treaty of Tordesillas and the Argentine-Brazilian Boundary Question," *Hisp. Amer. Hist. Rev.,* V (Feb., 1922), 19-20; Rebouças, *op. cit.,* sec. 8.

decision which was cause for great relief to the Emperor,[26] who was at this time much concerned over finding a successor to João Alfredo as head of the government.

The Visconde de Ouro Preto, to whom the task fell, was fully aware that he had a military question on his hands, in addition to a constitutional one. He apparently realized also that further concessions to the army officers might prove fatal to the nation. A policy of resistance, reform, and discipline was, according to the views of the Liberal cabinet, decidedly in order. Therefore, when a clash came in the city of Ouro Preto, Minas, between the police and the soldiers, and demand was made that the chief of police be removed, the imperial government, instead of complying, sent the twenty-third infantry in support of the police.[27]

The plan of Ouro Preto apparently was to weaken the seditious regular army by dividing the battalions and distributing them among the provinces, and as a counterpoise to reorganize, arm, and drill the national guard, and to rely upon it, as the government had done back in the period of the regency when the imperial troops had proven seditious and undependable. This seemed a logical and sound solution of the vexatious military question,[28] but the mutinous spirit was by now so deep and widespread that there was considerable risk in putting the program into effect.

Unfortunately, however, the cabinet had, in a sense, made a concession to the military: after the tension between Bolivia and Paraguay had abated, the troops under Deodoro, which had been on the frontier for several months, were ordered back to the capital. This was done partly through the influence of Visconde de Maracajú, Minister of War, with the idea of mollifying the General by giving him a position more in harmony with

[26] Rebouças, *op. cit.*, sec. 24.
[27] dos Santos, *op. cit.*, pp. 197-98.
[28] *Correio do Povo*, Oct. 1, 1889; Ottoni, *O advento da republica no Brasil*; p. 105; dos Santos, *op. cit.*, p. 198; Ouro Preto, *op. cit.*, pp. 90-103, 134-35.

his long service.[29] The forces reached Rio de Janeiro on September 13, and were received with great acclaim by the disaffected members of the regular army who had remained there.[30] Deodoro was again where he could make his influence felt.

By now, as José Maria dos Santos put it, the military attitude had reached a stage of "perfect hallucination." It no longer had a specific objective; it was a simple ostentation of force, regardless of consequences. The military class, drunk with its own pride, needed continually to exult in the sacrifice of the civil authority.[31]

It was not to be expected that the soldiers and their sympathizers would receive with docility the plan for their submission. On November 10, the hostile *Paiz* referred to a supposed scheme "to secure the throne for the Princess Imperial," consisting in scattering the army over the Empire; and it remarked, "A denial from the Government will be next in order." Military officers, when rumors of the plan reached them, became greatly concerned and fearful that the army was to be completely dissolved.[32] They and their supporters began to pour letters and telegrams upon Deodoro, many of them urging him to take action before it was too late. There was a general sentiment among the military that the Ouro Preto government was deliberately hostile to them. Deodoro de Fonseca shared in this feeling, and, perhaps recalling the resignation of the Cotegipe government in March, 1888, decided to try to get rid of the existing one. He, therefore, wrote a long letter to Dom Pedro calling attention to the unrest and bitterness in the army over its treatment. But he received no reply; and none came to a second letter. Neither the Ouro Preto ministry nor the Emperor intended to make further concessions to the army.[33]

[29] Ouro Preto, *op. cit.*, p. 34.
[30] dos Santos, *op. cit.*, pp. 196-97.   [31] *Ibid.*, p. 197.
[32] *Ibid.*, p. 198; Ernesto Senna, *Deodoro: subsidios para a historia*, pp. 27-28.
[33] dos Santos, *op. cit.*, pp. 198-99.

Failing to gain the sympathy of Dom Pedro against the cabinet, the leaders among the disgruntled army officers began to discuss direct action as a means of removing the Ouro Preto government. But some were hesitant because of the possible dire results to the army itself from resignation of the ministry before a display of military force. At first, none of the leading officers thought of deposing the Emperor, from whom several, especially Deodoro, had received many favors.[34] There was, in fact, considerable affection for Dom Pedro in military circles. It even existed among the radical cadets of the military academy. On September 22 of the preceding year a party of the students had scaled the steep sides of the Sugar Loaf Peak—a feat rarely, if ever, accomplished before—and displayed the word "Salve!" (Hail!) to welcome the Emperor on his return from Europe.[35]

Lieutenant-Colonel Benjamin Constant Coelho de Maga-

[34] *Ibid.*, p. 199; Senna, *op. cit.*, pp. 27-28; Oliveira Vianna, in *Contribuições para a Biographia de D. Pedro II*, Pt. I, p. 870; Jardim, *op. cit.*, pp. 255-58.
[35] *Rio News*, Nov. 18, 1889.
Dom Pedro's sympathetic kindness was the secret of his popularity. An anecdote told by a cadet in the first regiment of cavalry illustrates this. It was customary for the Empress and Emperor to dine once a week with Princess Isabel at her palace in Laranjéiras. Their cavalry guard left São Christovão before dinner time and received nothing to eat at Isabel Palace, and therefore, they waited, hungry, outside the entrance to the park at Laranjéiras until Dom Pedro and Dona Thereza should come out for the return across the city to Boa Vista. One day a bold young soldier named Carlos Maria Oliva decided to forage within the Isabel Palace for food. When he was leaving the dining room with a bunch of bananas, a bottle of wine, and other booty, he met the Emperor face to face. Though not abashed, he returned the things to their places, drew himself up and saluted his sovereign, saying: "Your Majesty, please pardon me. I was hungry and saw those fine bananas and could not restrain myself."
Between smiles and severity, Dom Pedro asked him why he had not waited until dinner time, which would not be long, whereupon the youth explained that they were not given dinner at the Isabel Palace and had no money with which to buy food. The Emperor frowned and said nothing more, and Carlos Maria Oliva, convinced that he was in a bad scrape, returned to his post at the palace gate.
Soon, however, a good dinner was brought out to the cavalrymen; and ever afterwards when the Emperor dined with his daughter a full meal was ordered from the Isabel Palace for the imperial guard.—Rego Barros, "Reminiscencias de ha 50 annos, de um cadete de primeiro regimento de cavallaria," *Rev. do Inst. Hist. e Geog. Bras.*, vol. 152, pp. 95-96.

lhães, a teacher at the military academy, was also indebted to Dom Pedro and had a certain fondness for him. But he was dominated by the desire for a republic and by the conviction that the government had outraged military "honor," which was intolerable. A well-meaning zealot, Benjamin Constant was less fearful of consequences than were the others and was anxious to bring about, at once, justice to the military and a republican "Utopia."

Late in October, 1889, occurred an incident which showed Benjamin Constant's temper and brought the military question more definitely to the fore. The Chilean government, anxious to capitalize the strained relations between Brazil and Argentina, with which Chile likewise had a boundary dispute, had sent the cruiser "Almirante Cochrane" on a friendly visit to Rio. A banquet was given at the military academy for the officers of the vessel, at which was also present Candido de Oliveira, the Minister of Justice, then acting as Minister of War for Maracajú, who was ill. Benjamin Constant, in his speech of greeting to the visitors, expressed bitter resentment over the treatment of the Brazilian army, and over the charges of the government that the army was insubordinate. "The soldiers are armed citizens, not Janizaries," he is reported to have said.[36]

The next day, October 26, the cadets and the officers of the second brigade showed their approval of this criticism by enthusiastic demonstrations, during which they pelted the teacher with flowers.[37] The ministry, apparently afraid to take formal notice of the students' and officers' actions, referred the matter to the brigadier-general, who censured them on October 28.[38] Ouro Preto wished Benjamin Constant likewise punished, but the Emperor was opposed. "Benjamin is an excellent creature," said he, "and very much my friend; he has certain ideas, but

---

[36] Senna, *op. cit.*, pp. 30-31; Serrano, *op. cit.*, p. 455.
[37] Serrano, *op. cit.*, p. 455; *Correio do Povo*, Oct. 30, 1889.
[38] Senna, *op. cit.*, p. 31.

they do no harm."[39] The Minister was insistent, however, and Dom Pedro finally agreed that the teacher should be rebuked, but matters reached a climax before the measure was carried out.[40]

Very shortly after the first rumors of the ministry's plan had spread, army circles learned that the twenty-second battalion of the infantry was to be sent to the far northern part of the Empire, where there were disorders resulting from drought and famine. They also heard that one other battalion was soon to go to the north, and one to the south. The twenty-second was to depart on November 10.[41] On the 9th, at a meeting of the Military Club, with more than one hundred and fifty officers present, Benjamin Constant got himself named to represent the organization, ostensibly in a final effort to come to terms with the government. But evidently he did not try to get in contact with the ministry. Instead, he proceeded to plot for the overthrow of the Empire. On November 11, a meeting arranged by him was held at the home of Marshal Deodoro, with a number of civilians present, among them, Ruy Barbosa and Quintino Bocayuva. Benjamin now suggested to Deodoro that he head a revolt in favor of a republic. According to one account, the General at first refused, mentioning his affection for the Emperor, but finally consented; but, judging from another version, he agreed only to help force the Ouro Preto ministry from office. The next day Benjamin Constant conferred with Eduardo Wandenkolk, chief of the naval squadron, who also agreed to coöperate, at least to the extent of action against the ministry.[42]

Ouro Preto was quickly informed, through letters, that some sort of conspiracy was afoot among the military, and he at once

[39] Verissimo, "D. Pedro II," *Jornal do Brasil*, Dec. 8, 1891.
[40] Monteiro, *Pesquisas e depoimentos para a historia*, p. 229.
[41] Ottoni, *O advento da republica no Brasil*, p. 105.
[42] Ouro Preto, *op. cit.*, p. 44; Amaral, "O Imperador e a proclamação da republica," *Rev. do Inst. Hist. e Geog. Bras.*, vol. 152, pp. 460-61; dos Santos, *op. cit.*, pp. 199-201, 252-53; Oliveira Vianna, in *Contribuições para a Biographia de D. Pedro II*, Pt. I, pp. 871-72.

spoke about it to Maracajú, who had within the last few days resumed the portfolio of war. Maracajú replied reassuringly, and quoted the Adjutant-General, Floriano Peixoto, as saying that nothing was wrong. On November 14, the Visconde de Ouro Preto received a letter written by Floriano to the Minister of Justice, Candido de Oliveira, the day before, which admitted that plotting was going on among the members of the army, but told him not to pay any attention to it, and added, "As much as necessary trust the loyalty of the chiefs, who are already on the alert."[43] It is quite clear that the Adjutant-General worded this letter for the express purpose of misleading the ministry, for he was by now deeply involved in the conspiracy. Indeed, he seems to have been the very pivot of it among the military officers— much more so than was Deodoro;[44] but he was less popular. It is very probable that when Floriano sent the letter of assurance to Ouro Preto a plot to take action against his ministry on November 16, or the 20th, when Parliament was to convene, was already arranged.[45]

While resentment against the ministry and the crown was thus approaching a climax Dom Pedro apparently remained quite unaware of the gravity of the situation. During the past winter he had appeared in public more than formerly, especially at the theatre. This was to help counteract the false reports about his health, and probably likewise the rumor, started by the republicans, that he would abdicate on his next birthday in favor of his daughter.[46]

He was, however, quite well enough to follow his usual routine, even when the hot season approached, and on October 15, Dona Thereza's saint's day and the birthday of the Prince

[43] Ouro Preto, *op. cit.*, pp. 45-46; Amaral, "O Imperador e a proclamação da republica," *Rev. do Inst. Hist. e Geog. Bras.*, vol. 152, p. 462.
[44] Ouro Preto, *op. cit.*, pp. 46-56; dos Santos, *op. cit.*, pp. 252-53.
[45] Amaral, "O Imperador e a proclamação da republica," *Rev. do Inst. Hist. e Geog. Bras.*, vol. 152, p. 464; Ouro Preto, *op. cit.*, p. 81.
[46] Rangel, *Gastão de Orléans, o ultimo Conde d'Eu*, p. 385; Rocha Pombo, *Historia do Brasil*, X, 102.

From a photograph taken at Petropolis

THE IMPERIAL FAMILY SHORTLY BEFORE THE REVOLUTION

Back row, left to right: the Empress, Princess Isabel, Dom Pedro II, Prince Pedro Augusto, the Comte d'Eu; *Front row, left to right:* the sons of Princess Isabel and the Comte—Dom Antonio, Dom Luiz, and Dom Pedro de Alcantara

of Grão Pará, he received at the City Palace, as was customary. A week later the press reported him as visiting the orphan asylum, where the children greeted him with flowers and gave him samples of their handiwork.[47] Because of the need to conserve his strength, on November 5, he and the Empress settled in Petropolis for the summer, a little earlier than usual.[48] But this did not remove him much from ordinary happenings in Rio, for he went down at frequent intervals. On the 7th, he was there for the meeting of the Historical and Geographical Institute,[49] and on the 8th, he presided over a session of the commission to revise the civil code, and fixed November 22 as the date for the next meeting. The 9th was an unusually full day for him in Rio. He, with the Empress and their daughter and son-in-law, attended the inauguration of the new yellow fever hospital.[50] They also listened to a demonstration of the phonograph by Thomas Edison's agent, and Dom Pedro expressed himself as much pleased with the invention.[51] In the evening they were all present at a dance at the Ilha Fiscal for the Chilean officers. Here took place an incident that was later vividly recalled. As the Emperor was entering the ballroom he slipped on a mat and was in danger of falling. Several persons rushed to his aid. Recovering his balance, he turned smilingly to the press representatives and remarked, "The monarchy scarcely slipped, and did not fall!"[52]

On November 14, he and the Empress attended mass in the imperial chapel for the soul of his sister Queen Maria II of Portugal. On the same day he visited the national printing office to see various recently-introduced improvements, and was present at the Collegio Dom Pedro II for an examination of a

[47] *Diario Official*, Oct. 15, 22, 1889.
[48] *Ibid.*, Nov. 6, 1889.
[49] Fleiuss, *Paginas de historia*, p. 485.
[50] *Rio News*, Nov. 11, 1889.
[51] *Ibid.*
[52] *Diario Official*, Nov. 9, 10, 1889; J. M. M. F., "D. Pedro II," *Rev. do Inst. Hist. e Geog. Bras.*, vol. 152, p. 743.

teacher of English.[53] That night he and Dona Thereza returned to Petropolis as usual.

Meanwhile the Princess Imperial and Prince Gaston, who were not yet moved to the summer capital, had been helping entertain the Chilean visitors, and they were arranging to give a grand ball in their honor on the 16th of November.[54]

[53] *O Paiz*, Nov. 15, 1889; *Diario Official*, Nov. 15, 1889.
[54] *O Paiz*, Nov. 15, 1889.

XVII

THE REVOLUTION

IN SPITE of Floriano Peixoto's attempt to allay the suspicions of Ouro Preto, the Prime Minister promptly, on November 14, took precautions against rebellion in the regular army. He called upon the Minister of Justice to have the police force and the national guard ready for any emergency, and upon the president of the Province of Rio de Janeiro to send to the imperial capital the troops under his command; and he also ordered the Minister of War to investigate Deodoro's activities and intentions. If the General's reply was not satisfactory Maracajú was to take precautionary measures against him, and, if necessary, to discharge him.[1]

These preparations seem to have caused Benjamin Constant and other leaders in the conspiracy to move ahead of schedule. The disgruntled were primed for action by a report circulated in the afternoon of the 14th that Deodoro was to be imprisoned and that various corps of garrisons in the capital were to be sent at once to the provinces.[2] When Major Solon Ribeiro, who had helped spread the false report in the city, imparted it to the second brigade, quartered at São Christovão, two of the regiments decided to resist being sent away, by marching in arms to the Campo da Acclamação the next morning. General Deodoro, who was sick in bed, was notified and told that the soldiers counted upon his assistance in the revolt.[3]

At midnight on the 14th Ouro Preto learned by telephone that the first regiment was armed in its quarters and that the

---
[1] Ouro Preto, *op. cit.*, p. 47.
[2] *Ibid.*, p. 49; *Rio News*, Nov. 18, 1889; Amaral, "O Imperador e a proclamação da republica," *Rev. do Inst. Hist. e Geog. Bras.*, vol. 152, p. 464.
[3] *Rio News*, Nov. 18, 1889; Ouro Preto, *op. cit.*, p. 57.

army chiefs were gathered in conference. Somewhat later he was informed that other military units had mutinied. He instructed Floriano to order the insurgents to lay down their arms, and he also began to consider their punishment.[4] At about four o'clock in the morning he sent to the Emperor at Petropolis a telegram marked "Urgent," stating that the first and ninth regiments of cavalry and the second battalion of artillery were in armed rebellion, but that the government was taking the precautions necessary to curb the insubordination and to make the laws respected.[5]

The telegram was sent from the marine arsenal, which Ouro Preto had ordered put in a state of defense; and this was done. Here the ministry met and planned to remain; but Maracajú declared that his place was at the quarters-general of the army on the Campo da Acclamação, and he urged that the other members of the cabinet go there, where, he said, Ouro Preto's presence was needed to stimulate resistance to the insurgents. After being assured that the army barracks were likewise prepared for defense, Ouro Preto, with the other ministers, went there. It was now about seven o'clock in the morning of the 15th. Gathered in the Campo were the police force and the firemen's corps of the city, armed, and here also were the troops of the Campo barracks, under command of Marshal Floriano. Upon his arrival Ouro Preto learned that the mutinous soldiers had left their quarters at São Christovão and were marching towards the city, and that no forces had been sent against them. The reason given by Maracajú for this omission was that none of the troops at the quarters-general could be trusted.[6]

At about eight o'clock General Deodoro, carrying the imperial flag, arrived at the Campo; and following him came the two mutinous regiments and the battery of artillery, the students from the military school, and also some marines. Among the rebels were seen a few leading republicans, including Quin-

---

[4] Ouro Preto, *op. cit.*, pp. 51-53.
[5] *Ibid.*, p. 56.
[6] *Ibid.*, pp. 57-60.

tino Bocayuva and Benjamin Constant. The newcomers surrounded the barracks in which the ministry was gathered.[7]

Barão de Ladario, who had remained at the arsenal to attend to some official duties, reached the war headquarters after the building had been encompassed by the troops led by Deodoro. As he alighted from his carriage one of the rebel officers attempted to arrest him, and Ladario fired his pistol. There were return shots, and the Minister of Marine, wounded, fell to the ground.[8]

Again and again Ouro Preto gave orders, which were repeated by Maracajú, for the troops under Floriano to attack the insurgents, but the Adjutant-General ignored the command, as did the other officers connected with the barracks. Instead, they and their men fraternized with the disloyal forces and admitted Deodoro, who was greeted with vivas as he rode into the courtyard of the barracks.[9]

Meeting to deliberate, the cabinet was informed by Maracajú that the rebellious troops could not be subdued without great bloodshed. This caused all of the members to favor resignation. Floriano, who had been sent for, told them that Deodoro demanded their retirement. Shortly after this Ouro Preto sent a second telegram to the Emperor, telling of the attack by Deodoro and wounding of Ladario, the desertion of the barracks troops, and the capture of the war office by the rebels; and he asked that his government be dismissed.[10]

A little later Deodoro himself appeared and, according to Ouro Preto's account, informed the ministers that, because they had greatly wronged the army, they were dismissed; and he added that it was his intention to ask the Emperor—whose rights

---

[7] *Ibid.*, pp. 60-64; *Rio News*, Nov. 18, 1889; Monteiro, *Pesquisas e depoimentos para a historia*, p. 235.

[8] Amaral, "O Imperador e a proclamação da republica," *Rev. do Inst. Hist. e Geog. Bras.*, vol. 152, pp. 467-68.

[9] Ouro Preto, *op. cit.*, pp. 64-66; Adams to Blaine, no. 19, Nov. 20, 1889, Dept. of State, Despatches, Brazil; Monteiro, *Pesquisas e depoimentos para a historia*, pp. 235-36.   [10] Ouro Preto, *op. cit.*, pp. 67-69.

would be respected and guaranteed—to appoint a new ministry. Ouro Preto, admitting defeat, agreed to resign.[11] Following this, Deodoro left the barracks at the head of the mutinous troops, who marched through the streets to the marine arsenal, where they were welcomed by Admiral Wandenkolk and other naval officers.[12]

On the train from Petropolis which reached Rio at nine-fifteen that morning came André Rebouças, the abolitionist, who was an engineering expert and was due to examine some students at the polytechnic school. A few weeks later in a written account he stated that when he arrived the revolution was on: Barão de Ladario was reported dead; all of the shops were closed; and many of the people, frightened by the attack on the Minister, had locked themselves in their homes.[13]

It is fairly certain, however, that when General Deodoro led the rebellious troops to the Campo da Acclamação he aimed solely to get rid of the Ouro Preto ministry, for he seems not only to have carried the imperial flag, but also, after entering the barracks, to have waved his cap and shouted, "Viva sua Magestade o Imperador!"[14] This harmonizes with the statement of the Conde de Affonso Celso, son of Ouro Preto, who, as a deputy from Minas, was attending a preliminary session of the lower house when the soldiers led by Deodoro towards the marine arsenal marched past the building where the deputies met. According to the Conde, the troops were carrying the flag of the Empire, unfurled.[15] Furthermore, Deodoro's remarks to Ouro Preto seem to have been aimed en-

---

[11] *Ibid.*, pp. 69-70; Galanti, *op. cit.*, V, 120. Accounts of what took place are, naturally, conflicting, but there is no doubt that Deodoro gave an order of dismissal to the Ouro Preto government.

[12] Ouro Preto, *op. cit.*, p. 71; Amaral, "O Imperador e a proclamação da republica," *Rev. do Inst. Hist. e Geog. Bras.*, vol. 152, p. 470.

[13] Rebouças, *op. cit.*, sec. 11.

[14] dos Santos, *op. cit.*, p. 201. After the republic was established, Deodoro's relatives denied that he had done so, but the friends of Benjamin Constant insisted that he had.—*Ibid.*

[15] Affonso Celso, *Oito annos de parlamento*, p. 164.

tirely at ousting him and his government. Deodoro was almost wholly concerned with military matters; he was not interested in political principles or governmental forms; and he certainly was not partial to republicanism. After leading the disaffected military element to the marine arsenal, he seems to have returned to his home, for he was really ill and weak from a fever contracted out on the frontier.[16]

The radicals led by Benjamin Constant had, however, no intention of stopping with the overthrow of the cabinet. After the triumph at the barracks on the Campo, they met at his house and planned to set up a republic at once. Again they approached Deodoro da Fonseca, who was apparently still reluctant to coöperate, until they impressed him with the likelihood that Silveira Martins, who had resented his previous conduct and attacked him in the senate, would head the new ministry, and that all of the leaders of the uprising against the Ouro Preto government would be severely punished. Probably, as a further inducement, they offered him at this time the provisional headship of the republic. In any case, he agreed to go with them; and the revolutionaries proceeded to carry out their plans.[17]

Meanwhile, Dom Pedro, who was badly needed in the capital, had not arrived, though Ouro Preto's first telegram to him had reached Petropolis at five-thirty in the morning and had been at once given to one of the Emperor's private servants.[18] Later, the Emperor appears to have said that he had failed to receive this message and that he had not been informed of the seriousness of developments, else he would have descended to the capital at once.[19] Consequently, for a time some people

---

[16] Rebouças, *op. cit.*, sec. 11; *Rio News*, Nov. 18, 1889; Max Fleiuss, *Historia administrativa do Brasil*, p. 435.

[17] Oliveira Vianna, in *Contribuições para a Biographia de D. Pedro II*, Pt. I, p. 872; Fleiuss, *Historia administrativa do Brasil*, p. 434; Rebouças, *op. cit.*, sec. 11; Monteiro, *Pesquisas e depoimentos para a historia*, pp. 238-39.

[18] Escragnolle Taunay, *Pedro II*, p. 95.

[19] Dom Pedro II, Exponho exactamente o que commigo se passou nos dias de Novembro, Pedro d'Orléans Bragança Archives, A, CC, 9043; Monteiro, *Pesquisas e depoimentos para a historia*, p. 302.

charged that the Conde de Motta Maia had withheld from his patient the Prime Minister's telegram reporting the uprising of the three military units. But this was untrue. The message was delivered promptly.[20] Dom Pedro's statement seems to have been caused by misunderstanding, owing to the confusion and excitement of the day, and also by the facts that on the afternoon of the 14th when he was in Rio all had seemed quiet and peaceful there and that, despite the many previous troubles with the army, nothing disastrous had happened. Furthermore, Ouro Preto had stated in his message that all precautions were being taken to curb the insubordination and to make the laws respected.

Many months later, after discussion had cleared up the misunderstanding, the Emperor's good friends the Barão and Baroneza de Muritiba gave to Visconde Taunay an account of Dom Pedro's movements on November 15 after he had received the telegram. Anxious, but by no means alarmed by the message from Ouro Preto, he telegraphed for further word, and then proceeded to the baths as usual. After his return, he inquired whether, in case of necessity, he could get a train of the Northern Railroad for Rio—seemingly because this would make better time than his special train, and he received an affirmative reply. This arranged, he asked whether there had been any additional telegrams from the ministry, and was told that none had come. He then went to mass, intending to take a morning train for the capital. The second message from Ouro Preto, which reached Petropolis at ten-thirty, was brought to the Emperor at church. He left immediately and called for a special train with which to start as soon as possible for Rio.[21] When the train was ready, he and the Empress left with a small suite, which included Dr. Motta Maia. They seem to have reached the railroad station in Rio at about one o'clock in the afternoon, and here their car-

---

[20] Alberto de Carvalho, *Imperio e republica dictatorial*, p. 124; Escragnolle Taunay, *Pedro II*, p. 95; Olympio da Fonseca, "Medicos do paço," *Rev. do Inst. Hist. e Geog. Bras.*, vol. 152, p. 184, Motta Maia, *op. cit.*, pp. 271-80.

[21] Escragnolle Taunay, *Pedro II*, pp. 95, 104.

riages were waiting as usual. But the imperial guard was missing. It had gone over to the revolutionaries. To avoid disorders in the downtown section, the Emperor and his suite were driven in a roundabout way to the City Palace.[22]

The Princess and Comte, who were living in Laranjéiras, did not hear of the uprising until rather late in the afternoon. All had appeared as usual when the Comte and his sons Pedro and Luiz took their customary early morning horseback ride in the outskirts of the capital.[23] It was perhaps ten o'clock when word was brought to the Isabel Palace by the arrival there of the Barão and Baroneza de Muritiba accompanying two loyal officers of the forces, one from the army and the other from the navy. When the Comte d'Eu, who had been reading developments with unusual clarity, heard what had happened at the Campo da Acclamacão, he exclaimed, "Monarchy is ended in Brazil!"[24] Princess Isabel could not bring herself to believe this, but she realized that the situation was critical and gave thought to her sons. For safety, it was decided to send them to Petropolis, in charge of their tutor, Barão Ramiz Galvão, and they were started off almost at once, going by boat to Mauá to take the train there and thus avoid the dangers of the city.[25]

Shortly after the three princes had been started off for the mountains, Dona Isabel received a telegram from Dr. Motta Maia saying that the Emperor was leaving for Rio; so she and her husband set out for the São Christovão Palace to await him there, making part of the trip by launch on the Bay. As the boat approached the older part of the city, the Comte d'Eu recognized in the distance the six-horse imperial carriage, which was approaching the City Palace. Therefore, he and the Princess and the Muritibas and others who had accompanied them landed and went to the palace likewise, arriving slightly after

---

[22] *Rio News*, Nov. 18, 1889; Galanti, *op. cit.*, V, 123.
[23] Rangel, *Gastão d'Orléans, o ultimo Conde d'Eu*, p. 395; information from Dom Pedro d'Orléans Bragança. [24] *Ibid.*, pp. 395-96.
[25] *Ibid.*, pp. 396-97; Autobiographie de la Comtesse d'Eu, Pedro d'Orléans Bragança Archives, A, CCIV, 9264.

Dom Pedro did. At the entrance they were received by the guards with the usual respect.[26]

Among the people at the palace was Visconde de Taunay, who, some hours before, had agreed with Rebouças upon a plan which they hoped might save the monarchy, and Rebouças had suggested it to the Princess while she was still at her home. It was that the Emperor form at Petropolis a ministry which should govern from there, unless it became necessary to retire farther towards the interior. Escragnolle Taunay now set the plan before him.[27] After Dom Pedro had been exiled, the proposal impressed him favorably, as one that he might have carried out with success.[28] Yet when Taunay offered the plan the Emperor apparently paid little or no attention to it, not because he thought that the time was past for such a recourse, but because he had not yet grasped the true state of affairs. He did not realize the extent to which his throne had been undermined, and he trusted to the loyalty of the great majority of his subjects. The first remedy he suggested for the military situation was dissolution of the battalions, and he mentioned this to his son-in-law.

"It is easy to say that," retorted the Comte. "But how can you dissolve corps that are in arms against you? It will be necessary to organize a government because the former one has resigned."

But Dom Pedro said that he would not accept its resignation, and he sent for Ouro Preto. It was now about three o'clock.[29] Apparently around this hour the Brazilian republic was proclaimed before a large crowd in the City Hall by a member of the city council. Somewhat later in the afternoon the officers of the republican provisional government were announced from the headquarters established in the treasury build-

---

[26] Rangel, *Gastão de Orléans, o ultimo Conde d'Eu*, p. 397.
[27] *Ibid.*, pp. 396-97.
[28] Monteiro, *Pesquisas e depoimentos para a historia*, p. 302; Autobiographie de la Comtesse d'Eu, Pedro d'Orléans Bragança Archives, A, CCIV, 9264.
[29] Rangel, *Gastão de Orléans, o ultimo Conde d'Eu*, pp. 397-98.

ing. General Deodoro had been made chief of the republic, and prominent revolutionaries filled all of the other national offices. Ruy Barbosa was in charge of finance; Benjamin Constant, of the war department; Wandenkolk, of the navy; Quintino Bocayuva was Minister of Foreign Relations.[30]

Seemingly after some delay, Ouro Preto was found, and when he appeared before the Emperor he repeated his request for dismissal of his government. Dom Pedro, opposed to dictation by the military, at first declined to comply, and ordered him to continue, but he consented after the Prime Minister had argued that the cabinet was scorned and could not be responsible for public order without the threat of armed force, or by actual use of it. Asked whom he would suggest to take his place, Ouro Preto named Senator Silveira Martins, former president of Rio Grande do Sul, whom the Emperor approved. The senator was absent in the south and would not be back for a day or two, but Dom Pedro told Ouro Preto to notify him (Silveira Martins) as soon as he arrived that the Emperor wished to see him, and Ouro Preto promised to do so.[31]

The fact that Ouro Preto apparently thought it safe to await the coming of Silveira Martins shows that he, likewise, did not realize how serious the crisis was. Neither he nor any of the people in the City Palace were, at the time, aware of the revolutionary developments of the last few hours. It was somewhat after six o'clock when Ouro Preto learned that the republic had been proclaimed. At about that hour he was arrested, as was also Candido de Oliveira, and the two were held in prison to await deportation. Later on the same day the provisional government threw a cordon of soldiers around the City Palace, to prevent the imperial family from escaping.[32]

[30] *Rio News*, Nov. 18, 1889; Amaral, "O Imperador e a proclamação da republica," *Rev. do Inst. Hist. e Geog. Bras.*, vol. 152, pp. 472-73.
[31] Ouro Preto, *op. cit.*, p. 72. Silveira Martins was arrested by revolutionary leaders in Santa Catharina and imprisoned, and was later sent into exile.—*Rio News*, Nov. 18, 25, 1889.
[32] *Rio News*, Nov. 18, 1889; Monteiro, *Pesquisas e depoimentos para a historia*, p. 252; Ouro Preto, op. cit., pp. 73-74.

When Dona Isabel and the Comte learned of the Emperor's plans for a new ministry, they were much disturbed, and urged him not to wait for Silveira Martins, since a government was needed at once; but he remained unmoved. The Comte then told him that a republican provisional government was already formed, composed of Deodoro and others of the disaffected, but Dom Pedro, according to Alberto Rangel's account, based on the Comte's papers, merely displayed irritation.[33] Asked if he would not at least call a meeting of the council of state, the Emperor replied, "Later," and turned his attention to a scientific review which he had in his hands. Apparently at about the same time the president of the council, Lourenço de Albuquerque, and another of its members also tried, but in vain, to get him to change his mind.[34]

After dinner, served at about five o'clock, the Princess and Comte decided to act on their own responsibility, and they sent, in the name of Dona Isabel, calls to the members of the council of state to meet the Emperor at the City Palace as soon as possible.[35]

While Dom Pedro's daughter and son-in-law were trying to induce him to take steps to meet the crisis, various members of the council of state besides the two or three who were at the palace were feeling much concern over the delay, and one of them, the Visconde de Cruzeiro, called a meeting of the members at his house. Most of those not already with the Emperor attended, and they decided to go to him and point out the dangerous situation and suggest that he form a cabinet headed by Saraiva, with General Deodoro included as Minister of War.[36]

Whether this meeting was influenced by the messages sent out by the Comte and Princess is not apparent, but it seems unlikely, for the councilors were probably gathering, or in con-

---

[33] Rangel, *Gastão de Orléans, o ultimo Conde d'Eu*, p. 398.
[34] *Ibid.*; Moniz, *A côrte de D. Pedro II*, pp. 194-95.
[35] Rangel, *Gastão de Orléans, o ultimo Conde d'Eu*, p. 399.
[36] Escragnolle Taunay, *Pedro II*, p. 100.

ference, at Cruzeiro's home at about the time that Dona Isabel's call to them was issued.[37]

Practically all of the councilors who were at the meeting went to the Emperor, but he replied to their suggestion by stating that he had agreed with Ouro Preto that Silveira Martins should be called to form the new government.[38] Informal discussion followed among Dom Pedro, the councilors, and others, during which, according to Alberto Rangel,[39] Dom Pedro urged calmness, adding, "The thing will not last"— meaning the rebellion. But he soon began to give way on the question of waiting for Silveira Martins and to consider asking that Saraiva form a ministry; and at about nine o'clock he had a tentative conference with Saraiva. Some councilors, however, seemed to think it desirable that Deodoro be first approached and sounded out. The Comte d'Eu had suggested this some time before,[40] but Dona Isabel had opposed the idea.[41] Visconde de Taunay now broached the plan to the Emperor, who was likewise against it. Apparently in spite of that fact, it was arranged that two of the councilors, a Conservative and a Liberal, should go to see Deodoro; but they failed to find him at home.[42]

Finally, Dom Pedro decided to call a formal, official meeting of the eleven councilors who were still at the palace, and they assembled in the council room. By now, it lacked only a half hour of midnight. The Princess attended the session, but her husband remained away.[43]

---

[37] In a note made in his diary on April 19, 1890, Escragnolle Taunay stated that Cruzeiro had that day told him of the meeting. No mention was made in the entry of messages from the Princess.—*Ibid.*

[38] *Ibid.*

[39] *Gastão de Orléans, o ultimo Conde d'Eu,* p. 399.

[40] d'Orléans Bragança, *op. cit.,* p. 20; Affonso Celso, in *Contribuições para a Biographia de D. Pedro II,* Pt. I, p. 888.

[41] Rangel, *Gastão de Orléans, o ultimo Conde d'Eu,* p. 399.

[42] *Ibid.*

[43] *Ibid.* Braz do Amaral says that the Comte attended, but this is certainly an error.—"O Imperador e a proclamação da republica," *Rev. do Inst. Hist. e Geog. Bras.,* vol. 152, p. 476.

The plan agreed to at Cruzeiro's home was discussed and adopted by the council, though the Emperor, when the others urged the necessity for conferring with Deodoro, replied, "For my part, No; I don't negotiate with insurgents."[44] But he favored Saraiva as head of the government. The Marquez de Paranaguá was commissioned to go to the residence of the venerable statesman on Santa Thereza Heights and notify him and bring him back to the City Palace.[45]

By now, Dom Pedro and the others connected with the government probably saw only a small chance for saving the monarchy. During the evening the Emperor replied to an expression of despair, "Well, if all is lost, be calm. I have no fear of misfortune."[46] But many in the palace did have a hope, for they believed that Deodoro's aim was merely to get rid of the Ouro Preto ministry. Furthermore, no official word had been received by the Emperor that a republic had been proclaimed, so it seemed that reports of such a proclamation were simply the result of popular demonstrations and general excitement.

It was between one and two o'clock in the morning of the 16th that the messenger from Dom Pedro arrived at the home of Saraiva, who at once returned with him to the City Palace. Dom Pedro told Saraiva the results of the meeting of the council of state and offered him a free hand. The statesman agreed to try to form a new government, but felt that he must first know Deodoro's intentions. Therefore, he wrote immediately to the General, stating that he had undertaken to organize a ministry and adding, "I do not wish to, and I must not, do anything without an understanding with your excellency." He hoped for an early conference with Deodoro.[47] The message

[44] Escragnolle Taunay, *Pedro II*, p. 101.
[45] Rangel, *Gastão de Orléans, o ultimo Conde d'Eu*, p. 400.
[46] Escragnolle Taunay, *Pedro II*, p. 103.
[47] Affonso Celso, in *Contribuições para a Biographia de D. Pedro II*, Pt. I, pp. 888-89.

was sent at once, carried by Major Trompowsky, son-in-law of one of the members of the council of state.[48]

At half past three in the morning of the 16th, a little after Trompowsky had departed, some of those who were awake in the City Palace heard sounds of shooting. A number of marines who had cheered for the Emperor in the praça in front of the building had been arrested.[49]

At about dawn Trompowsky returned. He had no formal reply from Deodoro; but the fact that he had found the latter heading the republican government made an answer unnecessary.[50] The prediction of Prince Gaston, made the day before, had proved true: monarchy was indeed ended in Brazil!

In spite of the great concern felt by many over the Emperor's delay in acting after he reached the City Palace, it is quite clear that he could not have saved his crown even if he had gotten in touch with Deodoro as soon as he reached Rio, around one o'clock on the 15th; for Deodoro had certainly gone over to the republicans by then. If he had come to the capital as soon as possible after receiving Ouro Preto's first telegram and had at once communicated with the sulky General, he probably could have prevented Deodoro from coming to terms with Benjamin Constant and his faction. But a sop to Deodoro in the form of a cabinet position would hardly have solved the "military question," though it might have delayed its climax for the remainder of Dom Pedro's life.

Some Brazilian writers imply that feebleness of mind, caused by illness or old age, was the reason for the Emperor's long delay before he called the council of state, but there is no basis for such a view. His intellect seems to have been but slightly less vigorous in 1889 than it was during his middle years, in spite of the propaganda to the contrary spread by his political

---

[48] Rangel, *Gastão de Orléans, o ultimo Conde d'Eu*, p. 400.
[49] *Ibid.*; *Rio News*, November 18, 1889.
[50] Affonso Celso, in *Contribuiçoes para a Biographia de D. Pedro II*, Pt. I, p. 889; Rangel, *Gastão de Orléans, o ultimo Conde d'Eu*, p. 400.

enemies. Furthermore, his reactions on November 15 were such as might have been expected, in view of his temperament and principles, and of the facts that he underestimated the seriousness of the military question and counted too much upon the loyalty and affection of his subjects for keeping him on the throne. He delayed calling his council of state largely because, as civil head of the Empire, and under the constitution its "perpetual defender," he abhorred the thought of giving way to dictation of the military. For that reason he was most reluctant to accept the resignation of the Ouro Preto ministry, and, having done so, he objected to giving up the arrangement which he had made with the outgoing Minister as to his successor. Most of all, perhaps, the Emperor resented the idea of bribing Deodoro into loyal conduct by giving him a position in the cabinet. The attitude shown by Dom Pedro at this time was identical in spirit with that which he had taken towards Francisco López twenty years before, during the Paraguayan War, and with that displayed towards the bishops in the 1870's. In every case, the Emperor held out on principle—possibly accentuated by a touch of obstinacy.

Finally, though he had been confident that the love and loyalty of his people assured him the throne for the rest of his life, and though he really wanted to end his days as ruler of Brazil, he had taken a consistently indulgent attitude—mixed with gentle cynicism—towards the growth of republicanism. Repeatedly he had said that he wished the people to have the type of government that they desired. Perhaps they really preferred a republic. This attitude tended to prevent him from working energetically on November 15 to save the monarchy, just as it had disinclined him earlier to combat anti-monarchist developments.

The revolution, however, was not a popular uprising. Save for a few republican leaders, the civil element had practically no part in it. Perhaps most of the people thought that the soldiers were on parade when they saw them marching through the streets to the marine arsenal. "The spectators were rather indifferent," remarked the *Rio News*, of later events in the day, "and there was a noticeable lack of enthusiasm everywhere."[51] There was, on the other hand, practically no resistance. The one instance of it in Rio de Janeiro was that of Barão de Ladario, and his was the only blood that was shed in the revolution of November 15.[52] In the provinces, notably in Rio Grande do Sul and Bahia, there were reports later of conflicts between monarchists and republicans,[53] but the country as a whole received the change in government in about the same spirit as did the capital.

Dom Pedro was right in believing that most of his people loved him, and if vigorous champions had come to his defense the masses would have rallied around them, but, lacking leaders, the rank and file calmly acquiesced in the new order. This general acceptance of the republic was reflected in the press. The monarchist dailies saw it as an accomplished fact, of which the best must be made; the radical sheets welcomed it with shouting, exultant headlines.[54] Here and there the customary opportunism showed itself. When the morning papers of November 16 came out with the proclamation of the republic and the names of the officers of the provisional government, merchants who had counted it an honor to have the imperial coat-of-arms over their places of business made haste to remove the emblem of monarchy. Various recent prominent monarchists also now seemed to believe that they had long yearned for a republic.

[51] Issue for Nov. 18, 1889; "Pedro II e os operarios," *Rev. do Inst. Hist. e Geog. Bras.*, vol. 152, pp. 981-82.
[52] His wounds were but slight and he fully recovered.
[53] *Rio News*, Nov. 18, 25, 1889.
[54] "Revolutionary Incidents," *Rio News*, Nov. 18, 25, Dec. 2, 9, 1889; *Gazeta do Povo*, Nov. 16, 1889; *Diario Popular*, Nov. 16, 1889; *A Provincia do São Paulo*, Nov. 16, 20, 1889; *Correio do Povo*, Nov. 16, 1889; *Diario de Noticias*, Nov. 16, 1889; *Correio Paulistano*, Nov. 18, 1889; *Cearense*, Nov. 22, 1889; *Gazeta do Norte*, Nov. 16, 20, 1889.

"There is an astonishing amount of driftwood on this new flood!" remarked the *Rio News*.[55]

While the revolution was spreading in the Empire, the situation was becoming more serious for Dom Pedro and his family. At nine o'clock on the morning of November 16 the City Palace was placed in rigorous incommunicado and orders were given that no one should enter or leave the building. Sentries were placed at the doors and along the outer walls, and cavalry troops patrolled the neighboring streets.[56]

This treatment hurt the Emperor more than anything else in connection with his overthrow. Later he referred to the

soldiers a-foot and on horseback guarding all of the doors, menacing me and my family with arms, as if we were criminals likely to escape. Would not my word have been sufficient security for them? . . . There was a cavalry officer who, from the praça, watched all of my movements, his eyes following me like a shadow if I passed from one room to another. I felt a strong desire to go into the street and say to him: "Surely you do not know me. I am not a man who flees or hides himself. Do not trouble yourself for my sake. You may rest assured that I shall always be found in the place where I am supposed to be."[57]

In spite of the vigilance of the guards, however, two close friends of the imperial family, the Conde and Condessa de Carapebús, slipped by and joined the prisoners. But the situation caused much concern, especially to those who, from the palace windows, saw relatives and friends who tried to reach them turned back by the sentries. Concern became alarm when it was reported by the Conde de Carapebús that there was talk in the city of placing the imperial family aboard a small, un-

[55] Nov. 25, 1889.
[56] Rangel, *Gastão de Orléans, o ultimo Conde d'Eu*, p. 400. That morning some of the foreign representatives proposed that the diplomatic corps make a demonstration in behalf of the Emperor, by going in a body to the palace and demanding to see him. This, the French chargé d'affaires and the American minister declined to do; and the plan was given up. Later, these two men went separately to the palace, were refused admission, and sent their cards to the Emperor.—Adams to Blaine, no. 21, Nov. 27, 1889, Dept. of State, Despatches, Brazil.
[57] Affonso Celso, *O Imperador no exilio*, pp. 58-59.

seaworthy cruiser, the "Solimões." In view of this, he suggested that arrangements be made to have them take refuge on the Chilean vessel "Almirante Cochrane." Prince Gaston favored this, and he seems to have helped plan for the Emperor to issue a communication to the Brazilians, preparatory to asking for such protection. Two drafts of a proclamation,[58] varying considerably in content, were made, probably without consulting Dom Pedro, who seems to have ignored them both and indignantly refused to consider going aboard the Chilean cruiser. He was unwilling to turn entirely to strangers, as if he were unsafe amidst his own people. And Dona Isabel said that she would sooner be shot like Ladario than desert her father.[59] The Comte, therefore, merely instructed Carapebús to have the three little princes brought from Petropolis and placed aboard the "Almirante Cochrane" for safety, and to have them embark later for Europe on another vessel which was expected soon.[60] But new developments in the situation prevented this from being done.

[58] These exist in the Pedro d'Orléans Bragança Archives, A, CC, 9044. The shorter, and probably first-written of the two, expressed the Emperor's desire to end his days in Brazil; whereas the second referred to the deep grief he felt at being denied his liberty, and stated that he would seek refuge under the flag of a friendly nation since he was not permitted any other alternative.

[59] Rangel, *Gastão de Orléans, o ultimo Conde d'Eu*, p. 401; Escragnolle Taunay, *Pedro II*, pp. 105-6.

[60] Escragnolle Taunay, *Pedro II*, p. 103.

XVIII

BANISHMENT OF THE IMPERIAL FAMILY

THE VAGUE fears of greater woes which had harassed the prisoners in the City Palace since morning on the 16th were soon realized. At three o'clock in the afternoon a squad of cavalry appeared before the building and its commander, Major Solon Ribeiro, dismounted and asked to see the Emperor. Taken to the salon where the imperial family was gathered, he handed Dom Pedro a communication from the republican government and departed. After reading the paper, the Emperor conferred with Franklin Doria, Barão de Loreto, for a few minutes and then announced to those present that he and his family were ordered into exile and must leave for Europe within twenty-four hours. The letter, signed by Deodoro, remarked in conclusion: "The country expects that you will know how to imitate, in submission to its desires, the example of the first Emperor, on April 7, 1831."[1]

The notice could not have surprised Dom Pedro greatly, for he well knew that banishment was the usual fate of fallen monarchs, but, though he managed to appear fairly calm outwardly, he was much upset by the definite order to leave his native land which he had ruled so long. Dona Isabel, who, like her father, had been overconfident as to survival of the monarchy, burst into tears and wept convulsively; and the other women joined her. Since the Empress had kept entirely aloof from politics, she was the least prepared for the blow and was dazed and bewildered as well as deeply stricken with grief.[2]

---

[1] Account written by Princess Isabel aboard the "Alagôas," Nov. 22, 1889, Pedro d'Orléans Bragança Archives, A, CC, 9043; *Rio News*, Nov. 18, 1889.

[2] Rangel, *Gastão de Orléans, o ultimo Conde d'Eu*, p. 401; Heitor Lyra, "Quéda do imperio e deposição do Imperador," *Jornal do Commercio*, Nov. 18, 1934.

It seems that no one suggested resistance, since that would have been worse than useless. The only discussion taking place related to the terms of the reply. Franklin Doria helped Dom Pedro with the phrasing, which finally stood as follows:

> In view of the written statement delivered to me at three o'clock this afternoon, I have decided to yield to the force of circumstances, and to depart, with my whole family, for Europe tomorrow, leaving this country, loved extremely by all of us, to which I have tried to give constant testimony of my affection and dedication for almost half of a century, during which I have discharged my duties as chief of the state. Absenting myself, then, I, with all the members of my family, will cherish for Brazil the deepest, most yearning remembrance, while praying earnestly for its greatness and prosperity. Rio de Janeiro, November 16, 1889. D. Pedro de Alcantara.[3]

The Emperor set two o'clock the next afternoon, Sunday, November 17, as the hour for departure, and obtained for himself and his family permission to attend mass in the morning at the Capella do Carmo.[4] Dr. Motta Maia volunteered to accompany his patient into exile, and therefore the provisional government granted him a year's leave of absence from the medical school in which he was a teacher.[5] Various others undertook to accompany the imperial family, including the Baroneza da Fonseca Costa, now eighty-one years old, who, during half of her life, had served the Empress as lady-in-waiting. The Visconde do Bom Retiro had been dead for three years,[6] and black Raphael, very aged and feeble, died suddenly on November 16, upon hearing that a republic had been proclaimed and that the Emperor was a prisoner in the City Palace.[7] Among the close friends who decided to go with the exiles were the Loretos and the Muritibas.

After the reply had been sent to Deodoro, most of the remainder of Saturday, the 16th, was given to preparations for

---

[3] *Rev. do Inst. Hist. e Geog. Bras.*, vol. 152, p. 975.
[4] *Rio News*, Nov. 18, 1889.   [5] *Ibid.*
[6] Jonathas Serrano, "O amigo do Imperador," *Rev. do Inst. Hist. e Geog. Bras.*, vol. 152, p. 110.   [7] Teixeira, *op. cit.*, p. 23.

departure. The members of the imperial family were not permitted to leave the palace, but the others were, and they helped arrange for the departure of all. Dom Pedro and Dona Thereza signed an authorization giving Nogueira da Gama charge of their financial interests, and the Comte and Princess made similar arrangements. Dona Isabel also wrote a short note of affectionate farewell to the Brazilians, which was published in the press, and her husband sent to Benjamin Constant, Minister of War, his resignation as commandant-general of artillery.[8] One of the last instructions of the Empress was in behalf of those to whom she had regularly given alms.[9]

During the afternoon or evening of the 16th, General Lassance, major domo of the Comte d'Eu, apparently under instructions, took up with the republican government the question of the Comte's and Princess's financial rights under the contract for their marriage and the existing laws; for the Prince owed a large sum to the Bank of Brazil, and Dona Isabel seemed fearful that imperial property might be confiscated to meet the debt.[10] Following Lassance's initiative, the provisional government voted that five thousand contos of milreis be given to the imperial family in a lump sum for covering financial obligations in Brazil and helping them get settled in Europe. According to a statement attributed to Lassance, the Prince and Princess were told of the decree by an army officer who came to the palace for the purpose. Apparently they acquiesced in the arrangement, but Dona Isabel remarked, "It is not a question of money with us. What afflicts me is having to leave the land of my birth and my affections. It is this that I lament, not the throne, nor ambitions—which I do not possess."[11] The incident of the five thou-

[8] *Rev. do Inst. Hist. e Geog. Bras.*, vol. 152, p. 975; Monteiro, *Pesquisas e depoimentos para a historia*, pp. 264-65.

[9] Fleiuss, *Paginas de historia*, p. 391.

[10] The Comte's indebtedness began through a loan obtained in 1875 to help pay the French surgeon who attended Dona Isabel when their eldest son was born.—Rangel, *Gastão de Orléans, o ultimo Conde d'Eu*, p. 416.

[11] *Ibid.*, pp. 402-3; Monteiro, *Pesquisas e depoimentos para a historia*, pp. 312-24.

sand contos at once became the basis of a false report, which was promptly circulated, that the Emperor had, in return for that sum, agreed to leave the country.[12] Through the press, Lassance and Saraiva at once denied the story, stating that the money was offered spontaneously and was not contingent on exile.[13] In fact, when the report started Dom Pedro was probably not even aware of the action of the provisional authorities.

At about half past one the next morning, Sunday, the Comte d'Eu was roused by Lassance with word that General José Simeon and Colonel Mallet had arrived with orders that Dom Pedro and his family must embark without delay. The republican government, it was explained, feared a demonstration in favor of the Emperor at the time of departure, and the students of the military school were arming themselves for the purpose of preventing such an outbreak. Talk was heard, Lassance whispered, of assassinating the Emperor. To prevent bloodshed, the imperial family were to be placed aboard ship under cover of darkness.[14] Deodoro and his associates were, in fact, somewhat fearful of a counter revolution.

Those who were to go into exile were awakened in turn, and were assembled, under guard, in the main room of the palace. Prince Pedro Augusto, eldest son of Princess Leopoldina, and Dona Isabel and her husband were among the first to reach there. The Princess was greatly distraught by the fact that her three children were still in Petropolis, and she refused to go without them. Mallet promised that the family would not be sent away until the boys had arrived, and the government at once ordered that the Princes be brought to Rio by special train and that there be guards at the stations for their protection.[15]

---
[12] *Rio News*, Nov. 18, 1889; Adams to Blaine, no. 20, Nov. 19, 1889, no. 21, Nov. 27, 1889, Dept. of State, Despatches, Brazil.

[13] *Rio News*, Nov. 18, 1889; Monteiro, *Pesquisas e depoimentos para a historia*, pp. 313-16.

[14] Comte d'Eu to the Condessa de Barral, Pedro d'Orléans Bragança Archives, A, CCVIII, 9337; Lyra, "Quéda do imperio e deposição do Imperador," *Jornal do Commercio*, Nov. 18, 1934.

[15] *Ibid.*; Monteiro, *Pesquisas e depoimentos para a historia*, pp. 271-72.

Presently Dom Pedro entered the salon, walking slowly, with Dr. Motta Maia by his side. For some years his hair and beard had been snowy white; his majestic figure was slightly stooped at the shoulders; and his eyes were now faded to a bluish gray.

"What is this?" he inquired. "Am I to embark at this hour of the night?"

"The government asks that Your Majesty embark before dawn," said Mallet. "It is necessary to do so."

"What government?"

"The government of the republic."

"Deodoro is mixed up in this too, is he?"

"He is; yes, Senhor," Mallet replied. "He is chief of the government."

"Then all have lost their senses," said Dom Pedro.

As for departing at once, he declared, "I am not a fugitive slave. I will not embark at this hour."

But after he had been told of the danger from the military students he ceased protesting.[16]

Last of all came the Empress with one of her ladies. Shortly afterwards, shots were heard in the praça in front of the palace. Mallet, who went to investigate, found that Major Solon Ribeiro had just arrested fifteen sailors from a man-of-war, apparently because they had cheered for the Emperor.[17]

All were now ready, but no one wished to make the first move. Finally, however, Dom Pedro was induced to start down the stairs, and the others slowly followed. When he paused for a moment on the landing, the guards, standing below, presented arms to him, and he recognized the salute.[18] The praça and adjoining streets had been cleared by the military, and there was

---

[16] Escragnolle Taunay, *Pedro II*, p. 93; Monteiro, *Pesquisas e depoimentos para a historia*, pp. 274-75.

[17] Monteiro, *Pesquisas e depoimentos para a historia*, p. 275.

[18] Comte d'Eu to Condessa de Barral, Pedro d'Orléans Bragança Archives, A, CCVIII, 9337; Monteiro, *Pesquisas e depoimentos para a historia*, p. 275.

no demonstration when the imperial family entered the carriage outside, to be driven the short distance to the water's edge, where a launch from the arsenal waited. When there was an attempt to hurry them, Dom Pedro protested. "There is no haste," he said; "we are not fleeing." As he was getting into the carriage he quietly remarked to Mallet and the others, "You men have all lost your heads; you are crazy."[19] The Princess, still worried about her sons, was less calm, and excitedly told Mallet and the others that they would repent their actions.[20] The gray-headed Empress, ill and lame, sobbed brokenly, and the palace employes who had accompanied her to the boat wept with her. Just before she entered the launch, says one writer, the little old lady knelt and silently kissed the soil of the land she had adopted when she came as a bride forty-six years before.[21]

The night was dark and rainy, and the officers in the boat had difficulty in finding the cruiser "Parnahyba," on which the prisoners were to be placed. It was at last reached, after considerable zigzagging about the harbor, but the darkness added to the difficulty of boarding the vessel. When the Emperor, unsteady from weakness, was stepping from the launch to the ship's gangway, he would have fallen into the water but for the quick action of a sailor. Dona Thereza also had difficulty getting aboard, but with aid she and the others reached the deck of the "Parnahyba."[22]

At about four o'clock in the morning came Lieutenant França, the last agent of the provisional government to call upon the Emperor. He boarded the cruiser to bring a copy of the decree regarding the grant of five thousand contos to Dom

---

[19] *Autobiographie de la Comtesse d'Eu*, Pedro d'Orléans Bragança Archives, A, CCIV, 9264; Escragnolle Taunay, *Pedro II*, p. 120; Alvaro Bomilcar, "A partida do Imperador," *Jornal do Commercio*, Nov. 11, 1934.
[20] *Correio Paulistano*, Nov. 18, 1889.
[21] Fleiuss, *Paginas de historia*, p. 399.
[22] Monteiro, *Pesquisas e depoimentos para a historia*, pp. 277-78.

Pedro, and he found him with the members of his family. According to *Novidades* for November, 1889, the conversation between them was as follows.

"The government did me the honor of commissioning me to place in your hands this document, which I hereby present," said França.

"What government?" asked Dom Pedro, as before, thus revealing his contempt for the methods used to bring in the new régime.

"The government of Brazil."

"What is the document?"

"This document," replied the soldier, "is the decree which regulates the future of your family."

"The decree which regulates . . .?" said Dom Pedro doubtfully.

". . . the future of your family," repeated França.

Then, seeing that the dethroned sovereign still hesitated to take the sealed envelope held towards him, França added, "You can accept this document, Senhor; it is very honorable for you individually."

"Very well. Give it here." Dom Pedro took it,[23] and França departed without waiting for a reply.[24]

The dethroned monarch read the paper at once and handed it to Dr. Motta Maia, and he passed it to Prince Gaston. Later, the Prince and the physician agreed that it should be locked in one of the portmanteaus of the Emperor's chamberlain, the Conde de Aljezur.[25]

The fact that Dom Pedro took the envelope offered to him by Lieutenant França seemed to support the story, already in circulation, that he had accepted the five thousand contos and, thus, had abdicated.[26] It is questionable, however, whether

---

[23] *Ibid.*, pp. 322-24; Rangel, *Gastão de Orléans, o ultimo Conde d'Eu*, p. 407.
[24] Rangel, *Gastão de Orléans, o ultimo Conde d'Eu*, p. 407.
[25] *Ibid.*
[26] *Rio News*, Nov. 18, 1889; Adams to Blaine, no. 20, Nov. 19, 1889, no. 21, Nov. 27, 1889, Dept. of State, Despatches, Brazil.

Dom Pedro even knew that the document concerned money, for this was the first governmental communication with him about it—though it is possible that his daughter or son-in-law had mentioned the matter to him. To have accepted the money would have been quite unlike the Emperor; and the best explanation for his failure to send a refusal at once seems to be that the Princess and her husband were reluctant to give up the chance to wipe out the latter's debts by means of part of the sum, for evidently General Lassance's inquiry as to their financial rights under the marriage contract and subsequent legislation had not been definitely answered. It is probable that there was much discussion before the Princess and Comte saw the matter as did the Emperor—if they ever did so. It may be also that after the voyage across the Atlantic began, Dom Pedro got from some of the accompanying friends word of the report that the five thousand contos was the price of exile, and that this led him to an adverse decision; but it is not likely that such a stimulus was needed. In any case, just before reaching the Cape Verde Islands he wrote to Nogueira da Gama as follows:

Having received information, at the moment of departing for Europe, of the decree by which was granted to the imperial family, at one time, the quantity of five thousand contos, I order that you declare that neither I nor my family will receive anything except the settlement and other assets to which we have right under existing laws, agreements, and contracts; and, therefore, if you have received the sum, you must return it without loss of time. I charge you, furthermore, that, complying strictly with the terms of this communication, you order that it be published immediately, and send me a copy of the publication.—D. Pedro de Alcantara. Aboard the Alagôas, approaching S. Vicente, Cape Verde Islands, November 29, 1889.[27]

The message was cabled from São Vicente and was published in *O Paiz* and the *Jornal do Commercio*.[28]

[27] Teixeira, *op. cit.*, pp. 219-20. What seems to be the original draft of the letter, in Dom Pedro's hand, is in the Pedro d'Orléans Bragança Archives, A, CC, 9044.
[28] *Rio News*, Dec. 9, 1889; Teixeira, *op. cit.*, p. 219.

To return to the royal passengers on the "Parnahyba" in Rio Bay—at about nine o'clock on that Sunday morning, Dr. Ramiz Galvão arrived with the three princes—Pedro, now aged fourteen, Luiz, eleven, and Antonio, eight years old—and Frederico Stoll, another of their tutors, who was to go with them to Europe. Accompanying them were André Rebouças, who announced his intention to go into exile with the imperial family,[29] and the Austrian minister, Count Welsersheimb, who came to offer his respects and sympathy.

Welsersheimb, who remained aboard as long as he could, conversing with Dom Pedro and the others, was impressed with the serenity and dignity of the dethroned sovereign. Princess Isabel, though much disturbed by events, was greatly relieved by the arrival of her children and asked the diplomat not to think too badly of her country, for the revolutionaries had acted in a moment of folly. Dona Thereza, however, found it impossible to control her feelings, and, in tearful bewilderment, she repeated, "But what have we done that they should treat us like criminals?"[30]

Towards noon Barão de Ramiz Galvão and the other friends who were to remain behind went ashore, and the "Parnahyba" began to move towards the entrance of the Bay and the open sea. It was bound for Ilha Grande, to the southwest along the coast, where the passengers were to be transferred to the packet "Alagôas," which was to carry them to Portugal. Dom Pedro remained on deck, scarcely taking his gaze from the land. From

---

[29] Rangel, *Gastão de Orléans, o ultimo Conde d'Eu*, p. 404.

Rebouças, a mulatto, who had been one of the most ardent abolitionists, possessed deep sentiment and a sacrificial spirit. He had much love for Dom Pedro, and his admiration for Dona Isabel, because of her share in complete emancipation, almost amounted to worship. When making known his decision to leave Brazil, he stated that abolition had made him the permanent debtor of the Empire and that he would return only when Dom Pedro and the Princess and her sons did so. He kept his word—lived abroad in poverty, and died in the Island of Madeira.—Affonso Celso, in *Contribuições para a Biographia de D. Pedro II*, Pt. I, pp. 894-95.

[30] Lyra, "Quéda do imperio e deposição do Imperador," *Jornal do Commercio*, Nov. 18, 1934.

time to time he chatted about ordinary matters or commented to the captain on some point in the changing panorama, but he did not mention recent political events. For all the concern he seemed to show he might have been a passenger on a day's excursion.[31]

By sunset the "Parnahyba" had reached the island, and after dinner the exiles were transferred by the ship's boats to the "Alagôas," which rode at anchor near by. It was now dark, and the night was rather cloudy, with the occasional gleam of a star. The black silhouettes of the coastal mountains could be faintly seen. Since the water was rough, transferring the passengers was difficult, and Dona Thereza screamed with fright at the rocking of the boat. But they were finally all safe aboard the "Alagôas." The members of the imperial family shook hands with the captain of the "Parnahyba" and Dom Pedro urged him and the other officers to continue to serve their country well. His greatest hope, he added, was to receive word in Europe that there had been no bloodshed in Brazil. Prince Gaston sent back with the "Parnahyba" a farewell letter expressing forgiveness of enemies and affection and best wishes from himself and his family.[32]

The "Alagôas," which had orders not to touch at any point short of São Vicente, Cape Verde Islands, started out a little after midnight, and was followed for a short distance by the "Parnahyba." As dawn was breaking they passed the Bay of Rio de Janeiro, and the Comte called his little boys for a farewell look. Soon the "Parnahyba" was replaced by the "Riachuelo," which trailed and watched the "Alagôas" until November 22, when the packet left Brazilian waters.[33]

The exiles soon settled down for the long voyage. Captain

---

[31] Monteiro, *Pesquisas e depoimentos para a historia*, pp. 283-84.

[32] *Ibid.*, p. 287; Affonso Celso, in Fleiuss, *Contribuições para a Biographia de D. Pedro II*, Pt. I, p. 892; Escragnolle Taunay, *Pedro II*, p. 105.

[33] Monteiro, *Pesquisas e depoimentos para a historia*, pp. 287, 294-96; Rangel, *Gastão de Orléans, o ultimo Conde d'Eu*, p. 408; *Rio News*, Nov. 18, Dec. 2, 1889.

Pessoa of the "Alagôas" offered his cabin to Dom Pedro, who, however, declined it, for he was afraid of the wintry cold of northern waters, and he took quarters below, where he was made as comfortable as possible. At his invitation, the captain and the two marine officers who had been ordered by the provisional government to accompany the dethroned monarch to Europe had their meals at the same table as he and his family. The two officers at first tried to avoid the exiles, but the Emperor ignored this and chatted with them about matters unconnected with the revolution.[34] While the route followed the coast he spent much of the daytime sitting on deck looking at the land or gazing wistfully after passing vessels bound for Brazil.

The last part of his native soil that he saw was the island of Fernando de Noronha, one hundred and twenty-five miles east of the mainland. This was passed on November 24. After its outline was entirely lost to view, his grandson, the fourteen-year-old Dom Pedro de Alcantara, suggested that a message be sent back by one of the pigeons from the ship's supplies. It was a welcome idea. The Emperor wrote on a paper, "Saudades do Brasil!" (Dear, wistful remembrances to Brazil!) which, when signed by all, was tied to the bird. But the pigeon, after fluttering around for a few moments, beaten by the wind, sank under the waves, carrying with it the last loving message of the exiles. The incident left a depressing effect upon the family.[35]

Of more concern to the Emperor, however, was the condition of his eldest grandson, Prince Pedro Augusto. The young man, now twenty-three years old, had been trained as a mining engineer and showed considerable promise, for he was fond of learning and, unlike his brother, who had been a cause of worry

---

[34] Monteiro, *Pesquisas e depoimentos para a historia*, p. 301; Affonso Celso, in *Contribuições para a Biographia de D. Pedro II*, Pt. I, p. 895; d'Orléans Bragança, *op. cit.*, p. 12.

[35] Monteiro, *Pesquisas e depoimentos para a historia*, pp. 296-97, 309. Information confirmed by Dom Pedro d'Orléans Bragança.

BANISHMENT OF THE IMPERIAL FAMILY 355

to Dom Pedro II,[36] was steady in his habits. But he had shown occasional signs of mental unbalance,[37] which were greatly aggravated by the revolution. A new attack, which began on November 17, took the form of a mania of fear, which was especially pronounced while the "Riachuelo" followed the "Alagôas." There was talk of locking him up, but instead he was placed under two guards.[38]

During the voyage Dona Isabel continued bitter over what had happened, but the Empress, while sorrowing over her exile, was calmer. One day, talking with the captain, she mentioned the fate of Emperor Maximilian of Mexico, Dom Pedro's cousin, and of his wife Carlota, who was her own cousin. Then, referring to the plight of herself and her family, she added, "It might have been worse."[39] Prince Gaston preserved the calm which he had shown from the first, and supervised his sons with strict discipline, requiring that they follow a regular schedule for lessons and recreation.[40]

The Emperor spent much of the time in reading from a collection of recent books which Barão de Loreto had, at his request, gathered to be taken along. One of them was Chandordy's *La France en 1889*, in which he wrote many marginal notes. Regarding the authority given the French president in the effort to eliminate corruption, Dom Pedro commented, "How much it cost not to have that in Brazil!"[41] In another connection he remarked, "It is easy to be a profound statesman *post factum*."[42] He also mentioned on one margin that he in-

---

[36] Teixeira, *op. cit.*, pp. 157-58; *Rio News*, Nov. 15, 1886.
[37] Monteiro, *Pesquisas e depoimentos para a historia*, p. 301.
[38] *Ibid.*, pp. 285-86, 298-301; Escragnolle Taunay, *Pedro II*, pp. 92-93. His mind improved after he reached Europe, but later he became permanently afflicted. He died in 1934.—Escragnolle Taunay, "Dom Pedro Augusto de Saxe Coburgo Gotha," *Jornal do Commercio*, Sept. 30, 1934.
[39] Monteiro, *Pesquisas e depoimentos para a historia*, pp. 303-4.
[40] *Ibid.*, p. 304.
[41] P. 35. The annotated copy of the book is in the library of the Instituto Historico e Geographico Brasileiro in Rio.   [42] P. 65.

tended to write, when he had time, of his relations with notable people, such as Frederick Wilhelm of Germany.[43] His last note, at the end of the book, was "28th of November, 1889, aboard the "Alagôas," on the way. . . ."[44]

Dom Pedro also talked for hours on end with André Rebouças, who was avoided by most of the others, because, though talented, he was rather bizarre in manners, and they resented his attaching himself to them.[45] He also conversed often with the captain outside of meal times. And with both Pessoa and Rebouças he discussed the revolution, though he did not like the members of his family to bring it up, and usually he changed the subject when they did so. His belief that the events of November 15 were the result of a minority movement, which most of the people regretted, gave him much comfort.[46] To him, exile was far worse than loss of his throne, and he told Pessoa that he thought he might have saved himself from it, if, on November 15, instead of going to Rio he had retreated to the interior.[47] Asked by the captain whether he would return promptly if the republic failed by a counter-revolt, he replied, "Yes; if they call me, I will return."[48]

Pessoa also reported that the Emperor's famous memory had seemed admirably preserved, and that he had seen in him no signs of the mental decline about which there had been so much talk for some time before the revolution.[49] Indeed, the pithy comments inspired by Chandordy's book seem sufficient evidence that Dom Pedro had not lost much intellectual vigor.

On the morning of November 30 the "Alagôas" reached the dreary island of São Vicente, where the Portuguese authorities

[43] Pp. 215-16.   [44] P. 280.
[45] Monteiro, *Pesquisas e depoimentos para a historia*, pp. 302-3.
[46] Dom Pedro II, Exponho exactamente o que commigo se passou nos dias de Novembro, Pedro d'Orléans Bragança Archives, A, CC, 9043.
[47] Autobiographie de la Comtesse d'Eu, Pedro d'Orléans Bragança Archives, A, CCIV, 9264; Monteiro, *Pesquisas e depoimentos para a historia*, p. 302.
[48] Monteiro, *Pesquisas e depoimentos para a historia*, p. 302.
[49] *Ibid.*, p. 30.

saluted with twenty-one guns.[50] Close behind the packet came the German vessel, the "Montevideo," on which Ouro Preto and his son the Conde de Affonso Celso had been sent into exile. Affonso Celso, who had for many years been a republican, blaming and attacking the Emperor for most of the national ills, had become a contrite monarchist as a result of the revolution,[51] and was now anxious to pay his respects to the throneless monarch, who, with some of the others, had gone ashore. The health officer of the port would not, however, let any one land from the "Montevideo," but he carried to Dom Pedro a disinfected message from Ouro Preto. Some hours afterwards the Barão de Loreto brought a reply, in which the Emperor said, "Console yourself, as I do, in trying to serve Brazil in whatever part of the world you may be."[52] In the afternoon, the two vessels parted, with waving of handkerchiefs, the German one leaving a little before the other.[53]

By December 2, the "Alagôas" was so far north as to encounter cold, stormy weather, and Dona Thereza, who was a poor sailor, was sick in bed. But it was Dom Pedro's sixty-fourth birthday, and it was celebrated as well as possible. All joined in a written tribute to him, and the Barão de Loreto composed a sonnet in his honor. Dona Isabel and the Comte wrote him a special letter of good wishes; and from their sons came the following note:

Dear Grand Daddy: We have no flowers here to offer you on this day which is so dear to us; but, as always, we offer you our hearts.
Your little grandsons, who love you very much,
Pedro,
Luiz,
Antonio.
Aboard the steamship *Alagôas*, December 2, 1889. [54]

[50] Affonso Celso, O Imperador no exilio, pp. 6-9.
[51] Ibid., p. 5.   [52] Ibid., pp. 8-12.   [53] Ibid., p. 12.
[54] Pedro d'Orléans Bragança Archives, A, CCVI, 9318.

At the birthday banquet, prepared at Captain Pessoa's orders from the best to be had in the ship's stores, the Emperor drank to the prosperity of Brazil.[55]

After a voyage of almost three weeks, the "Alagôas" approached its destination,[56] and Dom Pedro made preparations for disembarking. On looking over the list of employes to whom tips were to be given, he missed the name of the man who cared for the vessel's livestock, and instructed that he not be forgotten.[57]

As the "Alagôas" neared Lisbon on December 7, King Carlos[58] and his court came out on the Tagus in the royal ceremonial barges to meet his dethroned kinsman. Dom Pedro declined the King's invitation to occupy apartments in one of his palaces, because he was not in a position to reciprocate. But Dona Isabel, thinking of the greater comfort to be had for all through accepting, begged her father—whom she repeatedly addressed as "Papa"—to take advantage of the offered hospitality. The Emperor, however, bluntly replied, "It doesn't help to 'Papa' me; I won't accept it, and I won't go."[59] He likewise refused exemption from the customary inspection of baggage. The first to disembark, he walked with difficulty and, to the press reporters, seemed feeble. Though he had been outwardly serene during the voyage, his physical appearance betrayed the mental suffering he had undergone. The Empress likewise was weak, and her lameness was very apparent as King Carlos helped her ashore.[60]

---

[55] Affonso Celso, *O Imperador no exilio*, pp. 79-81.
[56] The poor progress was caused by the fact that the "Riachuelo," which was practically unseaworthy, was very slow, and that the "Alagôas" had been ordered to keep within sight of her.—Monteiro, *Pesquisas e depoimentos para a historia*, pp. 295-96.
[57] *Ibid.*, pp. 308-9.
[58] The great-nephew of Dom Pedro. His father, King Luiz, had died about six weeks before, and Carlos was not yet crowned.
[59] Monteiro, *Pesquisas e depoimentos para a historia*, p. 304.
Translated literally, he said, "It is not 'Papa,' nor a half 'Papa,'" which has no meaning in English.
[60] *Jornal de Noticias* (Oporto), Dec. 8, 1889.

With the newspaper men who crowded around him, hoping for a sensational pronouncement, Dom Pedro chatted about the landscape and Portuguese literature, but he declined to comment on the revolution. When asked, however, whether he would issue a manifesto regarding recent developments in Brazil, he replied,

"Why should I? My *life* is my manifesto."[61]

[61] Affonso Celso, in *Contribuições para a Biographia de D. Pedro II*, Pt. I, pp. 895-96.

XIX

DOM PEDRO IN EXILE

AFTER GOING in public hacks to pray at the Church of São Vicente de Fóra, where many of their ancestors had been buried, the exiles established themselves at the Hotel Bragança. Here, George B. Loring, the American minister, vacated an apartment for the greater accommodation of the Emperor. Writing John Greenleaf Whittier about him, Loring said: "He looks very old, has no light or joy in his face, and dwells on the past with touching devotion. He talks of you and Longfellow and Agassiz, and Alexander Agassiz and Quincy Shaw, as if you had all been his brothers."[1]

Ouro Preto and his son, having transferred in the Canaries to a vessel bound for Lisbon, reached there on December 14, and, at Dom Pedro's request, went to see him at once. To Affonso Celso, the exile seemed resigned to the loss of his throne, and referred to his plans for study and for visits in Portugal. When there was mention of the possibility of his restoration, he interrupted with—"I shall never conspire to return, and I do not want any one to conspire in my name; but, if they call me spontaneously, I shall not hesitate a second: I shall go at once and with pleasure."[2]

Dona Thereza, however, who was just recovering from an attack of influenza, was not reconciled. With tears in her eyes and her voice, she repeated her old question: "But what wrong did we do those people that they should treat us so? ... I do not know what crime I committed against those people whom I love so much. It came in such an unexpected manner! I did not know that they hated us. ... I feel so friendly towards

[1] Pickard, *op. cit.*, II, 743-44; *Jornal de Noticias*, Dec. 8, 1889.
[2] Affonso Celso, *O Imperador no exilio*, pp. 12-14.

Brazil! I shall never forget it. . . . I have had such longings for everything, for all. I want to end my days in Brazil."[3]

When Ouro Preto and Affonso Celso were calling on him, December 20, the Emperor commented upon a manifesto to the Brazilians regarding the events of November 15 which the former minister had published through the *Commercio de Portugal*. He approved most of it, but thought that Ouro Preto had not been just to Maracajú, and he feared that those reading the communication might get a wrong impression regarding the part played by the Minister of War. He was very hesitant, he said, to believe conscious, premeditated treason on the part of certain people, and he did not think Maracajú had been guilty of treason. With this last Ouro Preto agreed.[4]

A day or two later there came from the provisional government at Rio the cabled copy of a decree issued on December 21, after it had received Dom Pedro's refusal of the five thousand contos. This declared Dom Pedro and his family banished from Brazil; ordered that within two years they dispose of all the property in real estate possessed there; revoked the grant of five thousand contos; and also declared ended, as of December 15, 1889, the regular income which the imperial family had received from the public treasury.[5]

Since the Emperor had refused the five thousand, the revocation of that grant was merely an empty form. The cancellation of the imperial civil list, however, though natural, was of serious import, since it left the exiles with decidedly limited funds. Dom Pedro's only remaining source of revenue—income from property inherited from his father—was not only small, but uncertain, for he had long been opposed to having any one "harassed or oppressed for the sake of getting the rents collected."[6]

[3] *Ibid.*, pp. 14-15.
[4] *Ibid.*, pp. 15-17. Maracajú's reply is given in Ouro Preto, *op. cit.*, pp. 186-211.
[5] "Traços biographicos de D. Pedro II," *Rev. do Inst. Hist. e Geog. Bras.*, vol. 152, pp. 660-61.
[6] C. B. Ottoni, *D. Pedro de Alcantara*, p. 59.

He protested to the republican authorities against the order to sell his landed property in Brazil, and apparently remained undisturbed in his possession of it.[7] But for the rest of his life he was financially handicapped, and at times he lacked the money needed to pay regular bills. At least twice he got loans from the Visconde de Andrade Machado, a wealthy Portuguese who had spent many years in Brazil.[8] Though he received offers of palaces from various European sovereigns, he declined them all and spent most of his time living in hotels.[9] Since he cared but little for money, his chief concern over lack of it came from the fact that he had so little to give to charity and to other worthy causes.[10]

After about two weeks in Lisbon, Dom Pedro and Dona Thereza left for Coimbra, since the festivities connected with the coronation of King Carlos would soon begin, and they did not wish to cast a shadow over them by the presence of a dethroned uncle.[11] A number of the other exiles, including Affonso Celso, were at the railroad station to see them off, and to them the Empress still expressed longing for Brazil, adding that she felt farther away from there every minute. Apparently she had not yet been told of the decree of banishment recently passed by the provisional government.[12]

At the University of Coimbra Dom Pedro found a considerable number of young Brazilians, upon whom he urged the

---

[7] After the departure of the imperial family there seems to have been considerable looting of their movable possessions; furniture and valuables of various sorts are commonly reported to have found their way into other hands without compensation.—(Escragnolle Taunay, *Pedro II*, pp. 158-59.) There are stories still afloat in Brazil regarding this pillaging.

[8] *Ibid.*, pp. 96, 97, 106-7; Motta Maia, *op. cit.*, pp. 296-97, 310-12, 319-23.

The second loan was asked after he had failed to get aid from Rothschild's, who wanted Princess Isabel and the Comte to assume responsibility, as Dom Pedro's heirs, for payment of the debt. This they were unwilling to do because of their own financial limitations.—Escragnolle Taunay, *Pedro II*, p. 118.

[9] Affonso Celso, in Fleiuss, *Contribuições para a historia de D. Pedro II*, Pt. I, p. 898.

[10] Affonso Celso, *O Imperador no exilio*, pp. 85-91.

[11] *Ibid.*, p. 17; *Jornal de Noticias*, Dec. 25, 1889.

[12] Affonso Celso, *O Imperador no exilio*, pp. 17-18.

importance of studying hard for the sake of their native land. The new régime was experimental, he reminded them, and they must work hard to keep the country from being dismembered and to preserve the glory of Brazil. "You must maintain that great legacy united and strong," he is reported to have said; "you must make happy the land which I left free from slaves."[13]

From Coimbra, they went to Oporto, where, when Dom Pedro was at the academy of fine arts on the afternoon of December 28, a new calamity befell him. Receiving word that the Empress was in a coma, he hurried back to the hotel where they were staying, and found her already dead, from lesion of the heart. Her last words were, "Brazil, my beautiful land! I cannot return there."[14]

Great was the grief of Dom Pedro who, during their many years together, had developed for his wife a deep appreciation and a tender attachment. Her death, he said, was a heavier blow than the loss of his crown. The fact that Dona Isabel and her husband were absent visiting in Spain made the bereavement harder to bear.[15] His self discipline caused him to turn to his diary almost at once, to unburden his anguished soul; for he would not give way before others; and he made this entry:

> I do not know how I can write. A half hour ago the Empress, that saint, died! . . . No one can imagine my affliction. I can only weep the lost happiness of forty-six years. I cannot say more. It is hard for me to write, but I must not collapse. I do not know what I shall do now. Only study will console me in my woe.
> It is hard for me to believe. I always wanted to precede her in death. It has produced an emptiness in my life which I do not know how to fill. I must wait to embrace my daughter! . . . Nothing can express how much I have lost! . . . No one knows

---

[13] *Collectanea Rabello*, III, 395.

[14] Affonso Celso, in *Contribuições para a Biographia de D. Pedro II*, Pt. I, pp. 899-901; Heitor Lyra, "Exilio e morte do Imperador," *Jornal do Commercio*, Jan. 5, 1936.

[15] Autobiographie de la Comtesse d'Eu, Pedro d'Orléans Bragança Archives, A, CCIV, 9264; *Jornal de Noticias*, Dec. 29, 1889.

how good she was, and how the sufferings of others meant more to her than her own. Like her god-mother, the Queen of Savoy, she deserves to be sanctified. . . . I am certain that in Brazil they will feel as I do.[16]

I want to read, but cannot. . . . What did she do that she had to suffer for me? . . . I wish that my daughter would come.[17]

Ouro Preto and Affonso Celso received word in Lisbon of Dona Thereza's death, and hurried to Oporto. Here they found Dom Pedro, in a desolate hotel room, reading a new edition of Dante's *Divina Commedia*. He embraced his former Prime Minister and seated the two callers close beside him. And after some minutes of sorrowful silence, he began to talk about the poem before him, in which he found consolation. Ouro Preto, in confused embarrassment, presently asked,

"And you are not thinking of returning to Brazil?"

"I am banished, Senhor," said Dom Pedro.

Later, the talk turned to Oporto, and he suggested places for them to visit there. Only when they were leaving did he mention the Empress; then he told them that her body lay in an adjoining room, where mass would be performed the next morning at eight o'clock.[18]

A few minutes after they had departed, Affonso Celso returned for his hat, which he had dropped at the entrance to the imperial apartments. Glancing in, he saw the Emperor, his face in his hands, weeping; the tears, trickling between his fingers and down his snowy beard, were falling upon the strophes of Dante's poem.[19]

One of the finest of Dom Pedro's sonnets is "Na Morte da Imperatriz" ("On the Death of the Empress"), written in Jan-

---

[16] In spite of the recently-established censorship of the Brazilian press, the *Jornal do Commercio* of Rio published on December 29 a eulogy of the Empress in which it stated that during the forty-six years she had lived in Brazil no one had uttered her name except in praise and appreciation.

[17] Lyra, "Exilio e morte do Imperador," *Jornal do Commercio*, Jan. 5, 1936.

[18] Affonso Celso, *O Imperador no exilio*, pp. 21-24.

[19] *Ibid.*, p. 24.

Dom Pedro II and Dr. Motta Maia at the Hotel Beauséjour, Cannes, 1890

From a photograph

Empress Thereza in Old Age

From a painting at the Château d'Eu

uary, 1890. It is a tender and beautiful tribute. After likening her death to the snapping of a harp string, he addressed her as

"The gentle companion of fortune and exile,
And the true half of my saddened soul."

Separated from an august and ancient trunk and transplanted to Brazilian soil, he wrote, she had formed there an hospitable shade in which every unfortunate found refuge. After referring to the ingratitude and suffering which she had recently experienced, he concluded with

"Mother of the people, your martyrdom is ended;
Daughter of kings, you have won a great throne!"[20]

Shortly after the body of Dona Thereza had been laid away among the Bragança dead in São Vicente de Fóra in Lisbon, Dom Pedro went to Cannes, in southern France, where he spent most of the time thereafter. Over the door of his apartment in the Hotel Beauséjour was his name, "D. Pedro de Alcantara."[21] With him were Dr. Motta Maia and his family and a few others, among them, the Barão de Penedo, who was representing the Empire in Paris when the revolution came.

Mucio Teixeira, who was then Brazilian consul in Venezuela, had at once resigned and asked permission to serve the Emperor in exile. His former patron and protector had written—

"I accept the sacrifice of Penedo, because he is old and rich; I refuse yours, because you are young and poor. Our country needs talents such as yours. Serve the Republic with the same devotion as that with which you served the Empire. Forms of government are mere questions of aesthetics. . . ."[22]

To his grandson, Prince Augusto Leopoldo, who was absent on a naval cruise when the dethronement came and had cabled from Ceylon for instructions, the exile had sent a similar answer:

[20] Teixeira, *op. cit.*, pp. 96-97.
[21] José Pires Brandão, "O Imperador no exilio," *Collectanea Rabello*, IV, 515.
[22] Teixeira, *op. cit.*, p. 194.

"Serve Brazil. Affectionate greetings. Your grandfather, Pedro."[23]

Though he was greatly relieved to learn that no serious bloodshed had resulted from the change of régime in Brazil, Dom Pedro was much hurt when he found how readily most officers of the Empire had recognized the new order and sought its favor. Only two men in the foreign service, he wrote Mucio Teixeira—himself and Penedo—had shown him any proofs of esteem and a willingness to sacrifice social position to duties of the heart.[24]

Barão de Ladario, loyal but tactless, after recovering from his wounds, sent Dom Pedro a long letter of painful details about defections. The first Brazilian to telegraph from Europe congratulating Deodoro for having "liberated the patria from oppression," wrote Ladario, was Barão de Teffé, who had received special consideration from the Emperor. Various others whom Ladario mentioned by name as having shown much promptness in lining up with the republic were likewise indebted to Dom Pedro. "In the civil class, Senhor," wrote the blunt Barão, "we see the same disgraceful desertions—councilors of state, senators, deputies, and high functionaries silently witnessing the revolt and the change of institutions which they had sworn to maintain."[25]

But this account seems not to have hurt the Emperor as did the first shock of the revolution, when he found himself imprisoned in the City Palace. He had then composed a sonnet, "Ingratos" ("Ingrates"), in which he said that what cut him to the heart at being torn from the throne when but a few feet from the grave was the fact that it was done by those who, before, had kissed his hand in adulation.[26] This seems to be the only strong condemnation of the revolutionary leaders ever uttered by him.

[23] Lyra, "Exilio e morte do Imperador," *Jornal do Commercio*, Jan. 5, 1936.
[24] Teixeira, *op. cit.*, p. 194.
[25] Lyra, "Exilio e morte do Imperador," *Jornal do Commercio*, Jan. 5, 1936.
[26] Um Brasileiro, *Sonetos do exilio*, p. 15; Motta Maia, *op. cit.*, pp. 356-57.

Thereafter, he took an impersonal and forgiving attitude. Repeatedly, he excused the revolutionaries and minimized what had happened, at times citing history to show that the occurrences in Brazil were not exceptional. When Francisco Cunha, a journalist who had attacked him bitterly, appeared in Paris as agent of the republican government, he invited him to call, and received him cordially.[27] After Benjamin Constant died, much disillusioned,[28] early in 1891, and, according to report that reached the exiles, insane, Dom Pedro said,

"Poor man! I knew him well and appreciated him. I really believe that he had recently suffered mental disturbances. That would explain his treatment of me, to whom he had shown himself so attached. Cultivated intellect, pure heart! I do not think that ambition lured him."[29]

Although, as head of Brazil, the Emperor was repeatedly criticised as too unwilling to believe evil of others and too inclined to forgive, nevertheless, for nineteen centuries readiness to turn the other cheek had, in theory, been counted a high Christian virtue. Therefore, when Dom Pedro's capacity for rising superior to personal resentment, severely tested by his overthrow and exile, stood firm, and even seemed to increase, his friends named him "the Magnanimous."

Despite his charity towards the revolutionary leaders, however, he felt deeply the ingratitude that was in many cases combined with disloyalty to oaths of office. But some balm for his wounds came from the messages he received from distinguished people in many lands expressing high regard for him and indignation over the way he had been treated.

---

[27] Um Brasileiro, *Sonetos do exilio*, p. 14; Affonso Celso, *O Imperador no exilio*, pp. 39-40; Lyra, "Exilio e morte do Imperador," *Jornal do Commercio*, Jan. 5, 1936.

[28] After the imperial family had embarked for exile, Benjamin Constant said, "The saddest of our duties is completed." (José Maria Moreira Guimarães, "O Imperador e o exercito," *Collectanea Rabello*, IV, 519.) Several months later, meeting Visconde Taunay, he spoke bitterly about developments after the revolution, saying that he had counted upon sincere patriotism but, instead, had found only selfishness and greed.—Escragnolle Taunay, *Reminiscencias*, pp. 216-17.

[29] Affonso Celso, *O Imperador no exilio*, p. 60.

Furthermore, loss of his throne brought certain compensations: now, his occupations were entirely congenial. Though he was ill for several weeks early in 1890, he devoted considerable time, when his health permitted, to the study of Tupí, Hebrew, Arabic, and Sanskrit with Dr. Seybold.[30] His volume of *Poésies hebraïco provençales* was published in 1891. It was during his exile also that he made his plan for a universal language which Max Muller approved.[31]

There was time also for less heavy pleasures. He read extensively in many fields, attended lectures and concerts as avidly as of yore, corresponded with various Brazilians and numerous foreign intellectuals,[32] and received calls from friends and from strangers who were bound to him by scholarly interests.

He was very popular in Cannes, and was well known in bookshops and in flowershops, where he chose the finest blossoms to send to his daughter. Little children smiled at his approach and ran to kiss his hand, and often followed him to his hotel. Dona Isabel, who spent part of the year in Cannes, frequently dined with him.[33]

Dr. José Pires Brandão gives a few glimpses of the Emperor in Cannes during a visit to him there. Ferreira Vianna, a former cabinet member and a charming personality, was also a guest and did much towards cheering the spirits of the exile. One day Princess Isabel, who had taken dinner with them, sat near by crocheting and chatting with her friend the Baroneza de São Joaquim about literature, history, and politics, while her father played billiards with Ferreira Vianna, and played the game well. Occasionally he left the billiard table to join in the women's conversation and express his views. Another time, when they were discussing Cannes, Pires Brandão praised its

---

[30] Pedro d'Orléans Bragança Archives, B, XXXVII, 1057; Escragnolle Taunay, *Pedro II*, pp. 97, 99, 100. [31] See p. 254 of this book.

[32] The Comte de Gobineau had died in 1882, but his daughter Diane, Baroness de Guldencrone, wrote to the Emperor. Her letters to him are in the Pedro d'Orléans Bragança Archives at the Château d'Eu, France.

[33] Pires Brandão, "O Imperador no exilio," *Collectanea Rabello*, IV, 515.

climate and beauty, at which Dom Pedro quickly remarked, "Those who have Petropolis don't need to exalt Cannes."[34] The chance to stroll once more in his lovely garden amidst the majestic Organ Mountains would have meant more to him then than the whole land of France.

Silveira Martins who, while in exile, visited the Emperor in Baden-Baden gives a further illustration of his loyalty to Brazil. Dom Pedro took his guest to an especially notable concert, and when the dethroned monarch appeared the distinguished audience spontaneously rose to its feet, and the director sent him a copy of the program. The Emperor was moved by the demonstration, but he remarked to his guest, "It is not for me, but for our Brazil."

"As a most eloquent protest," added Silveira Martins.[35]

In September, 1890, Dom Pedro went to Paris to visit the Brazilian Conde de Nioac, formerly his chamberlain. Affonso Celso, who was there at the time, noted the contrast between the Emperor's broken physical condition and halting step and his alert, hungry mind. For he was engaged in an almost constant round of intellectual pleasures, and was likely to be found at every place where progressive ideas were being set forth.[36]

He was the despair of his devoted friend and chamberlain, the Conde de Aljezur, who confided his worries to Affonso Celso. After referring to the Emperor's worn appearance, Aljezur explained:

He spent the entire night in reading old books and in taking notes. He did not rest twenty minutes. And now, in a little while, we leave here to go through no-one-knows-what library. I am tired of telling him that it is not the life for one of his age. He will surely be sick again. Do try to convince him that he must not work so hard, and without necessity.[37]

[34] *Ibid.*; Serrano, *Historia do Brasil*, p. 525.
[35] José Pires Brandão, "O Imperador em Baden-Baden e a visita de Silveira Martins," *Rev. do Inst. Hist. e Geog. Bras.*, vol. 152, pp. 882-83.
[36] Affonso Celso, *O Imperador no exilio*, pp. 31-34; Motta Maia, *op. cit.*, p. 310.
[37] *Ibid.*, p. 33.

But the ex-republican, who, after he was exiled, finally came to know the Emperor, and now almost adored him, apparently did not try to abate his intellectual pursuits. He may have thought it would be futile; but he doubtless realized that Dom Pedro's assiduity came partly from his determination not to let disappointments and sorrows dominate him, and to prevent harassing memories and futile regrets from haunting his pillow.

One day Dom Pedro told Affonso Celso that Paris was not enough to keep him busy; that he had sought and failed to find publications about Brazil, regarding which he always longed for more and more information. No one seemed to remember to send them to him. By now, Deodoro had swept aside most of the liberties which the Emperor had struggled to preserve, and Affonso Celso explained that, since the dictatorship had been set up no information and intellectual works had been published in Brazil. The Emperor at once saw a possible silver lining to the cloud, and said, "The change could bring this advantage, at least: it could stimulate the imagination, encourage literary production, widen literary horizons, reveal rich, unexplored possibilities. . . . We shall see. . . . We shall see."[38]

Always popular in Paris, the loss of his throne made him more so. His mail was enormous, with letters, invitations, gifts from authors of their writings, and tributes of many kinds. His receiving hours were short, but in his guest book were thousands of names, including not only the most distinguished in France, but also the élite of Europe in all fields of culture.[39] He was especially touched by a visit of a commission from a scientific society. "You cannot imagine," he remarked after they left, "how pleased I am at being remembered by those gentlemen."[40]

His prestige and popularity were capitalized for various purposes. At the request of Dr. Henri Huchard, a celebrated Paris physician, he visited a very up-to-date hospital.

[38] *Ibid.*, p. 34.   [39] *Ibid.*, p. 35.
[40] Corrêa, in *Jornal do Brasil*, Dec. 2, 1924.

"The visit of His Majesty," said Huchard, "will call attention and public sympathy to the establishment, with advantage to the innovations introduced there."

At eight o'clock on a rainy morning Dom Pedro started out to go through the institution; and he roused much interest by the thoroughness with which he examined it and by the knowledge he displayed of what he saw there.[41]

Affonso Celso tells how in one case the Emperor even let another impose upon him rather than offend. A literary Mussulman who was a pasha announced a lecture on Oriental literature and stated in connection with it that His Majesty Dom Pedro de Alcantara would honor the occasion with his presence. Before the program began Dom Pedro appeared, accompanied by two members of the French Institute, and was observed with curiosity mingled with respect. Two little girls presented him with a bouquet tied with the Brazilian green and yellow, and he was seated in the section of honor. To Affonso Celso, whom he invited to sit near him, he murmured, smiling,

"Prepare yourself for a regular bore. I know this pasha and have already heard him. He has much good will—excellent intentions—, nothing else. . . . I came because he invited me very insistently, and to have refused would have offended. As you see, I am not entirely freed from the old perquisites."

"Sure enough," wrote Affonso Celso, "for almost two hours the Mussulman, with unheard of cruelty, martyrized the patience of the Christians there assembled."[42]

At a dinner party attended by Affonso Celso at the Conde de Nioac's Dom Pedro appeared unusually light-hearted, even playful in mood. He asked Affonso Celso whether he had heard the lecture on the reform of the Church by Jacintho Loyson, adding that he had missed the announcement, else he would have gone. Dona Isabel expressed herself as shocked at her father's heretical tendencies.

[41] Affonso Celso, *O Imperador no exilio*, pp. 35-37.
[42] *Ibid.*, pp. 37-38.

"Why not?" retorted Dom Pedro. "The ex-priest Jacintho aims to regenerate the Church, not to destroy it. To go and listen to him does not signify that one subscribes to his ideas, or gives force to his propaganda. With full knowledge of the matter one can more easily combat it. Besides, he is an intelligent man, a celebrated orator, well informed, and moved by earnestness of purpose. Don't you want to know about things? As for me, I would not hesitate to go to hear the Devil himself if he undertook to give public lectures."

"Oh! Papa!"

"Yes, Madam, the Devil in person," declared her father. "I should be extremely curious to hear what he had to say, especially about revolutions."

Even the Princess joined in the laughter that followed.[43]

The Emperor so enjoyed Paris that he wished to stay on; but the winter threatened to be unusually severe, so on the advice of his physicians and the pleadings of his friends, he returned to the south. He was back in Cannes in time to preside at the November examinations of the Institut Stanislaus, which were taken by his grandsons Pedro de Alcantara and Luiz and also by Manoel and Oscar da Motta Maia, the sons of his physician. To Oscar, the Emperor gave a premium, or souvenir, for his ability, consisting of a folder in which he had written quotations in twelve different languages each one emphasizing the importance of learning. That in English was Jeremy Taylor's, "Knowledge is the wing wherewith we fly to Heaven," which had been a part of his own education.[44]

In spite of Dom Pedro's varied occupations and his intemperate amount of reading, Brazil and its welfare was almost constantly in his thoughts. Shortly after he returned to Cannes he read of the recent experiments of Dr. Robert Koch, the bacteriologist, in Berlin, and at once he telegraphed Pasteur asking that a supply of the Koch vaccine be sent to the Santa

[43] *Ibid.*, pp. 40-41.
[44] Teixeira, *op. cit.*, pp. 103-7, 199-201.

Casa de Misericórdia, a large hospital in Rio.[45] In a letter to Visconde Taunay he showed all of his former interest in fostering immigration, but expressed opposition to bringing Chinese coolies to Brazil.[46] After a course of reading on political economy, he admitted that he was less of a free-trader than formerly, since the world trend was towards protection.[47] The dispute over the Missions Territory, which had been a matter of concern to him early in 1889, disturbed him much after the revolution, for the Argentine government had taken advantage of the weakness of the Brazilian provisional authorities and induced them to sign a new treaty agreeing to divide by a mean line the area in dispute.[48] Over this arrangement Dom Pedro was distressed and indignant.

"It was my sacred duty," he said, "to conserve Brazilian unity and territorial integrity. Our greatness rests on that indivisible homogeneity. I can't see why the people who govern don't understand that. . . ."[49] It was a great relief to him when, on August 10, 1891, the Brazilian congress rejected the arrangement, thus throwing the two countries back on the treaty of arbitration, which was the last international agreement that he, as Emperor, had signed.[50]

Though the exiled sovereign repeatedly declared that he would not conspire to return or countenance conspiracy,[51] he greatly longed to go back; and for more than a year he probably thought that he would be called home; but after the republican

---

[45] Dom Pedro to Louis Pasteur, Nov. 24, 1890, Inst. Hist. e Geog. Bras., case 396, no. 18, 405F.
[46] Roure, in *Contribuições para a Biographia de D. Pedro II*, Pt. I, p. 737.
[47] Affonso Celso, *O Imperador no exilio*, p. 49.
[48] Williams, "The Treaty of Tordesillas and the Argentine-Brazilian Boundary Settlement," *Hisp. Amer. Hist. Rev.*, V (Feb., 1922), 20.
[49] Affonso Celso, *O Imperador no exilio*, pp. 56-57.
[50] Williams, "The Treaty of Tordesillas and the Argentine-Brazilian Boundary Settlement," *Hisp. Amer. Hist. Rev.*, V (Feb., 1922), 20.
The award of President Grover Cleveland, made in 1895, was in favor of Brazil's claims.
[51] See pp. 360, 376, 379 of this book; also Affonso Celso, *O Imperador no exilio*, pp. 57-58.

constitution was adopted in February, 1891, he apparently lost hope.

Various things he did now show his adjustment to this conviction and preparation for his own passing. In April, 1891, while he was still at Cannes, he wrote his "Fé de Officio do Imperador do Brasil," which is the result of an examination of his reign and, to some extent, of his life, before the tribunal of conscience. It begins with, "I believe in God"; then summarizes what he achieved and aspired to achieve during his reign, and concludes with, "Scientific preoccupations and constant study consoled me and preserved me amidst moral tempests."[52] He sent a copy of the document to his loyal friend Visconde Taunay, who arranged for its publication in Rio de Janeiro, and it appeared on the front page of the *Jornal do Commercio* for May 28, 1891.

Later, writing to Taunay to thank him for taking care of the matter, he referred to the "Fé de Officio" as his confession before the Brazilian nation; and he added, "Posterity, noting my intentions, will absolve me from my errors."[53] A little before this, speaking to some Brazilian callers, he said, "History will do me justice; that is my consolation."[54] Earlier, he had hoped for vindication through being recalled to leadership in Brazil; now, he looked to the slower, but more certain, grinding of the mills of the gods.

In July, 1891, the Emperor disposed of various personal belongings, with the aid of a commission and of Alfredo de Escragnolle Taunay.[55] His numismatical and geological collections he gave to the Brazilian National Museum. His most cherished possession, the fine library which he so much missed

---

[52] Escragnolle Taunay, *Pedro II*, pp. 201-8, 231-32; Affonso de Escragnolle Taunay, "Dom Pedro II e a sua Fé de Officio de Imperador do Brasil," *Jornal do Commercio*, Sept. 2, 1934.

[53] J. M. M. F., "Dom Pedro II," *Rev. do Inst. Hist. e Geog. Bras.*, vol. 152, p. 766.

[54] Affonso Celso, *O Imperador no exilio*, p. 58.

[55] Escragnolle Taunay, *Pedro II*, pp. 145, 146, 240.

in exile, he arranged to have divided between the Bibliotheca Nacional and the Instituto Historico e Geographico Brasileiro, to which he had so long been devoted. And he stipulated that the portion of his books that went to the National Library should bear the name of the Empress Thereza Christina.[56]

Somewhat later, he obtained a small quantity of Brazilian soil, which he put away in a closet of his apartment, and beside it he left a note, found after his death, saying, "This is soil of my *patria;* I wish it placed in my coffin."[57] In a sonnet written on September 13, 1891, in Paris, he referred to the fact that he had lost all hope of returning to Brazil, and, therefore, was preserving the bit of earth from the homeland, to insure for himself peaceful slumber in death. In the final stanza he mentioned once again his faith that he would be vindicated before the world:

> "And 'midst visions of peace, of light, of glory,
> Serene I'll await in my resting place
> The justice of God in the voice of History!"[58]

This confidence did, on the whole, sustain him during his last year. But at times he was low spirited, for his Brazilian friends, one after another, returned home, as the ban against them was lifted or as the needs of business demanded. These partings emphasized his isolation and the permanence of his exile. He was chronically homesick, and suffered from deep, painful longings for the patria. Moreover, there was never enough news from Brazil. Though he had a number of correspondents there, most of whom were faithful, unless he re-

---

[56] Affonso Celso, in *Contribuições para a Biographia de D. Pedro II*, Pt. I, pp. 909-10.

[57] Lyra, "Exilio e morte do Imperador," *Jornal do Commercio*, Jan. 5, 1936. Information given the present writer by Dom Pedro d'Orléans Bragança.

[58] E entre visões de paz, de luz, de gloria,
Sereno aguardarei no meu jazigo
A justiça de Deus na voz da Historia!

"Aos Vindouros" ("To Those Who Come Later"), in Teixeira, *op. cit.*, p. 101. The same verses, found on p. 25 of *Sonetos do exilio*, compiled by "Um Brasileiro," bear the title "Terra do Brasil" ("Soil of Brazil").

ceived letters or papers and journals on every boat, he was disappointed. Once, early in 1891, he complained, rather bitterly, to Affonso Celso because two vessels had arrived from home without a single token for him.

"It is queer," he said, "that no one still remembers me enough to send me a few lines. They forget more quickly than I had thought they would."

The Visconde protested, "The name of Your Majesty will never be forgotten in Brazil. The respect and love of the nation for you increases daily."

But Dom Pedro repeated, "It is queer, very queer."[59]

He was, however, usually philosophical. In May, 1891, Ouro Preto left for home. About a month later, his son, who was departing also, called with his family to take leave. The Emperor, though loath to see Affonso Celso go, cheerfully remarked that he had, personally, profited immensely by the revolution. Since he was more free, he could do as he pleased without rousing criticism or incurring heavy responsibilities; and he was not now forced to sacrifice devotion to obligation. He enjoyed, furthermore, the rest which he was coming to need; but he added that here he complained because he had nothing to do.

When asked whether he was not troubled by the misfortunes which had come to Brazil since the revolution (through the dictatorial policy of the republicans), and whether he did not want to go there and restore liberty and justice, he replied:

> Certainly; events have taken place there from which I have suffered much. . . . As for returning, if they call me, I will go at once. I will respond instantly, and most happily, aiming to be still of use to our country. But only if they call me spontaneously, understand. . . . I will never conspire. That does not conform with my nature, my character, or my precedents. It would be the negation of my entire life. Neither will I permit others to conspire in my name or in the name of my family. The Brazilian people have full right to govern themselves as they think best. If they

[59] Affonso Celso, *O Imperador no exilio*, pp. 44-47.

should desire again my experience and my dedication to the country to be placed at the head of the government, and say so clearly and without reservation, I would obey unhesitatingly, even at great sacrifice. Otherwise, I would not go.[60]

When one of the callers mentioned that in writings and speeches in Brazil General Deodoro da Fonseca was called the "South American Washington," the Emperor smiled. Affonso Celso then remarked that he was convinced that the "only personality on the South American continent which can be compared with Washington's is that of Your Majesty."

Startled, Dom Pedro exclaimed, "O! I protest that! No! Washington was one of the most perfect and noble persons whom the world has produced."

"Then," retorted the Visconde, "history will place the two figures on the same pedestal, perhaps recognizing greater virtues in the Brazilian, to our pride."

"Don't say that. You are deceived by the ardor of your imagination."

"Washington, Senhor," the other insisted, "lacked the apotheosis of misfortune. He was always successful. His qualities were never subjected to the test of evil reverses." And Affonso Celso proceeded to contrast the careers of the two men, pointing out the sorrows and hardships that had befallen the ruler of Brazil.

Dom Pedro listened thoughtfully, nodding his head slightly now and then, and, when the Visconde had finished, he murmured sadly, "It is true; I never knew my mother. I was less than a year old when she died."[61]

Since the Emperor's health was decidedly bad, only his habitual self-discipline and his steadying philosophy of life, enabled him to maintain his usual serenity. The diabetes, for which there was then little medical relief, appears to have grown steadily worse and, according to his physicians, had caused

[60] *Ibid.*, pp. 55-58.   [61] *Ibid.*, pp. 60-62.

lesions of the nerves.[62] Though medical baths, massage, and other devices were used to keep up his physical condition, he gradually grew weaker.

From Versailles, where Affonso Celso took leave of him, Dom Pedro went to Vichy for treatment with the mineral waters. Here, for some time, he was seriously ill with gangrene of the left foot, caused by a corn. There was fear that the foot would have to be amputated. For his escape from this, he wrote Taunay, he gave credit to his "already two times savior, Dr. Motta Maia,"[63] who had loyally remained with him after the year's leave of absence granted by the provisional government had expired, and had promised never to leave him. On September 5, he wrote Taunay from Vichy that he was steadily improving.[64] Apparently in the latter part of the month he went to Paris, where he took apartments at the Hotel Bedford. The sore on his foot had not healed, however, probably owing to his diabetic condition, and he leaned on the arm of his physician when he arrived. But at the end of several weeks he was able to walk with the support of a cane.[65]

On October 28, he wrote enthusiastically to Visconde Taunay, "Though the body is feeble and not good for much now, the spirit is always young; today I go to study new mathematical processes with Picard of the Academy of Sciences. We must always try to attain precision."[66] Six months before, he had mentioned to the Visconde that after his serious illness in 1888 his mind was more apt for mathematics—that he had especially noticed the improvement when he examined financial reports.[67]

---

[62] Statement of Dr. Charcot, June 17, 1891, Pedro d'Orléans Bragança Archives, A, CCIII, 9154.

[63] J. J. M. F., "D. Pedro II," *Rev. do Inst. Hist. e Geog. Bras.*, vol. 152, p. 766.

[64] Motta Maia, *op. cit.*, p. 302; Escragnolle Taunay, *Pedro II*, p. 236.

[65] Escragnolle Taunay, "A morte do Imperador," *Rev. do Inst. Hist. e Geog. Bras.*, vol. 152, p. 194; Fonseca, "Molestia do Imperador," *Rev. do Inst. Hist. e Geog. Bras.*, vol. 152, p. 193; Escragnolle Taunay, *Pedro II*, p. 241.

[66] Escragnolle Taunay, *Pedro II*, p. 339.

[67] *Ibid.*, p. 224.

Now, his thoughts stirred by the possibility of greater exactness in applied science, he wrote prophetically to Taunay, "I see the problems of aerial and submarine navigation almost solved. We shall laugh at mountains and tempests."[68]

As autumn progressed, Dr. Motta Maia urged the importance of returning to Cannes, but the Emperor wished to remain longer in Paris. The autumn would advance gradually, without sharp changes, he argued; and, furthermore, he was observing medical regulations carefully, felt well, enjoyed the congenial atmosphere of the French capital, and greatly desired to attend the next meeting of the Academy of Sciences.[69]

So he stayed on in Paris, and read, with reviving expectancy, the reports of Deodoro's growing despotism. In a letter of October 28 to Alfredo de Escragnolle Taunay, he expressed complete approval of his friend's judgment regarding the disposal of his books, "which," he added significantly, "I will hope to gaze upon once more before my death, as if they were beloved children."[70]

Less than a week later came word of Deodoro's dissolution of congress on November 3, and his almost immediate declaration of martial law in the Federal District. In the Emperor's apartment at the Hotel Bedford Silveira Martins, Barão de Penedo, and Goffredo de Escragnolle Taunay (the brother of the Visconde) discussed the situation. Apparently one of them remarked that Dom Pedro was needed in Brazil, to help to save the country from disorder and militarism; and the others agreed. But the exiled monarch replied that he had not been called back, at which Penedo declared that, in a situation such as the existing one, it was not necessary to be asked to return; that it was the duty of the Emperor, as a Brazilian citizen and a patriot to go back at once. Taunay also took this view, empha-

---

[68] *Ibid.*, p. 240.
[69] Escragnolle Taunay, "A morte do Imperador," *Rev. do Inst. Hist. e Geog. Bras.*, vol. 152, pp. 194-95; Motta Maia, *op. cit.*, pp. 323-25.
[70] Escragnolle Taunay, *Pedro II*, p. 240.

sizing the urgency of the matter, and suggested that the presence of the Emperor in Brazil would give a new and unexpected turn to events. He added, "Your Majesty must go at once or never go at all."[71]

Dom Pedro was impressed by what they said, but he pointed out that, because of his advanced age and his illness, it would be impossible for him to accomplish what was needed. He could, however, present himself again in Brazil—for whatever aid his presence might give. But he could not think of himself only; he must talk with his daughter, who would have to go too. Also her son Pedro, though it would mean an interruption of his studies. Luiz must go likewise. They would all go. But he added that, since he could not perform the duties of government as formerly, he would go merely to prepare for the reign of his daughter, and would soon free himself from the responsibilities of office.[72]

This was the main tenor of the discussion, according to what Heitor Lyra wrote that Goffredo de Escragnolle Taunay told him;[73] and it seems very probable that the report is substantially correct, especially since the Emperor's alleged reactions to the remarks of the others are just such as might have been expected from him.[74] It is likely, however, that his acquiescence was not supported by his later reflections; and there seems to be no evidence that he took up the matter with Princess Isabel. But even if he had done so, the resignation of Deodoro from the presidency of Brazil, on November 23, would probably have caused him to give up again all thought of returning without

[71] Lyra, "Exilio e morte do Imperador," *Jornal do Commercio*, Jan. 5, 1936.
[72] *Ibid.*   [73] *Ibid.*
[74] In Goffredo de Escragnolle Taunay's article written in connection with the centennial of Dom Pedro's birth, his account of the discussion which took place is brief, gives fewer details than Heitor Lyra's report, and does not indicate any such definite thought of returning on the Emperor's part as Heitor Lyra indicates. Escragnolle Taunay does, however, quote Dom Pedro as saying that if he did return to Brazil he would try to satisfy an ardent desire to visit the provinces that he had not seen.—Escragnolle Taunay, "A morte do Imperador," *Rev. do Inst. Hist. e Geog. Bras.*, vol. 152, p. 195.

a special call from the leaders of the nation—if, at the time, he had been in a position to consider the problem.

November 23, 1891, was, however, unfortunate for Dom Pedro as well as for Deodoro. On that day he attended a session of the Academy of Sciences, which he greatly enjoyed, but when he emerged on the street he became chilled by the sharp air. The next day, however, he declared that he felt very well and insisted upon going for a drive to St. Cloud and for a walk in the park there. He likewise wrote to Visconde Taunay referring to his mathematical studies.[75] Influenza developed, however; but he rallied and was better by November 30. On December 1, the eve of his birthday, he made an entry in his diary—the last one. "A better year than the past one for me," he wrote, "and for all whom I esteem." He also referred to his family, and he mentioned that he intended to return to Cannes on December 6.[76] But his sixty-sixth birthday found him very weak, though he received some friends who called to congratulate him. By the 3rd it was apparent that he had pneumonia of the left lung.[77] Abbé David, a colleague in the Academy of Sciences, was called to hear his confession,[78] but on the afternoon of the 4th he seemed so much improved that Dona Isabel and her family, who had been with him, returned to Versailles, where they were then living.

A telegram called her back almost immediately, for the Emperor had begun to sink rapidly. During much of the time after that he was in a coma, but between eleven and twelve in the evening he regained consciousness, and a curé from the Church of the Madeleine administered extreme unction.[79] Dona

---

[75] Motta Maia, *op. cit.*, p. 325; Escragnolle Taunay, *Pedro II*, p. 241.
[76] Lyra, "Exilio e morte do Imperador," *Jornal do Commercio*, Jan. 5, 1936.
[77] Fonseca, "Molestia do Imperador," *Rev. do Inst. Hist. e Geog. Bras.*, vol. 152, p. 193; Lyra, "Exilio e morte do Imperador," *Jornal do Commercio*, Jan. 5, 1936.
[78] Lyra, "Exilio e morte do Imperador," *Jornal do Commercio*, Jan. 5, 1936; Escragnolle Taunay, "A morte do Imperador," *Rev. do Inst. Hist. e Geog. Bras.*, vol. 152, p. 198.
[79] Rectification de la Comtesse d'Eu, Pedro d'Orléans Bragança Archives, A, 9263.

Isabel, Dom Pedro Augusto, and the Emperor's two sons-in-law knelt beside the bed. In the room were his physicians, the members of his suite, and several close friends. His breathing, very faint towards the last, ended a little after midnight on December 5, 1891.[80]

Although, mentally, Dom Pedro was well above the average, he had no marks of intellectual genius. Yet he was one of the most notable people of his century. While not original or creative in his work as Emperor, he did his utmost to bring to his people the best results of human thinking throughout the world; and, in view of the national and constitutional handicaps against which he struggled, he should rank among the wisest and best rulers of the period. As a personality he was, however, more original than as a sovereign; as a man he was far more notable than as an Emperor. He was greater for what he was than for what he did. His modesty, simplicity, and democracy; tenacity of high purposes; devotion to duty as he saw it; unwearied enthusiasm for learning; subordination of material values to intellectual and spiritual ones; his integrity, magnanimity, understanding pity, and Christlike kindness made him one of the finest personalities of modern times. Because of this rare combination of individual qualities he was, in truth, a credit and an honor to humanity. For greatness of character is the supreme greatness.

[80] Motta Maia, *op. cit.*, pp. 325-27; Escragnolle Taunay, "A morte do Imperador," *Rev. do Inst. Hist. e Geog. Bras.*, vol. 152, pp. 198-99; Fonseca, "Molestia do Imperador," *Rev. do Inst. Hist. e Geog. Bras.*, vol. 152, plate facing p. 188.

He was buried in the Church of São Vicente da Fóra near Dona Thereza, with the bit of Brazilian soil he had saved for the purpose placed in his coffin, in the pillow on which rested his head. But in September, 1920, the government of Brazil revoked the decree of banishment against the imperial family and voted to have the bodies of the Empress and Emperor brought back to Brazil. This was accomplished in December of the same year, and they were placed in a church in Petropolis. Dona Isabel was ill at the time and was not able to escort them there; but her husband, now seventy-eight years old, and their son Dom Pedro de Alcantara made the journey.—Escragnolle Taunay, "A morte do Imperador," *Rev. do Inst. Hist. e Geog. Bras.*, vol. 152, pp. 200-7; Silva Costa, "Os funeraes de S. M. o Imperador, o Sr. D. Pedro II, na Europa," *Rev. do Inst. Hist. e Geog. Bras.*, vol. 152, pp. 208-11; Max Fleiuss, *Trasladação dos restos mortaes de D. Pedro II e de D. Thereza Christina*; Affonso Celso, *O Imperador no exilio*, pp. 105-14.

APPENDIX I

Pronunciation of Portuguese
(Based partly on Hills, Ford, and Coutinho's
Portuguese Grammar)

The following comments are offered merely to aid in pronouncing Portuguese words occurring in this book, and are concerned only with the pronunciations which vary most from English forms. The suggested pronunciations seem the best approximations to the actual ones that can be given briefly and simply—without phonetic elaborations.

Vowels. In general, single vowels have the same values as in Castilian. *I,* for instance, often has the sound of long "e" in English, and *e,* of long "a"; *a, e,* and *i* never have the long sounds given them in English.

Diphthongs. The *ai,* as in *pai,* father, combines the values of "a" in the English "ask" and the "e" in "met," and sounds much like the English word "pie," pronounced quickly. *Ei,* which occurs in many surnames, such as Oliveira and Pereira, is pronounced like "ai" in the English word "air." *Eu,* as in the Portuguese word for I, sounds like the English long "a" and long "u," pronounced together quickly, with accent on the latter.

Nasalizations. The most common and most marked are as follows. (1). *Ae,* as in *mãe, em,* as in *bem,* good; and final *en,* before *s,* as in *homens,* men. The tilde (~) and the *m* and *n* nasalize the vowels. (2). *Ão* as in *São Paulo,* St. Paul; final *am,* as in *falaram,* they spoke; and final *om* in dialectic pronunciations. They have a value much like "oun," in the English word "noun," pronounced quickly.

Consonants. H is always silent at the beginning of a word. *J* has the value of "z" in the English "azure"; that is, it has a "zh" sound. Thus, *João,* the Portuguese form of John, is pronounced very much as if it were spelled Zho-oun. Q has always the sound of "k" in English. X has commonly the sound of "sh" in English. *Lh,* as in *filha,* daughter, has the value of the double *l* in Castilian, and the approximate value of the "li" in the English word "filial." *Nh,* as in *senhor,* sir, is the equivalent of the Castilian *ñ,* and, approximately, of the "ni" in the English word "pinion."

APPENDIX II
Prime Ministers of Brazil
1847-1889

1. Manoel Alves Branco, Visconde de Caravellas, Liberal, 1847-1848.
2. José Carlos Pereira de Almeida Torres, Visconde de Macahé, Liberal, Mar., 1848-May, 1848.
3. Francisco de Paula Souza e Mello, Liberal, May, 1848-Sept., 1848.
4. Pedro de Araujo Lima, Marquez de Olinda, Conservative, Sept., 1848-May, 1852.
5. Joaquim José Rodriques Torres, Visconde de Itaborahy, Conservative, May, 1852-Sept., 1853.
6. Honorio Hermeto Carneiro Leão, Marquez de Paraná, later, upon his death, Luis Alves de Lima e Silva, Duque de Caxias, both Conciliation, Sept., 1853-May, 1857.
7. Pedro de Araujo Lima, Marquez de Olinda, Conservative, May, 1857-Dec., 1858.
8. Antonio Paulino Limpo de Abreu, Visconde de Abaeté, Conservative, Dec., 1858-Aug., 1859.
9. Angelo Muniz da Silva Ferraz, Barão de Uruguayana, Conservative, Aug., 1859-Mar., 1861.
10. Luis Alves de Lima e Silva, Duque de Caxias, Conservative, Mar., 1861-May, 1862.
11. Zacharias de Góes e Vasconcellos, Liberal, May 24, 1862-May 30, 1862.
12. Pedro de Araujo Lima, Marquez de Olinda, Conservative, May, 1862-Jan., 1864.
13. Zacharias de Góes e Vasconcellos, Liberal, Jan., 1864-Aug., 1864.
14. Francisco José Furtado, Liberal, Aug., 1864-May, 1865.
15. Pedro de Araujo Lima, Marquez de Olinda, Conservative, May, 1865-Aug., 1866.
16. Zacharias de Góes e Vasconcellos, Liberal, Aug., 1866-July, 1868.
17. Joaquim José Rodrigues Torres, Visconde de Itaborahy, Conservative, July, 1868-Sept., 1870.
18. José Antonio Pimenta Bueno, Marquez de São Vicente, Conservative, Sept., 1870-Mar., 1871.
19. José Maria da Silva Paranhos, Visconde do Rio Branco, Conservative, Mar., 1871-June, 1876.

20. Luis Alves de Lima e Silva, Duque de Caxias, Conservative, June, 1876-Jan., 1878.
21. João Lins Viera Cansanção de Sinimbú, Visconde de Sinimbú, Liberal, Jan., 1878-Mar., 1880.
22. José Antonio Saraiva, Liberal, Mar., 1880-Jan., 1882.
23. Martinho de Campos, Liberal, Jan., 1882-July, 1882.
24. João Lustosa da Cunha Paranaguá, Marquez de Paranaguá, Liberal, July, 1882-May, 1883.
25. Lafayette Rodrigues Pereira, Liberal, May, 1883-June, 1884.
26. Manoel P. de Souza Dantas, Liberal, June, 1884-May, 1885.
27. José Antonio Saraiva, Liberal, May, 1885-Aug., 1885.
28. João Mauricio Wanderley, Barão de Cotegipe, Conservative, Aug., 1885-Mar., 1888.
29. João Alfredo Corrêa de Oliveira, Conservative, Mar., 1888-June, 1889.
30. Affonso Celso de Assiz Figueiredo, Visconde de Ouro Preto, Liberal, June, 1889-Nov. 15, 1889, overthrow of the Empire.

BIBLIOGRAPHY

Primary Sources

Manuscripts

Much of the most valuable material on the life of Dom Pedro II is still unpublished. Some of that consulted for the present work is in the United States. The John C. Bancroft Davis Papers in the Manuscripts Division of the Library of Congress contain a little material. The despatches of diplomatic agents of the United States stationed at Rio de Janeiro from 1825 to 1889, found in the Department of State at Washington, have contributed much important information.

More source accounts exist in Brazil. The library of the Instituto Historico e Geographico Brasileiro in Rio de Janeiro has many pertinent writings. The following were consulted by the present writer: the Emperor's diplomas from learned societies; his translation into Portuguese of Longfellow's "Count Robert of Sicily"; his marginal notes in Chandordy's *La France en 1889*, in Pressensé's *Les origines*, and in Pereira da Silva's *Historia do Brasil, 1831-1840;* the day-to-day account of the "Viagem de D. Pedro II á Europa em 1871"; and the typed copy of the Dom Pedro-Pasteur correspondence. In the Bibliotheca Nacional of Brazil at Rio de Janeiro were consulted the expense accounts for the palace, orders regarding imperial galas, letters of Empress Amelia to Dom Pedro II, and a collection of more than one hundred notes and letters from the Emperor to the Visconde do Bom Retiro on public matters, written between 1867 and 1880, most of them when the Visconde was Minister of Empire. Materials examined in the Brazilian Archivo Nacional included the marriage contract of Princess Isabel and the Comte d'Eu, and also records of the Council of State, such as opinions and decisions rendered by it, ministerial reports, memoranda, and the like, much of which seems never to have appeared in print.

By far the most abundant as well as the most valuable of the manuscript sources used for the present volume were found in the Pedro d'Orléans Bragança Archives at the Château d'Eu, in France. These include the Emperor's educational exercise books ranging from his earliest boyhood to his last years; large numbers of his note books and diaries, usually written in pencil, in many places illegible; drafts of letters and verses by him; typed copies of seventy-eight notes and letters written from him to the Comte de Gobineau, the originals of which are in the Library of the University of Strassburg; thousands of letters to the Emperor, many of which are from European intellectuals; occasional family letters; petitions, complaints, and eulogies from his subjects; cabinet minutes; reports of government officers to the Emperor and notes of inquiry and instruction from him; the Condessa de Barral's "Diario de viagem dos soberanos do Brasil in 1871;" a brief autobiographical sketch of Princess Isabel; her "Rectification" of "Les Contemporains: Pedro II"; accounts by the Comte d'Eu, Princess Isabel, and the Emperor of the revolution of November 15, 1889; and other similar manuscript records.

Signed Printed Material

Adalbert, Prince, of Prussia, *Travels in the South of Europe and in Brazil, with a Voyage up the Amazon and the Xingú.* Trans. by Robert H. Schomburgk and John Edward Taylor. 2 vols. London, 1849.

Affonso Celso, Affonso Celso de Assis Figueiredo, Conde de, *Contradictas monarchicas.* Rio de Janeiro, 1896.

―――, *O Imperador no exilio.* Rio de Janeiro, 1893. Very favorable to Dom Pedro II.

―――, *Oito annos de parlamento (1881-1889).* New enlarged edition. São Paulo, (1928)? This also includes *Poder pessoal de D. Pedro II* and *Reminiscencias e notas.* On the whole, critical of the Emperor and hostile towards him.

―――, *Vultos e factos.* Rio de Janeiro, 1892. Includes part of the material found in *O Imperador no exilio.*

Agassiz, Elizabeth Cary, *Louis Agassiz, his Life and Correspondence.* 10th ed. Boston, 1895.

Agassiz, Louis, and Agassiz, Elizabeth Cary, *A Journey in Brazil.* Boston, 1868.

Alencar, Barão de, "Um livro annotado pelo Sr. D. Pedro II," *Rev. do Inst. Hist. e Geog. Bras.*, tomo 56, pp. 401-5.

Andrews, C. C., *Brazil, its Conditions and Prospects.* New York, 1887. The author was consul-general of the United States in Brazil for some years, beginning in 1882.

Annaes da Camara dos Deputados do Imperio do Brazil. Vol. IV, 1884. Rio de Janeiro.

Annaes do Parlamento brasileiro: Camara dos Srs. Deputados. Vol. I, 1888. Rio de Janeiro, Jan., 1888.

Barbosa, Ruy, *Quéda do imperio.* 2 vols. Rio de Janeiro, 1921. This is composed of articles which appeared in the *Diario de Noticias* in 1889.

Barroso, Francisco T., "O Conde d'Eu," *Jornal do Commercio,* Oct. 6, 1935.

Bennett, Frank, *Forty Years in Brazil.* London, [1914].

Bezerra Cavalcanti, João Alcides (ed.), *A Imperatriz Maria Leopoldina: Documentos interessantes publicados para commemorar o primeiro centenario da sua morte, occorrida no dia 11 de dezembro de 1826.* (Publicações de Archivo Nacional.) Rio de Janeiro, 1926.

——— (ed.), *Infancia e adolescencia de D. Pedro II: Documentos interessantes publicados para commemorar o primeiro centenario do nacimento do grande brasileiro, occorrido em 2 de dezembro de 1825.* (Publicações do Archivo Nacional.) Rio de Janeiro, 1925.

Bomilcar, Alvaro, "A partida do Imperador," *Jornal do Commercio,* Nov. 11, 1934.

Camara dos deputados: organisações e ministeriaes desde 1822 a 1889. Travalho organizado na Secretaria da Camara dos Deputados. Rio de Janeiro, 1889.

Candler, John, and Burgess, William, *Narrative of a Recent Visit to Brazil by John Candler and William Burgess to Present an Address on the Slave Trade and Slavery Issued by the Religious Society of Friends.* London, 1853.

Christie, W. D., *Notes on Brazilian Questions.* London, 1865.

Codman, John, *Ten Months in Brazil, with Notes on the Paraguayan War.* New York, 1872.

Coêlho Rodrigues, A., *A republica na America do Sul, ou um pouco de historia e critica offericido aos Latino-Americanos.* Rio de Janeiro, 1904. Based largely on hearsay and reminiscences.

Collecção das leis do Imperio do Brasil. Vols. for 1871, 1881, 1885, 1889. Rio de Janeiro, 1871, 1881, 1886, 1889.

Darwin, Francis (ed.), *The Life and Letters of Charles Darwin, including an Autobiographical Chapter.* 2 vols. New York, 1893.

Debanné, Nicolas, "D. Pedro II no Egypto," *Rev. do Inst. Hist. e Geog. Bras.,* tomo 75, pp. 130-57.

Debret, J. B., *Voyage pittoresque et historique au Brésil, ou Séjour d'un artiste française au Brésil depuis 1816 jusqu'en 1831 inclusivement.* 3 vols. and atlas. Paris, 1834-1839.

Declaração (A) de maioridade de Sua Magestade o Senhor D. Pedro II, desde o momento em que essa idea foi aventada no corpo legislativo até acto de sua realisação. Rio de Janeiro, 1840. Extracts from debates, documents, the press, etc., intended to show that the Brazilian people wanted D. Pedro made Emperor in fact.

Desmoulins (pseudonym), *Pedro II e Isabel I.* São Paulo, 1888. A bitter attack on the monarchy.

Dunn, S. Ballard, *Brazil, the Home for Southerners: or a Practical Account of what the Author, and Others, who Visited that Country, for the Same Objects, Saw and Did while in that Empire.* New York, 1866.

Escragnolle Doria, "Reminiscencias do palacio de São Christovam," *Rev. do Inst. Hist. e Geog. Bras.*, vol. 152, pp. 99-104.

Escragnolle Taunay, Alfredo de, Visconde de Taunay, *Pedro II.* São Paulo, 1933. Contains extracts from Taunay's diary, letters from D. Pedro II, and his Fé de Officio.

―――――, *Reminiscencias.* 2nd ed. São Paulo, 1923.

Escragnolle Taunay, Goffredo de, "A morte do Imperador," *Rev. do Inst. Hist. e Geog. Bras.*, vol. 152, pp. 194-207.

Ewbank, Thomas, *Life in Brazil; or A Journal of a Visit to the Land of the Cocoa and the Palm.* New York, 1856. Excellent description of contemporary Brazil.

Fallas do throno, desde o anno de 1823 até o anno de 1889, acompanahadas dos respectivos votos de graças da Camara Temporaria, etc. Colligidas na Secretaria da Camara dos Deputados. Rio de Janeiro, 1889.

Fleiuss, Max, "Notas do Imperador ao livro do Conselheiro Tito Franco de Almeida sobre o Conselheiro Francisco José Furtado," *Rev. do Inst. Hist. e Geog. Bras.*, tomo 77, pp. 249-89.

―――――, "O Imperador julgado pelos intellectuaes," *Rev. do Inst. Hist. e Geog. Bras.*, vol. 152, pp. 958-63.

―――――, *Paginas brasileiras.* Rio de Janeiro, 1919. Contains letters of D. Pedro to José Antonio Saraiva.

―――――, "O Imperador D. Pedro II no archivo do Conselheiro José Antonio Saraiva," *Annaes do Primeiro Congresso de Historia Nacional*, vol. 1, pp. 1500-40.

Fletcher, J. C., *See* Kidder, D. P.

Franco, Tito, *Biographia do Conselheiro Furtado.* Rio de Janeiro.
Gomes Carmo, A., "O Imperador: factos, reminiscencias, e anecdotas," *Jornal do Commercio,* July 21, 1935.
Graham, Maria, *Journal of a Voyage to Brazil.* London, 1824.
Hadfield, William, *Brazil and the River Plate in 1868, by William Hadfield, showing the Progress of those Countries since his Former Visit in 1853.* London, 1869.
Hilliard, Henry W., *Politics and Pen Pictures at Home and Abroad.* New York, 1892. Hilliard was United States minister to the Brazilian Empire.
Homenagem da Companhia "Correio do Brasil" á Sua Majestade Imperial o Senhor D. Pedro II, pelo seu regresso a capital do imperio. Rio de Janeiro, 1872.
James, Herman G., *The Constitutional System of Brazil.* Washington, 1923. Contains a copy of the constitution of the Brazilian Empire.
Jardim, Silva, *Memorias e viagens: campanha de um propagandista (1887-1890).* Lisboa, 1891.
Kendall, Phebe Mitchell, *Maria Mitchell: Life, Letters, and Journals.* Boston, 1896.
Kennedy, W. Sloane, *Henry W. Longfellow: Biography, Anecdote, Letters, Criticism.* Cambridge, 1882.
Kidder, Daniel P., *Sketches of Residence and Travels in Brazil, embracing Historical and Geographical Notices of the Empire and its Several Provinces.* Philadelphia, 1845.
Kidder, D. P., and Fletcher, J. C., *Brazil and the Brazilians, Portrayed in Historical and Descriptive Sketches.* Philadelphia, 1857. Good, especially for description of contemporary Brazil.
Kidder, D. P., and Fletcher, J. C., *Brazil and the Brazilians.* 9th ed., revised and brought down to date. Boston, 1879.
Lamas, Pedro S., *Contribución historica: etapas de una gran politica.* Sceaux, 1908. Pedro Lamas was son of Andrés Lamas, Uruguayan minister to Brazil, and was for a time secretary of the Uruguayan legation there.
Macedo Costa, Antonio de, "*Carta pastoral do Exmo. Bispo do Pará . . . contra os erros de um papel . . . sob o titulo de Protesto do partido Liberal,*" Belem, 1872. (Bound with *Obras do Bispo do Pará.*)
[————], *O Barão de Penedo e a sua missão á Roma.* Rio de Janeiro, 1888.

Maria Leopoldina, Empress. *See* Bezerra Cavalcanti, João Alcides (ed.).
Mattoso, Ernesto, *Causas do meu tempo (Reminiscencias)*. Bordeaux, 1916.
Monteiro, Tobias, *Pesquisas e depoimentos para a historia*. Rio de Janeiro, 1913.
Mordell, Albert, *Quaker Militant, John Greenleaf Whittier*. Boston, 1933.
Mossé, B., *Dom Pedro II, Empereur du Brésil*. Paris, 1889. This was based almost entirely on notes furnished by Barão do Rio Branco; contains some letters secured by Mossé. (Pedro d'Orléans Bragança Archives, A, CCI, 9087; Nabuco, *Um estadista do imperio: Nabuco de Araujo*, *II*, 390; III, 54.)
Motta Maia, Manoel A. Velho da, *O Conde de Motta Maia, medico e amigo dedicado de D. Pedro II: Reminiscencias do Segundo Reinado*, Rio de Janeiro, 1937.
Nabuco, Joaquim, *O erro do Imperador (Propaganda Liberal)*. Rio de Janeiro, 1886. Bound in volume marked *Miscellanea*.
Nogueira da Gama, Visconde, *Minhas memorias*. Rio de Janeiro, 1893.
Organisações ministeraes do Imperio. Rio de Janeiro, 1889.
d'Orléans Bragança, Louis, Prince, *Sous la Croix-du-Sud—Brésil, Argentine, Chili, Bolivie, Paraguay, Uruguay, avec une carte*. 6th ed. Paris, 1912. The writer was a grandson of Dom Pedro II.
Ottoni, Christiano, *O advento da republica no Brasil*. Rio de Janeiro, 1890.
Ottoni, C. B., *D. Pedro de Alcantara, segundo e ultimo imperador do Brasil*. Rio de Janeiro, 1893. In the introduction the author admits that the book is based largely on memory and tradition.
[————, and others], *Brazilian Republican Address*. Trans. by H. Quintanhila from the original "A Republica," published in Rio de Janeiro, Dec. 3, 1870. 2nd ed. London, 1890.
Ottoni, Theophilo Benedicto, *Circular dedicada aos srs. eleitores e senadores pela provincia de Minas Geraes no quadrennio actual, e especialmente dirigida aos srs. eleitores de deputados pelo segundo districto eleitoral da mesma provincia para a proxima legislatura*. Rio de Janeiro, 1860.
Ouro Preto, Visconde de, *Advento da dictatura militar no Brazil*. Paris, 1891. Largely an account of personal experiences and observations by the last prime minister of the Brazilian Empire.

Paton, Lucy Ellen, *Elizabeth Cary Agassiz: a Biography*. Boston, 1919. Contains several letters from Brazil written by Mrs. Agassiz.

Pedro d'Alcantara, S. M. Dom, Empereur du Brésil, *Poésies hebraïco-provençales du rituel Israélite Comtadin, traduites et transcrites par S. M. Dom Pedro d'Alcantara, Empereur du Brésil.* Avignon, 1891.

Pedro de Alcantara, Dom, *Sonetos do exilio*. Recolhidos por Um Brasileiro. Paris 1898.

Pedro II, Letter to João Alfredo, *Selecta*, April 12, 1919.

Pedro II, S. M. o Senhor D., *Poesias (originaes e traducções) de S. M. o Senhor D. Pedro II. Homenagem de seus netos.* Petropolis, 1889. Mostly translations.

Penedo, Barão de, *Missão especial á Roma em 1873*. Londres, 1881.

————, *O Bispo do Pará e a Missão á Roma.* Lisboa, 1887.

Pereira da Silva, J. M., *Memorias do meu tempo*. 2 vols. Rio de Janeiro [1895-1896]. Valuable because of the character of the subject matter, but contains many errors of fact.

Pickard, Samuel T., *Life and Letters of John Greenleaf Whittier*. 2 vols. Boston, c. 1894.

Pires Brandão, José, "O Imperador em Baden-Baden e a visita de Silveira Martins," *Rev. do Inst. Hist. e Geog. Bras.*, vol. 152, pp. 881-85. From *Correio da Manhã*, Dec. 2, 1925.

————, "O Imperador no exilio," *Collectanea Rabello*, IV, 515.

Queseda, Vicente de, *Mis memorias diplomaticas: Mision ante el gobierno del Brasil.* 2 vols. Buenos Aires, 1907.

Raeders, Georges (ed.), "D. Pedro II e o Conde de Gobineau (Cartas ineditas de D. Pedro e de Gobineau)," *Jornal do Commercio*, Oct. 20, 1935.

Ramiz Galvão, Benjamin Franklin, "Gratas reminiscencias," *Rev. do Inst. Hist. e Geog. Bras.*, vol. 152, pp. 859-61. Copied from *Jornal do Commercio*, Dec. 2, 1925.

Rebouças, André, *A questão do Brazil. Cunho escravocrata do attentado contra a familia imperial.* Lisboa, 1889-1890.

Rego Barros, João do, "Reminiscencias de ha 50 annos, de um cadete de primeiro regimento de cavallaria," *Rev. do Inst. Hist. e Geog. Bras.*, vol. 152, pp. 89-98.

Rezende, Marquis de, *Éclaircissements historiques sur mes négociations relatives aux affaires de Portugal depuis la mort du roi Jean VI, jusqu'à mon arrivée en France comme ministre près cette cour.* 2nd ed. Paris, 1832.

[Ruschenberger, W. S. W.] An Officer in the United States Navy, *Three Years in the Pacific, Containing Notices of Brazil, Chile, Bolivia, Peru, etc., in 1831, 1832, 1833, 1834*. 2 vols. London, 1835.
Saraiva, José Antonio, *Correspondencia e documentos officiaes relativos á Missão Especial de Conselheiro José Antonio Saraiva ao Rio da Prata em 1864*. Bahia, 1872.
Sargent [Mary Elizabeth] (ed.), *Sketches and Reminiscences of the Radical Club of Chestnut Street, Boston*. Boston, 1880.
Spix, Joh. Bapt. von, and Martius, C. F. Phil. von, *Travels in Brazil in the Years 1817-1820, undertaken by Command of His Majesty, the King of Bavaria*. 2 vols. Trans. by H. E. Lloyd. London, 1824.
Teffé, Barão de, "Reminiscencias de D. Pedro II," *Revista da Semana*, Nov. 28, 1925.
Teixeira, Mucio, Barão Ergonte, *O Imperador visto de perto: Perfil de D. Pedro de Alcantara*. Rio de Janeiro, 1917.
Um Brasileiro. See Pedro de Alcantara, Dom, *Sonetos do exilio*.
Vincent, Frank, *Around and about South America: Twenty Months of Quest and Query*. New York, 1890.
Walsh, R., *Notices of Brazil in 1828 and 1829*. 2 vols. London, 1830.
Wanderley Pinho (ed.), *Cartas do Imperador D. Pedro II ao Barão de Cotegipe*. São Paulo, 1933.
——— (ed.), "Pedro II e Cotegipe," *Rev. do Inst. Hist. e Geog. Bras.*, vol. 152, pp. 262-90.
Wilkes, Charles, *Narrative of the United States Exploring Expedition during the Years 1838, 1839, 1840, 1841, 1842*. 5 vols. Philadelphia, 1845.

Newspapers and Magazines

Alabama State Journal; Baltimore *American and Commercial Advertiser*; Baltimore *Sun*; Baltimore *Weekly American*; Boston *Daily Advertiser*; Boston *Journal*; Boston *Post*; *Brazilian American*; *Cearense (Orgão Liberal*, Fortaleza); Chicago *Tribune*; *Cleveland Leader*; *O Combate* (São Paulo); *Correio do Povo* (Rio de Janeiro); *Correio Imperial*; *Correio Mercantil* (Rio de Janeiro); *Correio Paulista*; *Correio Paulistano*; *Daily Alta California*; *Deseret Evening News*; *Diario da Noite* (São Paulo); *Diario de Noticias* (São Paulo); *Diario do Rio de Janeiro*; *Diario Mercantil*; *Diario Official do Imperio do Brazil* (Rio de Janeiro); *Diario Popular* (São Paulo); *Falha da Manhã* (São Paulo);

Freudenblatt (Vienna); *Gaçeta de Noticias* (Rio de Janeiro); *Gazeta do Norte* (Fortaleza); *Gazeta do Povo; O Gazeta* (São Paulo); *Iowa State Register; Jornal do Brasil* (Rio de Janeiro); *Jornal do Commercio* (Rio de Janeiro); *Jornal do Noticias* (Oporto); London *Times;* Montreal *Gazette;* Nashville *Daily American;* New Orleans *Republican;* New Orleans *Times;* New York *Herald;* New York *Times;* New York *Tribune; New York World; A Noite* (Rio de Janeiro); *O Paiz* (Rio de Janeiro); Philadelphia *North American;* Philadelphia *Public Ledger; O Platéa* (São Paulo); *O Primeiro de Janeiro* (Oporto); *A Provincia da São Paulo; Revista Illustrada* (Rio de Janeiro); *Revista da Semana* (Rio de Janeiro); *Rio News;* San Francisco *Daily Evening Bulletin;* Toronto *Globe;* Washington *Evening Star.*

Clippings and Compilations

Collectanea Rabello: D. Pedro II. In Memoriam. 5 vols. These mammoth scrapbooks of press clippings were collected by Sr. Rabello. Some of the articles are unsigned and in many cases their press origin is not apparent. Library of Instituto Historico e Geographico Brasileiro, Rio de Janeiro.

Dom Pedro II in the U. S. Scrap book of clippings from newspapers in the United States. Lima Library, Catholic University of America.

Senhor (O) Dom Pedro Segundo, Imperador do Brasil. Porto, 1871. A day-by-day account of Dom Pedro's trip in western Europe by press articles.

"Traços biographicos de D. Pedro II," published in the *Jornal do Commercio* (Rio de Janeiro), Dec. 2, 1925 and the *Revista do Inst. Hist. e Geog. Bras.,* vol. 152, pp. 606-63. Reprints from the files of the *Jornal do Commercio,* 1825-1891.

Secondary Sources

Abreu, Capistrano de, "Phases do segundo imperio," *Rev. do Inst. Hist. e Geog. Bras.,* vol. 152, pp. 432-45.

Affonso Celso, Visconde de, "Gloria ao Magnanimo," *Rev. do Inst. Hist. e Geog. Bras.,* vol. 152, pp. 786-89. From *Jornal do Commercio* and *Jornal do Brasil,* Dec. 2, 1925.

―――, "O Imperador como estadista," *Jornal do Brasil,* Nov. 24, 1925.

Akers, Charles Edmond, *A History of South America.* New ed. with additional chapters, by L. E. Elliott. New York [1930].

Alencar, Mario de, "D. Pedro II," *Rev. do Inst. Hist. e Geog. Bras.*, vol. 152, pp. 169-73.
Amaral, Braz do, "O Imperador e a proclamação da republica," *Rev. do Inst. Hist. e Geog. Bras.*, vol. 152, pp. 455-80.
Amaral, Leo de, *O Imperador*. São Paulo [1913?]. Effusive in its praise of Dom Pedro II.
Armitage, John, *The History of Brazil from the Period of the Arrival of the Braganza Family in 1808 to the Abdication of Dom Pedro the First in 1831*. 2 vols. London, 1836.
Azeredo, Magalhães de, *D. Pedro II*. Rio de Janeiro, 1923.
Báez, Cecilio, *Resumen de la historia del Paraguay desde la época de la conquista hasta el año 1880*. Asunción, 1910.
Behring, Mario, "Documentos preciosos," *Collectanea Rabello*, III, 218.
Bezerra, Alcides, *A vida domestica de Imperatriz Leopoldina (1797-1826)*. Conferencia realizada no Centro Cultura Brasileira a 28 de Julho de 1927. Rio de Janeiro, 1930.
Bibliotheca do *Jornal do Brazil, D. Pedro II*. Rio de Janeiro, 1892. Very high in praise of the Emperor.
Box, Pelham Horton, *The Origins of the Paraguayan War*. 2 vols. Urbana, Ill., 1927.
Brandenburger, Clemente, "Immigração e colonização sob o segundo reinado," *Rev. do Inst. Hist. e Geog. Bras.*, vol. 152, pp. 481-515.
Brasileinse, A., *Os programas dos partidos e o segundo imperio*. São Paulo, 1878.
Calmon, Pedro, *O rei cavalleiro: a vida de D. Pedro I*. São Paulo, 1933.
———, *O rei do Brasil: a vida de D. João VI*. Rio de Janeiro, 1935.
———, "Visconde de Septiba," *Rev. do Inst. Hist. e Geog. Bras.*, vol. 152, pp. 56-61.
Calogeras, João Pandiá, *A politica exterior do Imperio*. 3 vols. This is part 2 of *Contribuições para a Biographia de D. Pedro II*, and is a special issue of the *Rev. do Inst. Hist. e Geog. Bras.*, Rio de Janeiro, 1927-1928.
———, "O Brasil em 1840," *Rev. do Inst. Hist. e Geog. Bras.*, vol. 152, pp. 225-43.
———, "O poder pessoal e o lapis fatidico," *Rev. do Inst. Hist. e Geog. Bras.*, vol. 152, pp. 424-31.
Camara Cascudo, Luis da, *O Conde d'Eu*. São Paulo, 1933.

Cardozo, Vicente Licinio, "A margem do segundo reinado—historia politica," *Rev. do Inst. Hist. e Geog. Bras.*, vol. 152, pp. 1039-88. *(O Estado de São Paulo,* Dec. 2 and 3, 1925.)
Carneiro, Levi, "O Imperador e o federalismo," *Rev. do Inst. Hist. e Geog. Bras.,* vol. 152, pp. 371-84.
Carvalho, Alberto de, *Imperio e republica dictatorial.* Rio de Janeiro, 1891.
Carvalho, Austrichano de, *Brasil, colonia e imperio.* 2 vols. Rio de Janeiro, 1927. Bitter towards Dom Pedro II.
Carvalho, Delgado de, *Historia da Cidade do Rio de Janeiro.* Rio de Janeiro, 1926.
"Centenario (O) de Pedro II," *Rev. do Inst. Hist. e Geog. Bras.,* vol. 152, pp. 537-56. *(Jornal do Commercio,* reprint.)
Chateaubriand, Assis, "Um professor de élites," *Rev. do Inst. Hist. e Geog. Bras.,* vol. 152, pp. 14-16.
Coelho, José Maria Latino, *Elogio historico de José Bonifacio de Andrada e Silva.* Lisboa, 1877.
Contribuições para a Biographia de D. Pedro II. See Fleiuss, Max, and others.
Corrêa, Viriato, "Pedro II, o democrata," *Rev. do Inst. Hist. e Geog. Bras.,* vol. 152, pp. 111-14.
Cunha, Alfredo da, *Elogio historico de sua Magestade o Imperador do Brazil D. Pedro II.* Lisboa, 1893.
Dawson, Thomas C., *The South American Republics.* 2 vols. New York, c. 1903.
Escragnolle Doria, "Quero já," *Revista da Semana,* Feb. 16, 1924.
Escragnolle Taunay, Affonso de, "A formação intellectual de Pedro II," *Rev. do Inst. Hist. e Geog. Bras.,* vol. 152, pp. 886-93. *(Correio da Manhã,* Dec. 2, 1925.)
————, "Dom Pedro Augusto de Saxe Coburgo Gotha," *Jornal do Commercio,* Sept. 30, 1934.
————, "D. Pedro e a guerra do Paraguay," *Rev. do Inst. Hist. e Geog. Bras.,* vol. 152, pp. 291-301.
————, "Dom Pedro II e a sua Fé de Officio de Imperador do Brasil," *Jornal do Commercio,* Sept. 2, 1934.
————, "Pedro II: os grandes factos de seu reinado (1840-1889)," *Rev. do Inst. Hist. e Geog. Bras.,* vol. 152, pp. 987-1016. *(Correio Paulistano,* Dec. 2, 1936.)
Escragnolle Taunay, Alfredo de, *O Visconde do Rio Branco, gloria do Brasil e da humanidade.* 2nd ed. São Paulo, [1930].

Faría, Alberto de, *Irenêo Evangelista de Souza, Barão e Visconde de Mauá, 1813-1889*. 2nd ed. São Paulo, 1933.
Faría, Zeferino de, "O Imperador e a Sociedade Amante da Instrucção," *Rev. do Inst. Hist. e Geog. Bras.*, vol. 152, pp. 592-98. (*Jornal do Commercio*, Dec. 2, 1925.)
Ferreira da Rosa, "Rio de Janeiro em 1889," *Rev. do Inst. Hist. e Geog. Bras.*, vol. 152, pp. 516-28.
Fialho, Anfriso, *Dom Pedro II, empereur du Brésil*. Bruxelles, 1876.
Fleiuss, Max, "D. Pedro II," *Rev. do Inst. Hist. e Geog. Bras.*, vol. 152, pp. 1088-1119. (*O Globo.*)
———, "D. Pedro II e as letras patrias," *Rev. do Inst. Hist. e Geog. Bras.*, vol. 152, pp. 894-903. (*Correio da Manhã*, Dec. 2, 1925.)
———, "D. Pedro II—seu nascimento—seus irmãos," *Rev. do Inst. Hist. e Geog. Bras.*, vol. 152, pp. 20-31.
———, *Historia administrativa do Brasil*. 2nd ed. Rio de Janeiro, 1925.
———, *Historia da Cidade do Rio de Janeiro* (Districto Federal). Rio de Janeiro, 1928?
———, *Paginas de historia*. 2nd ed. Rio de Janeiro, 1930.
———, "Pedro II e o Instituto Historico," *Rev. do Inst. Hist. e Geog. Bras.*, vol. 152, pp. 843-47. (*Jornal do Brasil*, Dec. 2, 1925.)
———, *Trasladação dos restos mortaes de D. Pedro II a de D. Thereza Christina* (*Rev. do Inst. Hist. e Geog. Bras.*, tomo especial), 1925.
———, and others, *Contribuições para a Biographia de D. Pedro II*, Pt. I. Special volume of *Rev. do Inst. Hist. e Geog. Bras.*, Rio de Janeiro, 1925.
Fonseca, Olympio da, "Medicos do paço," *Rev. do Inst. Hist. e Geog. Bras.*, vol. 152, pp. 174-85.
———, "Molestia do Imperador," *Rev. do Inst. Hist. e Geog. Bras.*, vol. 152, pp. 186-93.
Freire, Laudelino, "Desvelado e magnanimo," *Rev. do Inst. Hist. e Geog. Bras.*, vol. 152, pp. 420-23.
———, *Pedro II e a arte no Brasil e discurso de recepção no Instituto Historico*. Rio de Janeiro, 1917.
———, "Pedro II e o conceito universal em que foi tido," *Rev. do Inst. Hist. e Geog. Bras.*, vol. 152, pp. 866-69. (*Jornal do Brasil*, Dec. 2, 1925.)

Freyre, Gilberto, *Casa Grande & Senzala: formação da família brasileira sob o regimen de economia patriarchal.* 2nd ed. Rio de Janeiro, 1936.
———, *Sobrados e mucambos: decadencia do patriarchado rural no Brasil.* São Paulo, 1936.
Galanti, Raphael M., *Compendio de historia do Brazil.* 5 vols. São Paulo, 1896-1910.
Gallega, A., *The Pope and the King; the War between Church and State in Italy.* 2 vols. London, 1879.
Garcia, Rodolpho, "D. Pedro II e as linguas americanas," *Rev. do Inst. Hist. e Geog. Bras.,* vol. 152, pp. 126-31.
———, "Viagens de D. Pedro II," *Rev. do Inst. Hist. e Geog. Bras.,* vol. 152, pp. 115-25.
Gonzaga Duque-Estrada, L., *A arte brasileira: pintura e escultura.* Rio de Janeiro, 1888.
Grimke, Charlotte Forten, "Personal Recollections of Whittier," *New England Magazine,* N. S., Vol. VIII.
Guimarães, José Maria Moreira, "O Imperador e o exercito," *Rev. do Inst. Hist. e Geog. Bras.,* vol. 152, pp. 350-62.
Gurgel, Leoncio, *D. Pedro II e tempo! (Appello a nação brasileira).* São Paulo, 1902.
Hill, Lawrence F., *Diplomatic Relations between the United States and Brazil.* Durham, 1932.
J. M. M. F., "D. Pedro II," *Rev. do Inst. Hist. e Geog. Bras.,* vol. 152, pp. 696-785. (*Jornal do Commercio,* Dec. 2, 1925.)
Laet, Carlos de, "A Imperatriz," *Rev. do Inst. Hist. e Geog. Bras.,* vol. 152, pp. 790-92. (*Jornal do Brasil,* Dec. 25, 1925.)
———, "O Imperador," *Revista da Semana,* Nov. 28, 1925.
———, "O Imperador e a imprensa," *Rev. do Inst. Hist. e Geog. Bras.,* vol. 152, pp. 409-11.
Levene, Ricardo, *Lecciones de historia argentina.* 2 vols. 9th ed. Buenos Aires, 1925.
Lima Barbosa, Mario de, *Ruy Barbosa na politica e na historia, 1849-1916.* Rio de Janeiro, 1916.
Lima Barbosa, Sobrinho, "Pedro II e a imprensa," *Rev. do Inst. Hist. e Geog. Bras.,* vol. 152, pp. 835-42. (*Jornal do Commercio,* Dec. 2, 1925.)
Lisboa, Arrajado, "O Imperador em Petropolis," *Rev. do Inst. Hist. e Geog. Bras.,* vol. 152, pp. 162-68.
Lopes, Aurelio, "D. Pedro II e os seus livros," *Rev. do Inst. Hist. e Geog. Bras.,* vol. 152, pp. 576-91. (*Jornal do Commercio,* Dec. 2, 1925.)

Lyra, Heitor, "Exilio e morte do Imperador," *Jornal do Commercio*, Jan. 5, 1936.
————, "Quéda do imperio e deposição do Imperador," *Jornal do Commercio*, Nov. 18, 1934.
Mackenzie, Catherine, *Alexander Graham Bell, the Man who Contracted Space*. Boston, 1928.
Magalhães, Basilio de, "D Pedro e a egreja," *Rev. do Inst. Hist. e Geog. Bras.*, vol. 152, pp. 385-408.
Magalhães de Azeredo, Carlos, *Dom Pedro II: traços da sua physiognomia moral*. Rio de Janeiro, [1923]?
Manchester, Alan K., *British Preëminence in Brazil, its Rise and Decline: a Study in European Expansion*. Chapel Hill, 1933.
————, "The Paradoxical Pedro, First Emperor of Brazil," *Hisp. Amer. Hist. Rev.*, XII (May, 1932), 176-97.
————, "The Rise of the Brazilian Aristocracy," *Hisp. Amer. Hist. Rev.*, XI (May, 1931), 145-68.
Martin, Percy Alvin, "Causes of the Collapse of the Brazilian Empire," *Hisp. Amer. Hist. Rev.*, IV (Feb., 1921), 4-48.
————, "Slavery and Abolition in Brazil," *Hisp. Amer. Hist. Rev.*, XIII (May, 1933), 151-96.
Mecham, J. Lloyd, *Church and State in Latin America: a History of Politico-Religious Relations*. Chapel Hill, 1934.
Moacyr, Primitivo, *A instrucção e o Imperio (subsidios para a Historia da educação no Brasil), 1823-1853*. Vol. I. São Paulo, 1936.
Moniz, Heitor, *A côrte de D. Pedro II*. Rio de Janeiro, 1931.
————, *O segundo reinado*. Rio de Janeiro, 1928.
Monteiro, Mozart, "A familia imperial," *Rev. do Inst. Hist. e Geog. Bras.*, vol. 152, pp. 69-88.
————, "A infancia do Imperador," *Rev. do Inst. Hist. e Geog. Bras.*, vol. 152, pp. 32-44.
————, "O casamento do Imperador," *Rev. do Inst. Hist. e Geog. Bras.*, vol. 152, pp. 62-68.
Monteiro, Tobias, "A tolerancia do Imperador," *Rev. do Inst. Hist. e Geog. Bras.*, vol. 152, pp. 150-51.
————, *Historia do Imperio: a elaboração da independencia*. Rio de Janeiro, 1927.
Moraes, Evaristo de, "A abolição e o Imperador," *Rev. do Inst. Hist. e Geog. Bras.*, Vol. 152, pp. 862-65. (*Jornal do Brasil*, Dec. 2, 1925.)
————, *A campanha abolicionista (1879-1888)*. Rio de Janeiro, 1924.

———, "Pedro II e o movimento abolicionista," *Rev. do Inst. Hist. e Geog. Bras.*, vol. 152, pp. 323-42.

Moraes, E. Vilhena de, "Frei Pedro de Santa Marianna, o preceptor de Pedro II," *Rev. do Inst. Hist. e Geog. Bras.*, vol. 152, pp. 45-55.

———, *O gabinete Caxias e a amnistia aos bispos na "Questão religiosa"; a attitude pessoal do Imperador.* Rio de Janeiro, 1930.

Nabuco, Carolina, *A vida de Joaquim Nabuco.* 2nd ed. São Paulo, 1929.

Nabuco, Joaquim, *O abolicionismo.* Londres, 1883.

———, *O eclypse do abolicionismo.* (Reprint.) Rio de Janeiro, 1886.

———, *Um estadista do Imperio: Nabuco de Araujo, sua vida, suas opiniões, sua época.* 3 vols. Rio de Janeiro [1897].

Nascimento, Alfredo, "Magna nominis umbra," *Rev. do Inst. Hist. e Geog. Bras.*, vol. 152, pp. 664-89. (*Jornal do Commercio*, Dec. 2, 1925.)

———, "O patriotismo do Imperador," *Rev. do Inst. Hist. e Geog. Bras.*, vol. 152, pp. 132-41.

Normano, J. F., *Brazil: a Study of Economic Types.* Chapel Hill, 1935.

Oliveira Lima, Manoel de, *Dom João VI no Brasil, 1808-1821.* 2 vols. Rio de Janeiro, 1908.

———, *Dom Pedro e Dom Miguel: a querela da successão (1826-1828).* São Paulo, c. 1925.

———, *Formation historique de la nationalité brésilienne.* Paris, [1911].

———, *Historia diplomatica do Brazil: o reconhecimento do Imperio.* 2nd ed. Rio de Janeiro, 1902.

———, "O Imperador e os sabios," *Rev. do Inst. Hist. e Geog. Bras.*, vol. 152, pp. 145-49.

———, *O Imperio brazileiro, 1822-1889.* São Paulo [1927].

———, *O movimiento da independencia, 1821-1822.* São Paulo [1921?].

Oliveira Vianna, F. J., "D. Pedro e a propaganda republicana," *Rev. do Inst. Hist. e Geog. Bras.*, vol. 152, pp. 412-19.

———, "D. Pedro e os seus ministros," *Rev. do Inst. Hist. e Geog. Bras.*, vol. 152, pp. 874-80. (*Correio da Manhã*, Dec. 2, 1925.)

———, *Evolução do povo brasileiro.* São Paulo, 1933.

――――, *O occaso do Imperio.* São Paulo [1925].
――――, *Pequenos estudos de psycologia social.* São Paulo [1921].
Oneto y Viana, Carlos, *La diplomacia del Brasil en el Rio de Plata.* Montevideo, 1903.
Ortíz, Fernando, "Introducción biográfica," to James J. O'Kelly's *La Tierra del Mambi.* Habana, 1930.
Ottoni, Christiano, *O advento da republica no Brasil.* Rio de Janeiro, 1890.
Ottoni, C. B., *D. Pedro de Alcantara, segundo e ultimo Imperador do Brazil.* Rio de Janeiro, 1893.
Patrocinio, José de, *L'affranchisement des esclaves de la province de Ceará au Bresil: notes.* Paris, 1884.
"Pedro II e os operarios," *Rev. do Inst. Hist. e Geog. Bras.,* vol. 152, pp. 967-83. (*Imparcial,* Dec. 2, 1925.)
Pereira da Silva, J. M., *Historia da fundação do Imperio brazileiro.* 3 vols. 2nd ed. Rio de Janeiro, 1870.
――――, *Historia do Brasil de 1831 á 1840.* Rio de Janeiro, 1878.
Pereira Pinto, Antonio, *Politica tradicional: intervanções do Brasil no Rio da Prata.* Rio de Janeiro, 1871.
Peterson, Harold F., "Efforts of the United States to Mediate in the Paraguayan War," *Hisp. Amer. Hist. Rev.,* XII (Feb., 1932), 2-17.
Pimentel, Alberto, *A côrte de D. Pedro IV.* Porto, 1896.
Pimentel, Mesquita, "D. Pedro II," *Rev. do Inst. Hist. e Geog. Bras.,* vol. 152, pp. 565-70. (*Jornal do Commercio,* Dec. 2, 1925.)
――――, *D. Pedro II: seu caracter, seu governo, sua influencia sobre a politica e as costumes do seu tempo.* Petropolis, 1925.
Pinto de Campos, Monsenhor Joaquim, *O Senhor D. Pedro II, Imperador do Brasil.* Porto, 1871.
"Placa collocada no caixão de S. M. o Imperador," *Rev. do Inst. Hist. e Geog. Bras.,* vol. 152, pp. 983-86. (*Imparcial,* Dec. 2, 1925.)
Primeiro centenario do nacimento de D. Pedro II, 1825-1925. Recife, 1925.
Raffard, Henri (ed.), *Homenagem do Instituto Historico e Geographico Brasileiro á memoria de Sua Magestade o Senhor D. Pedro II.* Rio de Janeiro, 1894.

Ramiz Galvão, Benjamin Franklin, "O Imperador e a instrucção publica," *Rev. do Inst. Hist. e Geog. Bras.*, vol. 152, pp. 363-70.

Rangel, Alberto, *D. Pedro I e a Marquesa de Santos*. São Paulo, 1916.

———, *Gastão de Orléans, o ultimo Conde d'Eu*. São Paulo, 1935.

Rocha, Pinto da, "A politica brasileira no Prata até a guerra contra Rosas," *Rev. do Inst. Hist. e Geog. Bras.*, tomo especial (1917), Pt. V, pp. 565-621.

Rocha Pombo, José Francisco de, "A maioridade, desde quando se cogita da maioridade," *Rev. do Inst. Hist. e Geog. Bras.*, vol. 152, pp. 217-24.

———, *Historia do Brasil*. 10 vols. Rio de Janeiro, 1906.

Rodrigues, A. Candido, "O maior dos brasileiros," *Rev. do Inst. Hist. e Geog. Bras.*, vol. 152, pp. 11-13.

Roure, Agenor de, "O Brasil em 1889," *Rev. do Inst. Hist. e Geog. Bras.*, vol. 152, pp. 529-36.

Rudge, F. M., "Cardinal Giacomo Antonelli," *The Catholic Encyclopedia*.

Ryan, Edwin, *The Church in the South American Republics*. Milwaukee, c. 1932.

Saldanha Marinha, Joaquim, *O rei e o partido liberal*. Rio de Janeiro, 1869.

Sampaio, Theodoro, "A cultura intellectual do Imperador," *Rev. do Inst. Hist. e. Geog. Bras.*, vol. 152, pp. 142-44.

Santos, José Maria dos, *A politica geral do Brasil*. São Paulo, 1930.

Schemann, Ludwig, *Gobineau: eine Biographie*. 2 vols. Strassburg, 1913-1916.

Schmidt, Maria Junqueira, *A segunda imperatriz do Brasil: Amelia de Leuchtenberg*. São Paulo [1927].

Senna, Ernesto, *Deodoro: subsidios para a historia—notas de um reporter*. Rio de Janeiro, 1913.

Serpa Pimentel, Antonio de, *Alexandre Herculano e o seu tempo: estudo critico*. Lisboa, 1881.

Serrano, Jonathas, *Historia do Brasil*. Rio de Janeiro, 1931.

———, "O amigo do Imperador," *Rev. do Inst. Hist. e Geog. Bras.*, vol. 152, pp. 599-605. (*Jornal do Commercio*, Dec. 2, 1925.)

Shaw, Paul Vanorden, "José Bonifacio and Brazilian History," *Hisp. Amer. Hist. Rev.* VIII (Nov., 1928), 527-50.

Silva, Lafayette, "Vida, educação, governo, e morte de Pedro II," *Rev. do Inst. Hist. e Geog. Bras.*, vol. 152, pp. 911-48. (*Correio da Manhã*, Dec. 2, 1925.)

Sousa Carvalho, Visconde de, *A historia des dissoluções da Camara dos Deputados*. Rio de Janeiro, 1885. A bitter attack on the personal power of the Emperor.

Souza Carvalho, A. A. de, *O Brazil em 1870: estudo politico*. Rio de Janeiro, 1870.

[Souza Carvalho], *O imperialismo e a reforma*. Bound in volume entitled *Opúsculos politicos*. Rio de Janeiro, 1865.

Spring, Gerald M., *The Vitalism of Count de Gobineau*. New York, c. 1932.

Suetonio (Pseud. for Antonio Ferreira Vianna), *O antigo regimen (Homens e coisas)*. Rio de Janeiro, 1896. Critical of Dom Pedro II.

Süssekind de Mendonça, Carlos, *Quem foi Pedro II, golpeando, de frente o "saudosismo."* 2nd ed. Rio de Janeiro, 1930. A bitter attack on Dom Pedro II.

"Syllabus," *Encyclopedia Britannica*, 13th ed.

"Syllabus. The Syllabus of Pius IX," *Catholic Encyclopedia*.

Tavares de Lyra, Augusto, "A phase inicial do reinado e a acção individual do Imperador," *Rev. do Inst. Hist. e Geog. Bras.*, vol. 152, pp. 244-49.

————, *Deodoro da Fonseca*. (Lecture delivered at *Inst. Hist. e Geog. Bras.*, Aug. 5, 1925.) Rio de Janeiro, 1927.

Texeira Mendes, R., *Benjamin Constant: Esboço de uma apreação sintetica da vida e da obra do fundador da republica brazileira*. Rio de Janeiro, 1892. A eulogy dedicated to Benjamin Constant's widow.

Vasconcellos, Mario de Barros (ed.), *Motivos de historia diplomatica do Brasil*. 1st series. Rio de Janeiro, 1930.

Williams, Mary Wilhelmine, "The Treaty of Tordesillas and the Argentine-Brazilian Boundary Settlement," *Hisp. Amer. Hist. Rev.*, V (Feb., 1922), 3-20.

Wolf, Ferdinand, *Le Brésil littéraire: histoire de la littérature brésilienne*. Berlin, 1863.

INDEX

ABAETÉ, Limpo de Abreu, Visconde de, 232.
Aberdeen Act, 102-3.
Abolition, by Rio Branco Law, 270-72; in Ceará, 273; in Amazonas, 274; in Rio Grande do Sul, 274; by Cotegipe Law, 277-78; total, 282-84; effect of on slave owners, 288; effect of on imperial throne, 288.
Abrantes, Miguel Calmon du Pin e Almeida, Marquez de, 108, 112.
Academy of Sciences, French, 262, 381.
Acto Addicional, 47, 128.
Adalbert of Prussia, Prince, impressions of regarding Pedro II, 59-60.
Affonso, Prince, of Brazil, 89.
Affonso Celso, Conde de, and the republican revolution, 330; on the way to exile, 357; cited or quoted, 360-77, *passim*; calls on Pedro II in Lisbon, 360, 361; calls on Pedro II in Oporto, 364; calls on Pedro II in Paris, 369-70; departs for Brazil, 376.
Agassiz, Alexander, 206, 207.
Agassiz, Elizabeth Cary, quoted, 94-95, 97, 203; Pedro II calls on, 206; attends lecture given by her husband in Rio, 223-24.
Agassiz, Louis, in Brazil, 223-24; comment of on Pedro II, 246.
Agriculture, Brazilian, in the 1840's, 70; efforts of Pedro II to improve, 229-30.
Aguirre, Atanasio Cruz, 114, 115, 117.
"Alagôas," 299, 352, 353.
Alencar, José Martiniano de, 49, 137.
Aljezur, Conde de, 369.
"Almirante Cochrane," 322, 343.
Amadeo, King, of Spain, 153.
Amelia, Empress, of Brazil, marries Pedro I, 15; popularity of, 15; departure from Brazil, 19; farewell letter of, 24; Pedro II visits, 151-52.

Americo, Pedro, protégé of Pedro II, 219, 220.
Anagnos, Michael, 205.
Anderson, Mary, 199.
Andrada e Silva, Antonio Carlos de, exiled by Pedro I, 11; sent on mission to Lisbon, 46; agitates for shortening of period of Pedro II's minority, 52, 53; as member of Pedro II's first ministry, 58-59.
Andrada e Silva, José Bonifacio de, member of cabinet of Kingdom of Brazil, 7; stands for independence, 7; opposes Pedro I's policy and is exiled, 11; return of, 15; attitude towards Marchioness of Santos, 15; and death of Pedro I, 25; as tutor of Pedro I's children, 18, 28-29, 34; dismissal of and death, 29 and note 24; as a poet, 74.
Andrada e Silva, Martim Francisco de, 11, 52, 53.
Andrade Machado, Visconde de, 362.
Antonelli, Giacomo, Cardinal, 179-80.
Antonio, Prince, son of Princess Isabel, birth of, 186; sent to Petropolis for safety, 333; rejoins parents, 352; birthday letter from to grandfather, 357.
Araujo Lima, Pedro de, Marquez de Olinda, as sole regent, 48; attitude towards shortening period of Pedro II's minority, 50, 52, 55; and slavery, 266.
Araujo Vianna, José de, 55, 60.
Architecture, Brazilian, 79-80.
Argentina, wars with Brazil over Uruguay, 6; refuses permission for Paraguayan troops to cross Corrientes, 117; enters war against Paraguay, 118; part played by in war, 119; friction of with Brazil over Paraguay, 122, 125.

[405]

Augusto Leopoldo, Prince, son of Princess Leopoldina, mentioned, 158; returns to Brazil, 165; and military question, 316-17; asks for instructions from Pedro II, 365.
Aurora Fluminense, 16, 45.

BALTIMORE, Pedro II visits, 197-199.
Bancroft, George, 207.
Banda Oriental del Uruguay. *See* Uruguay.
Barbosa, Ruy, refuses place in Ouro Preto ministry, 303; and federation, 308; and censure of army officers, 315; and plot against the government, 323; made minister of finance in republican government, 335.
Barral, Condessa de, accompanies Empress to Europe, 150; quoted, 156, 157.
Bedini, Monsignor, 75-78.
Beija mão, 41, 48.
Beija mão mortuario, 22.
Bell, Alexander Graham, 205, 210-11, 235.
Beneplácito, 174, 178.
Bennett, James Gordon, 187.
Bezerra Cavalcanti, Amaro, 138.
Bocayuva, Quintino, 233, 318, 328-29, 335.
Bom Retiro, Luiz Pedreira do Couto Ferraz, Visconde de, selected as playmate for Pedro II, 27; accompanies Pedro II to Europe, 150; in United States with Pedro II, 160; as minister of empire, 214; death of, 345.
Boston, Pedro II visits, 203-7.
Botelho de Magalhães, Benjamin Constant, made tutor of Pedro II's grandsons, 295-96; favors shown to by Pedro II, 321-22; hostility of towards Ouro Preto ministry, 322; attitude of Pedro II towards, 322-23; plotting of against the Empire, 323, 329; as leader in plot to establish a republic, 331; made minister of war in republican government, 335; disillusionment and death of, 367; comment of Pedro II on 367.

Boulanger, Luiz Alexio, 34.
Braga, Guilhermo, 164.
Braganças, royal family of Portugal, flee to Brazil, 4.
Brazil, condition as a colony, 5; made a kingdom, 5; becomes an empire, 7-8; independence recognized by Portugal, 12; description of, 66-68; population of, 68, 237; economic activities in, 70-71; transportation in, 71-72, 234-35; sanitation in, 78, 239; food and clothing of inhabitants of, 81-82; amusements and diversions in, 82-83; war of with Paraguay, 117-27; becomes a republic, 334-35.
Brazilian Society against Slavery, 272.
Brazilians, characteristics of, 71-72, 82.
Brugsch, Heinrich Karl, 249.

CAETANO, José, Bishop, 75, note 18.
Caravellas, Francisco Carneiro de Campos, Marquez de, 44.
Caravellas, Carlos Carneiro de Campos, Visconde de, 178.
Carlos, King, of Portugal, 358, 362.
Carlota Joaquina, Queen, characterized, 5; political ambitions of, 6; dislike of for Brazilians, 6.
Carneiro Leão, Honorio Hermeto, 51, 52, 59.
Carpebús, Antonio Dias Coelho Netto dos Reis, Conde de, 243, 342.
Carroll, John Lee, 198.
Carvalho, João Manoel de, 304.
Carvalho Borges, Antonio Pedro de Carvalho Borges, Barão de, 195, 198.
Castello Branco, Camillo, 164.
Caudillismo, 310.
Caxias, Luis Alves de Lima e Silva, Barão de, pacification of Brazil by, 63-65; as commander-in-chief in war against Paraguay, 124; ministry of and Pedro II, 144; and bishops' controversy, 183-84.
Centennial Exhibition at Philadelphia, Pedro II decides to visit, 186; Pedro II helps open, 196; Pedro II visits, 196-97, 208-12.
Channing, William Ellery, 169.
Chaves, Alfredo Rodrigues Fernandes, 315.

INDEX

Childs, George W., 197, 209.
Christie, W. D., 104.
Church, Roman, in Brazil, condition of in the 1840's, 75-78; policy of Pedro II towards, 173-85, *passim*; Free Masonry and the, 173-78; friction between the government and the, 176-85.
Cisplatine Province. See Uruguay.
Club da Johanna, 61.
Club da Maioridade, 49.
Club de Lavóura e Commercio, 277.
Club Militar, 282, 317.
Coimbra, Pedro II visits, 164, 362-63.
Collegio Dom Pedro II, dedication of, 40; early importance of, 72-73; Pedro II's interest in, 217, 218.
Confederação Abolicionista, 272-73.
"Confederation of the Equator," 11-12.
Conservatives, origin of, 46; and slavery, 268; and the Empire, 136; and the Ouro Preto government, 307.
Constant, Benjamin. See Botelho de Magalhaes, Benjamin Constant.
Constitution of the Brazilian Empire, 11, 129-30.
Corporations, 233, 234.
Corrêa de Oliveira, João Alfredo, 176-78, 282-84.
Correio Imperial, 281.
Costa Carvalho, José de, 48.
Cotegipe, João Mauricio Wanderley, Barão de, and the Caxias ministry, 144; and abolition, 278; opposes total abolition, 284; and troubles with the army, 314, 316.
Cotegipe Law, 277-78.
Cunha Mattos, Colonel, 313.

Darwin, Charles Robert, 247, 248.
Deodoro da Fonseca, Manoel, and censure of the army officers, 314, 315; sent with troops to the frontier, 317; return of to Rio, 319-20; complains to Pedro II, 320; obligations to Pedro II, 321; plotting of against the Ouro Preto ministry, 323, 327; as leader of military revolt, 327-28; orders resignation of ministry, 329-30; becomes chief of republican government, 335; message of Saraiva to, 338-39.

Dias, Gonçalves, 74-75, 219, 220.
Droughts, 229-30.
Durant, H. F., 204.

Eads, James Buchanan, 201.
Education, in Brazil, in the 1840's, 72-74; under Pedro II, 214-25.
Edward, Prince, of Wales, 239.
Elizalde, Rufino de, 114.
Equay, Maria Catharina, 21.
Escragnolle Taunay, Alfredo de. See Taunay.
Escragnolle Taunay, Goffredo de, 379, 380.
d'Eu, Prince Louis Gaston d'Orléans, Comte, marries Princess Isabel, 116; joins Pedro II in Rio Grande do Sul, 120; as commander-in-chief in the Paraguayan War, 124-25; and abolition in Paraguay, 269; unpopularity of, 290-93; and growth of republicanism, 297-98; travels in Brazil to combat republicanism, 298-300; attempt of to have army reduced, 311; reaction to military revolt, 333, 334; financial difficulties of, 346-47, 351.
Evolution, views of Dom Pedro on, 170, 247.
Ewbanks, Thomas, quoted, 63, 80-81.
Exaltados, 46.

"Fé de Officio do Imperador do Brasil," 374.
Feijó, Diego Antonio, 47, 64.
Ferdinand I, Emperor, of Austria, 84.
Fernando, King, consort of Maria II da Gloria, 164.
Financial crises, 231-32.
Fish, Hamilton, 189, 195.
Fletcher, J. C., 224, 252.
Flores, Venancio, 110, 118, 121.
Fonseca Costa, Josephina, Baroneza da, 188, 198, 345.
"Forte," 103-05, 107.
França, Lieutenant, 349.
Francis Joseph, Emperor, of Austria, 158.
Francisca, Princess, birth of, 10; at acclamation of Pedro II, 3, 23; as playmate of Pedro II, 26; education of,

34; marriage of, 89; and marriage plans for her nieces, 116; meeting of with Pedro II in France, 154.
Franck, Adolphe, 162-63, 168.
Franco, Tito, 137.
Free Masonry, 173-78, *passim.*
Frothingham, Richard, 203.

Gobineau, Joseph Arthur, Comte de, meets Pedro II in France, 153; Pedro II buys his "Mima," 258; congeniality of and Pedro II, 260; visits at São Christovão while minister to Brazil, 260-61; later correspondence of and Pedro II, 261-62.
Góes e Vasconcellos, Zacharias de. *See* Zacharias de Góes e Vasconcellos.
Gomes, Carlos, 211-12, 221-22, 272.
Gonçalves de Oliveira, Vital Maria. *See* Vital.
Grant, President U. S., 190, 195.
Great Britain, aids Portugal against Napoleon Bonaparte, 4; uses influence for Uruguayan independence, 12; Brazilian relations with under Pedro II, 101-7.
Gregory XVI, Pope, 85
Grito do Ypiranga, 7.

Henning, Karl, 188, 192, 252.
Herculano, Alexandre, visit of to Pedro II in Lisbon, 152; religious views of, 167-68.
Huchard, Henri, 370-71.
Hugo, Victor, 259-60.

Immigration, early Brazilian, 68; under Pedro II, 236-37, 242.
Institute, Egyptian, 160, 249.
Instituto Historico e Geographico Brasileiro, 40, 225-27.
Intellectual ability of Pedro II, 244-45.
Intellectual interests and achievements of Pedro II: in science, 245-48; geography, 248; archaeology, 248-49; history, 250; linguistics, 250-54; literature, 254-55; his creative writing, 255-57; final estimate of, 262-63.
Intellectuals, friendships of Pedro II among, 257-62.

Irmandades, 78.
Isabel, Princess Imperial of Brazil, alleged rebuke of to father, 88; birth of, 89; education of, 95-96, 116; characteristics of, 116; marriage of, 116; made regent for first time, 149; and bishops' controversy, 183, 184; made regent for second time, 186-87; made regent for third time, 279; attitude of Brazilians towards, 289-90; and military question, 316-17; reaction of to military revolt, 333, 336; refusal of to desert father, 343; distress over banishment, 344, 347, 349, 355; in Cannes, 368; at deathbed of father, 381-82.
Itaborahy, Joaquim José Rodrigues Torres, Visconde de, 139.
Itanhaén, Manoel Ignacio de Andrade, Marquez de, made tutor of Pedro II, 28, 29; characteristics and education of, 29-30; educational policy for Pedro II, 30-34, and 35-42, *passim.*
Itaúna, Candido Borges Monteiro, Visconde de, 229.

Januaria, Princess, birth of, 10; at acclamation of Pedro II, 2, 23; as playmate of Pedro II, 26; education of, 34; movement to make regent, 50; marriage of, 89; meeting with Pedro II in England, 154; meeting with Pedro II at Carlsbad, 158.
Jesuits, 177.
João, Prince, son of Pedro I, 10.
João VI, King of Portugal and Brazil, as regent for mother, 4; characteristics of, 4-5; flight of to Brazil, 5; as ruler of Brazil, 5-6; return of to Portugal, 6-7; death of, 12.
José Fernando, Prince, son of Princess Leopoldina, 158.
Justice, administration of in Brazil, 233-34, 288.

Ladario, José da Costa Azevedo, Barão de, made minister of Marine, 303; wounded by insurgents, 329; report of to Pedro II on the revolution, 366.

Lamartine, Alphonse Marie de, 258.
Lamas, Pedro, 99.
Lapis fatidico, 137-38, 300.
Lassance, General, 346, 347.
Latour, Madame de, 258.
Learned societies, membership of Pedro II in, 262.
Lee, Richard Henry, 211.
Leopold I, King of the Belgians, 107.
Leopold II, King of the Belgians, 156.
Leopoldina, Empress of Brazil, aids movement for independence of Brazil, 7; ancestry of, 8-9; appearance and character of, 9; education and intellectual interests of, 9; marriage of, 9; influence of on the Brazilian court, 9-10; popularity of, 10; children of, 10; unhappiness of marriage of, 10; death of, 14.
Leopoldina, Princess, birth of, 90; education of, 95-96, 116; characteristics of, 116; marriage of, 116; death of, 149.
Liberals, origin of, 46; and movement to shorten period of Pedro II's minority, 49; and Paraguayan War, 112; aims of to reform constitution, 128-29; and the Empire, 129; factionalism among, 139; movement of to weaken power of Emperor, 140-41, 142-43; and electoral reform, 145; and abolition, 274; and republicanism, 303, 307.
Lima e Silva, Francisco de, 48.
Lisbon, Pedro II visits, 151-52, 164-65, 213 note 83, 358-62.
Literature, Brazilian, in early years of Empire, 76-77; efforts of Pedro II to foster, 221-22.
Livro de Ouro, 278-79.
London, Pedro II visits, 154-55.
Longfellow, Henry Wadsworth, 207, 255.
López, Carlos Antonio, 108.
López, Francisco Solano, characteristics and policy of, 111-12; protests of against Brazilian policy, 117; aggressions of against Brazil, 117; policy of in war against Triple Alliance, 122; death of, 125.

Loreto, Franklin Doria, Barão de, and abolition, 281-82; and the order banishing imperial family, 344, 345; accompanies Pedro II into exile, 345; at São Vicente, Cape Verde Islands, 357.
Loring, George B., 360.
Loyson, Jacintho, 371-72.
Luiz, Prince, son of Princess Isabel, birth of, 186; sent to Petropolis for safety, 333; rejoins parents, 352; birthday letter from to Pedro II, 357; in Cannes, 372.
Luiz I, King, of Portugal, 151.
Luiz Gaston, Prince, son of Princess Leopoldina, 158.

McCULLOUGH, John, 193, 194.
Macedo, Joaquim Manoel de, 219.
Macedo Costa, Antonio de, Bishop, and Free Masonry in Brazil, 175-84, *passim*.
Machado, Francisco Alvares, 51.
Magalhães, Gonçalves de, 74-75, 221.
Magalhães Coutinho, Joaquim José, 21.
Magalhães Coutinho, Marianna Carlota Verna de, arrival of in Brazil, 21; in charge of Pedro II on day of his acclamation, 23; as head nurse of Pedro II, 25-27; and Pedro II's marriage, 86.
Mallet, Colonel, 347, 348, 349.
Manufacturing in Brazil, 70, 230-31.
Manzoni, Alessandro, 161.
Maracajú, Rufino Enéas Gustavo Galvão, Barão de, made minister of war, 303; efforts of to conciliate Deodoro da Fonseca, 319-20; illness of, 322; reassures Ouro Preto regarding the military, 324; instructions of Ouro Preto to regarding Deodoro, 327; and the military insurrection, 328; opinions of Pedro II and Ouro Preto regarding, 361.
Maria I, Queen, of Portugal, insanity of, 4; death of, 5.
Maria II, da Gloria, Queen of Portugal, birth of, 10; becomes godmother of Pedro II, 21; Pedro I abdicates Portuguese throne in favor of, 12-13, betrothal of to Dom Miguel, 13; efforts

of to get support for claims to Portuguese throne, 19, note 37; last departure of for Europe, 19; death of, 151.
Mariette-Bey, Auguste Ferdinand François, 249.
Martins, Almeida, 174.
Mauá, Ireneu Evangelista de Souza, Barão de, 113.
Mendonça, Salvador de, 308.
Menezes, Cardoza de, 221.
Metternich-Winneburg, Clemens Wenzel Lothar, Prince, 84.
Miguel, Prince, brother of Pedro I, 13, 19.
Miguel, Prince, son of Pedro I, 10.
Military, little esteem for the in Brazil, 310; disaffection among the, 310-23; plotting of against the government, 323-24; revolution led by the, 327-346.
Missions Territory, Dom Pedro and, 373.
Mitchell, Maria, quoted regarding Pedro II, 208.
Mitre, Bartolomé, 115, 121.
Moderados, 46.
Moderating power, granted emperor by constitution, 129; movement to weaken, 140-41, 142-44; Pedro II's change of attitude towards, 147-48.
Moody, Dwight L., 190.
Mossé, Benjamin, 168.
Motta Maia, Claudio Velho da Motta Maia, Conde de, accompanies Pedro II to Europe in 1887, 279; said to exercise imperial authority, 300; falsely charged with withholding a telegram from Pedro II, 331-32; offers to go into exile with Pedro II, 345; accompanies Pedro II into exile, 348; gratitude of Pedro II to, 378; in Cannes with Dom Pedro, 365; urges Dom Pedro to return to Cannes 379; at death bed of Dom Pedro, 382.
Motta Maia, Manoel A. Velho da, son of the Conde de Motta Maia, 372.
Motta Maia, Oscar da, son of the Conde de Motta Maia, 372.
Mount Vernon, Dom Pedro visits, 201-2.
Muritiba, Baroneza de, 332, 333, 345.
Muritiba, Manoel Vieira Tosta, Barão de, 332, 333, 345.

Nabuco, Joaquim, opinion of on Pedro II's religious views, 170-71; champions abolition, 271, 272, 274, 275, 278, 283; quoted on weakness of the throne, 297.
Nabuco de Araujo, José Thomaz, and Liberal reform movements, 142-43; and the Roman Church, 173, 180; heads government committee to study methods for abolishing slavery, 267-68.
Napoleon Bonaparte, intervention of in Portugal, 4.
Nascimento, Francisco, 273.
Netto, Felippe, 111, 112, 113.
New Orleans, Pedro II visits, 200-1.
New York, Pedro II visits, 190-91, 212.
Niagara Falls, Pedro II visits, 202.
Nioac, Manoel Antonio da Rocha Faria, Conde de, 369, 371.
Nobility, Brazilian, 238-39.
Nogueira da Gama, Nicolão Antonio Nogueira Valle da Gama, Visconde de, with Pedro II in Portugal, 152; in Scotland, 155; in Italy, 160; in Southern France, 161; placed in charge of the finances of Dona Thereza and Dom Pedro, 346.
Nordenskjiöld, Nils Adolf Erick Baron, 248.

O'Kelly, James J., sent by New York *Herald* to Brazil, 187; report of on Pedro II's voyage to United States, 187-89; travels with Pedro II in United States, 189-209, *passim*.
Old Catholics, 168, 171, 181.
Oliveira, Candido Luiz Maria de, 322.
Oliveira Lima, Manoel de, comments of on Pedro II, 136, 226, 242.
Osorio, Manoel Luiz, Marquez de Herval, 310.
Ouro Preto, Affonso Celso de Assis Figueiredo, Visconde de, consents to head ministry, 303; characteristics of, 303; policy of, 303-5; and the military question, 319; and the military conspiracy, 323-24; and the military re-

volt, 327-31; telegraphs to Pedro II, 328, 329; exile of, 357; calls on Dom Pedro in Lisbon, 360, 361; calls on Dom Pedro in Oporto, 364; leaves for Brazil, 376.

PARAGUAY, strained relations of with Brazil, 117; war of with Triple Alliance, 118-27.

Paranaguá, Francisco Vilela Barbosa, Marquez de, 51, 56-57.

Paris, Pedro II visits, 162-63, 279-80, 370-72, 375, 378.

Partridge, James Rudolph, 271.

Pasteur, Louis, 246-47.

Patrocinio, José de, 272.

Paula, Princess, birth of, 10; at acclamation of Pedro II, 3, 23; death of, 26.

Pedro, Prince, son of Pedro II, 90.

Pedro I, Emperor of Brazil, as child accompanies parents to Brazil, 5; sympathizes with liberals, against father, 6; made regent of Brazil, 7; declares independence of Brazil, 7; proclaimed emperor of Brazil, 8; characterized, 8; education of, 8; marriage of, 9; political theories of, 8; and war over Cisplatine Province, 12; abdicates throne of Portugal, 12; political troubles of in Brazil, 11-13, 15-18; scandalous morals of, 8, 10, 13-15; second marriage of, 15; abdicates Brazilian throne, 18; later influence on children, 24, 25; war with brother over Portuguese throne, 19; death of, 19, 24.

Pedro II, Emperor of Brazil, ancestry of, 20; birth of, 10, 20; baptism of, 21; dedication of to Our Lady of Glory, 21; description of at three years, 22; affection of for stepmother, 22; for father, 22-23; acclamation of, 3, 23; first letter of to father, 24; formal education of, 30-39; health of during childhood, 39, 42; boyhood responsibilities of, 39-41; movement to shorten period of minority of, 48-56; agrees to assume imperial authority, 57; coronation of, 58; impressions of Adalbert of Prussia regarding, 59-60; appearance and character in 1847, 62-63; visits Rio Grande do Sul, 64; marriage of, 84-87; dress and daily routine of, 91-100; and relations with Great Britain, 103, 106-7; policy of towards Uruguay, 110; and war against Paraguay, 118-27, *passim;* effect of the war upon, 127; relations of with ministry, 130-33, 139-40; and the constitution, 134-37; attitude towards criticism, 141-42; and electoral reform, 143-48; change of attitude of towards moderating power, 147-48; visits Bahia and Pernambuco, 151; first visit of to Europe, 151-65; popularity of in Europe, 158-59; Church policy of, 173-85; travels of in United States, 186-213; work of for the education of Brazil, 214-17; promotion of internal progress, 228-43, *passim;* among the intellectuals, 244-63; and abolition, 264-79, 281-84, 285-87, *passim;* illness of, 279-80, 284-86, 300, 301; out of touch with political developments, 301,-2, 324; attempt on life, of, 306-7; and the military insurrection, 331-37; reluctance of to be coerced by the military, 334-38; attempts of to form new ministry, 335, 337-39; probable reasons for delay in acting to try to save throne, 339-41; receives and replies to order of banishment, 344-45; preparations of for departure, 345-46; departs from Brazil, 347-53; refuses grant of 5000 contos from revolutionary government, 350-51; voyage of into exile, 352-58; poverty of in exile, 361-62; distress of over death of Empress, 363-65; life of in Cannes, 365, 368-69; attitude of towards the revolution, 342, 366-67, 373, 374; activities of in exile, 368, 369, 370, 372, 373; preparations of for his end, 374-75; homesickness of for Brazil, 375-76; revived hopes of for return, 379-80; new illness of and death, 381-82; final estimate of, 382.

Pedro IV, of Portugal. *See* Pedro I, Emperor of Brazil.

Pedro V, of Portugal, 151.

Pedro Augusto, Prince, son of Princess Leopoldina, in Germany, 158; returns to Brazil with Pedro II, 165; accompanies Pedro II to Europe in 1887, 279-80; goes into exile, 347, 354-55; insanity of, 354-55; death of, 355, note 38.

Pedro de Alcantara, Prince of Grão Pará (son of Princess Isabel), birth of, 186; sent to Petropolis for safety, 333; rejoins parents, 352; suggests sending a message by a pigeon from the "Alagôas" back to Brazil, 354; birthday letter of to Pedro II, 357; in Cannes, 372.

Peixoto, Floriano, disaffection of, 318; participation of in plot against government, 324; fails to defend army barracks, 329.

Pellicano, 176.

Pelotas, José Antonio Corrêa da Camara, Visconde de, 315.

Penedo, Barão de, Francisco Ignacio Carvalho Moreira, Barão de, sent as special ambassador to the Pope, 178-79; serves Dom Pedro in exile, 365, 379.

Pereira, Clemente, 51.

Pereira de Vasconcellos, Bernardo, 50.

Pessoa, Captain, of the "Alagôas," 353-54, 356, 359.

Petropolis, summer capital of Brazil, 97-100.

Philadelphia, Pedro II visits, 196-97, 208-12.

Pires Brandão, José, 368.

Pius IX, Pope, audience of Pedro II with, 160-61; proclaims new dogmas, 168; condemns Free Masonry, 174; portrait of burned, 176; and bishops' controversy in Brazil, 180.

Pleasants, J. Hall, 198.

Poder moderador. See moderating power.

Political parties, weakness of in Brazil, 133-34.

Population of Brazil, in the 1840's, 68, 237-38.

Portugal, invaded by French, 4; flight of royal family of, to Brazil, 4-5; demands return of João VI, 6-7; reactionary policy of cortes of towards Brazil, 7; granted a constitution by Pedro I, 12; and war of succession, 13, 19.

Portuguese question, in Brazil, 15, 16.

Powers, Hiram, 160.

Press in Brazil, under Pedro I, 15; in the 1840's, 74; and Protestantism, 75-78; Pedro II's dependence upon, 92, 131-32.

"Prince of Wales," vessel, 104-5, 106.

Protégés of Pedro II, 218-19, 219-22.

Protestantism in Brazil, 75-78, 173.

Radical manifesto, 268.

Rafael, Negro, friend and servant of Pedro II, 27, 150, 345.

Ramiz, Benjamin Franklin Ramiz Galvão, Barão de, protégé of Pedro II, 219-20; as head of Imperial Public Library, 222; as tutor of Princess Isabel's sons, 251; and abolition, 282; brings the sons of Princess Isabel and the Comte d'Eu to their parents preparatory for exile, 352.

Rebouças, André, report of on revolution, 330; plan of to save the Empire, 334; goes into exile with imperial family, 352, 356; death of, 352, note 29.

Regency, provision for, 44; troubles of, 44-57, *passim*.

Religious views of Pedro II: childhood training and, 166; later factors influencing, 167-69; attitude towards the new dogmas, 168, 171-72; during mature years, 169-71.

Renan, Ernest, 169.

Republicanism in Brazil, growth of, 293-98; efforts to combat, 298-300; triumph of, 334-35.

Restauradores, 46.

Révy, J. J., 230.

Ribeiro, Solon, 327, 344.

Rio Branco, José Maria da Silva Paranhos, Visconde do, 150, 174, 180, 270-72.

Rio Branco Law, 270-72.

Rio de Janeiro, 67, 68, 239-40.

Rodrigues Pereira, Lafayette, 308.

Rosas, Juan Manuel, aggressive policy of in Plata basin, 108, 109; defeat and exile of, 109.

INDEX

Rose, Imperial Order of the, 63, 239.
Russell, John, Lord, 105, 106.

Sá, Simplicio Rodrigues de, 35.
Sabbatinas, 131.
Salles Torres Homem, Francisco de, 138-39, 232.
Salt Lake City, Pedro II visits, 192-93.
San Francisco, Pedro II visits, 194-95.
Sankey, Ira B., 190.
Santa Marianna, Pedro de, made headmaster of Pedro II, 31; qualifications of, 31; as instructor of Pedro II, 35; religious influence of, 166.
Santos, Domitila de Castro Canto e Mello, Marqueza de, 13-14, 15.
São Christovão Palace, 90-91.
São Vicente, José Antonio Pimenta Bueno, Visconde de, 266, 297.
São Vicente da Fóra, 151, 365, 382, note 80.
Saraiva, José Antonio, sent as special envoy to Montevideo, 113-15; and electoral reform, 146-48; and abolition, 277; and growth of republican sentiment, 301-3; and attempt to form a ministry after military revolt, 337-39.
Sargent, Mary Elizabeth, quoted regarding Pedro II, 206.
Saxe-Coburg-Gotha, Louis Augustus, Duke of, marries Princess Leopoldina, 116; accompanies Pedro II to Rio Grande do Sul, 120; meets Pedro II and the Empress in Europe, 158; returns with them to Brazil, 165; in the United States of America, 202.
Schenck, Robert C., quoted regarding Pedro II, 155.
Schliemann, Heinrich, 248.
Schreiner, Gustave Baron de, 253.
Schuch, Roque, 35.
Science, interest of Pedro II in, 222-23, 225.
Semmola, Dr., director of medical school at Naples, 285.
Senna Madureira, Colonel, 313, 314, 315.
Seybold, Christian Frederick, linguistic studies of Pedro II under, 252, 253,
note 34, 280; with Pedro II in exile, 368.
Silva, Rodrigo da, 283.
Silva Ferraz, Angelo Muniz da, quoted regarding Pedro II, 131.
Silva Lisboa, Bento da, 84.
Silva Prado, Antonio da, 281.
Silveira Martins, Gaspar da, and note of censure against military officers, 315; suggested to head new ministry, 335; arrest of by revolutionaries, 335; visits Pedro II in exile, 379.
Sinimbú, João Lins Viera Cansancão de Sinimbú, Visconde de, 145-46.
Slave trade, Great Britain and Brazilian, 102-4.
Slavery in Brazil, 68-69, 264-287, *passim*.
Sociedade Amante da Instrucção, 215.
Souza, Aureliano de, 60.
Souza Dantas, Manoel P. de, 276.

Tamandaré, Joaquim Marques Lisboa, Conde de, 122.
Taunay, Alfredo Maria Adriano d'Escragnolle Taunay, Visconde de, plan of to save the Empire, 334; gets Pedro II's "Fé de Officio" published, 374; helps Pedro II dispose of his library and museum collections in Brazil, 374-75.
Taylor, Bayard, 212.
Teffé, Antonio Luiz von Hoonholtz, Barão de, 366.
Teixeira, Mucio, incident connected with Pedro II described by, 218-19; republican affiliations of, 296; offers services to Dom Pedro in exile, 365.
Thereza Christina, Empress of Brazil, parentage of, 84-85; characteristics of, 85; marriage of to Pedro II, 84-87; popularity of in Brazil, 87-88; attitude of Pedro II towards, 88; ill health of, 149, 156, 158, 186; helps open Centennial Exhibition in Philadelphia, 196; accompanies Pedro II to Europe in 1887, 279; and illness of Pedro II in Milan, 285-86; distress of over banishment and exile, 344, 349, 352, 360-61; death of, 363-65.
Thiers, Louis Adolphe, 154.

INDEX

Thornton, Sir Edward, British minister, 114, 121, 197.
Transportation and communication in Brazil, 71-72, 234-35.
Travels of Pedro II: in Brazil, 64, 120-21, 187-88, 240-42; in Old World, in Portugal, 151-53, 163-65; in Spain, 153, 163; in France, 153-54, 161-62; in Great Britain, 154-56; in Belgium, 156; in Germany, 156-58; in Austria, 158-59; in Italy, 159, 160-61; in Egypt, 159-60, 249; in Palestine, 171; in Greece, 248; in other countries, 213 note 83; in United States of America—in New York, 190-91, 207-8; in Far West, 192-95; in Washington, D. C., 195-96, 201-2; in Philadelphia, 196-97, 208-12; in Maryland, 197-99; trip down Mississippi to New Orleans, 200-1; to New England, 203-7; to Canada, 202-3.
Triple Alliance. *See* Paraguay, Brazil, Argentina, Uruguay, López, Francisco, Pedro II.
Trompowsky, Major, 339.

União (A), 176, 177.
United States of America, relations of Brazil with, 107-8; Pedro II visits, 189-213.
Urquiza, Justo José, 110.
Uruguay, conflict of Brazil and Argentina over, 6; revolt of against Brazil, 12; becomes independent, 12; harassed by Rosas, 108; Brazilian policy towards, 109-17; and war with Paraguay, 118-19.

Valle, Adriano do, 306.
Vandelli, Alexander Antonio, 35.
Varnhagen, Francisco, 219.
Veiga, Evaristo da, draws up protest to Pedro I, 16; influence of, 45; as leader of *Moderados*, 46.
Victoria, Queen, of England, 154, 155.
Vital, Bishop, and Free Masonry in Brazil, 174-84.

Walsh, Robert, quoted, 22.
Wandenkolk, Eduardo, 323, 330, 335.
Washington, D. C., Pedro II visits, 195-96, 201-2.
Washington Monument, Pedro II contributes to fund for, 202.
Webb, James Watson, 107, 289.
Welsersheimb, Count, minister from Austria in Rio, 352.
Whittier, John Greenleaf, 206, 255.
Wilkes, Charles, 41.
Women, position of in Brazil, 69-70; attitude of Pedro II towards enlightenment of, 223-24, 242.
Writings of Pedro II, 255-57.

Zacharias de Góes e Vasconcellos, and Uruguayan question, 113, 115; ultimatum of ministry of to Paraguay, 115, 126; relations of with Pedro II, 138-40.